The National Dream

The National

"Size is not grandeur, and territory
does not make a nation."
– *Thomas Henry Huxley*

"Until this great work is completed,
our Dominion is little more than
a 'geographical expression.' "
– *Sir John A. Macdonald*

The Great Railway

1871-1881

Dream

By Pierre Berton

Anchor Canada

Copyright © 1970 by Pierre Berton Enterprises Ltd.
Anchor Canada paperback edition 2001

National Library of Canada Cataloguing in Publication Data

Berton, Pierre, 1920-
   The national dream : the great railway, 1871–1881

Includes index.
ISBN 978-0-385-65840-9

1. Canadian Pacific Railway Company – History. 2. Canada –
History – 1867-1914. 3. Railroads and state – Canada – History.
4. Railroads – Canada – History. I. Title.

HE2810.C2B48 2001   385'.0971   C2001-930606-7

Cover photo: Sir John A. Macdonald,
   courtesy National Archives of Canada (C-004154)
Cover design: CS Richardson
Printed and bound in the United States of America

Published in Canada byAnchor Canada,
a division of Random House of Canada Limited,
a Penguin Random House company

www.penguinrandomhouse.ca

Penguin
Random House
ANCHOR CANADA

Books by Pierre Berton

The Royal Family
The Mysterious North
Klondike
Just Add Water and Stir
Adventures of a Columnist
Fast Fast Fast Relief
The Big Sell
The Comfortable Pew
The Cool, Crazy, Committed
    World of the Sixties
The Smug Minority
The National Dream
The Last Spike
Drifting Home
Hollywood's Canada
My Country
The Dionne Years
The Wild Frontier
The Invasion of Canada
Flames Across the Border
Why We Act Like Canadians
The Promised Land
Vimy
Starting Out
The Arctic Grail
The Great Depression
Niagara: A History of the Falls
My Times: Living with History
1967, The Last Good Year

Picture Books
The New City (with Henri Rossier)
Remember Yesterday
The Great Railway
The Klondike Quest
Pierre Berton's Picture Book
    of Niagara Falls
Winter
The Great Lakes
Seacoasts
Pierre Berton's Canada

Anthologies
Great Canadians
Pierre and Janet Berton's
    Canadian Food Guide
Historic Headlines
Farewell to the Twentieth Century
Worth Repeating
Welcome to the Twenty-first
    Century

Fiction
Masquerade (pseudonym
    Lisa Kroniuk)

Books for Young Readers
The Golden Trail
The Secret World of Og
Adventures in Canadian History
    (22 volumes)

Contents

Maps

Drawn by Courtney C. J. Bond

To Arthur Irwin

Cast of Major Characters

The Politicians

LIBERAL-CONSERVATIVES (TORIES)

Sir John A. Macdonald, Prime Minister of Canada, 1867-73, 1878-91.

Sir George Etienne Cartier, Minister of Militia and Defence, 1867-73. Macdonald's Quebec lieutenant.

Doctor Charles Tupper, M.P. for Cumberland, Nova Scotia; President of the Privy Council, 1870-72; Minister of Inland Revenue, 1872-73; Minister of Customs, 1873; Minister of Public Works, 1878-79; Minister of Railways, 1879-84.

Sir Francis Hincks, Premier of United Canada, 1851-54; Minister of Finance, 1869-73.

Hector Louis Langevin, Minister of Public Works, 1869-73; Postmaster General, 1878-79; Minister of Public Works, 1879-91. Cartier's successor as Macdonald's Quebec lieutenant.

J. J. C. Abbott, M.P. for Argenteuil, Quebec. Sir Hugh Allan's legal counsel in 1873; legal counsel for the CPR Syndicate, 1880.

LIBERALS (CLEAR GRITS AND REFORMERS)

Alexander Mackenzie, Prime Minister of Canada and Minister of Public Works, 1873-78.

Edward Blake, M.P. for Durham West, Ontario; Premier of Ontario, 1871-72; Minister without Portfolio, 1873-74; Minister of Justice, 1875-77; President of the Privy Council, 1877-78. Succeeded Alexander Mackenzie as Liberal leader, 1880.

Sir Richard Cartwright (Conservative to 1869), Minister of Finance, 1873-78.

Lucius Seth Huntington, Solicitor General for Lower Canada, 1863-64; M.P. for Shefford, Quebec, 1867-78; President of the Privy Council, 1874-75; Postmaster General, 1875-78. His speech in 1873 touched off the Pacific Scandal.

James D. Edgar, chief Liberal whip, 1872-74; delegate to British Columbia on CPR negotiations, 1874.

The Pathfinders

Sandford Fleming, chief engineer of the government-owned Intercolonial; Engineer-in-Chief of the CPR, 1871-80; succeeded by Collingwood Schreiber. Devised a workable system of standard time.

Marcus Smith, in charge of surveys in British Columbia, 1872-76; Fleming's deputy in Ottawa, 1876-78. Strong proponent of Bute Inlet as CPR terminus.

Walter Moberly, assistant surveyor-general of British Columbia, 1865-66; in charge of mountain surveys for CPR, 1871-72. Discovered Eagle Pass.

Henry J. Cambie, in charge of British Columbia surveys after 1876, replacing Marcus Smith.

Charles Horetzky, photographer and explorer. Conducted exploratory surveys in the Pine Pass and Kitlope River regions.

The Entrepreneurs

Sir Hugh Allan, Montreal ship owner and financier whose syndicate was awarded the CPR contract in 1872. His heavy subscriptions to the Conservative Party implicated him in the Pacific Scandal.

Jay Cooke, Philadelphia banker who financed the Northern Pacific Railroad and hoped to control the CPR.

George W. McMullen, Canadian-born promoter from Chicago who produced American backers for Sir Hugh Allan's company.

Senator David L. Macpherson, Toronto railway builder and rival of Sir Hugh Allan. He made a fortune in Grand Trunk Railway construction contracts and headed the Interoceanic Company, which bid unsuccessfully for the CPR contract in 1872.

James J. Hill, Canadian-born fuel and transportation merchant in St. Paul, Minnesota. Member of the CPR Syndicate, 1880.

Norman Kittson, early Minnesota fur trader; Hill's partner in Red River Transportation Company and subsequent ventures. Member of the CPR Syndicate, 1880.

Donald A. Smith, M.P. for Selkirk, 1871-78; Labrador fur trader who rose to become resident governor and Chief Commissioner of the Hudson's Bay Company in Canada. He was a partner of Hill and Kittson in Red River Transportation Company and subsequent railroad ventures. Member of the CPR Syndicate, 1880.

George Stephen, Donald A. Smith's cousin; president of the Bank of Montreal, 1876-81. He helped Smith, Hill and Kittson organize the St.

Paul, Minneapolis and Manitoba Railway. Member of the CPR Syndicate and president of the CPR, 1881-88.

John S. Kennedy, New York banker who represented Dutch bondholders of the bankrupt St. Paul railway and arranged reorganization. Member of the CPR Syndicate, 1880.

Duncan McIntyre, president of Canada Central Railway. Member of and spokesman for the CPR Syndicate, 1880.

The Builders

Joseph Whitehead, Liberal M.P., awarded contracts on the Pembina Branch of the CPR and on Section Fifteen between Cross Lake and Rat Portage, west of Lake Superior.

Adam Oliver, Liberal M.P.P., awarded telegraph contracts west of Fort William. Implicated in "Neebing Hotel" scandal.

J. W. Sifton, awarded construction contract west of Fort William (with his brother Henry) and telegraph contract west of Winnipeg (with David Glass, M.P.). Father of Sir Clifford Sifton, founder of Sifton newspapers.

John Shields, Conservative Party fixer, member of contracting firm of Manning, Shields and McDonald. Involved in behind-the-scenes manipulation for Contract Forty-two for construction of the CPR line between Eagle River and Rat Portage, west of Lake Superior.

Michael Haney, construction boss who took over and completed Section Fifteen for the government after Joseph Whitehead suffered financial reverses.

The Bystanders

Frederick Temple Blackwood, Marquess of Dufferin and Ava, Governor General of Canada, 1872-78. Succeeded by the *Marquess of Lorne*.

George Brown, former leader of the Reform Party; publisher and editor of the *Globe,* Toronto. Alexander Mackenzie's mentor. Murdered in May, 1880.

George Walkem, Premier of British Columbia, 1874-76, 1878-82. A strong advocate of the Bute Inlet route for the CPR, his first term was marked by a long battle with Alexander Mackenzie over delays in commencing the railway.

George Monro Grant, minister of St. Matthew's Church, Halifax, 1863-77; secretary to Sandford Fleming on the chief engineer's transcontinental trip, 1872. His book, *Ocean to Ocean*, describes that journey.

John Macoun, self-educated botanist; companion of Fleming and Grant on their trip from ocean to ocean. Examined the fertility of the North West for the government.

Father Albert Lacombe, Oblate missionary whose parish was the Far West. Appointed pastor to railway workers east of Winnipeg in 1880.

Goldwin Smith, independent journalist, critic and editor of several publications, such as the *Bystander*. A Regius professor from Oxford who made his home in Toronto's Grange, he actively espoused the cause of commercial union with the United States.

Jesse Farley, receiver for the bankrupt St. Paul and Pacific Railroad. He later sued James J. Hill and Norman Kittson, claiming the reorganization of the railroad was his idea. The suit failed.

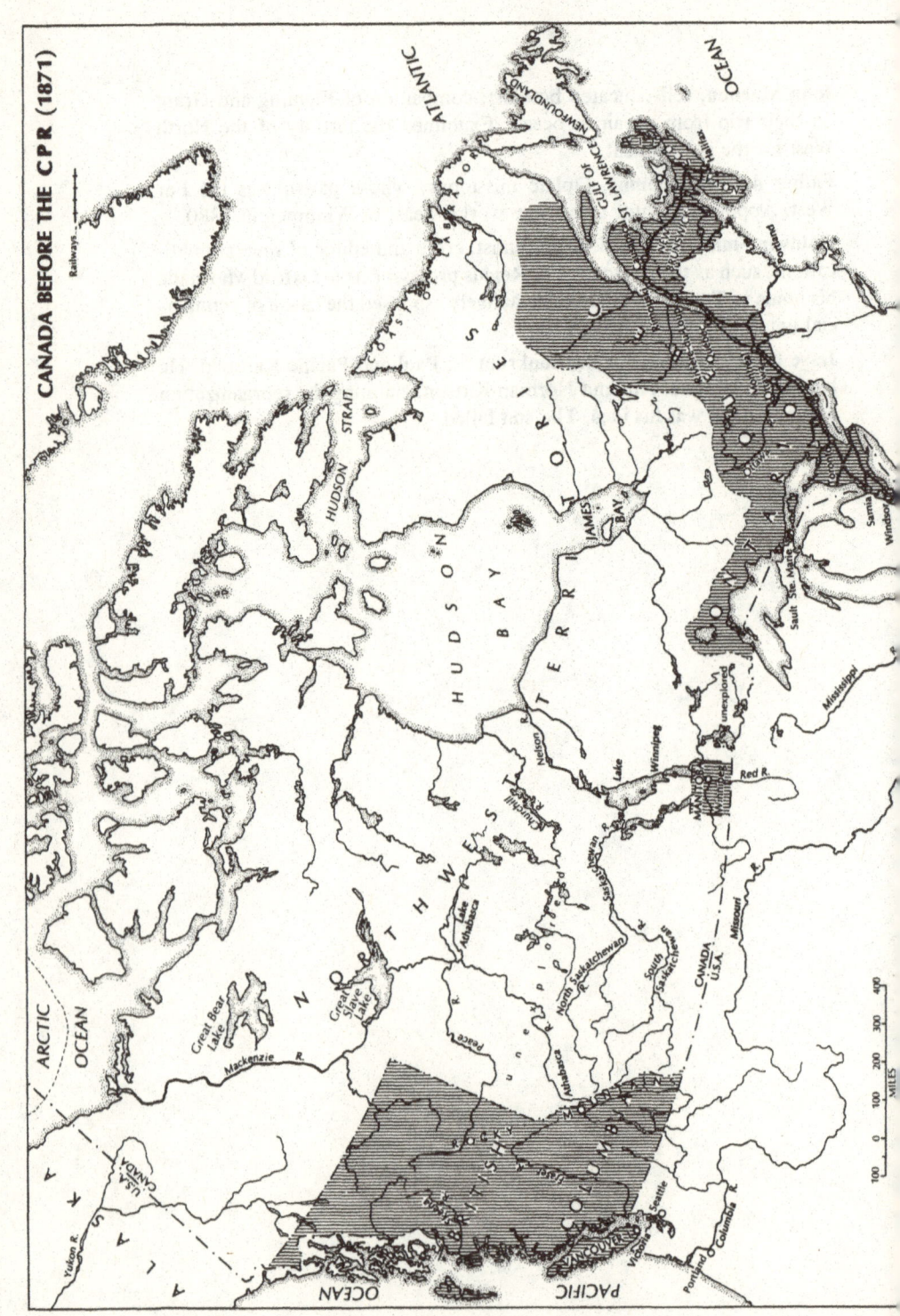

CANADA BEFORE THE CPR (1871)

Railway

ARCTIC OCEAN

YUKON R.

ALASKA

Mackenzie R.

Great Bear Lake

Great Slave Lake

Peace R.

Athabasca R.

Lake Athabasca

NORTH WEST TERRITORIES

unexplored

BRITISH COLUMBIA

Fraser R.

Columbia R.

Portland

Seattle

Victoria

VANCOUVER

PACIFIC OCEAN

North Saskatchewan R.

South Saskatchewan R.

Nelson R.

Lake Winnipeg

Red R.

MANITOBA

unexplored

Missouri

Mississippi

CANADA U.S.A.

HUDSON BAY

JAMES BAY

HUDSON STRAIT

LABRADOR COAST

UNGAVA

NEWFOUNDLAND

ATLANTIC OCEAN

GULF OF ST. LAWRENCE

Halifax

Sarnia

Windsor

Sault Ste. Marie

Toronto

MILES
100   0   100   200   300   400

From Sea to Sea

It is New Year's Day, 1871, the year in which Canada will become a transcontinental nation, and in most of British North America it is bitterly cold. In Ottawa, where it is 18 below, the snow, gritty as sand, squeaks eerily beneath the felted feet of morning church-goers. A cutting wind, blowing off Lake Ontario, is heaping great drifts against the square logs of the Upper Canadian barns, smothering the snake fences and frustrating the Grand Trunk's Montreal-Toronto passenger schedule. On the St. Lawrence, in front of Quebec City, that annual phenomenon, the ice bridge, is taking form. In the harbour of Saint John, the rime hangs thickly upon the rigging, turning schooners and barquentines into ghost ships.

Only at the colonial extremities is New Year's Day a green one. In the English gardens of Victoria, British Columbia, the occasional yellow wallflower still blooms shyly, and in the verdant colony of Prince Edward Island the fields are free of frost. The editorial comments are as salubrious as the climate. The potato farmers of Souris and Summerside read their Saturday Islander with approval: "In our cosy little Island we have scarcely experienced anything but the blessings of Providence," it says. "It is probable that never at any previous period of our existence were we as rich a community as we are at the moment." There is cause for rejoicing: the colony is eagerly awaiting new proposals from Canada calculated to entice it into Confederation; the rumours say that these will be far more liberal than the ones that have been rejected. And why not? After all, British Columbia has been promised a railway!

Three thousand miles to the west, the steam presses of the British Colonist are pumping out a New Year's salutation for the morrow. For British Columbia, the editor writes, the outlook has never been brighter: "Clad in bridal attire, she is about to unite her destinies with a country which is prepared to do much for her." The paper carries a reprint from a Tory journal back east, praising the Government for the nuptial present it is about to bestow.

The world is in its customary turmoil – the Germans at the gates of Paris, the insurrectionists bedevilling Cuba – but in Canada there is nothing but good humour. Even George Brown, the caustic editor of the Globe, is in a mellow mood. One can almost surmise a half-smile lighting up those long, Scottish features as he scribbles an

1

unusually benign editorial in his Toronto office. "Peace and plenty prevail," he writes, "and there is nothing for us but hope and encouragement as we welcome the advent of another year."

It is the Lord's Day and all across settled Canada the curtains are drawn and the church bells are sounding. Only an eccentric would resist their summons. Because of the Sabbath, all the elegant and sometimes lusty New Year's rituals of the Canadian social classes have been postponed for a day. The brass and rosewood, the sterling and cut glass have all been polished to a high gloss by an army of servants, making ready for Monday's "calling." Then will the gentlemen of the towns, frock-coated and convivial, trudge unsteadily from threshold to threshold, to be greeted by well-bustled matrons with puckered lips and full decanters. The temperance movement is crying out against such debauchery. In Montreal, it is reported, some of the ladies have been persuaded to serve coffee. That city, a correspondent notes, has already given the New Year "a sober and orderly welcome."

Far off beyond the sombre desert of the Canadian Shield, at Fort Garry in the new province of Manitoba, the welcome is not so orderly. Fiddles screech, pipes skirl and the settlers caper like souls possessed to an endless succession of Red River reels, while nearby tables groan with smoking joints of venison and buffalo. The great Scottish feast of Hogmanay—New Year's Eve—is far more important than Christmas.

For one Scotsman, there is a special reason to celebrate. Donald A. Smith, late of Labrador, has just won a federal seat in his adopted province's first election. It is a significant victory. The events set in motion by the decisions of 1871 will change the current of Smith's life and enshrine his likeness in the history books of a later century, linking him forever with a symbolic railway spike in a distant mountain pass.

That pass is one thousand miles to the west of the Red River and for all that thousand miles scarcely a light flickers or a soul moves. Awesome in its vastness and its isolation, the newly acquired North West — the heart of the new Canada — sleeps beneath its blanket of snow. Walled off from the Pacific by the vertebrae of the Cordilleras and from the settled East by a granite Precambrian wasteland, the great central plain is like an unconquered island.

The North West! The name is beginning to take on overtones of romance. In the winter, when the blizzard strikes and the heavens

2

are blotted out, it can be a white hell; in the summer, by all accounts, it is an enchanted realm. One can travel for days, they say, along the ruts of the Carlton Trail between Fort Garry and Fort Edmonton without encountering human kind – only ridge after ridge of untrammelled park land rolling on towards the high arch of the sky. Out there, they say, the eye can feast upon acres and acres of tiger lilies and bluebells, stretching to the horizon "as if a vast Oriental carpet had been thrown across the plains." The prairie chickens, they say, are so numerous that they mask the sun, while the passenger pigeons roost so thickly on the oaks that the very branches snap beneath their weight. And there are exquisite lakes, speckled with geese and swans, broad meadows where the whooping cranes stalk about in pairs, and everywhere the ultimate spectacle of the buffalo, moving in dark rivers through a tawny ocean of waist-high grass. Only a privileged few have gazed upon these marvels; the events of 1871 will ensure that they will soon be just a memory.

How many white men inhabit this empty realm? Perhaps twenty-five hundred. Nobody knows for certain because there has never been an accurate census. The North West is a scattered archipelago of human islets, each isolated from the others by vast distances and contrasting life-styles – Scottish farmers, Métis buffalo hunters, Yankee whiskey traders, French missionaries, British and Canadian fur merchants. In the lonely prairie between these human enclaves the nomadic and warlike Indian bands roam freely.

For all of the decade, this wild, misunderstood domain will be the subject of endless speculation, curiosity, political manoeuvre and debate. There are few Canadians yet who care greatly about it; most provincial politicians, indeed, are "either indifferent or hostile to its acquisition." Yet by the fact of its acquisition, the young Dominion has set itself upon a new course. The Conservative Prime Minister, Sir John A. Macdonald, has just promised British Columbia a great railway across the North West to Pacific tidewater. Once that decision is confirmed, as it must be in this pivotal year of 1871, nothing can ever again be the same.

Chapter One

1

Its political opponents pretended to believe that the Macdonald government had gone mad. "Insane" was the word the Liberal leader,
Alexander Mackenzie, used, time and again for most of the decade of
the seventies, to describe the pledge to build a railway to the Pacific.
It was, he said in the House that spring of 1871, "an act of insane
recklessness," and there were a good many Canadians, including
some of John A. Macdonald's own supporters, who thought he was
right.

Here was a country of only three and a half million people, not
yet four years old, pledged to construct the greatest of all railways.
It would be longer than any line yet built – almost one thousand miles
longer than the first American road to the Pacific, which the United
States, with a population of almost forty million, had only just managed to complete.

The Americans had more money, shorter mileage and far fewer
obstacles than the Canadians. For one thing, they knew where they
were going: there were established and sophisticated cities on their
Pacific coastline. But neither John A. Macdonald nor his surveyors
had any idea where they were headed. The only settlement of account
on the Canadian Pacific coast was on an island; the indentations in
the mainland were uncharted, the valleys were unexplored, the passes
were unsurveyed.

For another thing, the United States was not faced with any barrier
as implacable as that of the Precambrian Shield. If the railway followed an all-Canadian route, its builders would have to blast their
way across seven hundred miles of this granite wasteland, pocked by
gunmetal lakes and overlaid with a patchy coverlet of stunted trees.
There were ridges there that would consume three tons of dynamite
a day for months on end; and, where the ridges ended, there was
another three hundred miles of muskegs, which could (and would)
swallow a locomotive at a single gulp. This was land incapable of
cultivation. There were many who held with Alexander Mackenzie
that to build a railway across it was "one of the most foolish things
that could be imagined."

After the Shield was breached, the road was to lead across the
North West – a tenantless empire of waving grass (which many
thought to be unproductive desert) bordered by the thinly forested

valley of the North Saskatchewan River. Every sliver of timber – railroad ties, bridge supports, construction materials – would have to be hauled, league after league, across this desolate land where, it seemed, the wind never ceased.

At the far limits of the plains the way was blocked by a notched wall of naked rock, eight thousand feet high. Beyond that wall lay a second wall and beyond that wall a third. Here were gloomy trenches to be bridged, cataracts to be thwarted and alpine buttresses to be dynamited. At the end of that sea of plumed mountains lay the unknown coastline, tattered like a coat beyond repair. George Etienne Cartier, acting for his ailing leader, had promised British Columbia that the railway would reach that coastline, ready to operate, within ten years. It was, cried Edward Blake, the intellectual giant of the opposing Liberal (or Reform) Party, "a preposterous proposition."

Some of Macdonald's parliamentary followers tended to agree with Blake. The Prime Minister was absent in Washington during the debate over the railway in April, but Alexander Morris, his Minister of Internal Revenue, reported to him that it was the hardest fight since Confederation. Some twenty Government supporters, enough to cause the administration's defeat, were "weak kneed and alarmed." Morris rallied them with a tough speech, telling the caucus it was no time to stab an absent leader in the back; but the decision to build the great railway was a near thing.

The Government had promised the railway to British Columbia in order to lure that colony into the new confederation of Ontario, Quebec, New Brunswick, Nova Scotia and Manitoba. Macdonald's vision of Canada did not stop at the Great Lakes; his dream was of a transcontinental British nation in North America – a workable alternative to the United States. To achieve this dream, the railway was a necessity, or so the Prime Minister insisted: it would stitch the scattered provinces and empty territories of the West together, as the government-owned Intercolonial was intended to do in the East; it would be the means of colonizing the prairies; it would forestall American expansion; it would be the spine of empire, an Imperial highway linking the British Isles with the Orient and avoiding the appalling voyage round the Horn.

There were, almost certainly, more pragmatic reasons. Macdonald needed the diversion of the railway to maintain himself in office. The project was clearly a gamble; but the stakes were high. If he succeeded in fulfilling his pledge, the Conservative Party could probably look forward to a generation of power. No other *fait accompli*, even that of Confederation, could compete with such a triumph. The Government had bungled its handling of Louis Riel, the Métis leader whose prairie uprising in 1869-70 had brought about the formation of the new province of Manitoba. It could not afford to stumble again in the case of British Columbia; the terms to that colony had to be generous. That may have been one reason why, in the summer of 1870, the Government actually offered more than British Columbia asked for. The delegates who visited Ottawa that summer would have been content, initially at least, with a wagon road from the Rockies to the Pacific; it was Cartier, the tough little Quebecker, who talked them into demanding something more ambitious. "No, that will not do," he told them. "Ask for a railway the whole way and you will get it." The Government's explanation was that, since a railway was inevitable, it would be cheaper to build it immediately and save the expense of a road. The Prime Minister, in fact, had already settled on the idea of a transcontinental line. It was to his political advantage to have British Columbia insist upon a railway; it made it easier to convince a sceptical public that the national dream demanded it.

The sceptics had considerable logic on their side; Macdonald had emotion. Could a country of three and a half million people afford an expenditure of one hundred million dollars at a time when a labourer's wage was a dollar a day? Perhaps not; but Macdonald meant to persuade the country that it could not do without a railway if it wanted to be a nation in the true sense of the word. Besides, the Government insisted, the railway would not bring any rise in taxes: it could be paid for with land from the North West.

Why the fixed date of ten years? As Macdonald's opponent Mackenzie said, most of the railway would run through an uninhabitable wilderness: "It wouldn't be necessary to construct the greater portion of the line for another thirty years." That was also perfectly true; but Macdonald's attitude was that there might be no nation in thirty years without a railway. The corner-stone of his transcontinental policy was the settlement of the North West and he and his Ministers pressed the view that without a railway the land would remain empty until the Americans moved in to fill the vacuum. Besides, they had the assurance of the chief British Columbia delegate, Joseph Trutch, that the ten-year clause was not a "cast iron contract" but more a

8

figure of speech; the province would not hold the Canadian government to the letter of the wording.

It was the apparent insistence on an all-Canadian line that brought the harshest criticism. Few Canadians really believed that any railway builder would be foolhardy enough to hurdle the desert of rock between Lake Nipissing and the Red River. No white man had ever crossed it on foot and few reliable maps of the region existed. Macdonald's opponents were all for diverting the line south of Lake Superior, through United States territory, and then heading northwest into Manitoba from Duluth. If North America were one nation that would be the sensible way to go. But Macdonald did not believe that Canada could call herself a nation if she did not have geographical control of her own rail line. What if Canada were at war? Could troops of a belligerent nation be moved over foreign soil? The memory of the Métis uprising of 1869 was still green in the Prime Minister's memory. Unable to use the colonists' route through St. Paul, the troops sent to the Red River had taken ninety-six days to negotiate the forty-seven portages across the Canadian Shield. A railway could rush several regiments to the North West in less than a week. Macdonald did not rule out another rebellion or even a border dispute with the Americans. The Fenian brotherhood had, since 1866, mounted a series of skirmishes across the boundary and would try again on the Manitoba border in the fall of 1871.

The Prime Minister, as he was to say so vehemently on more than one occasion, was born a British subject and meant to die one. His nationalism had two sides. On the positive side he was pro-Canadian which, in those days, was much the same as being pro-British. On the negative side he was almost paranoic in his anti-Americanism. The Americans, to Macdonald, were "Yankees" and he put into that term all the disdain that was then implied by its use: the Yankees were upstarts, money grasping, uncouth, anti-British; and they wanted to grab Canada for themselves, throw off the monarchy and turn solid Canadians into shrill, greedy, tinsel copies of themselves.

Macdonald's opponents might feel that the price of holding the newly acquired North West was too high to pay, but he himself was well aware that some Americans, especially those in Minnesota, saw it as a ripe plum ready to fall into their hands. He believed, in fact, that the United States government "are resolved to do all they can, short of war, to get possession of the western territory." That being so, he wrote in January, 1870, "we must take immediate and vigorous steps to counteract them. One of the first things to be done is to show unmistakeably our resolve to build the Pacific Railway."

There was reason for Macdonald's suspicions. In the very year of Confederation, W. H. Seward, the United States Secretary of State, fresh from his successful purchase of Alaska, had told a Boston audience that the whole continent "shall be, sooner or later, within the magic circle of the American union." His successor, Hamilton Fish, was an expansionist, as was the President himself; though they were not prepared to fight for a piece of Canada, they were delighted to countenance, if not to encourage, a powerful group of Minnesota businessmen and politicians who saw their burgeoning territory extending north of the 49th parallel as a concomitant of the Red River uprising of 1869. In J. W. Taylor, Washington's undercover agent in Winnipeg, they had an ardent sympathizer.

As Macdonald well knew, there were powerful influences working in the United States to frustrate the building of any all-Canadian railroad. In 1869, a United States Senate committee report declared that "the opening by us first of a Northern Pacific railroad seals the destiny of the British possessions west of the ninety-first meridian. They will become so Americanised in interests and feelings that they will be in effect severed from the new Dominion, and the question of their annexation will be but a question of time." A similar kind of peaceful penetration had led eventually to the annexation of Oregon.

It was the railwaymen who coveted the North West. "I have an awful swallow for land," the Northern Pacific's General Cass told the Grand Trunk's Edward Watkin (Watkin later reproduced the despised Yankee vernacular as "swaller"). In 1869 – during the Red River uprising – the Governor of Vermont, John Gregory Smith, who also happened to be president of the Northern Pacific, determined to build that line so close to the Canadian border that it would forestall any plans for an all-Canadian railway. In a conversation with Charles Brydges, a leading Canadian railway man, he made no secret of Washington's willingness to take advantage of the uprising and subsidize the line in order to get possession of the North West for the United States.

By the following year, Jay Cooke, the banker who was the real power behind the Northern Pacific, was so sure of capturing the same territory as a monopoly for his railroad that he was using the idea to peddle the company's bonds. A Northern Pacific pamphlet decried

10

the whole idea of a railway north of Lake Superior: the Americans, it said, would send any branches needed into British territory to service their neighbours.

On one side of the mountains, the railway would siphon off the products of the rich farmlands; on the other side it would drain the British Columbia mining settlements. "Drain" was the operative verb; it was the one the Senate committee used. As for the Minnesotans, they saw their state devouring the entire Red River Valley. Their destiny lay north of the 49th parallel, so the St. Paul *Pioneer Press* editorialized. That was "the irresistible doctrine of nature."

But it was Macdonald's intention to defy nature and fashion a nation in the process. His tool, to this end, would be the Canadian Pacific. It would be a rare example of a nation created through the construction of a railway.

In the Canada of 1871, "nationalism" was a strange, new word. Patriotism was derivative, racial cleavage was deep, culture was regional, provincial animosities savage and the idea of unity ephemeral. Thousands of Canadians had already been lured south by the availability of land and the greater diversity of enterprise, which contrasted with the lack of opportunity at home. The country looked like a giant on the map, second only in size to China. For most practical purposes, it stopped at the Great Lakes.

The six scattered provinces had yet to unite in a great national endeavour or to glimpse anything remotely resembling a Canadian dream; but both were taking shape. The endeavour would be the building of the Pacific railway; the dream would be the filling up of the empty spaces and the dawn of a new Canada.

2

For almost forty years before Macdonald made his bargain with *The* British Columbia, there had been talk about a railway to the Pacific. *dreamers* Most of it was nothing more than rhetoric. It cost Joseph Howe little, in 1851, to utter his remark about some of his listeners living to hear a steam whistle in the passes of the Rockies. A century later, public figures were prophesying with equal recklessness and incidental accuracy that their children would live to see a man land on the moon. The comparison is a reasonable one: for most colonial Canadians at mid-century the prospect of a line of steel stretching off two thousand miles into the Pacific mists was similarly unreal.

Thomas Dalton, the editor of the Toronto *Patriot*, has been credited with the first vision. He talked vaguely, in 1834, of an all-steam route by river, rail and canal from Toronto to the Pacific and thence to the Orient. His friends dismissed him as a mere enthusiast, by which they probably meant he was slightly demented. Every far-sighted scheme has its quota of eccentrics and the railway dream was not immune. In 1845, a prodigious pamphleteer who called himself Sir John Smyth, Baronet, popped up in Toronto with a long printed tract urging a line of steam communication around the globe, including a rail and water route through British North America. Smyth was not taken seriously, possibly because of the string of titles he arranged to follow his by-line. These included "moral philosopher" and the initials "P.L.," which, Smyth insisted, stood for "poet loret." In those days just about anybody could afford to publish a pamphlet.

Between 1848 and 1850, however, a series of works was published by three sets of authors, and these *were* taken seriously. The first of these, and the most prescient, was by another Smyth – Major Robert Carmichael Smyth, a 49-year-old British engineer. A career soldier since the age of sixteen, Carmichael Smyth had just returned to England from service in Canada with the 93rd Highland Regiment. He first posed his idea of an "Atlantic and Pacific Railway" in 1848, in a series of letters to his shipboard acquaintance, the humorist Thomas Chandler Haliburton, creator of Sam Slick. Carmichael Smyth gathered the letters into a pamphlet early the following year and his enthusiastic advocacy of this "great link required to unite in one chain the whole English race" appealed to the imperialism of London editors and their readers. The *Daily Mail* called it "a noble plan," the *Morning Herald* endorsed the idea and so did the *Economist*, although the latter said that the actual job of building should be left to the colonists and not the mother country. Since Carmichael Smyth had reckoned the cost at seven hundred million dollars and since the colonists at that point had built only a few miles of railway, the suggestion was not immediately practical.

Nevertheless he lived to see his prophecies come true. In his pamphlet he asked: "Who will be the first locomotive engineer to inscribe upon the Rocky Mountains: 'Engineer A.B. piloted the first locomotive engine across the Rocky Mountains'?" Carmichael Smyth was still alive, thirty-five years later, when on a warm July day,

12

Robert Mee stepped from his CPR cab and, with a can of red paint, answered the query.

Although Carmichael Smyth overestimated the cost of the line, he was uncannily accurate about its route. It took more than ten years of surveys and untold squabbling to arrive at roughly the same location he scrawled across his map. His pencil even crossed the Rockies in the approximate vicinity of the Kicking Horse and Rogers passes, which at that time had not been discovered. And he also saw, quite clearly, that the road could be made to pay for itself through the traffic of the colonists it transported to the new land.

Almost simultaneously, an Irish subaltern in the Royal Engineers, Lieut. Millington Henry Synge, proposed a vast rail and water highway across the continent. Synge, who rose to be a major-general, was a member of the many-branched Millington Synge family, whose genealogical tree is studded with bishops and baronets and not a few imaginative writers of whom John Millington Synge, the Irish playwright, is the best known. His plan, though treated with respect at the time, bordered on the fanciful. Synge was stationed at Bytown near the famous flight locks of the Rideau and this proximity may have been the source of his mind-boggling suggestion for a canal through the Rockies – "steps of still water," as he airily described it.

Synge suggested importing the surplus unemployed of England to build the railway while Carmichael Smyth had advanced the idea of using convict labour. Both schemes were united, with scrupulous detail, in 1850, in a tome entitled *Britain Redeemed and Canada Preserved*. The authors were F. A. Wilson, an old Hudson's Bay Company man, and A. B. Richards of Lincoln's Inn, London. In 556 weighty pages, the authors contemplated the employment of twenty thousand convicts to break ground and rough-hew the line. In addition, a body of sixty thousand volunteers from "among the suffering poor of our most distressed counties" would be signed on for three years, at soldier's pay. An accompanying fold-out map showed the line running straight as a ruler from Halifax to the Pacific, oblivious of rock, muskeg, lake or mountain. The authors were so enamoured of the idea of a convict work force that they tended to dismiss geographical location.

Wilson and Richards were taking no chances on escapees. To protect the Canadian public there would be a network of forts and garrisoned barracks, constructed of "the gigantic logs of the country," vigilantly guarded and encircled by moats and palisades. Indian tribes would be encouraged to scour the country for missing male-factors. Canadian woodsmen would be formed into mounted patrols to assist the guards along the line of route. And, in case any of the fugitives tried to disguise their close-cropped heads with false hair, the promoters of the plan proposed to crop their eyebrows as well.

Once the railway was finished, the miscreants were to be shipped off to the bleak Labrador peninsula because of the "very remarkable and salutary influence which the contiguous climate of Nova Scotia seems to exercise upon the *morale* of persons inhabiting that country." A legion of five thousand "Pioneer Rifle Guards" would be recruited for Labrador, in case the climate failed in its work of rehabilitation.

These published parlour games were all very well but thus far nobody had invested a single dollar in a road to the Pacific. In 1851, Allan Macdonell, a Toronto mining man and promoter, made the first concrete move: he organized a company and applied to the Legislative Assembly of Canada for a charter to build a railway to the Pacific. It would cost more than eight million pounds, he estimated, and would have to be built in stages, paid for step by step by land subsidies and the tide of advancing settlement. The standing committee on railways reluctantly reported that the plan was premature. The land across which Macdonell's line would run belonged to the Hudson's Bay Company.

Macdonell was not finished; indeed, he had only just begun to fight. He was a resolute figure, a lawyer and one-time sheriff who had, during the 1837 rebellion, raised a troop of cavalry at his own expense. He knew the Lake Superior country well, having explored it in an open boat as a prospector before its waters were charted. With his mining background and his eternal optimism, he was, perhaps, the first of that authentic Canadian breed, the Toronto promoter. Nothing, it seemed, could keep him down. His prospectus glowed with the same kind of purple prose and starry-eyed confidence that was to distinguish later speculative literature from Bay Street. Macdonell called upon his readers to hark back to the construction of the pyramids of Egypt and the Great Wall of China, built by "a semi-barbarous people, centuries before the Christian era." In the light of such marvels, he hinted, the construction of a railway to the Pacific would be mere child's play: ". . . let us not insult the Enterprize of this enlightened age by denouncing as visionary and impractical the plan of a simple line of rails over a surface of no greater extent, without one-half the natural obstacles to overcome."

Macdonell *was* denounced as visionary and impractical and his scheme viewed "as an hallucination to amuse for a moment and then to vanish." Such criticism failed to daunt him. He applied again to the legislature and was again turned down. He applied a third time and was for a third time turned down. He would not quit. He went on the attack, addressing public meetings, denouncing the monopoly of the Hudson's Bay Company. He fired the Toronto Board of Trade into action. He brought old Red River settlers to Toronto to write letters to the press and speak out against the monopoly. When a government committee inquired into the Hudson's Bay lands in 1857, Macdonell was one of the chief witnesses before it.

He was perfectly confident that he would get his railway charter and he had reason to be, for the climate for railway building in Canada was undergoing a dramatic change. When Macdonell first applied for a charter in 1851, Canada had built only about two hundred miles of railway – this in spite of the fact that it had chartered thirty-four railway companies with a total capitalization of $12,800,000. The United States, by comparison, had built ten thousand miles. Two years later the dam burst and the country entered into an orgy of railroad building which saw the construction of the Grand Trunk, the Great Western and the Northern. It was, in the words of Thomas Keefer, himself a respected engineer, "the saturnalia of nearly all classes connected with railways." In this euphoric period was launched the partnership between railways, promoters, politicians and government that became the classic Canadian pattern for so many public works. Francis Hincks, the joint premier of the united Canadas until 1854, held thousands of shares of Grand Trunk railway stock; he was one of that company's most enthusiastic supporters. His successor, Allan MacNab, was at the same time the president of the Great Western Railway. George Etienne Cartier, who (with John A. Macdonald) became joint premier in 1857, was the salaried solicitor of the Grand Trunk. Three powerful politicians, Alexander Galt, David Macpherson and Luther Holton, all made fortunes out of Grand Trunk construction contracts.

It is no accident that four of these men were leading Tories and another, Galt, became one. Most Conservative politicians were business or professional men who welcomed the idea of a partnership between big business and government to build the country. Profits and politics tended to become inseparable. By 1871, when Macdonald launched his Pacific railway scheme, there were forty Members of Parliament and twelve Senators – promoters, directors, contractors or company presidents – with vested interests in railroads. The great majority were Conservatives; only eleven of the Members and four of the Senators called themselves Liberals.

The Liberal opposition to Macdonald's railway policy stemmed in part from the excesses of the railway boom of the fifties. The Clear Grits of Ontario, led by prudent Calvinists in the persons of George Brown and Alexander Mackenzie, became jaundiced over the avalanche of spending. They viewed the Conservative railway schemes as a device to stay in office. The Grits, who were to form the nucleus of the Liberal Party after Confederation, came mainly from the farming counties of western Ontario; they were zealous reformers – "all sand and no dirt, clear grit all the way through" – and they had reason to be outraged. Between 1854 and 1857 an estimated one hundred million dollars in foreign capital was pumped into Canada for the purpose of building railways. Much of it found its way into the pockets of promoters and contractors. The usual scheme was to form a company, keep control of it, float as much stock as possible and then award lush construction contracts to men on the inside. Thomas Keefer insisted that when the Speaker's bell rang for a division, the vast majority of the members of the legislature from Canada West were to be found in the apartments of an influential railway contractor who dispensed champagne as freely as if it were sarsaparilla. Keefer told of cabinet ministers accepting fees from promoters, contractors and railway officials and making such men "their most intimate companions, their hosts and guests, their patrons and protégés." One American contractor, he said, virtually ran the Upper Canadian government in the fifties.

The railways publicly wooed the politicians, carrying them free on the slightest excuse and planning luxurious excursions of which the Grand Trunk's three-week junket to the Maritimes in 1864 was perhaps the most memorable. Sixty-five politicians and forty newspapermen, many of them accompanied by their wives and children, accepted the railway's largesse and set off through Detroit, Chicago, Toronto, Montreal, Portland and Saint John on an odyssey which had a dual purpose: it popularized both the railway and the concept of a confederated Canada.

In such an atmosphere, it was inevitable that Allan Macdonell would eventually get his way. After his three rebuffs, he tried for a fourth time and was granted, in 1858, a charter to construct a railway linking the navigable waters to the North West. His board of directors included two former premiers, a chief justice and a future lieutenant-governor. In spite of this glittering display of political muscle, the enterprise was short lived. The promoter's ambitious plan to combine steamers, barges, locomotives and even wagons into one multi-faceted transportation system was blocked by his old adversary, the Hudson's Bay Company. Macdonell managed to put a single boat on the lakes but did not drive a foot of steel. By 1860 the scheme had collapsed.

In spite of such frustrations it had become fashionable by this time to talk of a Pacific railway. Edward Bulwer-Lytton, the English novelist and politician, Samuel Cunard, the Canadian shipbuilder, and Edward Watkin, the future president of the Grand Trunk, all followed Joseph Howe in paying lip-service to the principle. Both the British and the Canadian governments began to take an active interest in examining the North West with an eye to possible railway routes and a series of expeditions was launched at the end of the 1850's to explore all the country between Lake Superior and the Rockies – land still under the control of the Hudson's Bay Company.

Then, in 1862, Sandford Fleming entered the picture and placed before the government the first carefully worked out plan for building a railroad to the Pacific. Fleming was already a respected railroad engineer; he had just laid out the Northern, from Toronto to Collingwood. He had read Carmichael Smyth's pamphlet and it was this work that convinced him a railway across the continent was practical. Fleming, however, was not a man to lay a ruler across a map and call it a right of way. As a surveyor he knew that the ultimate location would depend upon the travail and, in some cases, the lives of hundreds of men toiling for years with aneroid and spirit-level, clawing their way up mountain slopes, struggling through impossible mires, clambering mile after bone-weary mile across acres of deadfalls. He had, after all, done it himself. What Fleming drew up was a combined work and cost sheet, together with a step-by-step scheme for development.

Of all the men connected with the active planning and construction of the great railway, only Fleming (apart from the politicians) was present at both the beginning and the end. His massive figure is to be seen in that most famous of all Canadian photographs, gazing down at Donald Smith hammering in the last spike – a mountain of a man in a stovepipe hat, his vast beard trimmed in the shape of an executioner's axe. It is surely no accident that Fleming is the only man in that historic picture dressed in formal clothes. If he had a sense of occasion it was because he had begun his involvement with the railroad a good seventeen years before any of the others who posed that day at Craigellachie in the mountains.

When Fleming wrote his "Observations and Practical Suggestions on the Subject of a Railway through British North America," he was only thirty-five and most of his awesome accomplishments (including the invention of standard time) lay ahead of him. Typically, his outline for a "highway to the Pacific" was carefully thought out, measured and detailed. It was to be built in gradual stages: a territorial road first, then a telegraph line, then a railway laid directly on the original roadbed. It would cost, he figured (with remarkable accuracy, as it turned out), about one hundred million dollars and it would take at least twenty-five years to build.

It was the cautious and meticulous plan of a cautious and meticulous Scot, for Fleming, in spite of his inventive record (he had designed the first postage stamp in Canada and founded the Canadian Institute), was nothing if not deliberate. He worked out every detail down to the last horse, cross-tie and telegraph pole, and, of course, to the last dollar. His gradualness, he conceded, would not "satisfy the precipitate or impatient," but he included in his memorandum a reminder of Aesop's hare and tortoise, pointing out that the line of the railway extended over forty-five degrees of longitude, which was "equal to one-eighth of a circle of latitude passing entirely around the globe." After all, wrote Fleming, "half a continent has to be redeemed and parted at least from a wild state of nature."

It was an impressive memorandum and it undoubtedly did a great deal to advance Fleming's considerable ambitions. Eight years later, when Canada's pledge to British Columbia passed the Commons, the Prime Minister appointed Fleming Engineer-in-Chief of the Canadian Pacific Railway in addition to his previous appointment to the same capacity with the government-owned Intercolonial, then being built to link the Maritime provinces with central Canada. Being a politician, though a Scot, Macdonald *was* both "precipitate and impatient" by Fleming's standards. George Etienne Cartier had, on his behalf, promised British Columbia that the railway would be commenced within two years and finished in ten. Certainly ten years had a more attractive ring than twenty-five; and the Prime Minister could reassure himself that he had Joseph Trutch's promise that the Pacific province would not hold him too firmly to that reckless schedule.

3

The Canada of 1871 was a pioneer nation without an accessible frontier. The Canadian Shield was uninhabitable, the North West virtually unreachable. The real frontier was the American frontier, the real West the American West. As the decade opened, a quarter of all Canadians in North America were living south of the border.

Some went for adventure. These included the father of Buffalo Bill Cody, who had once kept a tavern in Toronto Township, and, significantly, two Minnesota steamboat men from Rockwood, Ontario, and Sorel, Quebec – James J. Hill and Norman W. Kittson – who would, a few years later, help launch the Canadian Pacific Railway. Some went for greater opportunity. These would soon include the frustrated composer of *O Canada*, Calixte Lavallée. But most went for land. The good land ran out in Upper Canada in the 1850's and over the next generation the country began to feel a sense of limitation as farmers' sons trekked off to Iowa and Minnesota never to return. The nation's life-blood was being drained away.

A moving frontier is essential to the vitality of a burgeoning nation. It tends to draw to it the boldest and most independent spirits in the country and they in turn, stimulated and tempered by its challenge, become a regenerating force. Canada, by its geography, was being denied this kind of transfusion.

The call of the land was far stronger than the call of country. "The young Canadian leaving his native country to seek his fortune in the United States feels no greater wrench than a young Englishman would feel in leaving his county to seek his fortune in London," the novelist Anthony Trollope noted during a voyage to North America. Nationalism, in the seventies, was a sickly plant. Even W. A. Foster, the founder of "Canada First," the one authentic attempt at a nationalism of sorts, admitted that many Canadians were devoid of national feeling. In his famous address on the subject he quoted an English visitor who said that "to the Canadian it is of small concern what you think of his country. He has little patriotic pride in it himself.

Whatever pride of country a Canadian has, its object, for the most part, is outside Canada."

Indeed, the very utterance of the phrase "Canadian Nation" was denounced in some quarters. "Canada," said the *Globe*, "except by a mere play on words, is not a nation." The newspaper helped destroy the Canada First movement by attacking it as disloyal and anti-British. The whole idea of a national spirit or "national sentiment," to use the phrase of the day, was under suspicion as being slightly treasonous. William Canniff, who traced the growth of national feeling in a book published in 1875, wrote that after Confederation "there was hope that . . . the petty warfare of faction would be entirely submerged in a common Canadian sentiment. But this hope was short-lived." And Goldwin Smith, the Regius professor from Oxford who made his home in The Grange at Toronto, wrote sadly that "the province, the sect, Orangism, Fenianism, Free Masonry, Oddfellowship, are more to the ordinary Canadian than Canada."

If far off fields looked greener to many Canadians, it was because life at home often seemed drab and unrewarding. Trollope confessed that in passing from the United States into Canada one moved "from a richer country into one that is poorer, from a greater country into one that is less." An Irishman who had spent a brief period in Canada before succumbing to the lure of the United States set down, in 1870, his feelings about the land he had left behind: "There is no galvanizing a corpse! Canada is dead – dead church, dead commerce, dead people. A poor, priest-ridden, politician-ridden, doctor-ridden, lawyer-ridden land. No energy, no enterprise, no snap."

It was a harsh indictment but there was some truth in it. The country was controlled by the land-owning classes – the merchants, the professional people and the farm owners. In the United States manhood suffrage was universal; in Canada, the propertyless had no vote. An examination of the Parliament of 1871 shows clearly where the political power lay. Seventy-four Members were merchants or businessmen; eighty-seven belonged to the professions (half of these were lawyers); only fourteen were farmers.

The new dominion was not yet a cohesive nation but rather a bundle of isolated village communities connected by tenuous threads. Three-quarters of the population lived in comparative isolation on farms where, of necessity, most activity ceased at dusk and where, at certain times of the year, the condition of the concession roads made extended travel nearly impossible. There was scarcely a city worthy of the name "metropolis." Montreal with a population of one hundred thousand was really two cities – one French speaking, one English. Toronto, with half that population, was still largely an over-sized village dominated by men of narrow views – Methodists, Tories and Orangemen; it reeked, as most cities did, of fresh manure, discarded garbage and the stench of ten thousand outdoor toilets. Ottawa was beyond the pale. For a newly elected Member of Parliament, it was, in the words of George Rose, the British humorist, "simple banishment." Rose, who passed briefly through the new dominion after touring the United States, thought of Canada as "at best the Siberia of Great Britain." As for the new capital, he was baffled that anyone, especially a peer of the realm, would choose to spend time there at all: "One doesn't know what can induce a man to accept the post of Governor-General unless he should be a misanthrope or have hosts of relations at home whom he is anxious to make distant."

For the industrial worker, life in Canada was harsh and colourless: he toiled for longer hours and for lower pay than his counterpart across the border. (In Quebec the *annual* wage in industry was $185; in Ontario, $245.) But there was not much industry; in all of Canada it employed fewer than two hundred thousand people. Thus there was little opportunity for those who wanted to escape the drudgery of the farms.

In those days of dawn to dusk labour, there were three major spare-time activities: for the land holders, there was politics; for the women, there was religion; for the labourers on farms and in factories, there was strong drink. A man applying for a job was generally asked two questions, his politics and his religion. His chance of acceptance depended upon how he replied. Political animosities were bitter and party allegiance generally unyielding. Most of the space in the newspapers was given over to political comment, almost all of it shrill and carping. As for the church, it was a welcome respite for those women who enjoyed no other real reprieve from the desolation and travail of farm life. The church was the hub of every small community, providing a platform for visiting lecturers and thespians and a meeting place where an unattached young lady might encounter a prospective husband. A sermon was as good as a stage show and, for many, the only entertainment they knew.

Alcohol in the seventies was both the national pastime and the national problem. Half of all the arrests in the Dominion were for offences connected with liquor. Toronto had more than five hundred saloons, dispensing whiskey at two cents a shot. Barn raisings, picnics and work "bees" of all kinds were lubricated with barrels of what the flourishing temperance movement was calling "demon rum." Delirium tremens was a common ailment. Special police patrols were needed in the cities to trundle staggering workingmen off to jail, while others were left insensible or prostrate in the mud of the streets. Leading politicians – those who did not trenchantly advocate temperance – did not seem to mind being seen inebriated, nor did the spectacle appear to affect their popularity. Joseph Howe, D'Arcy McGee and Macdonald himself were all legendary tipplers.

But it was the labouring classes who drank the most. It was the only amusement that came within the reach of their pocketbooks. A newspaper cost five cents – for that price you could get a full quart of beer in a tavern. A minstrel show cost fifty cents and for *that* you could buy a gallon or two of whiskey. The link between strong drink and the grey quality of Canadian life is inescapable.

It is small wonder then that under these conditions many a Canadian looked with longing eyes across the border where the work opportunities were more varied, where social conditions were better, where every man had the vote and where the way to the frontier farmland was not barred by a thousand miles of granite and swamp.

It was a strangely intense love-hate relationship that the country had with the United States. Publicly the Americans were vilified; secretly they were admired. The very newspapers which attacked the hated Yankees published syrupy American serial stories on their front pages instead of solid Canadian news. The very people who scoffed at the ingenious Yankee labour-saving gadgets, such as the eggbeater, were the ones who bought them. Canadians sang Yankee songs, attended Yankee plays, minstrel shows and circuses, read Yankee authors and were beginning to accept Yankee customs – the "boarding house" rather than the British lodging, for example. And almost everybody wanted the return of reciprocity with the United States. It could open up an enormous and attractive market for Canadian products.

The Yankees were thought of as go-getters and, though this propensity was publicly scoffed at, many a Canadian – Alfred Waddington, the railway promoter was one – felt his own country's business leaders lacked something of the Americans' commercial zeal. The attitude was well expressed by a British travel writer, who reported

22

that "in Canada everyone skates well. The Yankee rarely snatches time from his business for such recreation."

If the Yankees were envied, they were also feared. The memory of the Fenian raids was still green in everyone's mind; the suspicion lingered that the Americans had secretly encouraged them. Canadians were still moving to the United States in disturbing numbers but, in spite of this – or perhaps because of it – any newspaper could be sure of a hearing if it launched a violent anti-American attack and any politician could secure a following by damning the Yankees. Making fun of the Americans was almost a national pastime and had some of the overtones of latter-day anti-Semitism. The cartoonist's stereotype, Brother (or Cousin) Jonathan, later to be renamed Uncle Sam, was pictured in unflattering terms in the pages of such short-lived *Punch*-style humour magazines as *Diogenes* and *Grinchuckle*. He was a sharp storekeeper with hard, cold eyes, whittling on a piece of wood. He was a lecherous roué, or an unshaven suitor, rejected by an innocent "Miss Canada." He was a red-nosed toper, kicked in the pants by a vigorous "Young Canada," the precursor of Jack Canuck. Yankee speech was lampooned in painfully laborious dialect stories, in which Americans invariably said "wall" for well, "fust" for first, "jest" for just, "thar" for there and never, *never* sounded the final "g." Americanisms such as "to velocipede" or "specimentary" came under attack from grammatical pedants while such Yankee habits as serving ice water with meals or chewing tobacco – habits also indulged in by large numbers of Canadians – were sneered at in print.

All these attacks on the Yankees underlined the undeniable truth that they were different from the British. Canada – aside from Quebec – was still very much a British nation, with British habits, attitudes, speech, mannerisms and loyalties. Almost all immigrants came from the British Isles, continued to think of the motherland as "home," and often returned to it. Such disparate public figures as Edward Blake, the Reform leader, and George Stephen, the CPR president, would, after spectacular careers in Canada, suddenly choose to move to the old country. The habit of giving three cheers for Queen and Country (the country being Great Britain), and for anyone else who was royal, at dinners, military parades and political gatherings was universal – among French-speaking Quebeckers as well as British born Canadians. Royal and vice-regal visits produced paroxysms of excitement. The Dominion was, indeed, more British than Canadian.

23

So lightly did some school texts take Confederation that, even in the seventies, they continued to use such obsolete names as Upper and Lower Canada and Rupert's Land. Cricket had not yet given way to baseball and only a few Canada Firsters thought Canadian scenery worth painting; the leading artists continued to portray English cows and Dutch windmills. Class was important; church and family traditions were often placed above money in the social scale and the "best" families flaunted coats of arms. Titles were coveted by politician and merchant prince alike. That was the great thing about Canada in their eyes: its British background provided the climate for a merchant nobility that served as a bulwark against the creeping republicanism from south of the border, which the newspapers decried so vehemently.

The newspapers, which mixed advertising with news and opinion with fact in the most ambiguous fashion, led the attack on the Americans. They published dire warnings to those who would emigrate south of the border. American commerce was declining, they declared; prices in the U.S. were excessively high; the rates of taxation were crushing. Most of all they harped on the dangers of "republicanism"; again and again they sought to demonstrate that it inevitably led to crime and corruption.

In this attempt to stem the flow across the border, no hair was too fine to split. Witness the Toronto *Leader*'s editorial in the first month of the new decade:

"Are any of our Canadian farmers thinking of migrating to the United States? Perhaps not. Certainly not if they have paid due attention to the intimations we, from time to time, have to make of the differences of living, which are perplexing the settlers in that country and of the distress that pervades all classes. But in case there should be any who will not heed our warnings, it may be well to remind them of a little matter to which we have not yet directed their attention . . . that farmers in the U.S. are not permitted to sell the produce of their own farms without first taking out a license as produce brokers. . . ."

It is doubtful if this kind of quibble prevented many young men from quitting the narrow concession roads of Canada for the broader highways to the south. "Antipathy to the Americans," wrote Goldwin Smith, ". . . does not hinder young Canadians from going by the hundreds to seek their fortunes in the United States." The railways were running west and prosperity followed them. In those halcyon days the building of a railway was automatically believed to spell good times: anyone who turned his eyes south and west could see that.

But railways meant something more. Out beyond that sprawl of billion-year-old rock lay an immense frontier, of which Canadians were dimly becoming aware. It was now their land, wrested in 1869 from the great fur-trading monopoly of the Hudson's Bay Company after two centuries of isolation; but they did not have the means of exploiting it. A railway could give them access to that empty empire. Canada in 1871 was a country whose population was trapped in the prison of the St. Lawrence lowlands and the Atlantic littoral. A railway would be the means by which the captive finally broke out of its cage.

4

The North West was, in 1871, an almost totally unknown realm. *The struggle* Until the sixties, it had been generally considered worthless to anyone *for the* but fur traders – a Canadian Gobi, barren, ice-locked, forbidding *North West* and totally unfit for settlement. In 1855 the Montreal *Transcript* wrote that it would not even produce potatoes, let alone grain. This attitude was fostered and encouraged by the Hudson's Bay Company, whose private preserve it had been for almost two centuries. The last thing the great fur-trading empire wanted was settlers pouring in. Even bridges were taboo: they might encourage colonists. When Father Lacombe, the saintly voyageur priest, finally had one built at the St. Albert Oblate mission near Fort Edmonton, the Governor himself tried to have it destroyed. At that time it was the only bridge in all of Rupert's Land.

James Young, the Galt M.P., in his reminiscences of those days, recalled that "even the most eminent Canadians were deceived by these representations. For example, up to the time of Confederation, Sir George Cartier strongly opposed its acquisition by this country. The Prime Minister himself, at that time, had no idea of the value of the North West from an agricultural, commercial or manufacturing point of view."

As late as March, 1865, Macdonald had written to Edward Watkin that "the country is of no present value to Canada. We have unoccupied land enough to absorb the immigration for many years, and the opening up of the Saskatchewan would do to Canada what the prairie lands are doing now – drain away our youth and strength."

George Grant, the Halifax preacher, himself a strong advocate of a transcontinental nation, collected, in 1868, a sum of three thousand dollars to alleviate the sufferings of the Red River settlers during the disastrous grasshopper plague of that year. The remoteness of the region struck home to him. "I could have collected the money quite as easily and the givers would have given quite as intelligently, had the sufferers been in Central Abyssinia," he recalled.

Historically, Montreal had dominated the North West through control of the fur trade; but in the mid fifties, Toronto moved to seize the initiative from its metropolitan rival. The lack of good land was one reason why Toronto's eyes turned westward; the last block of wild land was auctioned off in western Ontario in 1855. The completion of the Northern Railway to Collingwood on Georgian Bay in the same year was another; as the woodburners puffed into the wilderness, members of the Toronto business community – Allan Macdonell was typical – began to glimpse a new prosperity based on the opening of a trade and transportation route to the Red River and the eventual settlement of the prairie lands.

The leading Toronto expansionist was George Brown of the *Globe*, who had been interested in the North West since 1847 and had referred to it in his maiden speech in the legislature in 1851. In the summer of 1856, at the height of the railway-building spree, Brown launched a campaign designed to educate his readers to the potential of the North West and to make the Hudson's Bay Company, who controlled it, into the villain of the piece; it was no accident that his brother, Gordon, had an interest in a company planning a line of steamboats on the Lakes. The Browns had the support of the Toronto Board of Trade, which, after a fiery meeting in December, 1856 (addressed by the unquenchable Macdonell), petitioned the government to investigate the Hudson's Bay Company's title to the North West. The following year Brown rammed through a plank at the Reform convention in Toronto demanding the incorporation of the Company's territories into Canada.

It was this Toronto agitation that led to the government-sponsored exploration of the North West in 1857 and the appointment the same year by the British House of Commons of a Select Committee to examine the whole question of the Hudson's Bay territories in North America. Twelve years later the company ceded it all to Canada.

There is irony in the attitudes towards western expansion in the years before Confederation. The Brownite Liberals and the Toronto merchants and promoters had set their sights on far horizons beyond the prairies. "It is my fervent aspiration and belief," Brown said in a speech in Belleville in 1858, "that some here tonight may live to see the day when the British-American flag shall proudly wave from Labrador to Vancouver Island, and from our own Niagara to the shores of Hudson Bay." On the other hand, the Montrealers and the Conservatives, including Macdonald himself, looked eastward; they were far more concerned with federating the Atlantic provinces with the two Canadas. Yet it was Montreal, in the end, which captured the prize of the Pacific railway, Macdonald who became the advocate of precipitate western expansion and the Liberals, under Alexander Mackenzie (with Brown as his mentor), who opposed it.

Macdonald's indifference to the North West continued until 1869 when the Red River uprising inflamed the nation and launched the tragic odyssey of Louis Riel. No other figure in Canada's frontier past has so fascinated historians and writers, not to mention playwrights and even librettists. Villain or hero, martyr or madman – perhaps all four combined – Riel dominates the story of the opening of the prairies.

When he set up his independent state in the heart of North America he was just twenty-five years old, a swarthy figure with a drooping moustache and a shock of curly hair. Some scores of literary scalpels have since attempted the dissection of that perplexing personality. All agree that he was a solitary man with few confidants outside of his priest and his mother. All agree that his Roman Catholic religion – the narrow, ultramontane version absorbed during his college years in Montreal and at his mother's knee (she saw visions and heard the voice of God) – was a dominant force in shaping him; at the end of his life it was interwoven into his madness. The evidence shows that he was a passionate man with a quick temper and a love of popular adulation who liked to get his own way and who could be violent when crossed; it also shows that he preferred non-violence and on more than one occasion practised it to his own detriment. He could be as compassionate as he was pious but, as everyone knows, he was hanged for a crime which some called murder and others, execution. He was, by turns, politically pragmatic – the murder-execution was more pragmatic than vengeful – and mystically idealistic. A champion who was prepared to sacrifice himself for his people, he was also capable of taking a bribe (to quit the country) in 1871 and of asking for another (to abandon his people and his cause) in 1885. It is small wonder that it took a century before a monument was raised to him in the province he helped to found.

Riel was born a westerner and a Métis, which means he was a French-speaking Roman Catholic of mixed race. In his case his veins were tinctured with the merest dash of Cree blood. His father, who was to have been a priest, became an eloquent tribune of his people, and Louis, the eldest of eleven, inherited the mantle of political agitator. His schooling in Montreal, his brief period in the law office of a leading radical, and his own prairie heritage had shaped this clever, intense and apparently humourless youth into a racial patriot ready to champion the half-breed cause at Red River.

The Métis were in a state of turmoil when Riel arrived back at St. Boniface in 1868 because their status quo was threatened by the yeasty combination of events arising out of Confederation and the imminent sale of the Hudson's Bay lands to Canada. The settlement of the West, they knew, meant an end to their own unique society, the loss of the lands on which many of them had squatted, usually without title, and the eventual break-up of their race.

Métis society was built on the law of the buffalo hunt, a twice-yearly event, which was run with a military precision that produced generalship of a high order and led to the first stirrings of political organization among an essentially nomadic people. The statistics of such hunts are remarkable. The greatest employed four hundred mounted hunters, twelve hundred carts and sixteen hundred souls, including women and children. This vast, itinerant city crawled across the plains, stretching for miles, on its way to a border rendezvous with the Métis of Dakota; there, near Pembina, it formed itself into a gigantic circle, one thousand feet in diameter, ringed with oxcarts placed hub to hub and a triple row of teepees. Then, after four days of painstaking organization, which saw the election of captains, soldiers and guides, it rolled off once more – every cart in its exact place – towards the final encounter with the great herd. The climactic scene was awesome: the ground shaking as if from an earthquake, the sky blacked out by the immense clouds of dust, the phalanx of mounted hunters, muskets raised, galloping towards the stampeding beasts, the prairie running red with the blood of the animals. Such a spectacle would be unthinkable in a land of roads and railways, fences and furrows. By 1869, with the Hudson's Bay Company about to yield up its lands to Canada, surveyors from the East, without a by-your-leave, were already setting up their transits on Métis river lots.

The Métis were not Canadians and did not think of themselves as such. Neither did the white Selkirk settlers of the Red River or the Protestant half-breed farmers. Within the community there was a small "Canadian Party" whose orientation was white, Protestant, Orange and Upper Canadian. Its leader was a towering journalist and surgeon named John Christian Schultz. He and his colleagues had strong links with the Toronto expansionists and Canada Firsters (who were, really, Upper Canada Firsters) with whom they were working for annexation. Schultz and his shrill followers helped precipitate the Métis uprising which Riel did not begin but which he did organize and shape with consummate skill.

The details are familiar to most Canadian high school students. By the end of 1869, without a single act of violence, Riel and the Métis had raised their own flag over the Red River settlement and were preparing to treat on equal diplomatic terms with Donald A. Smith, the Hudson's Bay man from Montreal and Labrador, whom the Government had hastily dispatched. Since the great fur company had formally relinquished its territory and Canada had yet to take it over (the Métis prevented the erstwhile lieutenant-governor from crossing the border) Riel was in an interesting bargaining position. Soon he had the entire community behind him save for the incendiary members of the Canadian Party whom he had imprisoned. Had matters rested there, Louis Riel would undoubtedly have brought the community peacefully into Confederation on Métis terms and taken his place with men like Joseph Howe and D'Arcy McGee as a great Canadian statesman, his name enshrined on countless hospitals, ball parks, schools and expressways.

This was not to be. Schultz and some of his cronies escaped from Riel's prison and mounted a counter-movement. The Métis quickly put it down but one of the Canadians, a sinewy Orangeman named Thomas Scott, could not be put down. When he tried to murder Riel, he was summarily court-martialled and sentenced to be shot. In this single act of violence was laid the basis for a century of bitterness and controversy.

Of all the pivotal figures in Canadian history, Thomas Scott is one of the least engaging. His breed was not uncommon in Ontario – a bigoted Protestant Irishman, totally unyielding, always inflammatory, who was nourished by his own hatreds. Scott would have driven a less mercurial man than Riel into a fury: he attacked his guards, urged his companions to follow suit, taunted the Métis and vowed to escape and kill their leader. Riel made his death a deliberate act of policy: Canada must learn to respect his people. One can pity Scott, as he is dragged before the firing squad, faced for the first time with the realization that the Popish half-breeds actually mean what they say (his shocked cry, "This is cold-blooded murder!" was to echo for decades through the back roads of Ontario); but one can never like him. He makes his brief, incandescent appearance on the stage of history and is gone, writhing on the ground, not quite dead from the firing squad's volley, waiting for the *coup de grâce*. But his memory remains and his tragedy, mythologized out of recognition (as Riel's was to be), will kindle an unquenchable conflagration in Orange Ontario.

The massive demand for revenge, washing over Parliament Hill like a tidal wave, forced the Government to mount, in 1870, a largely unnecessary military expedition across the portages of the Shield to relieve a fort which Riel was preparing to hand over peacefully. The expedition did have one other purpose: Macdonald, now thoroughly alive to the perils of further indifference, was not unhappy about a show of military strength in the valley of the Red River which the Minnesota expansionists clearly coveted.

By January, 1870, Macdonald had determined that speedy construction of a railway across the new territory to the Pacific was a necessity. Charles Brydges of the Grand Trunk had warned him that Washington would try to use the Riel troubles to frustrate Canada's acquisition of the North West. Macdonald, whose own intelligence from the United States confirmed Brydges's fears, wrote that "no time should be lost in this."

Riel's own story almost exactly parallels that of the railway. Unwittingly, he helped to launch it; unwittingly again, fifteen years later, he helped to save it; he was hanged within a few days of the driving of the last spike. Forced into hiding and finally into exile in the United States, Riel was twice elected to Parliament from the riding of Provencher in the new province of Manitoba, of which he was the undisputed founder. He could not take his seat – the Ontario government had put a price of five thousand dollars on his head –

but before he vanished over the border, he indulged in one last, dramatic piece of stagecraft. The scene is Ottawa in 1874 – a snowy afternoon in January. Two muffled figures appear at a side door of the Parliament Buildings. One tells the clerk on duty that a new member has come to sign the roll. The bored clerk hands the stranger a pen: he scratches his name and slips away. Idly, the clerk glances at it and utters a startled cry. There are the words "Louis Riel" burning themselves into the paper. The clerk looks up; but the outlaw waves sardonically and vanishes. He will not return until 1885 to play his unknowing role at the most critical moment of all in the history of the Canadian Pacific Railway.

5

By 1871, with the events from Manitoba still making headlines week *The* after week, Canadians began to look upon their new North West *land beyond* with the same mixture of wonder, guilt and apprehension that they *the lakes* would bring to the country north of 55 in John Diefenbaker's day: *It must be wonderful to see it! Oh, if only one* COULD *see it, but it was so remote, so hard to reach! Something ought to be done about developing it; they said parts of it were very rich. But would you want to* LIVE *there – so far away from everything, in that dreadful climate? One day, of course, millions would live there – that was certain. One day . . .*

If the attitudes to the North West were vague, confused and uncertain, part of the reason lay in the conflicting reports about it. Some said it was little more than a desert; others saw it as a verdant paradise. Even the two official government explorations of the territory launched in 1857 – one by the British, one by the Canadians – differed in their assessments.

The best-remembered of these expeditions was that of the British, mounted by a dashing Irish bachelor named John Palliser, who left his name on a triangle of supposed desert in what is now southern Alberta. The expedition was Palliser's own idea and it came at the height of the restless mid-Victorian era – a period that saw the sons of the landed gentry striking out on voyages of exploration and adventure to the far corners of the globe, plunging through African jungles and veldt, attacking the Arctic ice pack, staggering across

31

the plains of Australia and North America, always with magnificent aplomb. The Palliser brothers were all seduced by this wanderlust. Two went off to shoot big game in Ceylon, another headed for the China seas where he rescued a French lady from pirates. A brother-in-law vanished into the Australian wilderness, a second was lost on Franklin's last polar expedition. John Palliser, fired by a relative's tales of the Missouri country, had already trekked across the western plains, living with the Indians, running the gantlet of war parties and bagging buffalo, three of which he brought back to Ireland alive in the company of a black bear, an antelope, two Virginia deer and an Indian dog.

What, then, was more natural than that this darkly handsome and muscular bachelor with the aquiline face and the romantic sideburns, seeing another intriguing blank space on the map, should view the Canadian North West as a new land to conquer? There was so much to learn out there, beyond the inland seas: where did the British territory end and the United States territory begin? Were there workable passes in the Rockies? Was a railway feasible across those plains and mountains?

There was only one problem: Palliser's family had fallen upon lean days; his father was being forced to sell the family estates to make ends meet. The expedition would cost at least five thousand pounds, and Palliser could no longer afford that amount. He approached the Royal Geographical Society for support. His credentials as a typical Victorian adventurer were impeccable. He was fluent in five languages, was a crack shot, could camp out and take care of himself in the wilds and had travelled the world. The Society, which was interested in both the climate and the geology of this unknown region of the continent, decided to back Palliser; and so did the Imperial government.

Palliser's commission was broad. He was to explore an empire from Lake Superior to the Rockies and he was to report on *everything* – agriculture, minerals, settlement possibilities, and, of course, possible transportation routes. He was to keep every conceivable kind of record, botanical, zoological, meteorological, magnetic. As companions he was given three ill-assorted but dedicated scientists. There was Eugène Bourgeau, a plump and unfailingly cheerful little naturalist known as "the Prince of Botanical Collectors." There was Dr. James Hector, a slender Scots geologist of twenty-three whose inner resolve belied his scholarly features; with Spartan discipline

32

Hector had trained himself to endure discomfort. Finally, there was a frosty-looking magnetical observer from the Royal Artillery, Thomas Blakiston, an able and ambitious Crimea veteran but such a terrible stickler for form and place that he finally parted company with the expedition and went off on his own.

Palliser and his companions were two years in the field and their accomplishments, though obscured at the time (the expedition's report was delayed in its publication until 1862 and Palliser's map until 1865), were monumental. They explored, by a variety of routes, all of the country between Lake Superior and the Pacific coast. Bourgeau collected 460 species and sixty thousand specimens, some of which are still to be seen in the museum and herbarium of the Royal Botanical Gardens at Kew. Hector discovered the Kicking Horse Pass and was almost buried alive as a result. His horse, stumbling in the frothing waters, dealt him a blow with its hoof which rendered him insensible. The Indians, believing him dead, popped him into a freshly dug grave and were about to shovel in the earth when the supposed corpse, conscious but unable to utter a word, managed, by a single prodigious wink of one eye, to shock the would-be burial party into less precipitate action. With Hector in great pain and his companions close to starvation, the party plunged on through the newly named pass, following the turbulent river along the line of the future CPR.

But the idea of a railway in the shadows of those rumpled peaks was far from Palliser's mind. He had been asked to judge whether or not, in the carefully non-committal prose of the Colonial Office, "the country presents such facilities for the construction of a railway as would at some period, though possibly a remote one, encourage her Majesty's government in the belief that such an undertaking between the Atlantic and Pacific Oceans will ever be accomplished."

His answer was bluntly negative. His knowledge of the country would never lead him to advocate a railway "exclusively through British territory." Across the prairies, certainly; but that armoured barrier north of Lake Superior "is *the* obstacle of the country and one, I fear, almost beyond the remedies of art." The sensible method was to go through American territory south of the lake and cut up to Manitoba through Pembina on the border, if and when the Americans built their own lines to that point.

Meanwhile the government of the united Canadas, prodded by George Brown and the Toronto expansionists, had mounted, in 1857,

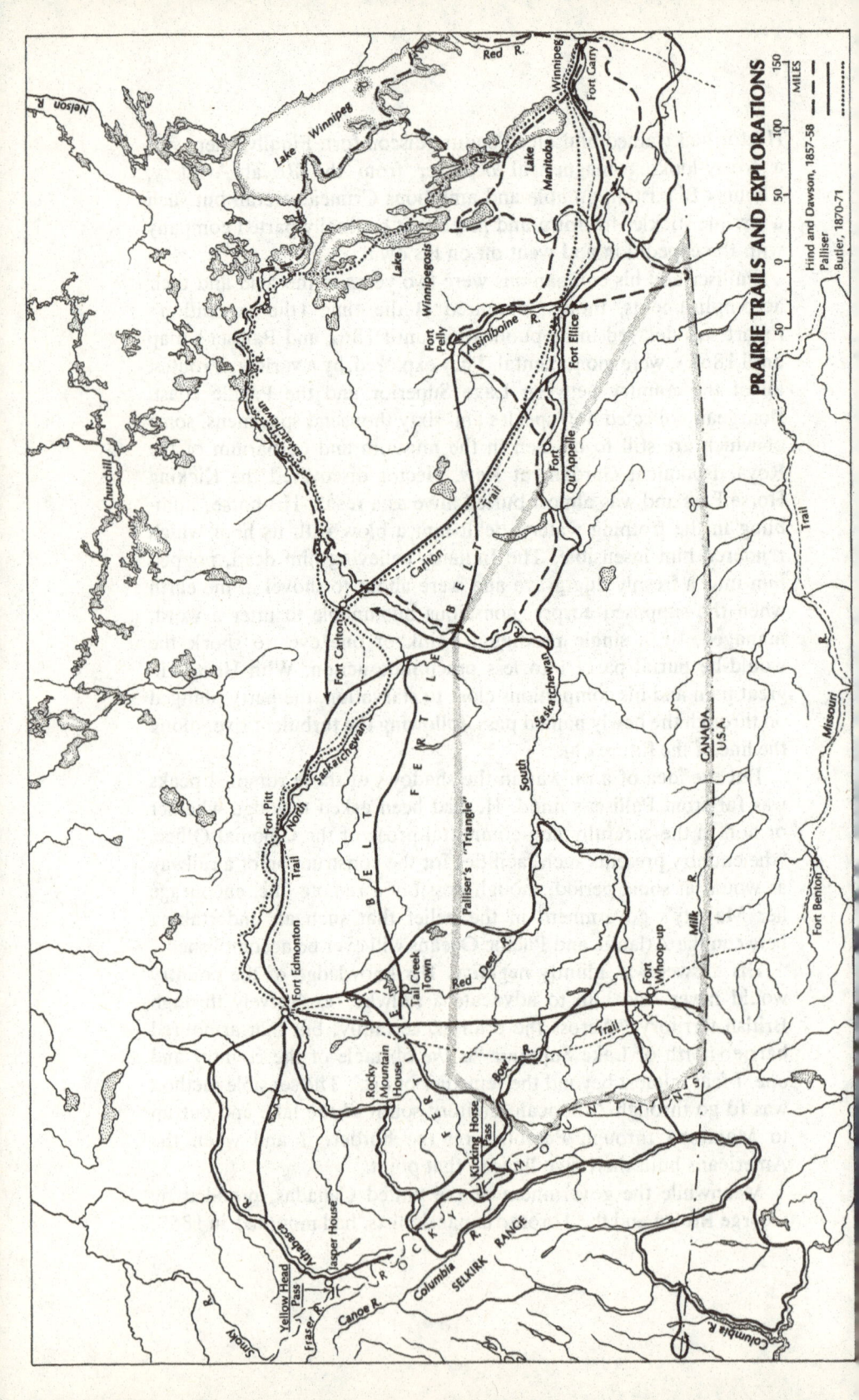

PRAIRIE TRAILS AND EXPLORATIONS

Hind and Dawson, 1857-58
Palliser, 1857-60
Butler, 1870-71

MILES
0   50   100   150

a similar expedition under George Gladman, a retired Hudson's Bay chief trader. Though he was the nominal head, the key men were Henry Youle Hind, a self-assured young professor of geology and chemistry from the University of Toronto, and Simon James Dawson, a sharp-featured civil engineer from Trois Rivières. The following year these two men, without Gladman, co-directed a second expedition made up of several parties which explored the Assiniboine and Saskatchewan river country.

In their separate reports, the Canadian explorers were, significantly, far more optimistic about an all-Canadian railway than the members of the British expedition. Gladman did not feel the difficulties to be "insuperable to Canadian energy and enterprise." Hind thought Palliser too sweeping in his condemnation of the route across the Shield, which was "of vast importance to Canada." Hind agreed with Palliser that the Great American Desert had its apex in the Far West but along the wooded valley of the North Saskatchewan and some of its tributaries there was "a broad strip of fertile country." Hind wrote in his report that "it is a physical reality of the highest importance to the interest of British North America that this continuous belt can be settled and cultivated from a few miles west of the Lake of the Woods to the passes of the Rocky Mountains." He was impressed enough by that statement to render it in capitals. In Hind's view this was the route that any railway must take to span the great central plain. He borrowed the magic name of "Fertile Belt," which Palliser had first used, and the name stuck. To the south was an "Arid Belt" – Palliser's Triangle, in truth – which Hind, too, felt was unfit for human habitation.

Hind's enthusiasm for the Fertile Belt was to have a profound effect on the railway planners; from that point on few gave serious consideration to taking the CPR farther to the south. Hind also helped promote the North West as a land of promise. "A great future lies before the valley of the Saskatchewan," he declared. "It will become the granary of British Columbia, the vast pasture field by which the mining industry of the Rocky Mountains will be fed."

In 1871, a decade after Hind wrote those words, his vision still belonged to the future. The land beyond the lakes had not changed greatly since he and Palliser explored it. To the men of the North West Canada remained a foreign country; their world ran north and south. In the Far West, the mail bore United States postage for it went out to civilization by way of Fort Benton, Montana, a situation that continued until the end of the decade. The Red River settlers' nearest neighbours lived in Minnesota and the most travelled of the prairie trails was the one that ran from Fort Garry to the railhead at St. Cloud, where the settlers did their shopping.

There were, in point of fact, several "Wests," each with its own social customs, way of life, traditions and loyalties. The truly wild West of the whiskey traders and wolf hunters in the foothills north of the Montana border bore no relation at all to the cultivated valley of the Selkirk settlers, eight hundred miles to the east. Even the mode of transportation was different: in the Far West bull trains took the place of Red River carts. The Métis buffalo hunters, who were beginning to quit the Red River country for the unsettled plains, had established Tail Creek town, the strangest of all communities, near the site of what is now Stettler, Alberta. Their West was as distinct from that of the Hudson's Bay traders as Belgium is from Yugoslavia. Beyond the mountain wall lay other "Wests": the lively camps of the Cariboo miners, complete with hurdy-gurdy girls and wide open saloons, and the fiercely British colony of Victoria with its pretty English gardens and its obligatory rituals of teatime and tiffin.

The whiskey traders lived in impregnable forts, which bore names like Robbers' Roost, Whiskey Gap and Whoop-up. They fought the nomadic wolf hunters with rifles and cannon and, on one memorable occasion, with the threat of a lighted cigar held over an open barrel of gunpowder. Their folkways reflected the frontier culture of the American West, of which they were a spiritual extension. They carried six-shooters on their hips and they believed that the only good Indian was a dead one.

The traditions of the Selkirk settlers in Manitoba, founded sixty years before by the fifth Earl, and still the only agricultural community in all the North West, were Scottish. The feast days were Scottish, the worship was Scottish, the music was Scottish and the chief mode of transportation, the Red River cart, had a Scottish ancestor.

Tail Creek town, by 1874, was the capital of the western buffalo hunt. Its floating population sometimes reached two thousand. Here, in four hundred huts of sod and log, the language was French, the accent Canadian, the religion Catholic and the institutions peculiarly Métis. When the season was at its height, men and women danced all night to the unceasing screeching of violins which were passed from one exhausted fiddler to the next until the dawn broke. It was a frenzy that contrasted sharply with the cool precision of the hunts themselves.

One hundred miles to the north lay the palisades of the Hudson's Bay Company's Fort Edmonton, a minor fief, feudal in its structure, sufficient unto itself. This was the chief centre for the sparse band of missionaries, traders and trappers who travelled the forested belt of the North Saskatchewan. South of that natural boundary lay the empty plains, dominated by the Indian tribes. As late as 1875 not a single white settler had yet ventured there.

To cross the North West, in the days before the railway, was a considerable feat attempted by only a hardy few. The chief form of transportation was by Red River cart, "scrub oak shaganappi and squeals," as John McDougall, the pioneer Fort Edmonton trader called them. The carts, pulled by oxen, were adapted from Scottish vehicles – light boxes, each perched on a single axle with wheels six feet high. There was one difference: they contained not a single nail nor, indeed, a scrap of iron. Instead, tough strands of buffalo hide – the all-purpose "shaganappi" – were used. The axles could not be greased because the thick prairie dust would quickly immobilize the carts; as a result the wheels emitted an infernal screeching, "the North West fiddle," as some pioneers dubbed it.

With the clouds of yellow prairie dust that were raised in their wake, the brigades of carts were made visible and audible for miles. Jean d'Artigue, a Frenchman who spent six years in the North West during the seventies, wrote that the sound had to be heard to be really understood: "A den of wild beasts cannot be compared with its hideousness. Combine all the discordant sounds ever heard in Ontario and they cannot reproduce anything so horrid as a train of Red River carts. At each turn of the wheel they run up and down all the notes of the scale without sounding distinctly any note or giving one harmonious sound."

The carts generally travelled in brigades, some of which were as long as railway trains. The most memorable, and surely the loudest, was the one organized in 1855 by Norman Kittson, the St. Paul trader. It contained five hundred carts and took one month to reach the Minnesota capital from Fort Garry.

The carts left deep ruts in the soft prairie turf, so deep that the wagons tended to spread out, the right wheel of one cart travelling in the wake of the left wheel of the cart ahead; thus, the prairie trails could be as much as twenty carts wide, a phenomenon that helps explain the broad streets of some of the pioneer towns. Portage Avenue in Winnipeg, the widest thoroughfare in Canada, is actually part of the old trail that led west to Portage la Prairie.

These trails furrowed the plains like the creases on a human palm. The well-rutted trail from the Red River settlement to Minnesota was paralleled in the Far West by a similar trail from Fort Edmonton to Fort Benton, Montana. Another trail ran southwest from the Red River settlement to Fort Benton. The most famous trail of all was the Carlton Trail, the aorta of the plains, winding for 1,160 miles from Fort Garry to the Yellow Head Pass in the Rockies by way of Fort Carlton and Fort Edmonton. It was slow going to travel that famous thoroughfare. It took a good forty days for an ox cart to negotiate the initial 479 miles to Fort Carlton – the halfway point – where the trail branched off for various destinations. But for half a century this was the broad highway used by every explorer, settler, trader or adventurer who set his sights for the West. When the railway was planned, almost everybody expected it to follow the general course of the Carlton Trail. This was not to be, but a later railway did just that: it forms part of the Canadian National system today.

The trails crossed the domain of the buffalo whose numbers, in the early seventies, were still legion. The open prairie was covered with their dried dung, which provided the only fuel for hundreds of miles; often, too, it was white with their bones – so many that, from a distance, it seemed as if a blizzard had covered the grass. As late as 1874, when the newly formed North West Mounted Police made their initial trek across the plains, their colonel estimated, within the range of his own vision, one million head stretching off to the horizon. And the sound of them! To the Earl of Southesk, "the deep, rolling voice of the mighty multitude came grandly on the air like the booming of a distant ocean." This was a domain which few men ever saw; it could not exist for men. The railway would mark its finish.

For the few who had come, nature might be idyllic but life was harsh. They huddled in drafty cabins, ill-lit by candles made of grease or buffalo chips and heated by a single box stove. They slept on mattresses stuffed with prairie grasses, spread out on bunks fashioned from green lumber whipsawed by hand. The price of groceries was so astronomical that they were, often enough, obliged to do without. In the words of Mrs. David McDougall, who bore the first white child along the Saskatchewan in 1872, it was "meat, morning, noon and night until I could have cried for joy to have seen some fresh fruit."

The savage blizzards of winter could fell the hardiest, as they did the respected prairie missionary George McDougall in 1876; in summer the clouds of mosquitoes could drive oxen mad. Then there were the great fires that could leave the land a blackened ruin and the grasshoppers that, in plague years, could eat everything, including the curtains on the windows, leaving no green or living sprout behind.

In the East such phenomena were not understood. By 1872, the trickle of settlers westward was reaching the thousands. The soldiers who had struggled over the portages at the time of the Métis uprising, returned with tales of the rich humus in the Red River Valley. Their colonel, Garnet Wolseley, had himself written in *Blackwoods* magazine that "as far as the eye can see, there is stretched out before you an ocean of grass, whose vast immensity grows upon you more and more the longer you gaze upon it." It brought, he said "a feeling of indescribably buoyant freedom [that] seems to tingle through every nerve, making the old feel young again. . . . Upon the boundless prairies, with no traces of man in sight, nature looks so fresh and smiling that youth alone is in consonance with it."

These were heady words but there were headier by far to come. Another dashing and romantic Irishman was back from the North West and very shortly the country would be agog with his descriptions of the region which he called "The Great Lone Land."

6

William Francis Butler has been called hot-blooded and impulsive. *Ocean to* He does not look it in his photographs; but then one must remember *Ocean* that the photographers of that era had to support their subjects on metal posing stands and hold their heads steady with neck clamps (later removed from the print by a retoucher) so that they could endure the time exposures necessitated by wet plate photography. The glazed eye and the frozen expression became the accepted portrait style. Long after a faster process was invented, people thought they had to maintain a corpse-like aspect, devoid of levity. Butler, *circa* 1870, is a solemn, dome-headed young subaltern, the long oval of his face exaggerated by his close-cropped Souvaroff-style side whiskers and moustache. Only the eyes are alive.

But he *was* impulsive. He was stationed in England when he

learned that the Canadian government was mounting an expedition against Riel. The news could not have come at a more propitious moment. A remarkably intelligent officer, who had seen twelve years' service in India, Burma and Canada (he had been there during the Fenian troubles of 1867), he ought to have been promoted long before. But in those days commissions were purchased, not earned, and Butler did not have the fifteen hundred pounds it would cost him to accept the proffered command of a company.

He was faced with a terrible dilemma: he could serve on as a junior officer, watching "the dull routine of barrack life grow duller," or he could quit the service and face an equally cheerless existence as the governor of a penitentiary or the secretary of a London club – and worse still, "admit that the twelve best years of life had been a useless dream." He was positively thirsting for adventure "no matter in what climate, or under what circumstances." The Red River uprising saved him from an irksome choice. The news of the expeditionary force had scarcely reached England before Butler was off to the nearest telegraph office, dashing off the cheapest possible cable, consistent with politeness, to the expedition's commander, Colonel Wolseley: *"Please remember me."* Then, without waiting for an answer, he caught the first boat for North America.

When Butler reached Canada he found to his chagrin that there was no job for him. Butler suggested one: that of an intelligence officer who, by travelling through the United States, might possibly enter Riel's stronghold from the south. Wolseley liked the idea and Butler leaped into his assignment with enthusiasm. He slipped past Riel and his men at the Red River, returned to the rebels' headquarters where he interviewed Riel himself and then, following the old voyageur route, paddled his way east to the Lake of the Woods where he made his report to Wolseley.

When the troops entered Fort Garry, Butler was with them; but he found the subsequent anti-climactic weeks irksome. One night during a dinner at the home of Donald A. Smith, he suddenly announced that he was returning to Europe to resign his commission and join the French forces at that time embroiled in the Franco-Prussian war.

Smith had a better idea. Out along the North Saskatchewan there had been continuing disorders, which the local Hudson's Bay Company factors had been powerless to prevent. The Indians were being ravaged by smallpox and cheap whiskey, to what extent no one knew.

Something in the way of troops might be needed. Why not send Butler to make a thorough report?

Shortly thereafter, the Lieutenant-Governor, Adams Archibald, sent for Butler, outlined Smith's plan and suggested he think it over.

"There is no necessity, sir, to consider the matter," responded the impetuous officer. "I have already made up my mind and, if necessary, will start in half an hour."

It was typical of Butler that he made his mind up on the instant, regardless of the circumstances. He would not wait for the summer, when the trails were dry, the grouse plentiful, the shadberries plump and juicy, and the plains perfumed with briar rose. It was October 10 "and winter was already sending his breath over the yellowed grass of the prairies." With a single Métis guide, Butler set off on a cold and moonless night, the sky shafted by a brilliant aurora, prepared to travel by foot, horseback and dog sled across four thousand miles of uninhabited wilderness.

"Behind me lay friends and news of friends, civilization, tidings of a terrible war, firesides, and houses; before me lay unknown savage tribes, long days of saddle-travel, long nights of chilling bivouac, silence, separation and space!" Butler loved every minute of it.

He acquitted himself handsomely. It was his recommendation to the government, following his return, that led to the formation of the North West Mounted Police. But it was his subsequent book, *The Great Lone Land*, with its haunting descriptions of "that great, boundless, solitary waste of verdure" that caught the public's imagination. The title went into the language of the day. For the next fifteen years, until the railway made the land lone no longer, no description, no reference, no journalistic report about the North West seemed complete without some mention of Butler's poetic title. It was as well that the CPR was built when it was; long before the phrase was rendered obsolete, it had become a cliché.

But Butler's description of what he saw and felt on that chill, solitary trek across the white face of the new Canada will never be hackneyed:

"The great ocean itself does not present more infinite variety than does this prairie ocean of which we speak. In winter, a dazzling surface of purest snow; in early summer, a vast expanse of grass and pale pink roses; in autumn, too often a wild sea of raging fire. No ocean of water in the world can vie with its gorgeous sunsets; no

41

solitude can equal the loneliness of a night-shadowed prairie: one feels the stillness and hears the silence, the wail of the prowling wolf makes the voice of solitude audible, the stars look down through infinite silence upon a silence almost as intense. This ocean has no past – time has been nought to it; and men have come and gone, leaving behind them no track, no vestige, of their presence."

Butler went back to England eventually, returned to write a second book, this one called *The Wild North Land*, and pursued, for the remainder of his years, a distinguished military career. Wealthy or not, his calibre was such that they had to make him a general and, when the great British river flotilla went up the Nile in its vain attempt to save Gordon from the Mahdi, Butler was in charge of it. He gathered many trophies and not a few decorations but his book was his monument and his closing words rang down the corridor of the decade like a trumpet call:

"Midst the smoke and hum of cities, midst the prayer of churches, in street or *salon*, it needs but little cause to recall again to the wanderer the image of the immense meadows where, far away at the portals of the setting sun, lies the Great Lone Land."

Butler's book was published in 1872. The following year another work on the North West made its appearance. It was so popular that it went into several editions and was serialized in the newspapers. Its title, *Ocean to Ocean*, also became part of the phraseology of the day. It was the saga of two bearded Scots, who, in one continuous passage by almost every conveyance available travelled entirely through British territory to the Pacific Coast – a feat which captured the public's imagination.

The author of *Ocean to Ocean* was a remarkable Presbyterian minister named George Monro Grant, who was to become one of the most distinguished educators and literary figures of his time. He was already an outstanding preacher whose sermons, at St. Matthew's, Halifax, were so eloquent and forceful that sinners of the deepest dye were seen to emerge from their pews actually beaming after suffering the scourge of his tongue.

Grant was Sandford Fleming's choice for the post of secretary to the transcontinental expedition that the Engineer-in-Chief organized in 1872 to follow the proposed route of the new railway. The surveyor had determined to see the country for himself and discuss the

42

progress of the field work at every point with the men on the ground. He could scarcely have chosen a better companion, for Grant had the same breadth of vision as his own. Many of his parishioners agreed with the elderly lady who said that Grant was "far too much taken up with the affairs of the world ever to have been a minister." In 1867 he had been a strong advocate of Confederation, a cause not popular with all of his congregation; one of them told him bluntly to "stick to your damn preaching and leave the politics to us." But Grant was already a Canadian first and a Nova Scotian second; he did not believe that the future of his province lay in petty sectionalism; the prosperity of the part, he was certain, depended on the development of the whole. His odyssey with Fleming resolved in his mind "the uneasy doubt . . . as to whether or not Canada had a future."

In Grant, Fleming had a trail-mate who was leather-tough and untroubled by adversity, a good man in the best sense, from whose bald brow there always seemed to shine the light of Christian good humour, in spite of an invalid wife and one retarded son. He himself had come through the fire, having been thrice at death's door in the very first decade of life: scalded half to death, almost drowned and given up for dead and mangled by a haycutter, which cost him his right hand. This accident-proneness – it sprang out of bubbling high spirits and an incurably restless energy, which saw him engaged in a score of boyhood scrapes – had a maturing effect on him. His mother firmly believed that God had a purpose in sparing him; Grant himself said that without the loss of his hand he would not have achieved the success that was later to be his. Confined by his accident, the handicapped boy brought to the world of books the same zestful curiosity with which he had examined the haycutter. At college he was known as an outstanding and intensely competitive student, debater, orator and, in spite of his missing hand, a good football player.

Grant was, in a London journalist's phrase, "the realized ideal of Kingsley's muscular Christian." When he joined Fleming's expedition, he was in the prime of life – a lithe thirty-seven, with a high, savant's dome, flat straight nose, intense Scottish eyes and the inevitable beard. He stood, at that moment, at the threshold of a great career which would lead him to the principal's chair at Queen's. The notes for *Ocean to Ocean* were transcribed late at night, at the end of a hard day's travel, by the light of a flickering campfire, but the

43

book itself, a polished and readable polemic for the new Canada, bore no sign of haste or hardship. In the words of Grant's son, "it revealed to Canada the glories of her northern and western territories, and did not a little to steel the hearts of many through the dark days that were to come."

The expedition set out across the Great Lakes by steamer into the stony wasteland of the Shield where Fleming's surveyors were already inching their way – and sometimes meeting their deaths – in a land untouched by white men's moccasins. The party included Fleming's son and a Halifax doctor friend of Grant's, Arthur Moren. Soon another remarkable figure was to be enlisted.

Not long after embarkation, Fleming's attention was attracted by the enthusiasms of an agile and energetic man with a brown beard and twinkling eyes. This creature invariably leaped from the steamer the instant it touched the shoreline and began scrambling over rocks and diving into thickets, stuffing all manner of mosses, ferns, lichens, sedges, grasses and flowers into a covered case, which he carried with him.

It was only because the steamer whistled obligingly for him that he did not miss the boat. Sometimes, indeed, he was forced to scramble up the side after the ship had cast loose from the pier. The sailors called him "the Haypicker" and treated him with an amused tolerance, but his enthusiasm was so infectious that he soon had a gaggle of passengers in his wake, scraping their shins on the Precambrian granite, as he plucked new specimens from between the rocks.

This was John Macoun, a botanist on the staff of Albert College in Belleville, enjoying a busman's holiday in the wilds. Fleming asked him casually if he would care to come along to the Pacific and Macoun, just as casually, accepted. Timetables in the seventies were elastic and, though the prospect of a twenty-five-hundred-mile journey across uncharted prairie, forest, mountain peak and canyon might have deterred a lesser man, it only stimulated Macoun, in the garden of whose lively mind the images of hundreds of unknown species were already blooming.

Macoun was a natural botanist, almost entirely self-taught. As a child he had been credited with the sharpest eyes among his fellows, able to find more strawberries and birds' nests than any other boy in the school. At thirteen he had quit school and shortly after that departed his native Ireland (then in the throes of the ghastly potato famine) to seek his future in Upper Canada. He began his new life

44

as a farmhand but he could not resist the lure of plants. He determined to become a teacher in order that he might devote his spare hours to a study of botany. It tells something of the educational system of those days that he had little trouble in achieving his ambition. After a three-day study of a plain grammar text, Macoun left his job, walked forty-three miles in the dead of winter to the home of the county school inspector and was given to understand that he was practically qualified. He received his certificate in just three weeks and began his new career teaching, of all subjects, astronomy.

In his spare moments, this enormously energetic and dedicated Irishman read his way through the standard scientific tomes, collected specimens by the hundreds, hobnobbed with every botanist he could find, talked botany with anyone who would listen, built himself a herbarium and, partly by trial and error, partly by osmosis, and partly by sheer, hard slogging, slowly made himself a botanist of standing in both Europe and America.

In 1869, just ten years after he had left the farm and set himself on his chosen path, John Macoun was offered the chair of Natural History at Albert College. That summer he began the series of Great Lakes vacation-studies that brought him, three years later, into the ken of Sandford Fleming.

This accidental meeting between Fleming and Macoun was immensely significant. Macoun, the perennial enthusiast, became enamoured of the North West. It was he, perhaps more than anyone else, who eventually convinced the Government, the public at large, and, finally, the men who built the Canadian Pacific Railway, that Hind and Palliser were wrong – that the land to the south of the Saskatchewan River was not an arid belt but a fertile plain. In doing so he helped change the course of the railway and thus, for better or for worse, the very shape of Canada. It is possible that the south Saskatchewan farmers, eking out an existence along the drought-stricken right of way during the 1930's, might have cursed his memory, had they been aware of it.

By the time they left the steamer and headed out across the rock and muskeg towards the prairie, Macoun, Grant and Fleming had become a close triumvirate. It makes a fascinating picture, this spectacle of the three bearded savants, all in their prime, each at the top of his field, setting off together to breast a continent: the comradeship was warm, the prayers earnest, the talk stimulating and the way challenging.

Of the three, Fleming was easily the most remarkable as well as the most impressive physically. He was forty-five years old at the time and he still had half of his life ahead of him in which to complete the Intercolonial and plan the Canadian Pacific, devise a workable system of standard time, plan and promote the Pacific cable, act as an ambassador to Hawaii, publish a book of "short daily prayers for busy households," become Chancellor of Queen's University, girdle the globe, and cross Canada by foot, snowshoe, dog team, horseback, raft, dugout canoe and finally by rail.

Fleming was a dedicated amateur whose interests ran the gamut from early steamboats to colour-blindness. (He himself was colour blind and once courted his future wife unknowingly wearing a pink suit.) He had a fling at a wide variety of pastimes and pursuits. A competent artist, he was rarely without his sketchbook. He dabbled in town planning and was a better than average chess player. He once acted as an amateur lawyer in a civil litigation. Indeed, if this insatiably curious yet singularly cautious man had a fault, it was that he had too many interests. He always seemed willing to take on something more, at a cost to his health and his abilities in his chosen profession of engineering. He loved his work and apparently saw himself as a strong, silent scientist – a doer and not a talker. "Engineers," he once said, ". . . are not as a rule gifted with many words. Men so gifted generally aim at achieving renown in some other sphere – the pulpit, the press, the bar . . . politics. . . . Silent men, such as we are, can have no such ambition. . . . Engineers must plod on in a distinct sphere of their own, dealing less with words than with deeds, less with men than with matter. . . ."

This was nonsense. Fleming was far wordier than most politicians – a graceful public speaker, a voluminous diarist and author who, at his death, had some hundred and fifty articles, reports, books and pamphlets credited to his pen. As a writer, Fleming again was the gifted amateur. In his diaries and reminiscences he showed a sharp eye for descriptive detail, for subtlety of character and for the revealing personal anecdote. When he was too occupied to write himself, he took along a "secretary," such as Grant, who would be sure to put it all down on paper.

Without this mountainous literary legacy, it is doubtful whether Fleming's reputation as one of the greatest Canadians of the century would have survived. In his quiet yet thorough way, Fleming, the expert on communication, knew a good deal about personal public relations. There is a revealing story of Fleming's curious role on behalf of members of the Red River's Canadian Party in the winter of 1862-63. He petitioned the Colonial Office and the Canadian government in their interest, representing himself as their delegate in Canada and England. His purpose, clearly, was to win public notice. Fleming paid the editor of the *Nor'wester* one hundred dollars to report that he had been given the post at large and enthusiastic public meetings. As the Governor of Rupert's Land put it, "Mr. Fleming virtually appointed himself to represent a country and a people he had never seen."

Finally, a decade later, he was about to see it, along with his companions. The prairie, which all had read about in Butler's book, lured them on like a magnet. One night, after supper, realizing that it was only thirty-three miles away, they decided they *must* see it and pushed on through the night, in spite of a driving rain so heavy that it blotted out all signs of a trail. The three men climbed down from their wagon and, hand in hand – the giant Fleming in the centre, the one-handed Grant on the right and the wiry Macoun on the left – trudged blindly forward through the downpour, leading the horse, mile after muddy mile, until a faint light appeared far off in the murk. When, at last, they burst through the woods and onto the unbroken prairie they were too weary to gaze upon it. They tumbled, dripping wet, into a half-finished Hudson's Bay store and slept. The following morning the party awoke to find the irrepressible Macoun already up and about, his arms full of flowers.

"Thirty-two new species already!" he cried. "It is a perfect floral garden."

"We looked out," wrote Grant, "and saw a sea of green, sprinkled with yellow, red, lilac and white. None of us had ever seen the prairie before and behold, the half had not been told us. As you cannot know what the ocean is without having seen it, neither in imagination can you picture the prairie."

In Winnipeg, the party picked up a new companion, a strapping giant named Charles Horetzky, with brooding eyes and a vast black beard. This former Hudson's Bay Company man was to be the official photographer for the party. Though everything went smoothly at the time, Horetzky was to be a thorn in Fleming's side for all of the decade. Eight years later, the generally charitable Grant referred to him as "a rascal and . . . a consummate fool combined."

The party set out along the Carlton Trail – a small brigade of six Red River carts and two buckboards. The meticulous Fleming had

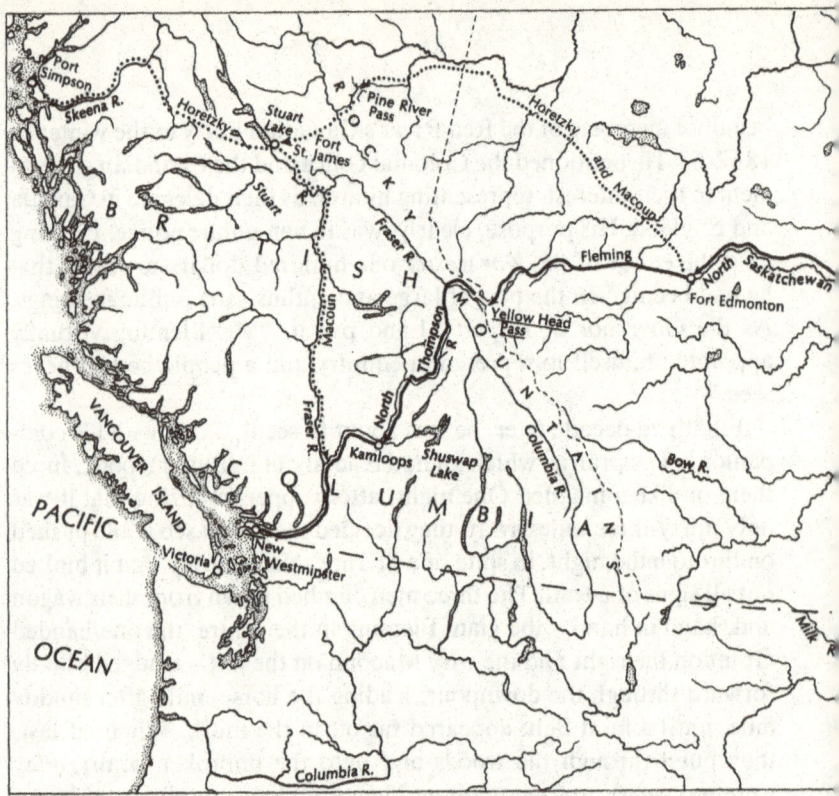

figured that they must make forty miles a day for a full month and, leaving nothing to guesswork, attached an odometer to one of the carts. They rose at sunrise and travelled until dark in three spells a day. There were surprises all along the line of route, some of them pleasant, some terrifying. At one point they happened upon a flat plain, twelve miles wide, which was an unbroken mass of sunflowers, asters, goldenrod and daisies – an Elysian field shining like a multi-coloured beacon out of the dun-coloured expanse of the prairie. At another they were struck by a hailstorm so strong that the very horses were flung to the ground and the carts broken. In this chill Hades, the stones pelting from the sky were so large that a single blow from one of them could stun a man.

All along the way, the travellers read and reread Butler's account of his journey. In addition they had the newly published journal of an early Peace River explorer, which had been edited by Malcolm McLeod, an Ottawa jurist. McLeod was a man to be taken seriously. His father had been one of the early Hudson's Bay men to cross the Rockies and he himself was familiar with that ocean of mountains. It was McLeod's memorandum to the Colonial Secretary in 1862

48

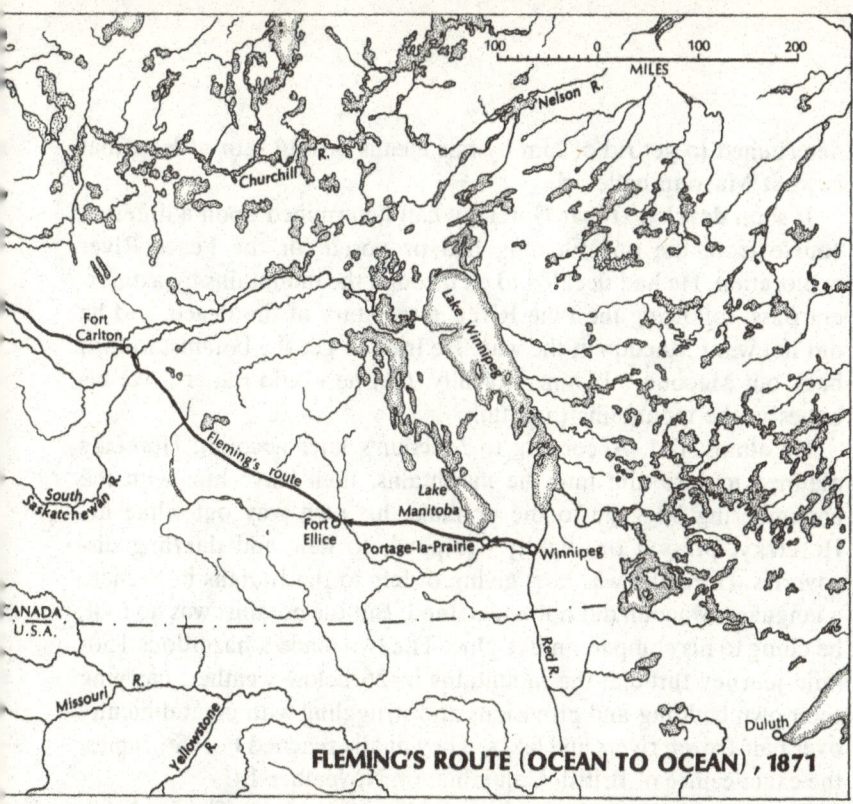

FLEMING'S ROUTE (OCEAN TO OCEAN), 1871

that was credited with helping to force the sale of Rupert's Land by the Hudson's Bay Company.

At Edmonton, the party split up. Fleming, intrigued by McLeod's views on the agricultural resources of the Peace, suggested that Horetzky and Macoun go north and try to get through the mountains by way of that great river and then head for Fort St. James and thence to the coast. He and Grant would go through the old Leather Pass, now called the Yellow Head – after a tow-headed Indian – to meet one of Fleming's survey parties.

For Macoun it became a bizarre journey. The hardy botanist was no stranger to punishment. As a schoolboy in Ireland he had been whipped unmercifully, almost daily. In spelling tests he would be given a slap on the hand with a ruler for every word he missed out of a selection of forty or more. It made him into something of a stoic; often he would take an undeserved whipping without a murmur to prevent a weaker boy from receiving it. But in the Peace River country, Macoun was subjected to a more subtle chastisement. It became increasingly clear, as the days wore on, that the swarthy Horetzky felt that the botanist was a drag on the expedition and had determined to get rid of him by fair means or foul – or at least that is what Macoun believed.

It soon developed that Horetzky had determined upon a different course from the one Fleming had proposed for the Peace River exploration. He had decided to go through the mountains by a different pass, following the Pine River, a tributary of the Peace, and he did not want Macoun in the way. He tried to get the botanist to turn back but Macoun told him, stoically, that he would rather leave his bones in the mountains than fail.

He almost did. According to Macoun's later account, Horetzky planned to lure him into the mountains, then leave him with the encumbering baggage to die or make his own way out while he, Horetzky, pressed on, lightly equipped, to new and dazzling discoveries. Horetzky was now giving orders to the Indians in French, a language Macoun did not understand. But the botanist was no fool; he clung to his companion like glue. The two made a hazardous 150-mile journey through the mountains in 26 below weather, carrying their own bedding and provisions and struggling with great difficulty over half-frozen rivers and lakes. They finally reached Fort St. James, the exact centre of British Columbia, on November 14.

It must have been a trying journey in other ways. The Hudson's Bay factor at the fort quietly let Macoun know that Horetzky, who was only a co-director of the expedition, appeared to have taken full charge, ordering all sorts of luxuries for himself but only minimal provender for the botanist.

"I told him I did not care what I got," Macoun later recalled, "as long as I got away from Horetzky with my life."

Horetzky was already planning to push on westward through virtually unknown country to the mouth of the Skeena but Macoun had no intention of accompanying him. He was penniless by now, totally dependent on the charity of the Hudson's Bay Company. Accompanied by two Indian guides, he fled south, wearing snowshoes seven feet long. He had never worn snowshoes in his life and soon abandoned them, content to flounder through the drifts which reached above his knees. Eventually, on December 12, he reached Victoria where he learned that, in his absence, his wife had been delivered of a fifth child. What she thought of her husband's impetuous and extended summer vacation is not recorded.

Both Macoun and Horetzky produced books about their adventures and, eight years later, Horetzky followed up with a much more bitter pamphlet in which he attacked both Macoun and Grant. The

50

latter, he wrote, made "from the very beginning . . . strenuous efforts to 'run' the whole affair, as fast as possible, being, as he said himself, excessively anxious to rejoin his parishioners at Halifax by the 15th of November following." Horetzky also became a zealous, indeed a fanatical advocate of the route he had first followed from the Pine Pass in the Rockies to the northern Pacific coast of British Columbia.

Grant made it back to his parish with two weeks to spare before the deadline of November 15. His journey with Fleming through the Yellow Head and down the Fraser lacked the cloak-and-dagger aspects of Macoun's struggle. When the pair reached Victoria they found that one of their party had preceded them and was cadging free drinks from the press in the local saloons on the strength of tall tales about the expedition. "He had conjured up a canyon . . . twenty miles long where no canyon is or ever had been; had described us galloping down the Yellow Head Pass till arrested by the sight of quartz boulders gleaming with gold."

The trip was not that exotic but it was certainly arduous. There were long swamps "covered with an underbrush of scrub birch, and tough willows . . . that slapped our faces, and defiled our clothing with foul-smelling marsh mud." At times, in the Albreda area, the nine-year-old trail was buried out of sight by "masses of timber, torrents, landslides or debris." The horses' hooves sank eighteen inches into a mixture of bog and clay, but "by slipping over rocks, jumping fallen trees, breasting precipitous ascents with a rush, and recklessly dashing down hills," the crossing of the Thompson River was reached. To the one-handed clergyman, the comfortable parish of St. Matthew's must have seemed to have been on the far side of the moon.

It was, by any standard, an impressive journey that he and his companions had made. In 103 days of hard travel they had come 5,300 miles by railway, steamer, coach, wagon, canoe, rowboat, dugout, pack and saddle horse and their own sturdy legs. They had made sixty-two camps on prairie, river bank, rock, brush, swamp and mountainside; and they were convinced that the future railway would follow their route across the Shield, up along the Fertile Belt and through the Yellow Head Pass, which was Fleming's choice from the moment he first saw it. This physical accomplishment was magnificent but its subtle concomitant was far more significant: in the most graphic and dramatic fashion, the clergyman and the surveyor had given the Canadian public a vision of a nation stretching from sea to sea.

7

It was one thing to have an itch to go west. It was quite another to
get there. At the start of the decade, the would-be homesteader had
a choice of two routes, both of them awkward and frustrating. He
could take the train to St. Paul and thence to the railhead and proceed
by stagecoach, cart and steamboat to Winnipeg; or he could take
the all-Canadian route by way of the lakehead and the notorious
Dawson Route.

The rail route was undoubtedly the most comfortable, though
"comfortable" in those days was a comparative word. The Miller
coupling and the air brake had not yet been invented so that passengers were jolted fearfully in their Pullmans. Having reached St.
Paul by a series of fits and starts – for there were many changes and
few through lines – the weary traveller could figure on at least
another week before arriving at Winnipeg. The service on the St. Paul
and Pacific Railroad was, to put it charitably, erratic. The faltering
line, plagued by bankruptcies and plundering, ran to nowhere in
particular, the exact location of the railhead being at all times uncertain and the condition of the rolling stock bordering on a state of
collapse. "Two streaks of rust and a right of way," they called it.
Who would have believed that this comic opera line would one day
become the nucleus of the two greatest transcontinental railways –
the Great Northern and the Canadian Pacific?

Once at the end of track, the passengers hoisted all their worldly
belongings onto a four-horse stage and bumped along through clouds
of acrid dust and flocks of whirring prairie chickens towards the
steamboat landing at Twenty-Five Mile Point. Along the trail one
was likely to encounter hordes of Winnipeggers travelling, a family
to a cart, to St. Cloud – "Father, mother and a troop of frowzy-
headed, brown-faced children, who, though shoeless and hatless and
half-naked, are as happy as larks singing in the meadows."

During the summer the Hudson's Bay Company's steamboat *International* plied the Red River at uncertain intervals. Butler described
it with his usual sharp eye: "Her engines were a perfect marvel of
patchwork – pieces of rope seemed twisted around the crank and
shaft – mud was laid thickly on boiler and pipes, little spurts of steam
had a disagreeable way of coming out from places not supposed to
be capable of such outpourings." The creaky vessel, 130 feet long,

had difficulty negotiating the hairpin turns. In winter, of course, she could not operate; and when the water in the Red fell below two feet, she ran aground and the passengers had to take the Burbank stagecoach out across the bumpy, uninhabited prairie, laying over during the night at the atrocious stopping places where, in a single undivided attic, men, women and children all slept together in beds jammed together side by side.

This ordeal was idyllic compared to that suffered by the luckless ones who chose the all-Canadian route (generally because it was cheaper). The steamer trip as far as Prince Arthur's Landing was pleasant enough, though a little nerve-racking at meal times: there were as many as four sittings and those who had not yet eaten were in the habit of hovering impatiently behind the seats of the diners. But after Prince Arthur's Landing, on the Dawson Route to Winnipeg, the real test of nerves began.

The route consisted of a corduroy road, interspersed with water stretches, and then a wagon road cut directly from the prairie turf. It was named for another Scot, the same Simon J. Dawson who, with Henry Youle Hind, had been sent out by the government in the late fifties to explore the North West. Dawson, who was later to become a Member of Parliament, was known as "Smooth Bore Dawson" because of his even temper and his quiet way of speaking. He needed to husband his reserves. The calumnies subsequently heaped upon him might have driven a more excitable man to dangerous excesses.

As the result of the report he made following his explorations of the Lake Superior country, Dawson was commissioned in 1868 to supervise the building of a series of corduroy links from Prince Arthur's Landing to connect the long chain of ragged lakes which lie between Superior and the Lake of the Woods. From that point the Fort Garry Road would lead on to the prairie and thence to Winnipeg.

When Wolseley and his soldiers set out on their 96-day overland journey to quell the Riel uprising, the Dawson road was still unfinished. The soldiers helped put part of it together, splitting rocks by lighting fires under them and sousing them with water, packing the corduroy under the roadbed, building bridges, and cutting cords of poplar poles on which they rolled their boats across the exhausting portages, each man masked like a hangman by a heavy veil to ward off the hordes of blackflies and mosquitoes.

From Wolseley's point of view, the odyssey was a success. Dawson

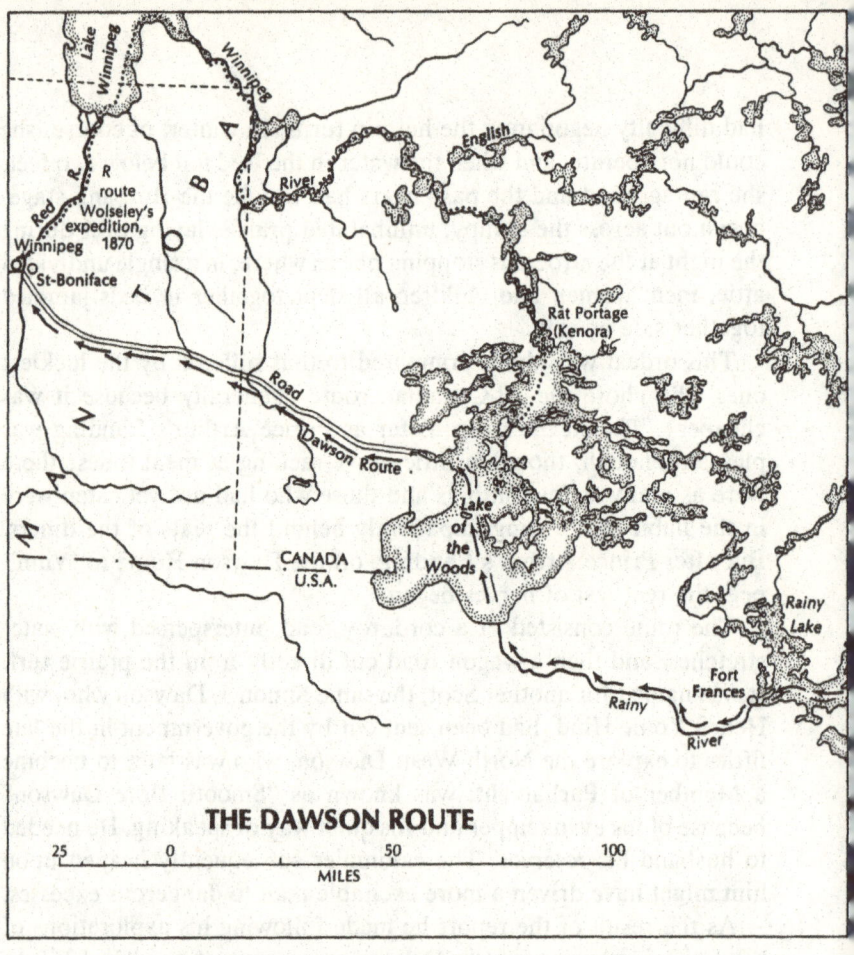

THE DAWSON ROUTE

25　　　0　　　　　　　50　　　　　　　100

MILES

had ordered one hundred and fifty boats specially built for the expedition on the Isle of Orleans and shipped to Sarnia, from where a crew of eight hundred skilled voyageurs brought them to Lake Superior and thence over the portages the soldiers had prepared (the same technique and some of the same voyageurs were later used to navigate the cataracts of the Nile during the attempt to rescue Gordon in 1884-85). But in the process Wolseley's troops destroyed as much of the road as they built and held up construction for the three months it took to move the sixteen hundred men through the wilderness. By the time the last soldier had moved on, the road was in such a state that it was useless.

Eventually, however, it was completed. Tugs and steamboats were placed on a dozen lakes. Dams were built on the Maligne River to raise the water levels around the falls and rapids as much as a dozen

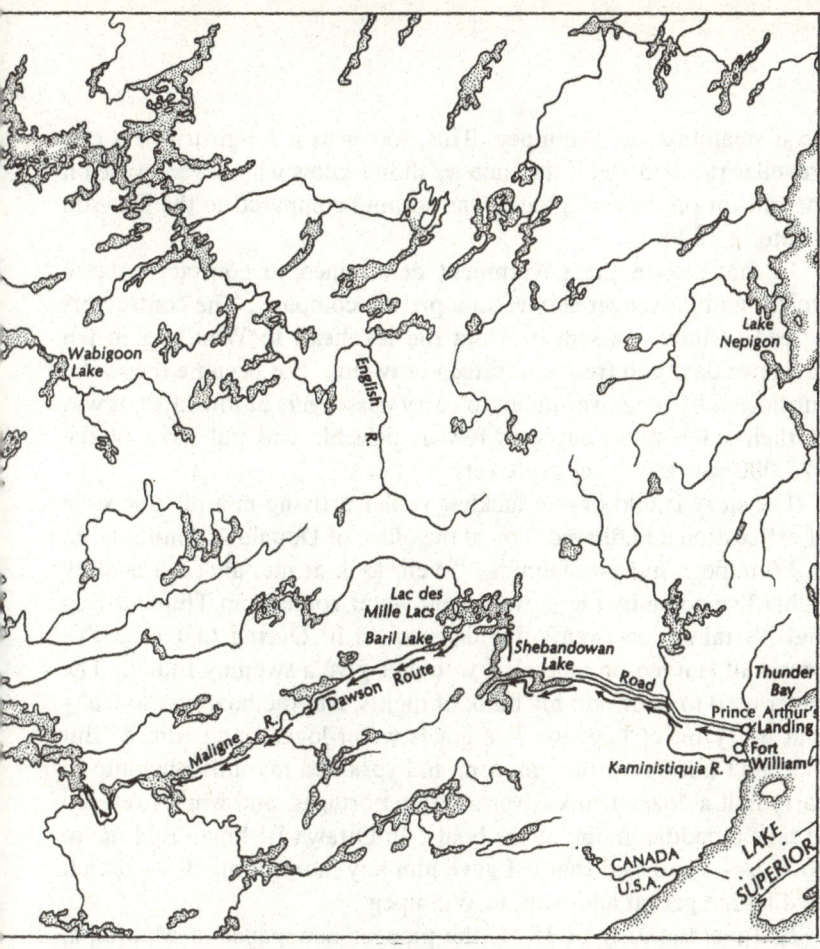

feet. Tents, houses and shanties were erected for the convenience of passengers. And two great locks, eight hundred and two hundred feet high, were planned at Fort Frances so that steamboats might eventually circumvent the rapids of the Rainy River. Between 1872 and 1873, a thousand settlers paid their ten dollars to use the Dawson Route between the lakehead and Winnipeg.

It was a formidable route. A tug or steamboat was required on every lake and a different team of horses, together with harnesses and wagons, at each of the ten portages. Throughout its brief existence, there was never a time when some section of the Dawson road was not in need of repair. Indeed, the route was scarcely open when the completion of a railway from Duluth to Moorhead on the Red River, in the spring of 1873, made it obsolete. Travellers could now take the lake boat to Duluth, proceed by rail to the river and there pick

55

up a steamboat to Winnipeg. This, too, was a rough trip. As one traveller recalled, "half the time we didn't know whether we were on the rails or on the ties"; but it was nothing compared to the Dawson Route in 1874.

In that season the government determined to contract out the freight and passenger service to a private company. The contractors agreed to move passengers from the lakehead to Winnipeg in ten or twelve days and freight in fifteen or twenty. But because they were subsidized by the government to carry passengers at low fares, it was in their interests to carry as few as possible and put most of the $75,000 subsidy in their pockets.

The story is told of one luckless settler arriving in a pitiable state of exhaustion and dilapidation at the office of Donald A. Smith, M.P., in Winnipeg, and proclaiming: "Well, look at me, ain't I a healthy sight? I've come by the Government water route from Thunder Bay and it's taken me twenty-five days to do it. During that time I've been half starved on victuals I wouldn't give a swampy Indian. The water used to pour into my bunk of nights, and the boat was so leaky that every bit of baggage I've got is water-logged and ruined. But that ain't all. I've broke my arm and sprained my ankle helping to carry half a dozen trunks over a dozen portages, and when I refused to take a paddle in one of the boats, an Ottawa Irishman told me to go to h––l and said that if I gave him any more of my d––––d chat he'd let me get off and walk to Winnipeg."

In June and July of 1874, the pioneer newspaper of Manitoba, the *Nor'wester*, began to carry the immigrants' complaints. They considered the station-master at Fifteen Mile shanty "a brute," and the men at the Height of Land "mean and surly." At Baril Lake, the baggage was flung helter-skelter into the hold of a barge where it rested in eight inches of water. On one passage across Rainy Lake where, true to nomenclature, a cloudburst descended, male passengers compassionately took the tarpaulin off a woodpile and placed it over the heads of the women and children. This so enraged the engineer that he seized an axe and threatened to chop away at the customers unless the covering were instantly replaced. It wasn't, whereupon the engineer "out of sheer spite" held up the boat for five hours.

So eager were the contractors – W. H. Carpenter and Company – to "make the most of the $75,000 bonus" (to quote the *Nor'wester*) that they were criminally careless of human life. One boat was so

56

overloaded with freight, horses and forty passengers that its gunwales were within three inches of the water, which could be seen pouring in at several places. Even then the pilot wanted to proceed and could only be persuaded to turn around after a heated quarrel.

James Trow, an Ontario Member of Parliament who took a lively interest in the North West, reported that paid American agents of the Northern Pacific were on hand at Prince Arthur's Landing to try to seduce immigrants away from the Dawson Route, saying that "if we persisted we might possibly get through before Christmas or New Year's but in all probability our bones would be left to bleach on some portage or sunk beneath the waves."

The Americans urged the travellers to give up any fancy of settling on the Canadian prairie and choose instead the more hospitable soil of Minnesota or Dakota. "These smooth-tongued interlopers succeeded in poisoning the minds of several," Trow reported. The burly M.P. patriotically chose the all-Canadian route and on its corduroyed right of way encountered an Englishman who exclaimed that "he would sooner be hanged in England than die a natural death on the Dawson Route."

Trow himself was forced to admit that the men stationed along the way seemed remarkably indifferent to the interests of the travelling community. Nevertheless, he retained his patriotism and wrote that "notwithstanding all its drawbacks, the Dawson Route affords one of the most enjoyable excursions on the continent of America." The scenery, all agreed, was beautiful and the region was to become, decades later, a major tourist resort.

Still, many a passenger was on the edge of revolt as a result of conditions on the trail. Scores arrived in Winnipeg in a state of semi-starvation, obliged to subsist on fish they caught themselves, their effects destroyed by leaky boats. They were forced to work their own passage, sleep in dirty, neglected shanties and walk when no wagons were available – all the time subjected to a volley of insults and threats by the employees of the contractors.

Complaints began to pour into Ottawa. In July, 1874, an alarmed government sent Simon Dawson himself out to investigate. When the surveyor arrived at the North West Angle of the Lake of the Woods, he was nearly mobbed by a crowd of infuriated and starving passengers who were vainly awaiting transportation to Winnipeg. Dawson scrambled about and found some half-breeds with Red River carts who arranged to handle the job, but his smooth-bore temperament must have been sorely tried. That year he quit in disgust and disappointment as superintendent of the route and advised the government that no further work should be done on it.

The road continued to operate in a desultory kind of way. The Marchioness of Dufferin, the Governor General's lady, went over it in 1877 and was knocked about so much on the corduroy that she preferred to get out and walk. Another traveller, Mary Fitzgibbon, wrote that she would never forget her own trip. The road by this time consisted of "round logs, loosely bound together, and thrown down upon a marsh, no two consecutive logs being of the same size." Originally there had been some foundation, and there were still deep drains on each side but "the logs had given way at different ends in some parts and altogether in others. It was bump, bump, bang and squash and squash, bang and bump; now up now down, now all on one side, now all on the other. Cushions, rugs, everything that could slide, slid off the seats . . . and one longed to cry out and beg to be stopped if only for a moment. . . ."

Finally the road was abandoned, and the locks at Fort Frances, on which the government had squandered three years and $289,000, were abandoned, too. The days of canals and corduroy roads were over. The railway was on its way.

Chapter Two

1

Poor
Waddington
The debate on the terms of admission of British Columbia was not yet over when the first of the entrepreneurs arrived in Ottawa. This was Alfred Waddington of Victoria, seventy-five years old and a fanatic on the subject of a Pacific railway. His scheme was premature and ill-considered and he himself was suspect in the eyes of the Canadian decision-makers; nonetheless his place as a minor catalyst in Canadian history is secure: his meeting in July, 1871, with Sir Francis Hincks and Sir John A. Macdonald touched off the complicated chain of events that led to the nation's first great political crisis.

"Old Waddy," as he was called, was a bland-looking man whose moon face was framed in ear-length locks and a little fringe of chin whiskers. Only the hard, resolute line of his mouth hinted at an inner stubbornness. He was obsessed, almost to the point of irrationality, by the idea of building the railway through the Yellow Head Pass to Bute Inlet, a precipitous indentation in the British Columbia coastline on whose beaches he had already been granted a townsite.

Waddington had been a trial to the Victoria political establishment ever since he had arrived in British Columbia from San Francisco, with the first wave of adventurers, after gold was discovered on the Fraser in 1858. The well-educated son of an English squire, originally lured across the Atlantic by the California gold rush, he came to the colony a wealthy man, free to plunge with zest into politics and pamphleteering. As a member of the colonial legislature he became a constant and pugnacious critic of the administration. He was more than a politician: he was also a railway engineer of sorts, an amateur fireman, a school inspector, the publisher of the first book printed on Vancouver Island, the founder of the colony's first gas-works and a pillar of the first old-people's home in Victoria.

He was, in short, a mover and a shaker, a tilter at windmills who attacked with equal pugnacity the Hudson's Bay Company, the medical profession, the pomp and circumstance of British colonial society and the restricted franchise – everything that Victoria held dear. For years old Waddy battered away at the unyielding ramparts of the tight little in-group that controlled the colony until, one autumn day in 1860, he suddenly abandoned it all and turned his attention to the promotion of what eventually became a transcontinental railway scheme.

60

The railway – he intended it first as a wagon road to the gold-fields of the Cariboo – took over his life. Its terminus was to be at Waddington Harbour, a paper community he had created at the head of Bute Inlet, the narrow fiord that springs out of the mouth of the Homathco River, some 150 air miles north of Vancouver. The inlet and the river seduced Waddington as they were to seduce later surveyors. At an age when most men seek retirement, he spent five years struggling through the Homathco's gloomy canyons, beggaring himself on trail-making and surveys.

The venture was marred by the Chilcoten Massacre of 1864. Nineteen of Waddington's men were slaughtered by Indians whose women had been molested and whose fears had been aroused by pranksters who had pretended to bottle enough smallpox to destroy the entire tribe.

But nothing seemed to deter Waddington, neither Indian ferocity nor the seventy-nine hairpin turns on the sheer cliffs of the mountain named after him. He was an incurable optimist, "one of the most sanguine imaginative men I have ever met; prompt to delude himself on any matter of which he makes a hobby," in the words of the colonial government's police inspector, Chartres Brew. Where realists would have reckoned the odds insurmountable and retreated, the quixotic Waddington galloped forward towards disaster. By 1868 he had squandered sixty thousand dollars on his scheme, but his projected road was little more than a series of blazed trees and surveyors' markers while his envisioned metropolis, in which some Victoria merchants had recklessly speculated, remained a pretty map.

By this time he had expanded his plans to encompass a transcontinental railway. Off he went to England where he read a paper before the Royal Geographical Society and tried, without success, to interest the Imperial government in the scheme. His attempts to sell the idea in Canada were equally fruitless. In the summer of 1869 he wrote to the government, inquiring about the possibility of building the railway, declaring that "financial parties of standing have promised me their assistance and co-operation." Waddington's letters went unanswered. The following year, he published an ambitious "Elements for the Prospectus" of the railway. The cost, he reckoned, would be twenty million pounds and the return on the investment would be three and a half per cent within two years.

Undeterred by the lack of response, Waddington bounced back to Canada, where he encountered William Kersteman, a promoter who had tried to interest some prominent Canadians in building a railroad from Pembina on the Manitoba–United States border to Fort Garry, and thence across the prairies to the Yellow Head Pass. The plan collapsed with the outbreak of the Red River uprising, but when the announcement of Macdonald's pact with British Columbia was made public, Waddington and Kersteman joined forces and descended on Ottawa. In March of 1871, during the debate on the admission of British Columbia into Confederation, they bombarded the Government newspapers with daily articles and extracts to which, Kersteman later wrote, "I may in a degree be vain enough to attribute the ultimate passing of that measure."

In a certain sense, the two irrepressible promoters might be called far-sighted. After all, they were the first to set to work actively on the railway idea. The Pembina line, which Kersteman dreamed of, was actually the first section of the Canadian Pacific to be constructed. The Yellow Head Pass was the one that Fleming was to choose. Bute Inlet, which Waddington championed, almost became the terminus of the CPR. But the truth is that both men were wildly overconfident and unrealistic. Though they themselves would never have believed it, there was no possibility of either or both successfully promoting the great railway to the Pacific. Historically, they were merely the means by which the sinister figure of George W. McMullen was introduced to the Pacific railway scheme.

McMullen was just twenty-seven years old, a stubby man with a pudgy face, luminous brown eyes and short cropped beard. He came from a prominent Conservative family in Picton, Ontario; his mother's relatives owned the local Tory paper. His father, Daniel, who had retired early from the Wesleyan Methodist ministry because, he said, his energetic revivalism had overtaxed his strength, was "greatly esteemed for his piety." The phrase scarcely applied to the son (though he was a trustee of the Picton Methodist Church all his life). Young McMullen – he was one of twelve children – had left with a brother for the United States several years before, a move which earned him the nickname of George "Washington" McMullen (the *W* actually stood for William). By 1871 he was a hard-nosed Chicago businessman, proprietor, among other things, of a newspaper, the *Evening Post*, one of a host of short-lived journals that sprang up and died like weeds in that city during the mid-century.

McMullen was interested in railways and canals. Indeed, he was interested in anything that might make him a dollar. He had an agile, inquisitive mind which, for all of his long life, intrigued him into the most curious ventures – the growing of aphrodisiacs, for example, and the development of a long-distance cannon. He had come to Ottawa in the spring of 1871 as part of a Chicago delegation seeking the enlargement of the Chicago and Huron Shipping Canal. Waddington and Kersteman were both ardent Yankeephiles. Kersteman was sure that only the Americans had the know-how to build the railway. Waddington's profitable years in California had convinced him that Americans were the kind of people who got things done.

Armed with surveys, maps, pamphlets and copies of speeches, the two enthusiasts approached McMullen, who was intrigued enough to seek further support in the United States. A series of meetings followed in Ottawa, Chicago, New York and Toronto. By July, McMullen had brought a covey of American businessmen into the scheme. His co-promoter became Charles Mather Smith, a Chicago banker. Smith brought in W. B. Ogden, an original incorporator of the Northern Pacific. Ogden brought in General George W. Cass, heir apparent to the presidency of the Northern Pacific, and, more important, Jay Cooke, the Philadelphia banker who controlled the railroad's purse strings and who had his clear, boyish eyes focused on the Canadian North West, which he hoped would become a tributary of his railroad.

Cooke's first hope was for out-and-out annexation, which would give the Northern Pacific a total monopoly of the land west of the lakes. Failing that, Cooke and his agents intended to work for a Canadian line which would be dependent on the U.S. road for an outlet. In his dreams, Cooke visualized an international railway, running from Montreal through American territory south of Lake Superior and then cutting back into Canada by way of the Red River to proceed westward across the prairies. The railroad, and eventually the territory itself, would be totally under American control. When Ogden wrote to Cooke in June, 1871, urging him to take preliminary steps to "control this project," it was exactly the opportunity that Cooke had been seeking.

It was an ironic situation. The first people to call on the Canadian government to offer to build the Canadian Pacific were the representatives of the very men whom the Canadian Pacific was intended to thwart.

The Americans arrived in Ottawa in mid-July about a week before the contract was signed (on July 20) with British Columbia. They came armed with a set of documents stating the terms on which they would undertake to build the railway. They had brought some extra political muscle along in the shape of a robust and red-bearded Irish lawyer, James Beaty, Jr., of Toronto. Beaty came of a powerful Conservative family. His uncle was editor of the daily Toronto *Leader* and he himself helped found both the *Monetary Times* and the Confederation Life Association. Before the end of the decade Beaty would be mayor of Toronto. But, in spite of his presence, the atmosphere in Sir Francis Hincks's office on July 13 was decidedly chilly and it began to dawn on McMullen and Smith that Kersteman and Waddington had over-represented their political leverage. Indeed, they turned out to be liabilities rather than assets. Hincks, who was Macdonald's Minister of Finance, later wrote to Beaty that Kersteman was "a man of straw" who was clearly trying to peddle an influence he did not have: "I am persuaded that owing to Mr. Kersteman's premature and most injudicious proceedings, the greatest injury has been done to a great undertaking." The day after the meeting with Hincks, the Prime Minister, at Waddington's urging, agreed to see the Americans "as a matter of politeness," but made it quite clear that any railway scheme, at that stage, was too premature for serious discussion. Moreover, any plan would have to be substantially Canadian and it was clear that Macdonald did not consider the present Canadian emissaries substantial at all. Waddington, he wrote to a friend, was a "respectable old fool" who had handled the whole matter most improperly. To Macdonald, the only value this patently Yankee delegation had was as a kind of lever to force Canadian capitalists to take the matter of the railway seriously.

The Americans did not give up. Through their lawyer, Beaty, they indicated that they were prepared to be generous: they would welcome some prominent Canadians on the board of their railway company. Beaty would be obliged if Hincks would name "such persons as you think proper to have associated in the matter, either from personal or political considerations." There was free stock to be distributed and a hint of ultimate profits for insiders. The questionable morality of all this seemed to escape the finance minister, who merely replied: "I fear that you are going altogether too fast." The ambiguity of that statement was to return to haunt Hincks when the correspondence was made public two years later.

At this point, the Americans unceremoniously dumped both Waddington and Kersteman, though they apprised neither of their fate.

Kersteman, with Macdonald's apparent encouragement, continued to attempt to raise funds to build the line, secure in the belief that he was to be made a provisional director of the new company when it was formed. He journeyed to England and came back, late in 1872, full of enthusiastic but vague promises of financial assistance. Macdonald palmed him off on Hincks. The promoter arrived on the finance minister's doorstep in Montreal on Christmas Day, where he found himself subjected to some unseasonable abuse. Events had passed him by; the Americans by this time had become a decided liability and the wretched Kersteman – the man who had brought them into the business in the first place – was dismissed as a trouble-maker. It began to dawn on Kersteman, after four years of unremitting labour and twenty-five hundred dollars spent out of his own pocket, that nobody at any time, Canadian or American, had ever had the slightest intention of cutting him in on the Pacific railway company.

As for Alfred Waddington, he died on February 26, 1872, a victim of smallpox, the same disease that had indirectly caused the massacre of his survey party eight years before. The reports of his death and funeral were meagre; the briefest of paragraphs mentioned his promotion of the railway. Back in Victoria, where he had for so long made news, the *British Colonist* gave him a cursory eulogy. "Poor Waddington," it called him. The reference was not unkind and certainly not inaccurate.

2

As Waddington and Kersteman fade into the wings, the formidable figure of Sir Hugh Allan strides out to stage centre. This vain, haughty and politically naïve shipping magnate was the richest man and the most powerful financier in Canada.

Sir Hugh Allan's shopping spree

In his Notman photograph, Allan looks like the prototype of the nineteenth-century robber baron. He is seen taking a pace forward as if to lunge upon the hapless photographer, and the fierceness of his terrier face is enhanced by a shaggy mane of hair and whiskers, snow white, which encircles his features like the frame of a picture. Allan's annual income was estimated at more than half a million dollars a year, a sum so immense that it is hard to grasp today. A dollar in 1871 was worth four or five in 1970; since there was no income tax, Allan's net income amounted to more than two millions annually in modern terms. It allowed him to build and maintain his baronial mansion in Montreal on which he bestowed the Gothic title of Ravenscrag. Here he had entertained Prince Arthur, a piece of hospitality which undoubtedly contributed to his knighthood in 1871.

Like so many Canadian financiers of the period, Allan was a Scot and a self-educated as well as a self-made man. His father had been a shipmaster, engaged in trade between the Clyde and Montreal and young Allan was raised in the company of sailors. He left school at thirteen, immigrated to Montreal three years later in 1826, and shortly after went to work for a firm of commission merchants and shipbuilders. Within a dozen years, Allan had risen to senior partner, a driving, hard-working man who studied furiously in his spare hours to make up for his lack of schooling. Unlike most English-speaking Canadians of that time, he made a point of learning French; it was to his advantage to become fluent in the language.

The history of the Allan Line, as his Montreal Steamship Company was popularly called, is substantially the history of Canadian maritime commerce in the nineteenth century. Under Hugh Allan's leadership, and that of his younger brother, Andrew, the original firm shifted direction, concentrating on shipbuilding and keeping pace with the disturbing changes in ocean transportation which saw steam replace sail and iron replace timber. The company was constructing iron screw steamships as early as 1851 and was the first to adopt the spar or flush deck on its new vessels. When it was awarded a mail contract between Great Britain and Montreal and acted as one of the chief troop carriers in the Crimean war, its future was secured. The penniless, half-educated Scottish boy had become the head of one of the principal fleets of the world. If he was proud, egotistical and single-minded he had reason to be. Starting with nothing he had amassed the greatest fortune in Canada. He was president of the Merchants' Bank, which he had founded, and of fifteen other corporations; he was vice-president of half a dozen more. His interests encompassed telegraphs and railways, coal and iron, tobacco and cotton, cattle, paper, rolling mills and elevators.

It was the heyday of the uncritical journalistic eulogy, when the title "merchant prince" was a panegyric, not an epithet; and Allan was hailed as the very prince of merchant princes. No muckraking scrivener delved into the working conditions of his employees. It would be almost two decades before a royal commission rapped the Allan Line on the knuckles for forcing its longshoremen to pay onerous premiums to an insurance company that Allan himself had headed. Basking in the adulation of press and peer group, praised for his business acumen, his public philanthropies and his regular church attendance, Allan could scarcely be blamed if he felt himself to be above other men. He *was* a good businessman – his habits so strict that he never acted on a question which involved the spending of money without first having the transaction reduced to writing; he *was* a good churchman – he often read the lesson or delivered a lecture from the pulpit. He was also imperious and uncommunicative. He had a healthy disdain for the public, the press and the politicians. The first could be ignored, the latter two purchased. He was accustomed to making handsome loans, with vague terms, to newspapers: the Montreal *Gazette* and the influential French journal *La Minerve* were two which enjoyed his largesse. His only real politics, as that acidulous commentator, Goldwin Smith, remarked, were the politics of steamboats and railways. Allan undoubtedly felt himself above politics, more powerful than any politician and certainly more astute. He was a man long accustomed to getting his own way and it certainly never occurred to him, in the summer of 1871, that this very bull-headed self-confidence would frustrate his ambitions and besmirch his name.

It was to Sir Hugh Allan that Sir Francis Hincks dropped the news, early that August, that some Americans were interested in building the Pacific railway. It was too bad, Hincks added casually, that a work of such importance should be entrusted to foreigners. Allan was immediately interested. As the country's leading shipowner he could benefit, perhaps more than anyone else, from a railway link to the Pacific. It would place him at the head of a transportation colossus and probably bring him other laurels. Allan had just received a knighthood; the successful construction of the Pacific railway would surely lead to a baronetcy and, perhaps more than anything else, the Lord of Ravenscrag, as the press had informally dubbed him, wanted a genuine title.

Allan lost little time in getting in touch with the Americans whose names Hincks had obligingly supplied. In September he met McMullen and Smith in Montreal and proceeded to form a company which, though ostensibly Canadian, would be almost entirely controlled and financed by the Northern Pacific; it was planned, in fact, that it would be part of the Northern Pacific complex. Allan's reward was to be a large block of stock, and a secret fund of forty thousand dollars – later raised to fifty thousand – to distribute, in McMullen's phrase, "among persons whose accession would be desirable."

McMullen, meanwhile, had held exploratory meetings with Macdonald. He and Allan also met some members of the Cabinet and were told that the Government was not yet ready to enter into negotiations to build the railway. McMullen later insisted that Hincks told him quietly that the Government would have to go through the motions of calling for tenders in order to avoid public censure, a conversation that Hincks himself heatedly denied, though he later admitted he probably did make some reference to the matter. There is no doubt that the aging Hincks, who had been out of the country for some fifteen years, was, more than any other member of the Cabinet, on Hugh Allan's side in these preliminary negotiations and that he, of all the Cabinet, was the most pro-American and the least concerned about American railway ambitions in Canada. Hincks had had a conversation with Jay Cooke in New York that summer, which convinced the U.S. financier that his scheme of building an American line through the Canadian North West was workable. Now, however, a series of "unauthorized conversations" (Hincks's phrase) took place between Hincks, McMullen and Allan from which it became clear to the Americans that the way would not be quite so smooth. A serious obstacle existed in the person of Sir George Etienne Cartier, Macdonald's dynamic but ailing Quebec lieutenant, who had done so much to launch the railway idea in the first place. Cartier's position as solicitor to the politically powerful Grand Trunk Railway, which would not give in gracefully to an upstart, was felt to be a stumbling block. Certainly he was unalterably opposed to any U.S. participation. "As long as I live," he had declared, ". . . never will a damned American company have control of the Pacific." He was prepared to resign rather than consent to it.

The Americans pressed on. They signed a formal agreement with Allan on December 23, 1871. The details were kept secret for good reason: Jay Cooke explained to his partner that "the American agreement has to be kept dark for the present on account of the political jealousies in the Dominion, and there is no hint of the Northern Pacific connection, but the plan is to cross the Sault Ste. Marie through northern Michigan and Wisconsin to Duluth, then build from Pembina up to Fort Garry and by and by through the Saskatchewan into British Columbia."

68

At the same time a pretense would be made that an all-Canadian route was being constructed north of Lake Superior: "The act will provide for building a north shore road to Fort Garry merely to calm public opinion." Its actual construction, however, was to be delayed for years while the Montreal-Duluth link through the United States was put into operation, financed by Canadian Pacific bonds sold in London to investors who believed they were promoting an Imperial project.

Jay Cooke was then at the peak of his meteoric career – a big, apple-cheeked financier, boyish-looking in spite of his flowing beard – dreaming dreams of a railway empire that would devour half of Canada for America's manifest destiny. He was known throughout the financial world as the Tycoon, a name that had yet to be vulgarized by American journalism. "As rich as Jay Cooke" was a common comparative of the day and well it might be, for Cooke, the empire builder, lived like a prince of old, surrounded by three hundred costly paintings, in a million-dollar, fifty-two-room Philadelphia palace, popularly known as "Cooke's castle." Here prayers were a morning ritual and religious service an evening duty, for Cooke was nothing if not pious. On the Lord's Day he engaged in a round of church and Sunday school services; on weekdays he worked hard at manipulating newspapers, politicians and governments, all of whom praised him to the skies.

"Manipulate" was a word that came easily to Cooke. The year before he had written to a colleague to invite his aid "in manipulating the annexation of British North America north of Duluth to our country." It could be done, he suggested, without any violation of treaties but "as a result of the quiet emigration over the border of trustworthy men and their families." Cooke was secure in the belief that "the country belongs to us naturally and should be brought over without violence or bloodshed." In this scheme, he planned to use the new Canadian Pacific railway in which he and his associates would have a fifty-five per cent interest. Among other things, Cooke believed that a union between the two railroads (for that is what he ultimately envisaged) would strengthen the Northern Pacific's chances for a loan in London. It was to have quite the opposite effect, engendering harsh opposition from the more powerful financial group that centred around the rival Grand Trunk. In the end, the opposition to him in London helped precipitate the failure of the Northern Pacific, which crashed in 1873 with a resonance that shook the North American financial world.

But in 1872 no cloud could be detected on the horizon and Jay Cooke's itinerant commissioner in Canada, Lycurgus Edgerton, found Sir Hugh Allan in a mellow mood. He wished "a perfect entente cordiale from the outset," Edgerton reported. If it ever occurred to Allan that he was engaged in a secret plot with American businessmen to deliver the Canadian North West into the hands of the United States (for this is what Cooke wanted), he was able to rationalize it magnificently. Business, after all, was business and American investment in Canada was not only desirable but also necessary. At one point he even wrote to General Cass, who was about to become the new president of the American railroad, that "the plans I propose are in themselves the best for the interests of the Dominion, and in urging them on the public I am really doing a most patriotic action." What was good for Sir Hugh was, in his eyes, good for the country.

By the time this letter was written – with unconscious irony on Dominion Day, 1872 – Allan had for almost six months been engaging in a lavish shopping spree, using the Americans' money in an attempt to buy up politicians, newspapermen and business opponents. On the question of who should be bought, and for how much, Allan differed with McMullen. The Chicago promoter was doing his best to suborn minor members of Parliament. Allan thought this "a waste of powder and shot." He preferred to concentrate on bigger game – Cartier, Charles Brydges and Senator David Macpherson, all of whom had close Grand Trunk connections and one of whom was being urged to put a rival company together to compete with Allan for the contract.

Charles John Brydges was, in a contemporary's words, "brought up in a railway age for railway use." He had been a railwayman all of his life, starting as a junior clerk on the London and Southwestern in England at sixteen and rising to become general manager of the Grand Trunk at thirty-four. Now this hefty man with the resolute face and the firm jaw was a commissioner on the publicly-owned Intercolonial. Allan saw him as a man "using all the influence he can with Cartier to thwart our views." On New Year's Day, 1872, he wrote to McMullen that he had seen Brydges the previous day and "found out pretty nearly what he will require to join our railway project. His terms are very high, but as they possibly include more than himself, we may have to concede them."

On January 24, Allan was more specific. He wrote to Smith and

McMullen that of the $1,450,000 in stock which he, Allan, was to receive, a sum of $200,000 would be earmarked for Brydges "on condition of his joining our organization and giving it the benefit of his assistance and influence." If Brydges didn't come through by April 15, or if he could be bought more cheaply, Allan would send half the money back, but keep the rest and use it "to secure any other influence that may be deemed by myself and you desirable or important. . . ."

Brydges, however, had plans of his own. He refused to believe that Allan's company was, as the shipping magnate kept insisting, free of American influence. Allan told McMullen that Brydges was starting to talk seriously about forming an all-Canadian company to bid for the railway contract – as was Senator Macpherson. Macpherson's Interoceanic company had a directorate of prominent Toronto and Ontario capitalists, including his partner, Casimir Gzowski, the railway contractor; William Howland, son of the Lieutenant-Governor of Ontario; John Carling, the brewer and Tory M.P., and others. His stated object was to defeat Allan's scheme, which the Liberal press, especially the Toronto *Globe*, was denouncing almost daily as a front for the Northern Pacific. Toronto, which had pushed so hard for the acquisition of the North West, now saw itself losing out to Montreal in the struggle for the railway. If Allan got the contract, the city feared it would be by-passed. Thus Macpherson's company had strong Toronto support.

It was not difficult for Macpherson or Allan to find partners for their ventures; they were clamouring to be let in. All directors of the successful company stood to make substantial profits with minimal risk. The plan was that each director would get a proportionate share of the stock without paying for it. Allan's lawyer, J. J. C. Abbott, ultimately objected to this. He feared that if "the present *immaculate* and *excellent* government" were defeated, the victorious Grits would have an excuse to force out the friendly directors, take back the stock and load the board with their own political supporters. But even if the stock were technically *bona fide*, Abbott said, it would be issued "with the hope certainly of escaping from paying."

It is also possible, in the light of Macpherson's previous record, that he incorporated the Interoceanic company at least partly for its nuisance value. That technique had paid off handsomely for him once before. In 1851, he, Galt and Holton had managed to secure a charter to build a railway from Montreal to Hamilton. Nothing came of the venture, but when the Grand Trunk entered the picture the three immediately took up 7,940 shares each in the dormant company, for which they expected handsome payment. The Grand Trunk could not be completed until it came to terms with them. All three, together with Gzowski, profited from a subsequent Grand Trunk construction contract.

Macpherson, in Allan's view, was "rather an important person to gain over to our side." He did his best to buy him off – or so he told his American backers on February 24. He claimed Macpherson had insisted on a quarter-million dollars worth of stock and threatened opposition if he didn't get it. A few days later Allan was back again with a list of a dozen other prominent Canadians he said would have to be paid off with fifty to one hundred thousand dollars in stock apiece. The names ranged from that of George Brown of the *Globe* to Donald A. Smith, the chief commissioner of the Hudson's Bay Company and independent member for Selkirk. "I think you will have to go it blind in the matter of money – cash payments," he wrote. "I have already paid $8500 and have not a voucher and cannot get one."

There is no evidence that Allan saw all or any of these men or offered them anything. Macpherson's subsequent account of their meeting was quite different. Allan, he said, had called upon him to join in forming the Canadian Pacific Railway Company with the understanding that he, Allan, would head it. There would be eleven directors – six Canadians, including Allan and Macpherson, and five Americans, all of them directors of the Northern Pacific. Macpherson objected strenuously to the Americans' involvement; all they needed to control the company was one vote, Allan's, and if they controlled the purse strings they certainly controlled that. The naïve idea that the Americans would own the company and yet allow the Canadians to run it was too much for Macpherson. He washed his hands of Allan and set about getting a charter for his all-Canadian company.

3

The downfall George Etienne Cartier, a fighting cock of a politician and a one-time
of Cartier rebel who had fought for Papineau in '37, was one of the leading

architects of Canadian Confederation and, next to Macdonald, the most important politician in Canada. His opposition to Allan's railway scheme could not be brooked; before Allan could succeed he must have Cartier with him; to achieve that end he was prepared to use brutal methods.

Cartier controlled the parliamentary action of forty-five Quebec members who voted in a solid phalanx. The Government needed this Quebec vote since its majority was considerably less than forty-five. The defection of half could, on a tightly fought issue, put it out of office. If Allan could win over a slice of Cartier's following he would then control the means to manipulate their leader. The lever, he shrewdly decided, would be the Quebeckers' hunger for a railroad along the north shore of the St. Lawrence from Quebec City, through Montreal to Ottawa. He himself headed the Northern Colonization Railway which planned to build the Montreal-Ottawa link of the coveted line. Cartier, with his Grand Trunk connections, could be presumed to oppose it. Allan began at once to spend the money provided by his American backers to stir up the French Canadians along the proposed route against Cartier.

He proudly reported to General Cass of the Northern Pacific the particulars of his successful campaign. He had, he said, paid several French-Canadian lawyers to write up the matter in the press. He had bought controlling stock in newspapers and subsidized others as well as their editors and proprietors. He had stumped the country through which his proposed railway would go, calling on the people, visiting the priests, making friends, sending paid agents among the more prominent citizens and making speech after speech himself, in French, to show the habitants "where their true interests lay."

The scheme began to bear fruit. Allan won over twenty-seven of Cartier's forty-five followers. He could now, in effect, control the Government, or at least he thought he could. An election was in the offing for the late summer of 1872 and Cartier, to his astonishment and dismay, woke up to the truth that he had lost his backing and much of his political power. According to Allan's account, the electors of Cartier's ward in Montreal told him bluntly that unless the contract for the Pacific railway was given in the interests of Lower Canada – which meant to Sir Hugh Allan – he need not present himself for re-election. Certainly Cartier's surrender was total. On June 12, Allan wrote to McMullen that it would not be necessary for either of them to talk to the Government in Ottawa: "I believe I have got the whole thing arranged through my French friends, by means you are aware of, and we now have the pledge of Sir G. that we will have a majority, and other things satisfactory. I have told you all along that this was the true basis of operations. . . ."

Meanwhile, Senator David Lewis Macpherson and his rival Interoceanic company were proving an embarrassment to Macdonald. Macpherson was an Inverness Highlander of heroic stature "in whose presence," Macdonald's astute secretary Joseph Pope recalled, "an ordinary mortal felt very small indeed." He had a massive head, a huge brow, pouched, Oriental eyes and a fantastic tangle of side whiskers, which, with his immense soup-strainer moustache, effectively concealed the weakness of his chin. Somewhat pompous in manner, overdeliberate in method, but generally sound in judgement, he could not be pushed an inch. He remained utterly convinced, in spite of all disclaimers, that Allan was prepared to deliver the railway into the hands of Yankee freebooters.

Macpherson's stubbornness posed a real dilemma for the Prime Minister, who was anxious to resolve the railway problem before the election; there was no doubt it would strengthen his hand politically in a tight contest. The Highlander was an old friend and a staunch Conservative who had, the previous winter, raised a testimonial fund of sixty thousand dollars to help free Macdonald from a crushing burden of political debt. Moreover, in the summer of 1871, Macdonald had actually pressed his friend to take up the question of the railroad in order to prevent the Americans from coming in. Now the Prime Minister was faced with an impossible choice: he could choose the Toronto group and alienate French Canada, or he could choose the Allan group and alienate Ontario. Once again, and not for the last time, the traditional Toronto-Montreal mercantile rivalry was bedevilling the country. Clearly an amalgamation of the two companies was indicated but here Macdonald came up against the stone wall of Macpherson's intractability. Macdonald genuinely believed that Allan was the only possible choice to head the venture. Only a man of his established wealth and apparent business know-how could command the confidence of the international financial community. But Macpherson continued to insist stubbornly that Allan was a tool of the American railway; and not even his own associates, who were moved to throw in with the Montreal group, could shake this belief. He would welcome amalgamation, but not with Allan as president.

As it turned out, Macpherson was right. It ought to have been clear to Allan by this time that the Government had no intention of allowing American control of the railway; and yet, while pretending publicly that his was an all-Canadian company, the imperious shipbuilder retained his secret ties with New York and Chicago. On August 7, he told General Cass that the Government was obliged to stipulate that no foreigner could appear as a shareholder in the company: "The shares taken by you and our other American friends, will therefore have to stand in my name for some time." To McMullen he sent a reassuring letter: the Americans were to be excluded but "I fancy we can get over that some way or other."

In vain Macdonald tried to effect a rapprochement between Macpherson and Allan. In July, with the election campaign underway, Macpherson suggested that the new directors – seven from his company and six from Allan's – elect their own president; but to this Allan would not consent. The Tory party desperately wanted to place the *fait accompli* of a strong railway company before the electors; but the principals remained deadlocked.

By this time Allan was hard at work trying to restore the political fortunes of the badly battered Cartier, who had been transformed from enemy into ally by his machinations of the previous spring. It was Allan's first and only entry into politics; indeed, he had rarely bothered to vote before this. But by August 9 he was so deeply involved in the campaign that he even appeared on the platform with Cartier at St. James Square. It was not a prepossessing beginning: both men had to duck a volley of stones and rotten eggs, and the taunts were so great that Cartier had difficulty being heard. Allan, it appeared, had done his work only too well.

It was this tortured alliance with Allan that was to cloud Cartier's reputation. He remains, save for this one fall from grace, an attractive figure: a wiry, compact, totally dedicated Canadian patriot with all the vivacity of his race. In the familiar portrait of the Fathers of Confederation he occupies the front row centre, next to Macdonald – a robust, almost dapper man with a mane of white hair. His black, darting eyes were a sign of his inner vitality: he was quite capable of working fifteen hours a day. His value to Macdonald was inestimable – together they forged and maintained the uneasy alliance between the French and English nations in British North America. But in the election of 1872, Cartier was robust no longer: the telltale symptoms of Bright's disease – the swollen feet, the impaired judgement – had already appeared. George Etienne Cartier had less than a year to live.

If Allan threw himself, heart, soul, and pocketbook, into the election, it was because he believed he had a pledge from the Government to give him the charter for the railway. The events of July 29 and 30, when promises were made by Cartier and Macdonald, and election funds were pledged by Allan, can only be understood against the background of the political morality and practice of the time.

Elections in post-Confederation Canada were fought with money and, often enough, it was the candidate who spent the most who cornered the votes. Dollars spoke louder than ideas and out-and-out bribery was not uncommon. At the end of the decade a contemporary historian wrote that "bribery at elections was scarcely regarded as an offense; both parties resorted to it freely and almost openly." During the seventies so many elections were controverted because of bribery that a kind of gentleman's agreement existed between the parties to keep them to a manageable number. As late as 1874, there were official charges of bribery before the courts in no less than twenty-nine constituencies in Ontario and Manitoba. Charles Clarke, who was clerk of the Legislature of Ontario, recalled that "for many years before Confederation, and after its creation, electoral corruption, gross intimidation, bludgeon arguments and brutal force had been employed at various elections to the detriment and loss of electoral strength by one or other of the opposing candidates." Of the early seventies, Clarke wrote that "nearly every active politician who had experience in Canadian Parliamentary elections was aware of the existence of bribery and intimidation. So common was this experience that, although never seeing money actually exchanged for a vote, its use was as well known to me as was the existence, say, of the Queen of England, or the fact that she occupied the throne."

In those days, before competing electronic pleasures, politics was *the* major pastime in city and village. The entire country was almost totally partisan which meant that, in the absence of any really burning issue, it was difficult to change a man's mind unless, in the euphemism of the period, you "treated" him – to a drink, a bottle, a dinner or a five-dollar bill. (In one election wagonloads of voters were paid off in the unnegotiable five-dollar bills of a defunct bank.) Treating was against the law, as was the practice of driving or dragging reluctant voters to the polls, but these expensive customs, as Macdonald himself admitted, were common to both parties. And each charged the other with committing identical crimes. Goldwin Smith, at a political picnic, drew a farmer aside to ask him what was the difference in principle between his party and the opposition. "He was a long time in answering but at last he replied: 'We say the other fellows are corrupt.'"

There was still no secret ballot in the 1872 election; it did not make its appearance until 1874. This meant that bribery was extraordinarily effective since the party agents could check on the loyalty of their paid supporters. Other devices were also in use to influence the results: agents of the party in power would resort to trickery to prevent opponents from voting before the polls closed – forcing septuagenarians to swear they were over twenty-one and British subjects, or, on occasion, actually driving voters from the booths with broken heads if they thought their votes would affect the outcome. Clarke recalled that he had known men, sworn in as special constables, "use their authority to force back, again and again, from the polls, voters of an opposite party." On another occasion, he heard twenty men, all Tories, sworn in as special constables, take an oath to keep the peace on election day towards all Her Majesty's subjects "except the d––d Grits." Frank "King" Cornish, the mayor of London, Ontario in the sixties, used to surround the polling booths on voting day with a private army armed with cudgels, batons, shillelaghs and brass knuckles, who effectively prevented the supporters of his perennial opponent, David Glass, from exercising their franchise. Glass finally became mayor by calling out the local militia to guard the booths before Cornish's party policemen were in place.

The election of 1872 was particularly hard fought. "I don't suppose," John A. Macdonald recalled, "that there ever was a fiercer struggle for the mastery than that which took place between the two parties, especially in Ontario." In that province, the Grits were on the rise: the Riel incident and, perhaps, the extravagant promises to British Columbia had hurt the Government. Macdonald thought that financially the Opposition had the best of it. On the other hand, George Brown, in a letter (later notorious) to the head of an Ontario bank, complained that the Liberals were having a hard struggle against "enormous sums" spent by Tory candidates: "A big push has to be made . . . if we are not to succumb to the cash of the Government. . . ." Certainly, money counted. When William Blumhart, who served on several Montreal election committees, was asked to give the reasons for the defeat of three candidates, he replied laconically that "they had not money enough."

Macdonald himself was hard pressed for funds and was scraping up every dollar he could find from reluctant friends. C. J. Campbell, the brother of the Postmaster General, Alexander Campbell, Macdonald's old law partner, wrote a worried letter to his brother revealing that he and a friend had co-signed a note for ten thousand dollars, a huge sum in those days, for the Prime Minister, "to enable him to supply funds to the several constituencies he hopes to carry, the only security we have being Sir John's undertaking in writing as a *member of the government to recoup us the amount loaned him.*" Campbell admitted that it was a foolish thing to do: "My object in writing is to make you aware of the circumstances so that steps may be taken for my protection when the subject comes up."

Cartier was equally desperate for funds and this desperation was increased by the knowledge that he faced an uphill battle in his own constituency. His friends, Macdonald among them, had urged him to seek an easier contest but he had stubbornly refused. For him the moment of truth came at the close of July. Allan had conferred with him in Montreal on several occasions, urging him to procure the amalgamation of the two companies "upon such terms as I considered would be just to myself" (in short, the presidency for Allan). On the thirtieth, some six weeks after Allan had told McMullen that Cartier had been brought to heel, he and his lawyer, the ever-present Abbott, visited Cartier once again for a meeting that was to become memorable. Cartier had a telegram scribbled by Macdonald who, in the midst of fighting his own election battle in Kingston, had managed to crowd in another interview with Macpherson. Again Macpherson had insisted that the question of the presidency be left to a board of directors. Macdonald made his decision.

"Under these circumstances," he wired on July 26, "I authorize you to assure Allan that the influence of the Government will be exercised to secure him the position of President. The other terms to be as agreed on between Macpherson and Abbott. The whole matter to be kept quiet until after the elections. . . ."

Four days later Cartier showed the wire to Allan. It was not quite enough for the shipping magnate. What if Macpherson continued to be stubborn? What would the Government do then? The ailing Cartier was forced to concede that, if a new amalgamated company could not be formed, then Allan's Canada Pacific company would be given the charter.

Allan wanted that promise nailed down: "If you can put these points in writing for me, as you state them, I think they will satisfy our friends."

78

Cartier suggested that Abbott draw up a document incorporating his pledge and return with it that afternoon. Allan and Abbott rose to leave, and as he saw them to the door, Cartier asked, in his abrupt way: "Are you not going to help us in our elections?" (Though later public testimony suggested that this was the first time the question of financial aid had been raised, the matter had undoubtedly been discussed earlier between Allan and Cartier, as Allan's various reports to Cass and McMullen make clear.)

Allan asked how much Cartier wanted. Cartier replied that he really did not know but, because of the opposition against him, it might come to one hundred thousand dollars. Allan, the model businessman, suggested he put that in writing, too.

That afternoon – the date was July 30, 1872, the day on which Fleming, Grant and Macoun first reached the open prairie – he and Abbott were back again with two letters. One, to be signed by Cartier, promised Allan the charter; the other, also to be signed by Cartier, asked for financial help in the elections. Cartier was not satisfied with either of the letters and both were rewritten. One was to become notorious:

"The friends of the Government will expect to be assisted with funds in the pending elections, and any amount which you or your Company shall advance for that purpose shall be recouped by you. A memorandum of immediate requirements is below.

NOW WANTED

Sir John A. Macdonald	$25,000
Hon. Mr. Langevin	15,000
Sir G. E. C.	20,000
Sir J. A. (add.)	10,000
Hon. Mr. Langevin	10,000
Sir G. E. C.	30,000."

In spite of promises to recoup, Allan did not really expect to see his money again.

Meanwhile, in Kingston, Macdonald was impatiently awaiting a reply to his telegram of July 26. When it finally arrived he was appalled. His immediate instinct was to go to Montreal at once and straighten out the mess into which Cartier had blundered; but the poll was about to begin and Macdonald could not afford to take time off from last minute electioneering. Instead he wired Cartier, repudiating the letter: his original telegram of July 26 must be "the basis of the agreement." *Agreement*. The ambiguity of that word would return to haunt Macdonald.

Cartier broke the news to Allan, who gracefully withdrew the letter; but he did not withdraw his financial support. He increased it. The additional fifty thousand dollars in Cartier's original NOW WANTED memo was swiftly paid over – ten thousand to Langevin, Macdonald's portly Minister of Public Works and Cartier's successor as the leader of the Quebec wing of the party, another ten thousand to the Prime Minister and thirty thousand to Cartier's central election committee. That was not the end of it. Allan left for Newfoundland at the height of the campaign but was pursued by a telegram from Abbott asking another twenty thousand dollars for the committee and ten thousand more for Macdonald. When Allan returned he learned that these sums had actually been exceeded. Cartier's committee received a total of $85,000 of Allan's money; Macdonald got $45,000; Langevin, $32,600. In addition Allan had pumped another sixteen thousand dollars worth of aid – perhaps more – into smaller election battles. Altogether he had distributed more than $350,000.

And for what? The Conservative government barely squeaked into power. In Ontario it was badly battered and in Quebec, where most of the Allan funds had been spent, it managed to capture only a bare majority. Without the West and the Maritimes, Macdonald would have been ruined politically. As for Cartier, he suffered a stunning personal defeat, which had its own ironies. By some mysterious process, a large slice of Allan's money had been appropriated by the other side. On the day of the election, the open balloting revealed that man after man who had been paid in good hard cash to work for George Etienne Cartier had actually been in the secret service of the enemy all the while.

4

George All that autumn, as Sir John A. Macdonald, freed at last from the
McMullen's campaign, struggled to effect a compromise between the two rival
blackmail companies, he was haunted by his secret promise to Allan. There was no way out of it. Senator David Macpherson remained utterly immovable and the Prime Minister had no leverage with which to budge him. He sent emissaries to Macpherson, he sent long concilia-

tory letters and, at last, he himself made a pilgrimage to the rambling and turreted Queen's Hotel in Toronto where the two Scots downed a formidable succession of brandies and soda. The attempt failed. Macdonald's personal charm was legendary but in this case every conversation foundered on the rock of Allan's presidency. Macpherson kept asking awkward questions. Why was the Government so committed to a man who was, in the Senator's furious phrase, the instigator of "one of the most unpatriotic conspiracies ever entered into in this Dominion . . . an audacious, insolent, unpatriotic and gigantic swindle." Macpherson could not understand it, nor could he believe, as Macdonald tried to make him believe, that Allan, as president, would have little influence.

If Allan were made president, Macpherson argued, time and again, the Canadian public would be "seized with apprehension that the R^y. would be handed over to the Americans"; that feeling alone would affect stock sales. Everybody, Macpherson pointed out, believed the Americans were behind Allan: "You yourself must believe it." At the height of the election campaign Macpherson had put his finger on the crucial point at issue: "If this Ring, owing to their electioneering influence, can force Allan upon you now, what will they do when they constitute a parliamentary phalanx, able under their leader to importune, embarrass and bully the Government from day to day?" Macpherson in later correspondence indicated that he knew the Prime Minister was bound to Allan by a secret promise. He was understandably bitter but, though his relations with Macdonald were marked for some years by a studied frostiness, he did not, as a good party member, rock the boat publicly or privately.

Nor was he to be moved by Macdonald's pleas about "putting your shoulder to the wheel," his threats ("if you hold back, you are in my opinion playing Allan's game"), his flattery (Macpherson's departure would be "a great blow to myself") or his hardheaded estimate of the prospects ("If you got the contract tomorrow it would do you no good, your friends would be defeated on the meeting of parliament.").

It was no use; Macdonald realized that he must form a new company without Macpherson. Like it or not, he had to keep his promise to the man who had been the biggest contributor to the Conservative coffers. At this juncture he ought to have entertained some doubts about Allan. On October 4, when the Interoceanic Company refused point blank to enter into any negotiations with the Canada Pacific, the Prime Minister realized that he must dispel the

81

rumours of American influence once and for all. Three days later he was shocked to discover that the Montrealer, in spite of all his pious proclamations, had not actually broken off relations with McMullen and the others. Allan's alibi to Macdonald was that he was trying to let the Americans down gradually, but he was later to testify under oath that he believed the proposition to exclude foreigners was impolitic and unnecessary and that the Government would not insist upon it. Macdonald did insist and Allan, at last, promised to obey. Was this the man who ought to be heading up the greatest of national ventures?

There was nothing the Prime Minister could do. He had made a promise, through Cartier – Allan kept using that awkward word "agreement" – and he would have to stick by it. Macdonald uneasily began to wonder just what the agreement consisted of; the memory of that ambiguous telegram, dispatched at the height of a fatiguing campaign, when whiskey and wine were flowing freely, began to nag at him. What actually *had* Cartier promised Allan? Macdonald realized that he himself did not know the exact details. Already there were rumours floating around Montreal about Allan's gifts to the Cartier campaign. "Allan and McMullen have done a great deal of harm by their foolish talk," James Beaty, editor of the Toronto *Leader* (his nephew had represented the Americans), wrote to Macdonald on November 4. Hincks reported to Alexander Campbell from Montreal on November 8 that "it is generally known in town that Cartier gave Allan some letter promising *something*" and that he took a receipt for a sum of money. Hincks added that Luther Holton, the leading Liberal in French Canada, was one of those who knew the story. If Holton had heard the rumours, it was safe to assume that the Liberals would start to dig. In December, Edward Penny, the editor of the Montreal Grit paper, the *Herald*, wrote to his party leader, Alexander Mackenzie, of a strong report "from a good and reliable source" that Allan had "put the screws on" by advancing $150,000 for electioneering purposes "which was in some way to be speedily repaid; but has not been repaid since." Allan had made up his mind, Penny reported, "to have the contract at any price hoping that when he once got command of it to be able to make his own terms." Macdonald, meanwhile, learned from Allan the full extent of Cartier's financial dependence upon him. The Prime Minister was horrified. Was it possible that the once astute Cartier could have been so foolish? He could not believe it and sought reassurance from his old friend, who had sailed for England to seek medical aid for his disease. Cartier's reply confirmed Macdonald's worst fears.

Meanwhile, in Chicago, George McMullen was experiencing little twinges of uneasiness as he studied Allan's reports of his lavish spending. On September 16, 1872 (Grant and Fleming reached the summit of the Yellow Head Pass that day), Allan informed him that he had paid out the staggering sum of $343,000 in gold for election expenses and other disbursements connected with the railway contract. He still had $13,500 to pay, "which will close everything off." The original fund of forty thousand – later boosted to fifty thousand – which Jay Cooke had contributed, had long since dried up. Allan's letter was really an expense account.

Startled by the magnitude of these figures, McMullen lost no time in getting to Montreal to confront Allan. There is considerable dispute as to what was said. According to McMullen's account, Allan filled him in on a long series of negotiations with Cartier, explaining that he had already supplied some two hundred thousand dollars in election funds before the "agreement" of July 30 was reached. He had secured the agreement, McMullen's account said, by refusing to pay any more of the drafts that were pouring in until Cartier, on the Government's behalf, put his promises in writing.

Whatever was said, McMullen was mollified. He returned to Chicago where, some weeks later, he suffered another shock. On October 24, Allan, under Macdonald's goading, finally broke the news to his American associates that he would have to dump them. McMullen was furious. There were angry letters, evasive replies and finally, on Christmas Eve, a face-to-face meeting between the two men in Montreal. Here, at last, Allan made it bluntly clear to McMullen that it was all over: he was closing off all arrangements with the Americans and repudiating any obligations they might feel he was under to them. McMullen was in a state of rage. He had squandered more than a year of his time and tens of thousands of his and his associates' dollars and now it appeared that he, like the frustrated Kersteman (who was at that very moment heading for Francis Hincks's doorstep and ultimate disillusion), had had no hope of success from the outset. Allan had deceived everybody. He had deceived the Government; he had deceived his friends; he had deceived his backers, and, above all, he had deceived himself – led on to greater and greater foolishness by what Lord Dufferin was to call "the purse proud and ostentatious notion of domineering over everybody and overcoming all obstacles by the brute force of money."

The apoplectic McMullen suggested that if Allan had a scrap of honour left he would either stick to the original agreement or step right out of the picture. This Allan refused to do, whereupon McMullen threatened to tell the entire story to the Prime Minister; after all, he had in his possession all of Allan's indiscreet correspondence. McMullen had for some time considered these damaging letters to be his ace in the hole. In August he had told his second cousin in Woodstock that "Sir Hugh Allan is a tricky fellow and not to be depended upon, but I think we have got him so tightly bound by these letters that he dare not go back on us."

Allan, apparently sure of his ground because of his deal with Cartier, remained obdurate. Perhaps he did not believe that McMullen would carry out his threat. But McMullen was not a man to shilly-shally. He wanted compensation and, if he did not get that, he wanted revenge. Off he went to Ottawa with no less a purpose than to blackmail the Prime Minister of Canada.

The encounter, which Macdonald had been half expecting and certainly dreading for all of that autumn, took place on New Year's Eve, 1872. The politicians and businessmen of the seventies seem to have had a certain insensitivity to festive occasions. Allan and McMullen had battled it out on Christmas Eve. Hincks had given Kersteman a dressing down on the Yule. Now McMullen was waiting to see the Prime Minister in the East Block while the rest of the nation was preparing jubilantly to usher in the new year of 1873 – the blackest in all of Macdonald's long political career.

It makes a striking picture, this pivotal meeting in the Prime Minister's office. The youthful McMullen, his round eyes coldly furious, faced a man thirty years his senior, whose languorous attitude gave no hint of his inner emotions. Physical opposites, the two antagonists had certain common qualities. Both were possessed of lively imaginations, which allowed them to glimpse future benefits in schemes others thought hare-brained. Both, as a result, enjoyed the steady nerves of committed gamblers. For Macdonald, the railway project had been an immense political risk; for McMullen, a considerable financial one. Oddly, McMullen, the apparently hard-headed businessman, was far more quixotic than the pragmatic politician who faced him across the desk. Macdonald's gambles – or visions or dreams (all three nouns apply) – had a habit of turning out far more successfully than McMullen's astonishing series of ventures, several of which certainly *were* hare-brained.

The interview took up two hours. McMullen came armed with Allan's letters to him; he proceeded to read the Prime Minister some compromising extracts. He produced the correspondence with General Cass. He unfolded the secret contracts made the previous year with the Americans. He talked mysteriously about strange stories that Allan had told him about paying off Members of Parliament. He said he could name names in that connection – names of persons "who are very near to you." Macdonald was inwardly aghast but, at moments like this, he knew enough to maintain a poker face. He denied that Allan had bribed the Government. In that case, McMullen replied smoothly, Allan must be a swindler – he had taken almost four hundred thousand dollars from the Americans on just that pretext. He urged Macdonald either to stick to the original agreement or leave Allan out of the new company. Macdonald replied that he could do neither; if McMullen thought he was badly used, that was his problem. The Americans, said the Prime Minister, had been out of the company for some time.

Not so, replied McMullen, and he produced Allan's own correspondence in evidence. Again, Macdonald was appalled, but he did not turn a hair.

"He [Allan] ought to have been more frank with you," Macdonald said. "He could not if he had tried obtained what he wanted to get. He must have ascertained that last session. He could not by any possibility have effected the purpose you wished him to effect of getting your associates, the American capitalists, interested in the company. He could not do so, the public feeling was so great."

McMullen grew more threatening. He began to talk about what would happen politically if the public knew all the facts "as they certainly would, if Allan was put in and allowed to break his sacred obligations with his associates." Macdonald made no comment but asked for time to consult with Allan and his lawyer, Abbott. On that note the encounter ended.

McMullen was back in Ottawa three weeks later. This time he brought along Charles Mather Smith and another colleague, Hurlburt, who had been privy to the early negotiations. Smith brought *his* correspondence with Allan and the three men indulged in a kind of Greek chorus of woe, bewailing their relationship with the perfidious Montrealer and crying out that they had advanced huge sums of money for the railway in good faith. Macdonald was properly sympathetic. He agreed that they had been badly used by Allan who should certainly be made to refund the money. McMullen began to talk wildly about seizing Allan's ships in American ports and suing him in the courts.

"I think you are quite right," said Macdonald. "If I were in your place I would proceed against him."

With this the atmosphere grew almost genial. McMullen and Smith denied that they were trying to blackmail the Government and asked, wistfully, if there was any chance they could be given an interest in the railway. That, Macdonald told them, would not be possible.

McMullen offered to let Macdonald have copies of all the damaging correspondence, including some new documents nailing down Allan's dishonesty regarding the extent of the American interest in his company. These showed that on October 12, at the very time when Allan and Abbott had assured Parliament that negotiations with the Americans had been terminated, Allan was paying over American money to incorporate the railway company.

Although none of the men involved knew it at the time, this was not the full extent of Allan's duplicity. The day before he finally dumped McMullen, Allan had a long talk with Lycurgus Edgerton, the Jay Cooke agent, about the new company Macdonald was forming. Allan assured the Northern Pacific man that there was nothing in the charter to affect Cooke's plans. "Certain, unreasoning public opinion had to be conciliated by an apparent concession . . ." but this was "more in form than in substance." Edgerton was able to report to Cooke that there would be no all-Canadian route via the north shore of Lake Superior, if Allan remained in control. It was a "useless expenditure . . . dictated by a sentimental patriotism, and a narrow minded jealousy and prejudice." For the next five or ten years "if not for *all time*, the Canada Pacific must be subservient and tributary to the interests of the Northern Pacific."*

Even without this knowledge it must have been clear by now to the Prime Minister that Allan was an unfortunate choice to head the new company. For almost a year Macdonald had been telling his colleagues, his friends, his political enemies and the country at large (as well as himself) that Allan was the only possible choice for the job – a man of business acumen, probity, sagacity and experience

---

* Allan was not the only Canadian prepared to sell out to the Americans for financial gain. According to General Cass, some of Macpherson's associates who had joined the amalgamated company were farming out some of their stock on the side to Northern Pacific people. Cooke himself wrote to a Minnesota congressman: ". . . the puzzle to me is that these men should have been so clamorous for the interest and then do just what they accused Sir Hugh of – selling out to the Americans. Under such circumstances, I do not think that the stock can be a very desirable thing to have."

who commanded the total respect of the financial community. Now he stood revealed as a blunderer, a conniver, a liar, a double-dealer and, perhaps worst of all, a Yankee-lover – a man whose imprudence, in Macdonald's own words, "has almost mounted to insanity." And this was the man who would shortly be setting off for London on a mission of the greatest delicacy to secure the underwriting of the world's largest railway project.

"Entre nous, Allan seems to have lost his head altogether," the dismayed Prime Minister wrote to Sir John Rose, Canada's unofficial spokesman in England. ". . . He is the worst negotiator I ever saw in my life . . . I fear that Allan's intense selfishness may blind him as to the true interests of the scheme; that is to say, I fear he will be inclined to think more about how much he can make out of the thing, than the success of the enterprise itself." Clearly, if the financial community or the public at large knew what Macdonald knew, the railway scheme would collapse like a soap bubble.

Would they find out? Worry gnawed at Macdonald as he prepared for the session of 1873. There was a bitter letter from Senator Asa B. Foster, a long-time railway contractor, regretting that he had not been included on the board of the new company. Both Cartier and Allan had promised him this plum, he claimed. For the past eighteen months, Foster revealed, he had had knowledge of Allan's dealings with the Americans and he had "seen all of the papers that were shown to you and some that were not." He himself had had an understanding with the Americans; they had promised him three and a half per cent of the company. There was no knowing what use the disgruntled Foster would make of that information.

There was a brief lull, then another brutal letter from Chicago, this time from Charles Mather Smith, pointing out that it was Allan, not the Americans, who had made the first overtures and that "He stated that he came to us by the direction of the Ministry. . . . The Government alone had the address of our Syndicate." They had accepted Allan, in effect, as a representative of the Canadian cabinet. Would Macdonald have any objection if the group petitioned Parliament for redress?

Macdonald naturally had every objection in the world. The Americans would have to be bought off, if, indeed, blackmailers could ever be bought off. He wrote to Hincks in Montreal and Hincks sought out Abbott, the lawyer who, more and more, was assuming the role of fixer in the various chapters of the continuing unpleasantness. Some bargaining then took place between Abbott and the Americans.

McMullen had wanted more than two hundred thousand dollars. Abbott pared the sum down to $37,500 U.S. He paid him twenty thousand down and placed Allan's cheque for the rest in an envelope which he gave to Henry Starnes of Allan's Merchants' Bank. McMullen then placed the offending correspondence in another envelope and gave that to Starnes. The banker's instructions were to wait until ten days after the end of the coming session and then deliver the envelope with the money to McMullen and the envelope with the correspondence to Allan. This was the best arrangement that Abbott could make to keep the story from becoming public before Allan completed his negotiations in England and while Parliament was in session.

The arrangement was concluded on the very eve of Allan's departure. Indeed, Hincks did not learn that the lawyer had been successful until the night before Allan sailed, at a dinner given in his honour. The circumstances did not lend themselves to a detailed report of exactly what occurred (though there was whispered agreement to destroy certain revealing memos by both Macdonald and Allan) and Hincks probably did not want to know anyway. Nor did Macdonald. One thing the Government could *not* be involved in was the paying of blackmail, since blackmailers were notoriously undependable. In the months and years that followed, a good many pundits and politicians asked aloud or in print why Macdonald did not buy off McMullen as soon as McMullen arrived in his office on New Year's Eve. The answer surely is that in Macdonald's shrewd view, McMullen was perfectly capable of taking the money and selling the correspondence later on. The view was absolutely correct. George McMullen did not bother to collect the second envelope from Henry Starnes, the banker. He had already received a higher bid from Macdonald's political enemies.

Chapter Three

1

The first session of the Second Parliament of Canada opened on March 6, 1873, with no hint of the storm that was gathering. The air was bracing and frosty and, though the snow was piled in soiled mountains along the sidewalks, the sky was blue and the sun bright. To Lord Dufferin, the dapper new governor general, setting off for Parliament Hill in his glittering four-horse state carriage, the weather was "quite divine."

He was deposited promptly at three o'clock before the main archway to the accompaniment of clanking swords, jangling spurs, brass band and Royal Salute and, as he entered the blood-red door of the Senate, he found himself proceeding through what one observer aptly called a "double file of living millinery." The crimson chamber had been cleared of desks and the senatorial chairs were now occupied by the wives and daughters of the parliamentarians and leading citizens, along with their sisters and their cousins and their aunts, all caparisoned in gowns from Paris, London or New York, every one of which would be allotted its own descriptive paragraph in the Ottawa press the following day. The crush in the gallery above was unprecedented. So great was the demand for tickets that some twenty-four hundred had been issued; there was scarcely room for a third that number of spectators.

It was Lord Dufferin's first Parliament and it was perhaps as well that he could not foresee the trials that lay before him. He had served as a diplomat at St. Petersburg, Rome and Paris, but nothing in his past had prepared him for the political hurly-burly of the Canadian scene. As he marched easily towards the canopied chair known as the Throne, followed by his entourage (the military brilliant in scarlet and gold), Dufferin, who was more than a little snobbish, looked about him with satisfaction. It was true that the Canadian Senators were not draped in the robes of English peers but "they looked a very dignified body in their sober court dress." Indeed, he was "rather surprised to see what a high bred and good looking company they formed."

The Governor General took his seat and looked out across an ocean of fluttering Parisian fans, glistening pearls and diamonds and silks in pale pastels framed against the darker velvets; it reminded him of a bed of flowers. Now, at the call of the Gentleman Usher of the Black Rod, the Members "swarmed in like a bunch of schoolboys" (there were four future prime ministers in that swarm). The Governor General read the speech from the Throne, feeling a little silly at having to repeat it in French.

One of the key paragraphs in the speech dealt with the railway: "I have caused a charter to be granted to a body of Canadian capitalists for the construction of the Pacific Railway. The company now formed has given assurance that this great work will be vigorously prosecuted, and the favourable state of the money market in England affords every hope that satisfactory arrangements may be made for the required capital."

Macdonald was not the only Member present who must have felt the hollowness of those words. By this time the Opposition was in on the secret and, as the session progressed, rumours began to flit around Ottawa about a coming political earthquake. Hincks anticipated trouble in a letter to Sir Charles Tupper, in which he suggested ways of countering the revelations ("You can testify that Sir John never tried to promote Sir Hugh Allan's views . . ."). The *Globe*, which called the railway scheme "financially the maddest, and politically the most unpatriotic, that could be proposed" hammered away daily, in editorial after editorial, its two points: first, that Allan was backed by Yankee dollars and, second, that the Government never had any intention, at any time, of dealing with anybody else.

Then, on March 31, the Opposition's intentions were revealed when, at the opening of the day's proceedings, Lucius Seth Huntington rose to give notice that before the House went into Committee of Ways and Means, he would move that a committee be appointed to inquire into matters generally affecting the Canadian Pacific railway. Huntington sat down amid Opposition cries of "Hear! Hear!"

A tingle of excitement rippled through the House. "Tomorrow is looked forward to as a grand field day in the Commons," the *Globe*'s Ottawa correspondent reported. That tomorrow came but Huntington did not get his motion before the House and the tension continued to rise. On April 2, the *Globe* reported that Huntington's notice "seems to have struck alarm through the ministerial camp." The newspaper said there were rumours that Huntington would charge that three hundred thousand dollars was handed over by the American promoters of the railway to pay Government members to corrupt the voters. But the *Globe* had in the past printed so many false political rumours that the general public scarcely gave it a passing thought.

All the same, when Huntington prepared to make his motion on the evening of April 2, the corridors of the House were filled to suffocation, the galleries were crowded, the Treasury benches were full and every Opposition seat was occupied. The Commons was silent and expectant. Seldom had any member faced such an attentive audience.

Huntington rose. At forty-six, he was a man of commanding presence, big-chested and handsome, with a classic head that a sculptor might covet – aquiline nose, poetic eyes, thick shock of light, wavy hair. He was a lawyer of long experience who had served as solicitor-general under Sandfield Macdonald for Canada East. He had opposed Confederation and had briefly worked for Canadian independence from the Crown. He was interested in railway matters and had had some dealings with Jay Cooke. One day, with his parliamentary career behind him, the eloquent Huntington would retire to New York and publish a political novel.

Huntington began to read from a paper in his hand. He was a polished speaker, resonant and melodious, though better at delivering carefully laboured set-piece addresses than in the cut and thrust of spontaneous debate. Now there was a tremor in his voice and he spoke so softly that the back-benchers had to lean forward to catch his words. He had every reason to be nervous for he was putting his career on the line. If he could not prove his charges, he would certainly be forced to resign his seat; but if he *could* prove them, his name would go down in history.

His speech was astonishingly brief; it ran to no more than seven short paragraphs and was supported by no documentary evidence. As he spoke, he paused occasionally and glanced uneasily about him as if to weigh the effect of his words: the reaction from the Government benches was one of stolid indifference. Huntington charged that the Allan company was secretly financed by American capital and that the Government was aware of that fact, that Allan had advanced large sums of money, some of it paid by the Americans, to aid the Government in the elections and that he had been offered the railway contract in return for this support. Lord Dufferin, who was a descendant of Richard Sheridan and had some of the eloquence of that great playwright, put the case more forcefully in his report to the Colonial Secretary. Huntington, he said, had charged that the Government had "trafficked with foreigners in Canada's most precious interests in order to debauch the constituencies of the Dominion with the gold obtained at the price of their treachery."

Dufferin did not believe a word of this. In spite of his official pose of strict impartiality he had been seduced by the Prime Minister's considerable charm. He thought the scene in the House, which he could not witness, "a very absurd one" and Huntington himself "a man of no great political capacity."

But it was not absurd, as events were to prove. Huntington called for a parliamentary committee of seven members to inquire into every circumstance connected with the railway negotiations with power to subpoena papers, records and witnesses. Then he sat down, "full of suppressed emotion," as an historian of the day recorded.

An oppressive silence hung over the House – a silence so deathly that some who were present recalled years later the solemn ticks of the parliamentary clock falling like hammer blows. James Edgar, the Liberal whip, thought he saw guilty looks on the faces of some of the Conservatives, but this may have been wishful thinking. Every eye had turned to the lean, sprawled figure of Macdonald. The Prime Minister, one hand toying with a pencil, remained "inscrutable as stone." There were those who said he was stunned by the charges but this is scarcely credible; he had been expecting them since Huntington gave his notice. More likely he was bothered by their lack of substance. Why was Huntington holding back? Why hadn't he read the evidence into the record? What was the Opposition plotting?

The silence was broken at last by the Speaker, asking in a calm, impersonal voice for the question. There was a spatter of nervous echoes from both sides of the House: "Question! Question!" The voting proceeded. The motion was lost by a majority of thirty-one – one of the largest the Government had enjoyed that session – and the House moved on to other business; but the oppressive atmosphere remained. "The feel of a hurricane was in the air," as the crowd in the gallery drifted uneasily into the corridors.

In "Number Nine," the smoking room reserved for Opposition members, excitement was mingled with outrage. James Young, the popular journalist from Galt, declared the country wouldn't stand for it; Macdonald must go. There were cheers of approval. Joseph Rymal, the caustic member from Wentworth South filled his pipe, uttered an oath and called Macdonald "the greatest corruptionist that America had produced." David Stirton, a pioneer farmer from Guelph, said Macdonald was a scoundrel "and ought to have been hanged long ago."

This was all very well but Huntington's motion, unsubstantiated by any evidence, had produced no result. The *Globe*, the following day, referred to the Pacific Railway Scandal (the title was eventually shortened to Pacific Scandal), and, as might be expected, laced into the Prime Minister for his silence in the face of Huntington's charges; but it confessed itself surprised "at the equally silent policy of Mr. Huntington." Surely, the Grit organ said, "the gravity and momentous importance of the motion should have been explained and urged upon the House before the vote was taken." The Governor General thought that Huntington was on a mere fishing expedition, hoping that a parliamentary inquiry would sniff out documents that he did not possess. "The House at large, including some of his own friends, thought he had got hold of a mare's nest," Dufferin later recorded. Macdonald himself thought Huntington had blundered by allowing the Government to shut off debate so subtly and treat the whole matter as a vote of non-confidence. The Government press took the view that the motion was nothing more than a device to needle the ministry.

As far as the public was concerned, the cry of bare-faced corruption had lost its potency from overuse by the newspapers. There was no such thing as an objective daily newspaper in the Canada of the seventies. The major papers were party organs, owned or subsidized by the Liberals or the Conservatives; their editors – men like White of the *Gazette* or Brown of the *Globe* – were up to their starched collars in politics, often sitting as members in House or legislature. The "news" stories emanating from Ottawa were no more impartial than the editorials and were not expected to be. Opinion, personal comment, prejudice and shrill invective enlivened every page and the charge of corruption, especially at election time, was made so often and so recklessly that the public had long since come to expect it and ignore it. Most people probably agreed with the Governor General himself who saw in the vote over the Huntington motion a great victory for the Government which "establishes them for the Session."

Macdonald, however, was having second thoughts. He had faced a rebellion from his own followers between sittings. Many felt that the Government had given the appearance of riding roughshod over its opponents and that its silence in the face of charges so serious could be taken as an admission of guilt. Accordingly, the Prime Minister rose a week later to announce the appointment of a select committee of five to investigate the Huntington charges. Edward Blake was one of the two Opposition members on the committee. The chairman was John Hillyard Cameron, a corpulent Scot who had long been a power within the Conservative Party – the ideal man, from Macdonald's point of view, to guide the committee in its deliberations.

Now Macdonald proceeded to set in motion a series of tactics of the kind that would eventually earn him the sobriquet – an affectionate one – of "Old Tomorrow." His was to be a policy of delay. When Mackenzie, the Opposition leader, urged that the evidence before the committee be taken under oath, Macdonald obligingly agreed. It sounded like a concession to the Opposition since Huntington's motion had not gone that far.

But before the witnesses could be sworn, a bill had to be introduced into the House providing for evidence to be taken under oath. That could occupy almost a month. Macdonald was reasonably confident that such a bill would be *ultra vires* and that Mother England, if prompted, would disallow it. Such a disallowance such would pave the way for a royal commission, which could, of course, examine witnesses under oath. From Macdonald's point of view, a royal commission composed of aging jurists of his own choosing was far preferable to a parliamentary committee with men of Blake's calibre ready to tear into the Allans, the Abbotts and the Langevins.

On April 18, Cameron introduced the Oaths Bill in the House and Macdonald chose that moment to demur. Before the second reading of the bill, he said, the matter should be carefully investigated and, if it were found that Canada did not have the necessary power to pass such a bill, then a royal commission could be obtained. On April 21, Cameron moved a second reading of the bill, explaining that he was satisfied the House could and should pass it. Macdonald made a point of disagreeing with his old crony but he added that he thought the bill should go through anyway. Macdonald had thus neatly covered himself. As Dufferin put it rather testily to Lord Kimberley, three days later: "Sir John's real object I imagine to be delay, but he did not like the odium of appearing to throw any impediment in the way of this enquiry but prefers to shelter himself behind my throne."

It was May 3 before the Oaths Bill received the Governor General's signature. The delay, frustrating to the Opposition, drove the *Globe* to a fury. "Every contemptible difficulty that an imagination frightened into creative activity could devise was thrown in its way," the newspaper cried. It thought the whole affair could have been accomplished in a single day.

On May 5, the committee met for the first time – but not for long. Again, Macdonald engineered a delay. He had by this time seen

95

Huntington's list of thirty-six witnesses and he saw at once that the Government faced something far more searching and exhaustive than a mere fishing expedition. Huntington was preparing to call McMullen, Allan, Abbott, Cartier, Hincks, the proprietors of the newspapers Allan said he bought, members of the Cartier election committee and even the managers of the Montreal and Ottawa telegraph offices who might have copies of compromising messages in their files. With Allan in England trying to raise funds for the railway (an increasingly difficult task in view of the disquieting news from Ottawa), the Prime Minister realized that, if the committee began its proceedings, he himself would have to take the witness stand before the absentee. That was a danger that must be avoided. He had no idea what the erratic Allan might blurt out on the stand. Their stories must dovetail and that could not be achieved until Allan and Abbott, who was with him, returned.

Macdonald determined to use the two men's absence, and that of Cartier, to force another delay. Here were the most important witnesses of all, he pointed out; would it be fair or just to proceed without them – to try them, in effect, in their absence? He got his way with the help of the Tories on the committee and his own parliamentary majority. The hearings were postponed until July 2.

Macdonald had successfully prevented the committee from sitting until midsummer and, if the Oaths Bill were disallowed, perhaps forever. The Opposition had not been able to get a shred of evidence on the record. Though the Liberal newspapers were screaming "scandal" (the ministerial press dubbed the affair "the Pacific Slander"), the public, numbed by a succession of spurious scandals and slanders, was not aroused.

The delay was more than frustrating: it was dangerous to the Opposition cause. Telegrams could be destroyed in the interval; originals of documents and letters could disappear, and, indeed, did. The Liberal leadership belatedly realized that it had made a tactical error in not placing some of the evidence on the record when Huntington first made his charges in early April. It is clear that he had seen copies of the Allan-McMullen correspondence and knew where the originals were stored. The evidence was to indicate that the Liberal party had purchased Allan's indiscreet correspondence from McMullen for twenty-five thousand dollars, using the aggrieved Senator Asa B. Foster as a go-between.

On May 13, Huntington tried to rectify his error, rising on a question of privilege to say that he knew of documentary evidence which was in the hands of a trustee and, because of the postponement, might be "beyond the reach of the Committee." He tried to read one of Allan's letters but Macdonald rose immediately to protest, in a soft, earnest voice, the impropriety of such disclosures being made in the House. The Speaker ruled Huntington out of order but in the course of his speech he did manage to get a good deal of titillating information on the record. If he only *could* read the letters, Huntington said, the House would see that they established that Allan had made a bargain for a sum of $360,000 which he wanted repaid. Amid cries of encouragement from his own party, Huntington went on to charge that Allan had manipulated priests and press for his own ends and that the letters – if he were only allowed to read them – would prove it. He moved that the committee subpoena the trustee and take over the documents, and to that the House agreed. The Liberal Party had cause to be jubilant. "They are done for," the Grit whip, J. D. Edgar, wrote to his wife that night.

In the preliminary bout of the great scandal, the Opposition had finally won a round. Macdonald was confident he would win the next one. On May 7 he learned, by telegram, that the Queen's legal advisers considered the Oaths Bill *ultra vires*. Could it be officially disallowed before the committee began cross-examining witnesses on July 2? Macdonald urged the Governor General to send a cable to London to hasten the British action and Lord Dufferin obligingly complied. Parliament adjourned until August 13.

Outwardly then, the Prime Minister was totally in command. Inwardly, he was sick at heart with grief, disappointment and foreboding. In May he suffered two terrible blows. Their force was not lessened by the fact he was braced to expect them.

By the middle of the month it was clear that Allan's negotiations with the English banking houses had met with total failure, destroyed by the whispers of scandal from across the water; and so Macdonald's railway policy lay in tatters. The settlement of the North West, the knitting together of the disunited provinces, the building of a workable, transcontinental nation, all these remained an elusive dream. Two years had already slipped by since the pact with British Columbia and there was now no chance in the foreseeable future of mounting the enterprise.

And the partnership of Macdonald and Cartier was no more. Macdonald's friend, confidant, bulwark, political comrade-in-arms and strong right hand, was dead in England of the kidney disease that had ravaged him for two years. At the nadir of his career, Macdonald had no one to turn to. Politically he stood alone, weary, overworked, tormented, dispirited. He wanted out; but his party could not let him resign; there was no one to replace him. When he suggested retiring to the back-benches, the Conservative hierarchy pointed out that his withdrawal could easily lead to a general exodus; and so, "very much harassed and out of health," he stayed.

He was, in fact, a Canadian fixture and it was unthinkable that he should go. In those days, before the newspaper half-tone engraving was invented, politicians were not always instantly recognizable; but everyone knew Macdonald, whom his own sister Louisa referred to as "one of the ugliest men in Canada." The long, rangy figure, the homely face, the absurd nose, the tight curls round the ears made him a caricaturist's delight. J. W. Bengough portrayed him week after week in *Grip* as a kind of likable rogue with matchstick legs and giant proboscis.

Likable he was, though often enough a rogue in the political sense. In those days of partisan hatreds, when one's political adversary really *was* the enemy, Macdonald's opponents found it hard to hate him. One Grit, Joseph Lister, who attacked Macdonald viciously in Parliament, confessed he was so attracted to the man's personality that he dare not trust himself in his company. Another, David Thompson of Haldimand, preferred him to his own leaders, Blake and Cartwright, who greeted him in the Commons corridors after a long illness with the chilliest of nods, while Macdonald slapped him on the back, called him Davy, said how glad he was to see him and declared: "I hope you'll soon be yourself again and live many a day to vote against me – as you have always done!" Said Thompson: "Hang me if it doesn't go against the grain to follow the men who haven't a word of kind greeting for me, and oppose a man with a heart like Sir John's." The twinkling eyes, the sardonic smile, the easy tolerance, the quick wit, and the general lack of malice made Macdonald an attractive figure in and out of Parliament. He did not believe that a politician could afford for long to harbour resentments; throughout his career he worked quite cheerfully with men who had slighted, insulted or betrayed him.

This singular absence of bile is remarkable when set against the tragedies and travails of Macdonald's private life. His personal vicissitudes would have broken a lesser man. His first wife had been a hopeless invalid, bed-ridden for most of the fourteen years of their married life. His second baby boy had died of convulsions. His daughter Mary, the only issue of his second marriage, was mentally retarded and physically deformed. After Confederation, Macdonald's life savings were wiped out, and he found himself plunged into heavy debt, partly because he had been forced by his political career to neglect his law practice, partly because of an unexpected bank failure. Never robust, always apparently on the cliff-edge of physical break-down, he had been felled for six months in 1870 by a nightmarish attack of gallstones, which brought him to the brink of death (his obituary set in type and ready for release) and weakened him for life.

Now, in the late spring of 1873, piled on top of all these adversities, Macdonald was burdened by the loss of his closest associate, the collapse of his national dream and the possible political destruction of himself and his party.

He turned, as he so often did in moments of stress, to the bottle; and for the next several weeks all who encountered him, from Governor General to hack reporter, were treated to the spectacle of the Prime Minister of Canada reeling drunk. "Indisposed" was the euphemism usually employed by the newspapers but the public knew exactly what *that* meant. After all, the stories about his drinking were legion: how he had once mounted a train platform so drunk and shaken that he had been seen to vomit while his opponent was speaking but had saved the day by opening his speech with the words: "Mr. Chairman and Gentlemen, I don't know how it is, but every time I hear Mr. Jones speak it turns my stomach." How he had told a public gathering during his campaigns against the former Liberal leader and *Globe* editor: "I know enough of the feeling of this meeting to know that you would rather have John A. drunk than George Brown sober." How, when his colleagues urged him to speak to that other great toper, D'Arcy McGee, about his alcohol problem, he had said: "Look here, McGee, this Government can't afford two drunkards and you've got to stop."

Macdonald's affinity for alcohol – he was a non-smoker – went back to his childhood when the Macdonald home dispensed what was then the universal form of hospitality: raw whiskey, obtainable at twenty-five cents a gallon and usually as easily available as water, being kept on tap or in a pail with a cup beside it. Macdonald's father "Little Hugh" was addicted to it and his life was shortened by it. Macdonald's own drinking bouts – he would sometimes retire to bed and consume bottle after bottle of port – were to become an endearing Canadian legend; but at the time they were a source of concern to his friends and colleagues and a perplexing embarrassment to his statuesque and highly moral wife, for whom, in the first glow of courtship, he had given up the bottle. To the sympathetic Dufferin, who was more than once publicly discomfited by the presence of his tipsy Prime Minister, Macdonald suffered from an "infirmity." The prim and granite-faced leader of the Opposition, Alexander Mackenzie, was not so tolerant. To him, Macdonald was, quite simply, a "drunken debauchee."

Yet his powers of recuperation were marvellous. He had the ability to pull himself together, even after days of drinking, when there was necessary business to attend to. And at the end of June, Macdonald needed his faculties: the Oaths Bill was officially disallowed just five days before the investigating committee was due to meet. Macdonald was now prepared to renew his offer of a royal commission.

The Dominion Day holiday, the sixth since Confederation, intervened – a day of picnics and street-dancing, quoits and croquet, train excursions and lacrosse games. Year by year, such national celebrations were giving the country a slight sense of community. The following morning, in the Montreal Court of Appeals, the select committee convened before a crowd of onlookers including such notables as Huntington, Macpherson, Alexander Galt, a gaggle of provincial and federal M.P.s but, noticeably, no member of the Government. Macdonald was in town, the *Globe* reported, but "indisposed." He was well enough, however, to send the committee a letter renewing his offer of a royal commission. A furious debate followed. The Government members wanted to pack up the committee until Parliament briefly reconvened on August 13. Parliament, they argued, had clearly meant the evidence to be taken under oath. Blake and his Liberal colleague, A. A. Dorion, wanted to dispense with the oath and examine unsworn witnesses. That was the way Parliamentary committees had always operated. The wrangle continued into the next day when the three Government supporters inevitably prevailed. Once again the Opposition had been frustrated in its attempts to get the evidence before the public. It was more than three months since Huntington had raised the issue and the country was in no sense aroused. There was only one course left open: the press.

On the morning of July 4, the faithful readers of the Toronto *Globe* Scandal!
and the Montreal *Herald* opened their slim papers to the scoop of the
decade. "PACIFIC RAILWAY INTRIGUES," the *Globe* headline read, and
there, for column after column, was laid bare the correspondence of
Sir Hugh Allan with his secret American backers. It was all in print
for the country to ponder: Allan's remarks regarding Brydges and
Macpherson . . . Allan's list of prominent Canadians who, he said,
were to be given free stock . . . Allan's detailed account of his victory
over Cartier . . . Allan's long report to General Cass (whose name
was withheld from the press) reporting on his coercion of the Quebec
press and public . . . Allan's disbursements of $343,000 . . . Allan's
double game with his American associates.

There were seventeen letters in total and they all but ended Sir
Hugh Allan's public career. One associate, the engineer Walter
Shanly, declared in Montreal that he would not be seen walking the
streets with Sir Hugh. The board of the new railway company met
hurriedly that afternoon while, not far away in Chaboillez Square, a
public meeting expressed its dissatisfaction with the investigation.
For the first time the public had something it could get its teeth into
and the Pacific Scandal, as it was now universally called, became the
major topic of the day.

The letters, the *Globe* insisted, showed that the Government
was "hopelessly involved in an infamous and corrupt conspiracy."
They scarcely showed that. Macdonald's name was mentioned only
three times and always innocuously. There was only one suspicious
paragraph in the letter of August 7 to General Cass, in which Allan
wrote that "we yesterday signed an agreement by which, on certain
monetary conditions, they agreed to form the company, of which I am
to be President, to suit my views, to give me and my friends a majority
of the stock." The letter was ambiguous enough to be capable of
innocent explanation.

Meanwhile, a much chastened Allan, at Macdonald's urgent behest
and with Abbott's legal skill, was preparing a sworn affidavit to be
published on July 6 in major Government newspapers. This lengthy
document, which was seized on with glee by the Government's
supporters, was designed to get the administration off the hook. It
largely succeeded. Allan's sworn denials were explicit and positive.

Though he certainly subscribed money to aid in the election of his friends, he had done so without any understanding or condition being placed upon such funds. None of this money, he swore, had come from the Americans. It was true that he had left the door ajar for his American friends until told specifically by the Government that they must be excluded; he felt honour bound to do so. As for McMullen, he had made such financial demands on Allan that "I declined altogether to entertain them." He was, of course, prepared to return all the money the Americans had expended but he was not prepared to pay McMullen an exorbitant fee for his time.

The statement, which bears the imprint of Abbott's sensitive legal mind, was a masterpiece of tightrope walking. "He [Abbott] has made the old gentleman acknowledge on oath that his letters were untrue," Macdonald wrote gleefully to Dufferin. "This was a bitter pill for him to swallow, but Abbott has gilded it over for him very nicely." It was not easy for Allan to wriggle out of correspondence written in his own hand but he did his best in a painfully contorted way: the letters, he said, were "written in the confidence of private intercourse in the midst of many matters engrossing my attention, and probably with less care and circumspection than might have been bestowed upon them had they been intended for publication. At the same time, while in some respects these letters are not strictly accurate, I can see that the circumstances, to a great extent, justified or excused the language used in them."

Allan, then, was the villain of the piece and the ministerial press cast him in that role. The Government's position was also immeasurably helped by the fact, easily substantiated, that the *Globe* and *Herald* had deliberately suppressed two other letters which showed that Allan had finally broken off negotiations with the Americans. McMullen, too, was reviled as a scoundrel and a blackmailer. His own relatives on the Picton *Gazette* attacked him, carefully refraining from any reference to his local family connections.

Though the *Globe* regurgitated the correspondence daily, it was clear that Macdonald's ministry, though bruised, was by no means broken. Indeed, Macdonald felt that the publication of the Allan correspondence was "very fortunate for the government" and Dufferin, in reply, agreed: "The unfolding of the drama is quite sensational and in spite of all the annoyance to which you have been put in this business, it must have afforded you a good deal of amusement. . . . Nothing can be more satisfactory than the way in which your own position and that of your colleagues remains unassailed in the midst of all these disreputable proceedings."

The weary Prime Minister now felt that he could afford a short holiday at Rivière du Loup. It was while he was there, in his small cottage by the riverside, that the world crashed in on him.

The blow fell on July 17, just as the public was growing weary of the newspapers' incessant harping on the scandal. It was devastating. The *Globe* ran a great bank of type on the right-hand column of its front page: "THE PACIFIC SCANDAL: ASTOUNDING REVELATIONS." The revelations appeared identically and simultaneously in the *Globe*, the *Herald* and *l'Evénement* of Quebec and they *were* astounding.

The story, which ran to several columns, took the form of a historical narrative by George McMullen, whose dubious presence had hung over the affair from the outset. McMullen, goaded by "the vilest slanders," laid about him with a scythe as he gave his version, often highly coloured and inaccurate, of his role in the drama. He claimed that Allan had lent Macdonald and Hincks $4,000 and $4,500 respectively "with very good knowledge that it was never to be repaid." He said that Allan had sounded out the finance minister regarding "the extent of his personal expectations" and that Hincks had asked for a flat fifty thousand dollars rather than a percentage of the ultimate profits plus a job for his son as secretary of the company for a minimum of two thousand dollars a year. He identified the newspapers, including *La Minerve* of Montreal, which Allan told him he had paid. He said that Allan had made an additional indefinite loan of ten thousand dollars to Hincks and had promised Langevin twenty-five thousand for election purposes, "on condition of his friendly assistance."

This was strong meat, though not of itself conclusive since McMullen, branded in the public mind as a blackmailer, was himself suspect. But unlike most newspaper stories, the sting of this one was in its tail. Appended to McMullen's narrative, deep inside the newspaper, was a series of letters and telegrams which contained political dynamite. They had been buried at the end by design in an attempt to divert suspicion from the source from which they had been obtained. They had been rifled from Abbott's safe in the dark of the night, during the lawyer's absence in England, copied by his confidential secretary, George Norris, Jr., and an assistant, and sold for hard cash to the Liberal Party.

Cartier to Abbott, Montreal, August 24, 1872: "In the absence of Sir Hugh Allan, I shall be obliged by your supplying the Central Committee with a further sum of twenty thousand dollars upon the same conditions as the amount written by me at the foot of my letter to Sir Hugh Allan of the 30th ult.

George E. Cartier

"P.S. Please also send Sir John A. Macdonald ten thousand dollars more on the same terms."

Terms? Conditions? What price Allan's sworn denials now?

Memorandum signed by three members of the Central Committee, J. L. Beaudry, Henry Starnes and P. S. Murphy: "Received from Sir Hugh Allan by the hands of J. J. C. Abbott twenty thousand dollars for General Election purposes, to be arranged hereafter according to the terms of the letter of Sir George E. Cartier, of the date of 30th of July, and in accordance with the request contained in his letter of the 24th instant."
Montreal, 26th Aug., 1872.

Again, that damning word: *terms.* It was well for the Government that poor Cartier was dead.

Telegram: Macdonald to Abbott at St. Anne's, Aug. 26, 1872, Toronto: "I must have another ten thousand; will be the last time of calling; do not fail me; answer today."

Reply: Abbott to Macdonald from Montreal, Aug. 26, 1872: "Draw on me for ten thousand dollars."

"Three more extraordinary documents than these . . . never saw the light of day," Lord Dufferin wrote to the Colonial Secretary. There was, in addition, a final clincher: a statement from the discontented Senator Asa B. Foster, commenting on the McMullen revelations and corroborating them: ". . . I was aware of the agreement with Mr. Langevin to which you refer as it was frequently discussed between us and Mr. Abbott. I was also aware from the first of Sir George E. Cartier's opposition to Sir Hugh Allan, and of the means by which Sir George was forced to forego this opposition.

"In regard to the payment of money for election purposes I was informed of the arrangement with Sir George Cartier, and was also shown a confirmatory telegram from Sir John A. Macdonald. I understand the affair to be substantially as you have related, and I have reason to believe that large sums of money were actually expended for election purposes under the arrangement."

The effect on the public of these revelations was incalculable. Dufferin was later to refer, in his dramatic fashion, to "the terror and shame manifested by the people at large when the possibility first dawned upon them of their most trusted statesman having been guilty of such conduct." The Pacific Scandal became the sole topic of conversation in those late July days and continued so into the fall. The carnage among the party faithful was devastating. Even schoolboys found themselves embroiled. Sir John Willison, who was to become editor of the *Globe*, was a youth at the time and remembered how his village school at Greenwood, Ontario, broke into factions. Those who clung to the Tory leader were denounced by their classmates as "Charter Sellers"; and Willison admitted, even though he had been reared in a Tory household and still clung desperately to the faith of his fathers, "I fear that I wavered as I found life-long Conservatives falling away from the standard." Many a loyal Tory was transformed, during that tempestuous summer, into a working Liberal.

All other news and comment was subordinated as the newspapers now took up the great scandal with what *The Times* of London called "colonial vehemence." The ministerial newspapers were badly shaken for they had been maintaining, day after day, that no money had been given Macdonald. The stooped and aging Hincks rushed into print to deny that he had ever asked or ever obtained anything from anybody, not even for his son, "though I did on one occasion casually say to Sir Hugh, as I had done to other friends, that if he ever happened to know of employment for my youngest son I would be glad if he would bear it in mind." The *Globe* maliciously reminded its readers that this was not the first time Hincks's name had been clouded by scandal. In his days as premier of the united Canadas he had, on more than one occasion, used his official knowledge for his personal profit, as a subsequent investigating committee discovered. Ironically, it had been John A. Macdonald who had attacked the Hincks ministry of that day as "steeped to the very lips in infamy" and "tainted with corruption."

Now at Rivière du Loup the echoes of those words were dinning in Macdonald's ears. In all his long career nothing hit Macdonald so hard as the McMullen revelations. The news, which reached him in condensed form in a hurriedly scribbled letter from Langevin, "fairly staggered" him. It was, he later told Dufferin, "one of those overwhelming misfortunes that they say every man must meet once in his life." He had expected trouble but nothing so cataclysmic as this. He had certainly sent the telegrams; but he had never expected to be found out.

Alexander Campbell, Macdonald's old law partner and Senate leader, was in touch with his chief immediately with a call for a hurried conference with Langevin in Quebec City. It was "very necessary to consider immediately what action should be taken." The strategy was clear: a royal commission was now an absolute necessity, preferably one that included "safe" judges. The indispensable Abbott was hurriedly called upon to assist in the negotiations. He reported a Montreal rumour that fresh revelations, in the form of more injudicious telegrams from Macdonald, were due to appear at any moment: "The sooner the Commission is appointed, the sooner these periodical galvanic shocks will cease." He had written "very guardedly" to Charles Dewey Day, a retired Superior Court judge, who was Chancellor of McGill University. Abbott had every confidence "in his acting judiciously." A sympathetic letter to Macdonald from the judge himself, two days later, made clear just what the cautious Abbott meant. Judge Day was squarely on Macdonald's side, disturbed by the fact that the correspondence as published in the press was "in a shape which tells against you." The judge wrote that "no time should be lost in endeavouring to change the current of public opinion. If you think I can be of service in helping to place the matter upon a true and just footing I willingly accept the duty." Obviously, from Macdonald's point of view, Charles Dewey Day was the proper choice to head the Royal Commission.

Abbott was indefatigable. He was in constant touch with Thomas White, the editor of the Montreal *Gazette*, practically dictating that paper's editorial attitude on the scandal. He was searching around for two more royal commissioners, suggesting to Macdonald that Upper Canada judges "would be safest on our account," since Lower Canada judges had a nasty habit of accepting all evidence and deciding on its admissibility at a later date, after it had been aired in the press. Then there were damaging papers to be destroyed (probably Cartier's); Abbott wanted both Macdonald and Campbell on hand in Montreal to preside over this delicate matter. At the same time he was dangling all sorts of "greatly attractive bait" in front of his former clerk, George Norris, in an attempt to publicize the full story of the theft of the documents. Norris wasn't budging, and this led Abbott to believe that "he must have been greatly well paid to enable him to resist temptation." Subsequently, Abbott and his men did succeed in rounding up Alfred Thomas Cooper, the man who had helped Norris copy out the letters, telegrams and notes from the shorthand book in Abbott's office. Cooper swore in a deposition that Norris had been paid five thousand dollars and promised a government job when the Liberals took power by the prominent Liberal legal firm of Laflamme, Huntington and Laflamme. When news of Cooper's defection leaked out, the Liberals tried to bribe Abbott's bookkeeper to find out exactly what Cooper had revealed. The harried Conservative press made as much as it could of the burglary, countenanced as it was by a party whose leaders, Mackenzie and Blake, preached the highest standards of morality. But the public, sickened by scandal, could not be persuaded that two wrongs made a right.

Meanwhile the persistent McMullen was back in print with a new charge: John Hillyard Cameron, the chairman of the abortive investigating committee, himself bore investigation. After the elections, Cameron had applied to Allan for a five-thousand-dollar loan, which Allan, following a series of urgent wires and letters from Macdonald, reluctantly paid. The note was discounted a fortnight before Allan got his charter and renewed on April 23, after Cameron had been named committee chairman.

It was all too much. With the crisis swirling around him, Macdonald took to the bottle and vanished from sight. No member of his cabinet could reach him or learn of his plans or purpose. The press reported that he had disappeared from Rivière du Loup. His wife had no idea where he was. The frantic Governor General, in the midst of a state tour of the Maritimes, could get no answer to an urgent and confidential letter. He followed it with an equally urgent telegram; silence. On August 5, the Montreal *Daily Witness* published in its two o'clock edition a rumour that Macdonald had committed suicide by throwing himself into the St. Lawrence. The story, concocted by his political enemies, vanished from the next edition but was widely believed at the time; it seemed to confirm the Government's guilt. Suicide or no, the fact was that for several days, in a moment of grave political crisis, the Prime Minister of Canada could not be found by anyone. Dufferin finally unravelled the mystery and put it delicately in a private letter to the Colonial Secretary: "He had stolen away, as I subsequently found, from his seaside villa and was lying perdu with a friend in the neighbourhood of Quebec."

3

The The elegant Lord Dufferin was a sorely perplexed man. Prince
memorable Edward Island, the crucible of Confederation, had, rather tardily,
August 13 made up its mind to become the sixth province and the Governor General was off on the kind of mission he loved best: official ceremonies, graceful off-the-cuff remarks, state dinners, carefully staged addresses punctuated by cheers and applause. As the Queen's representative, His Excellency saw himself as a kind of walking flag, a unifying national force in a sea of petty provincialism. All this pomp and circumstance was rudely shattered by the McMullen revelations. "We are in a devil of a mess here and my position is not to be envied," he wrote to Lord Kimberley, the Colonial Secretary, from Halifax. "The whole country is in a violent state of excitement from one end to the other and the language of the Newspaper Press is becoming perfectly rabid."

The Governor General's immediate problem was the reassembly of Parliament on August 13, just one week away. Originally all members had agreed that the sitting would be a mere token – a legal device to allow the investigating committee to meet, since it could not legally continue to sit if Parliament were prorogued. Macdonald had suggested that the House reassemble briefly in August, conduct no business and prorogue; presumably by the thirteenth the committee's work would be complete. Indeed, he said – and there was no dissent – those members who did not live in Ottawa need not go to the trouble of returning; a quorum could be found in the immediate neighbourhood.

All this was agreeable to the House on May 23; but by the end of July the whole political complexion of the country had changed. The "Party of Punishment," as some papers now called the Opposition, was out for blood. It wanted a *bona fide* session of Parliament to air the charges that had been made, and it was determined to get one. Mass meetings were being called in the major cities attacking the idea of prorogation. In Montreal, the Mayor himself addressed a crowd of

108

five thousand urging that the session be prolonged. Public sympathy was clearly with the Opposition.

Since it was he who must officially prorogue the House, the Governor General had become the key figure in the controversy. What would he do? Would he take the advice of his ministers, who certainly wanted the session to end without any discomfiting debate? Or would he follow another course?

When the McMullen thunderbolt was first launched, Dufferin had just reached Prince Edward Island. He at once called in the two leading Maritime politicians, Leonard Tilley of New Brunswick and Charles Tupper of Nova Scotia, who were in his entourage. Both men were astounded by the revelations "and seemed half inclined to throw in the sponge." Tupper's explanation was that "during the excitement of the election Sir John being on the drink must have written and telegraphed these strange things, a whisper of which he himself had never hitherto heard. . . ." Tupper, of course, *had* heard from Hincks the previous February that Allan had made large contributions to the election "simply because the Opposition . . . were publicly avowed enemies of the scheme, determined to upset it." Now, he recovered himself sufficiently to tell Dufferin that matters could be satisfactorily explained. The troubled Governor General grasped at this, though not without misgivings: he was beginning to sense that if he prorogued Parliament his cherished popularity would suffer a severe wrench. He wrote to Macdonald that the next session could not be put off until the following February. If prorogued, it must meet again as swiftly as possible. He added a word of encouragement: "I do not for a moment doubt the result."

By August 9, Macdonald had pulled himself together. He wrote Lord Dufferin in Halifax that he might as well continue his tour and not bother attending in Ottawa; he had no intention of prolonging the session in spite of the rising public outcry. But Dufferin was of a different mind: "At such a critical state of affairs it is not fair to my ministers to remain at a distance and so I go," he answered. His intentions were misinterpreted by the public; the news that the Governor General was coming to Ottawa strengthened the belief that the session would be more than a mere formality.

Dufferin arrived in the capital on the very day of the session – "the memorable 13th of August" as it came to be called. He saw his shaky Prime Minister who submitted the Government's unanimous advice that Parliament should conduct no business. The Governor General did not feel justified in withdrawing his confidence from his ministers on the basis of newspaper reports, but he extracted a price for his assent: Parliament must meet again within eight weeks. Macdonald agreed. With Dufferin's acquiescence, the Cabinet later lengthened the interval to ten.

The city itself was in an unprecedented state of excitement. No one could guess the Governor General's intentions but it was obvious that, if prorogation were planned, the Opposition intended to do its best to frustrate it. Already the Liberals were chipping away at Macdonald's majority. Thirteen members who normally supported the ministry had joined the ranks of the enemy. These were numbered among the ninety-two who signed a memorial to His Excellency. A delegation, headed by Richard Cartwright, a one-time Conservative with a great beak of a nose and prodigious side whiskers, waited upon Lord Dufferin that morning to read it. The honour of the country, said the memorial, required that there be no further delay. Four months had elapsed; nothing had happened. Parliament must remain in session until an investigation was forced. Cartwright had broken with Macdonald when the latter had made Hincks, and not himself, Minister of Finance. Since then he had pursued an independent course in Parliament. Now the Pacific Scandal was helping to turn him into a die-hard Grit; for the remainder of his long life the memory of these days would continue to haunt and embitter him; and he would never forgive Macdonald. Years later, when Parliament discussed the erection of a statue to Canada's first prime minister, Cartwright kept insisting that the details of the Pacific Scandal should be engraved upon the base; it took all the powers of persuasion his colleagues could summon up to talk him out of it.

Dufferin, listening to Cartwright's delegation, realized that he would be damned if he prorogued Parliament and damned if he did not; but he had made up his mind: to act against the advice of his ministers would be "an act of personal interference on my part." What guarantee could the delegation give him that Parliament would endorse it?

"What right has the Governor-General, on his personal responsibility, to proclaim to Canada – nay, not only to Canada, but to America and Europe, as such a proceeding on his part must necessarily do, that he believes his Ministers guilty of the crimes alleged against them?" he asked. The bellicose Cartwright and his delegation retired with bad grace.

By noon that day the Ottawa streets were crowded and the corridors of the Parliament Buildings swarming with people. The city was like a furnace but the public ignored the heat and debated the question: *What would the Governor General do?* At one o'clock the word spread that the entourage had been called out; prorogation was certain; once again, investigation had been stifled.

The spectacle that took place in the House of Commons that afternoon was one of the strangest the country had known. Both the Government and the Opposition were braced for it. On each side the tacticians had planned every move, all of them based on the hoary British pageantry and make-believe that accompanied the official end of a parliamentary session. Alexander Mackenzie, the solemn Sarnia stonemason who would become Liberal prime minister if Macdonald's ministry fell, knew exactly what he had to do. He must leap to his feet and start talking the moment the Speaker took the chair and before the Speaker could answer the traditional summons of the Gentleman Usher of the Black Rod. For as soon as Black Rod knocked three times on the Commons door, inviolable custom decreed that all debate must give way.

But there was more than this: it was usual for a House assembling to proceed with routine business – the reading of formal communications, the receiving of committee reports, the introduction of new members. The gaunt Mackenzie could not afford to wait for this; he must seize the floor and hold it the instant the House was organized. Even then he could be stopped unless he rose on a question of privilege, which, by the rules of Parliament, did not require the usual two days' notice.

That, then, was Mackenzie's plan: the instant the ample rump of the handsome and burly James Cockburn grazed the velvet of the Speaker's chair, he must be on his feet and in full voice.

It was the Government's intention to frustrate this tactic by a counter-gambit that required equally delicate timing: the Speaker must reach his seat and Black Rod must hammer on the door of the House almost simultaneously. Such was the mood of the House that the strategists were prepared for the most far-fetched eventuality. Black Rod would be guarded by a detective en route to the Commons to make sure he was not kidnapped by the Grits; and, in defiance of all custom, police would be stationed at every door.

In the Commons, the tension began to mount. Three o'clock came and went but there was no sign of the Speaker. The members, like spectators at a tennis match, switched their eyes back and forth between the door of the House and the parliamentary clock. Macdonald's seat was empty; he was at the entrance to Parliament waiting to greet the Governor General. Across the floor, facing the empty seat, was the spare figure of Mackenzie, wound tight as a spring, nervously gripping his glasses in one hand and a sheaf of papers in the other. The clock ticked away; still no Speaker. Then, at 3.20, a ripple of movement could be discerned behind the doors. It was the diminutive figure of René Edward Kimber, the Gentleman Usher in person, mace in hand, detective in tow, peeping through the glass of the central doorway. The Government's strategy was plain.

Another five minutes ticked by. Finally the Speaker made his entrance and mounted to the dais. He was scarcely seated before Mackenzie was on his feet, talking at top speed in his heavy Scots brogue:

"I propose to address you and the House on a very important question (*Hear, hear*). In the present grave phase of the history of our country and the extraordinary circumstances under which we are called together, I think it incumbent upon me to place the following motion in your hands."

Pandemonium! The Speaker had tried to interrupt Mackenzie and the Opposition, in full throat, was baying: "Go on! Go on!" But Mackenzie, in his eagerness to seize the floor, had moved too soon. The doors of the Commons were not yet open and thus, technically, the House was not in session. The Opposition leader stood his ground, fearful of losing his advantage, while the Sergeant-at-arms pushed the cumbersome doors aside. Now, reading swiftly and in his loudest voice, Mackenzie plunged into his motion: Parliament itself must investigate the charges of corruption. "Any tribunal created by the Executive would be a flagrant violation of the principles of this House."

The House remained in an uproar as Mackenzie kept on. The Speaker's handsome, heavy face was a picture of confusion. Black Rod, nonplussed by the stormy scene around him, was hammering with his mace the three knocks that tradition required. These could scarcely be heard, but the Government's supporters, relief on their faces, began to cry that the messenger had arrived from the Senate. The Opposition maintained its chant of "Privilege! Privilege!" Mackenzie continued to talk. "No messenger shall interrupt me in the discharge of my duty," he roared in a cracked voice.

112

A little pantomime now took place. The Speaker, unable to make himself heard above the uproar, engaged in dumb show with the Sergeant-at-arms, who dutifully admitted Black Rod. The messenger advanced to the Speaker's Table, as custom decreed, and vainly tried to shout his summons. Mackenzie, barely stopping for breath, continued to talk while the Speaker, again in dumb show, persuaded the Sergeant-at-arms to pick up the great mace. By now even the galleries were in an uproar; but the charade continued with Black Rod doing his best to maintain some grace, bowing his customary three bows and retreating backward towards the doors. The Speaker followed from his dais; some of the Government's supporters trooped out behind him. But the Opposition members remained in their seats and so did some Tories. In the Senate chamber, its galleries bright once more with millinery and silks, the rites of prorogation limped to their formal close.

Tactically, Macdonald had won every parliamentary skirmish since Huntington had risen in his place the previous April. He had managed to squelch a parliamentary investigation and he could now proceed with the kind of royal commission he had always wanted. But at what a cost! He had lost the sympathy of the public and, indeed, of some of his own followers. "I fear we cannot expect people to believe that the money he got was applied to any other purpose than bribery," Dufferin recorded. "Here, as in most other places, to do the thing is a lesser sin than to be found out, and although I believe as much bribery went on on the other side; that fact, however patent − will not go far to help Macdonald even here where the standard of public morality is much lower than in England."

On Parliament Hill, the uproar continued. The Opposition moved out of the Commons in a body and reconvened in the railway committee room where a marathon indignation meeting was mounted. Hour after hour, until ten-thirty that night, the heavy guns of the Liberal Party assailed the Government and the Governor General. Luther Holton, the Lincolnesque leader of the Quebec wing, attacked Lord Dufferin for "acting upon the advice of men who were themselves under impeachment for crimes which almost amounted to treason." Mackenzie, his voice almost gone from his verbal exertions in the House, croaked that "a cry would go out from end to end of the land against the indignity which had been put upon [Parliament]." Blake, who was at his best on such occasions, called, amid cheers, for an investigation "not by men chosen by the accused, not by men

113

named by the gentlemen in the dock – but by those chosen by Parliament." After the meeting broke up, the discussion continued in the streets. Little knots of people gathered under lamp posts all over town to argue that, had the Ministers of the Crown been innocent of the charges against them, they would have hastened the inquiry instead of delaying it. "It looks very black," people kept saying to each other as the arguments continued, far into the humid Ottawa night.

By the following day, the Governor General felt he had "pulled through this abominable business better than I had expected." But he had to suffer the slings and arrows of the Liberal press, which charged he had interfered with the freedom and privilege of debate. History books were scoured to find fittingly heinous parallels and the embattled Governor General found himself likened to King John, James II and even Charles I. In Montreal, the *Herald* called his action "the greatest outrage on the constitution since Oliver Cromwell ordered 'that bauble' to be taken away." On August 15, the *Globe*, perturbed at the spectacle of the Crown being dragged into politics, drew back a little and confessed that, though His Excellency had committed an error, it was not one of intention. Bit by bit, the press cooled off.

As for Macdonald, he was, in Dufferin's phrase, "in a terrible state." He was very shaky and "it seems to me his political supporters are very shaky, too." For the first time, the Governor General was pessimistic about the future of his ministry. "I don't think," he wrote, "the regime can last much longer."

4

The least satisfactory Royal Commission The three Royal Commissioners appointed under the great seal of Canada on August 14 began to take evidence at noon, on September 4, in the same railway committee room that three weeks before had echoed with the angry cries of the Opposition. On this very day, the general public was treated to an additional peek at the political morality of the period. In Montreal, the Grits had stolen another letter; or, at least, somebody had found the letter in the wrong postal box and turned it over to the Grits, who, ignoring the post office, turned it over to the Montreal *Herald*. The letter itself provided a fascinating glimpse behind the political scenery. It was from John A. Macdonald to John Henry Pope, the square-jawed minister of agriculture; it dealt with Macdonald's scheme to pressure the resignation of John Young, a Liberal member for Montreal West, by threatening to deny him the post of flour inspector, which he had held for nine years. Macdonald proposed to invoke a new act (from which Young later insisted he had been promised immunity) which prohibited Members of Parliament from receiving an outside salary. In the subsequent by-election Macdonald hoped to run William Workman, an extremely well-heeled Montreal businessman, whose person and pocketbook would be tempted into the fold by offering him the bribe of an early Senate appointment. The letter ordered Pope to hold up Young's appointment until all of Macdonald's plans were laid. The cold-blooded political manoeuvring exposed in this letter was to a large extent cancelled out by the Liberals' act of tampering with the mails; but it added to the public's general sense of outrage at the outset of the Commission's deliberations.

In his choice of commissioners, Macdonald was not able to escape the shrill charge of collusion. Oddly, Judge Day, the chairman, who had at the time of his appointment come down so firmly on Macdonald's side, was not attacked by the press. The aging jurist with the big, luminous eyes and domed head was generally felt to be above politics, perhaps by virtue of his position as Chancellor of McGill; Mackenzie himself felt he could be relied upon to do his duty without fear or favour. The other two choices were greeted with more scepticism. The *Globe* dismissed Judge Antoine Polette, another ex-politician and retired Superior Court judge from Lower Canada, as "a bitter, prejudiced French Conservative and . . . a very dull man." It reserved its heaviest ammunition, however, for the Honourable James Robert Gowan, a cadaverous-looking county court judge from Simcoe, Ontario, known to have been Macdonald's close friend for twenty-five years, whom the newspaper saw as a hack political appointee and party follower: "The bailiffs and clerks in his county have always been strong John A. men – the most active electioneering agents of the Conservative Government in all the countryside." Lord Dufferin, on his part, felt that "the length of time all three have been removed from politics frees them from the suspicion of political partisanship."

And so commenced "the least satisfactory of all Royal Commissions." It was unsatisfactory on several counts. There was no commission counsel to cross-examine witnesses. Huntington had been expected to assume that role but Huntington, along with all members of the Opposition, was boycotting the entire proceedings on principle; the matter, he continued to insist, ought to be in the hands of a parliamentary committee. The commission had Huntington's list of witnesses but the commissioners did not really know what to ask them. Their opening query was generally vague: "Have you any knowledge relating to an agreement between Sir Hugh Allan and Mr. G. W. McMullen, representing certain American capitalists, for the building of the Canadian Pacific Railway with American funds?" Apart from the three elderly judges no one else, save the Government in the person of Macdonald, was allowed the right of cross-examination. Several of the other principals would not be heard from. Cartier, who might have told so much, was in his grave. McMullen ignored the subpoena. Senator Asa B. Foster found it inconvenient to attend. George Norris, the clerk who had rifled Abbott's safe, replied through his lawyer that he was too ill to appear. Of the thirty-six witnesses called, fifteen contributed nothing whatsoever to the proceedings, nor were they pressed to contribute more. They only knew, as the saying goes, what they had read in the papers.

It was obvious from the beginning why Macdonald had preferred a royal commission to a parliamentary inquiry. As Dufferin summed it up in his colourful way, ". . . elderly judges have hardly the disembowelling powers which are rife in a young cross-examining counsel." Dufferin added that the commission's determination to allow the Government, through Macdonald, to question all witnesses "gave an unavoidable, one-sided aspect to the conduct of the case." Judge Day took the casual attitude that it was the other side's fault if they refused to claim a similar advantage. No wonder then, that Macdonald had "no fear but that the report must be a satisfactory one."

Day after day, for all of September, the public was treated to the spectacle of powerful business figures and important politicians, by nature and training supposedly men of precision, fumbling about on the stand, delivering fuzzy or evasive answers, testifying to receipts that were "lost" or missing, prefacing their remarks with such phrases as "I cannot remember," or "It is not very likely. . . ."

The first witness was Henry Starnes, the president of Allan's Merchants' Bank, and the chairman of Cartier's election fund. Starnes

116

was shrewd of feature, with lidded lizard's eyes and a beaked nose but he was a mountain of uncertainty when asked about contributions to the Cartier campaign: "I cannot say how all the money came but it was deposited with me, and by what means I do not exactly know."

This was the city's leading banker talking! Starnes, a lieutenant-colonel in the militia and a former mayor of Montreal, came empty-handed to the witness stand; he had no financial statement for the fund, no record of receipts or disbursements and, apparently, no memory of them. "When the receipt was published in the Montreal newspapers, I was astonished as I had forgotten all about it. I was surprised, for I had signed it I suppose in the hurry of the election; I might have signed more than one."

Starnes could not name the exact amount the committee had received, or how much of that money Allan had supplied, nor was he asked by the commission to file any account.

Sir Francis Hincks was the second witness. He had arrived from Montreal, according to the *Globe*, "much put out by things as they are and consequently in a very bad humour." Small wonder: he was approaching the twilight of a long career in business and politics (he was the only one of five brothers who did not enter the Church) and once again there was a cloud across his name. Where railways were concerned, Hincks the politician never seemed to let his public position interfere with the interests of Hincks the speculator. In 1854 a series of irregularities, all involving railways, had brought about his downfall as joint premier of the united Canadas. He had been accused of corruption for accepting one thousand shares of Grand Trunk stock while actively pushing for the railway. He was further charged before a special committee of the legislature with having speculated in another railway stock after getting inside information that it would be sold to the Grand Trunk. And he was also accused of spending public money to re-route a short line of railroad through some property he had purchased. For fifteen years after that Hincks exiled himself to the Caribbean where he served as governor, first of Barbados and then of British Guiana.

Now this shrivelled old man with the sharp features and the stooped shoulders once again saw his name connected with shady political manoeuvring. Because of his fierceness in debate he was known as "the Hyena," but he was positively calflike on the witness stand. He did not "think it at all likely" that he had discussed Cartier's alleged antipathy towards the CPR with McMullen. He professed ignorance that Allan had been "a liberal contributor to the election funds." Yet he must have known the money was coming from somewhere; he had got some himself. No commissioner thought to question him about that. Nor was he asked about the indefinite loan of ten thousand dollars that McMullen claimed Allan told him he had advanced. He denied everything and was excused.

Louis Beaubien, M.P., a provisional director of Allan's company, had got seven thousand dollars from Allan as a "loan" to cover his own election expenses. Ill at ease on the stand, nervously correcting himself over and over again, he swore that he could not locate the receipt for the money, although he had seen it a month earlier. Who was to repay the loan? Beaubien started to say that he supposed the Government would, then corrected himself and said he meant "the friends of the Government." Had he asked Allan for help? Again the evasive reply: "I suppose I must have said a word for myself at that time."

When the managers of the Ottawa and Montreal telegraph companies took the stand, it developed that copies of the telegrams of the previous year had been destroyed under new rules which had "nothing to do with the elections" but which provided that originals could only be kept for six months. Thus all copies of telegrams for the period under investigation were gone. The reasons given were lack of storage space and to prevent "our operators being dragged up to Court." The ubiquitous Allan, it turned out, was also president of the telegraph company.

Hector Louis Langevin, a bulky man with pouchy eyes, a page-boy hair style and a tiny *mouche* beneath his lower lip, was another public figure who destroyed most of his mail. Macdonald's Minister of Public Works testified; "I don't keep any of these letters, nor any letters that are mere formal letters. It has always been a rule with me as soon as I have finished with a letter to destroy it, unless it is an official letter to be filed in the Department. But my own letters I destroy, and I think, from what I have seen since, that I was perfectly right in this."

Langevin admitted getting election funds from Allan but "as far as I can recollect" there were no conditions attached to them. When he had pointed out to Abbott that he needed help, Abbott had remarked "that it would not be fair that the burden should all fall on my shoulders but that certainly I should be helped by my friends." In the end, Allan, through the ever-present Abbott, turned over $32,600 to Langevin. This was an enormous sum to receive from a single source; in modern terms it would be equivalent to some two hundred thousand dollars. But nobody thought to ask Langevin what his feelings were when he received such a purse, or whether he felt indebted to Allan or suspicious of him. Nor was he asked to tell where the money went. Did he favour some candidates over others? Did he leave some out in the cold? What was it used for, exactly? Since Langevin kept no records, the record did not say. Eighteen years later another scandal would abruptly end Langevin's career.

The tendency of the commissioners to take statements at their face value without further searching inquiry did not go unremarked. The manager of the Merchants' Bank gave no useful testimony at all; but he might have been asked to furnish a list of payments made by drafts on Allan's account during the period in question. He was not. Joseph Hamel spoke of several thousand dollars subscribed for the election in Kamouraska riding. Did it come in small sums or was a large portion subscribed by some one friend of the Government? He was not asked to break the figure down. Peter Murphy, a member of Cartier's election committee, took the stand to testify that forty thousand dollars had been given by Allan to the Montreal fund but there was no attempt made by the commission to tie up the series of payments referred to and the dates of the alleged agreements between Allan and the Government. In the *Globe*, George Brown and his editorial writers pounded these points home daily. Brown had just returned from England, where he had been sent for health reasons immediately following his publication of the McMullen revelations. The Scandal had worn *him* down, too. Once across the water, Macdonald's old adversary dined with one of *The Times*'s chief editorial writers, supplied him with documents dealing with the Scandal and then went after the lesser dailies and periodicals. "Putting the press men right," he called it. The result was that when Macdonald testified before the commission, the major British papers were ready to pounce.

It was Macdonald's testimony that the country was waiting for. The Prime Minister, who had attended every session of the commission, delivered himself of a long narrative, starting with his first meeting with Alfred Waddington and taking the story down past the election of 1872. He denied or qualified many of the statements in the McMullen account and he denied that Allan's election contributions had influenced the Government in any way. He also made it clear that the Government had never had any intention of allowing the Americans to control the railway. But there were two damning

119

accusations that he could not and did not deny. He had asked Allan for election funds and he had promised Allan the presidency of the company. Macdonald strove to put these awkward truths in the best possible light; Allan was the obvious man for the job: his business experience, his financial standing in the community, his ability to command confidence among English financiers, all these qualified him above any others. It was natural that he should supply the Conservative Party with election funds; it was in his own interest to support the one party that had promised to push the railway through to completion.

Macdonald swore that he had not used one cent of Allan's money for his own election; but he was forced to make one other damaging admission: Allan's money had been spent in a manner "contrary to statute," in bringing voters to the polls and in "dinners and things of that kind." The Prime Minister's euphemisms and deliberate vagueness could not cover up in the public mind the obvious deduction that the money had been used to bribe the voters. In his second capacity of Minister of Justice, he had knowingly broken the law.

Even Lord Dufferin, who had been leaning over backwards on Macdonald's behalf, thought his testimony had "a very bad appearance." Though he still did not believe his chief minister intended to sacrifice the interests of the country to Allan, "he cannot very well escape from the imputation of such an act, except by admitting that he was bleeding Allan very severely at the very time he was preparing to hedge him out from a participation in the benefits Allan was anticipating."

The British press came down very hard on the Prime Minister. *The Times* declared that his testimony had confirmed the McMullen revelations. The *Pall Mall Gazette* followed: "If even we were to know no more than the admission made by Sir John Macdonald himself, we should be compelled to say that the scandal of his conduct is without precedent . . . it will be the business of the honest people of Canada to take care that none of the persons who are concerned in the proceedings of which Sir George Cartier was the agent shall ever again obtain power in Canada." These opinions, originating with supposedly disinterested papers, and reprinted in the Opposition press, did incalculable damage to the Government cause. George Brown's spade-work had paid off for the Liberal Party.

Two days later, Allan took the stand. The tiger of the Notman photograph was now a chastened witness; and, like so many who had preceded him, a forgetful one. He even forgot that he had signed a supplementary contract with his American backers on March 28, 1872, in which he was authorized to accept, if necessary, a smaller land grant for the railway than that originally proposed.

"I had no recollection of this contract until the last few days," the laird of Ravenscrag declared. "And if I had been asked would have said I had never seen it." But there was no question that the contract existed and that the most astute business leader in Canada, who insisted that everything be in writing, had put his signature to it.

As for the notorious correspondence with McMullen, Smith and Cass, they were "private letters for private information and not for publication at all," and, in Allan's view, that seemed to take care of that. He admitted that some of the statements in the letters "may appear to conflict" with his own evidence and then repeated his previously published explanation that they had been written carelessly.

In his testimony, Allan showed himself a master of double talk. McMullen had charged that a secret agreement had been made between Cartier and Allan, with Macdonald's blessing, between July 30 and August 6, 1872, by which, for certain monetary considerations, Allan was to get the charter. And there, staring at him, was Allan's own letter to Cass of August 7, stating that "we yesterday signed an agreement by which, on certain monetary conditions, they agree to form a company of which I am to be President to suit my views, to give me and my friends a majority of the stock, and to give the company so formed the contract for building the road. . . ."

He had also used the word "agreement" in an August 6 letter to McMullen. But in Allan's curious interpretation "yesterday" no longer meant "yesterday," "signed" didn't really mean "signed" and an "agreement" was actually, on second thought, not an agreement at all.

The word "yesterday," Allan insisted, was used inadvertently for "recently" or "some time ago." It was "merely a slip of the pen." "Signed an agreement" was an expression "used in the hurry of the moment." And though Allan was faced with a letter in which he had written that the contract decision was ultimately in the hands of one man – Cartier – he now denied that he ever thought that an agreement with Cartier was equivalent to an agreement with the Government. Then he added that until Macdonald sent the wire refusing to accede to it he really *had* looked on it "as a kind of agreement."

121

Again the commissioners dealt lightly with the witness. What had made him discount Cameron's note? Did he expect Beaubien to pay back his "indefinite" loan? What happened, exactly, to the money he paid to three cabinet ministers? Why, if it was a free gift freely given, did he make so much fuss about getting receipts? Was the nominally paid-up capital of the Canada Pacific all in cash or was some of it bogus? Was he normally in the habit of spending almost four hundred thousand dollars at election time? The Reform press asked these questions rhetorically. The commissioners did not bother.

John Joseph Caldwell Abbott, M.P., took the stand following Allan's testimony. Even though the correspondence, telegrams and testimony showed that he had been handing out cash on behalf of Allan by the tens of thousands, he denied that he was Allan's confidential agent with respect to money.

"No, I don't think I was. Sir Hugh asked me to assist him in this affair. . . ." With these carefully chosen words Abbott subtly moved to dissociate himself from the discredited knight. He was the most powerful corporation lawyer in Canada – his clients included the Hudson's Bay Company and the Bank of Montreal as well as the Allan Line – and he knew how to hedge. His testimony was peppered with "not likelys."

A remarkable man, Abbott sprang from a remarkable lineage. His father was a pioneering missionary, a distinguished scholar, a well-known writer, first librarian and Vice-Principal of McGill. (His father-in-law, the tempestuous Dean John Bethune, was the Principal.) His mother was the daughter of another minister, a former midshipman with Captain Cook. Abbott himself, a voracious reader who knew a bit about everything, had an extraordinary range of interests – the merchandising of calico, the buying of grain, the packing of apples: he had done all these things himself. An enthusiastic gardener, he cultivated rare orchids in a specially constructed conservatory. He was not content to pursue his hobby of salmon fishing on public waters: he *owned* a salmon stream. His fine tenor voice had been a feature of Christ Church Cathedral, English Montreal's principal place of worship; he not only sang in the choir, he also directed it. A pillar of Montreal's military society, he raised and commanded his own regiment. A lecturer at McGill, he became Dean of Law. He was the kind of man who liked to be in charge of things and, obviously, he had the ability for it.

He claimed to be unhappy in politics. "I hate politics," he said, late in his career. "I hate notoriety, public meetings, public speeches, caucuses, everything ... [to do with politics] except doing public work to the best of my ability." Yet he could not avoid it; a corporation lawyer in those days was automatically immersed in politics. Abbott had started young, as a Liberal, and switched to the Conservative Party after Confederation. His dislike of politics seems to have been genuine – he was a man who automatically did his best (not terribly successfully) to stay out of the public eye; but he remained in politics all of his life. For, above all else, Abbott was a survivor. The Pacific Scandal, in which he was immersed to the ear lobes, failed to sink him, even though his own role was among the least admirable. In all of the shady background manoeuvring, from the time of Allan's dealings with Cartier to the final denouement of the Royal Commission, Abbott's guiding hand is to be seen. When secret agreements are drawn up, Abbott composes them. When election funds are promised, Abbott hands over the cheques. When damaging letters are purchased, Abbott negotiates. When indiscreet papers must be destroyed, Abbott presides. When dissident clerks defect, Abbott dangles the bribe. When friendly commissioners are needed, Abbott comes up with the names. Seven years later, Abbott the fixer would still be around to draw up new railway charter; "the most perfect organ of its kind" it would be called. By 1887 he would become mayor of Montreal and in 1891 he would enjoy a brief and not too glorious moment as the first native-born prime minister of Canada, in spite of his late leader's declared belief that he had not a single qualification for the office. But then, Macdonald never warmed to Abbott. He was an extraordinarily ugly man with a face like a homely John Bull – a big pudgy nose and hard metallic eyes – but as Macdonald's secretary Joseph Pope remarked, his nature was agreeable and his smile was sweet. Macdonald slew Abbott with a single phrase: "Yes," he said, "a sweet smile. All from the teeth outward."

There was one moment of comic opera in Abbott's testimony when the lawyer took it upon himself to comment on the McMullen charge "respecting an agreement . . . written by three clerks in my office so that none of them might know its contents."

Although he had, the previous November, specifically referred in a letter to Allan's "arrangement with Cartier," Abbott swore that there was no such agreement ever prepared or written. Then he added that Cartier's letter of July 30, promising Allan the presidency whatever Macpherson might do, actually *had* been written by three different clerks. Why? Abbott's straight-faced explanation was that he "placed one sheet in the hands of each clerk to save time."

By this time, however, interest in the Royal Commission was fading fast. Very little had emerged from the tangle of evasion, hedging and double talk that the public did not already know. The newspapers were still publishing verbatim accounts of the proceedings (the leader writers were concentrating on little else) but the people were bored. When Abbott returned on September 27 to read and correct his deposition – a task that occupied two hours – one of the commissioners went into a calm sleep from which, at intervals, he would rouse himself to take snuff. Another paced the floor at the rear of the bench pausing to help himself from the snuff box of his slumbering comrade. Only Judge Day, the chairman, managed to stay alert.

The voice that was the pride of Christ Church Cathedral droned on and on. The messengers nodded. The secretary of the commission read listlessly from the *Canada Monthly*. One of the three or four newspapermen present laid himself out on one of the cushioned seats that the public had abandoned and he, too, slept.

Thus did the proceedings of the Royal Commission grind slowly towards their close. The commissioners made no report but simply published the evidence without comment. It was left to Lord Dufferin to write its epitaph as he sent his account of the affair off to the Colonial Secretary: "A greater amount of lying and baseness," he remarked, "could not well be crammed into a smaller compass."

5

Battle The final act was played out on Parliament Hill from October 23 to
stations November 5 in what James Young, the parliamentarian-historian, called "one of the most remarkable and profoundly exciting debates of that period." There would be only one subject discussed in this new session of Parliament: the evidence taken before the Royal Commission.

The Governor General spent two days going over the evidence with Judge Day. On Sunday, October 19, he wrote Macdonald a brutal note in which he said that "what has occurred cannot but fatally affect your position." The Prime Minister's first impulse was to resign on the spot. Had it not been for Dufferin's "imperative commands to the contrary" he would have done so. But Dufferin wanted a meeting and on

Monday morning a painful interview took place at Rideau Hall. Dufferin pointed out to his prime minister that there were four charges against him: first, personal corruption; second, selling the railway to an American ring; third, granting corrupt and improper concessions to Allan; and, fourth, "having obtained money from a suspicious source and having applied it to illegitimate purposes." On the first three counts Macdonald had not been found guilty; on the fourth he had. Worse, he had been acting as Minister of Justice at the very time he had, by his own admission, broken the law by "treating" the voters. His letter, added the Governor General, was not to be seen as a dismissal but as a warning to save Macdonald from humiliation.

Dufferin felt that Macdonald ought to have the honesty to admit his guilt on the fourth charge and call an election; such frankness might just save him. And "having paid the penalty and received absolution you'll return to office under circumstances both more honourable and more favourable to you than if you seek to prolong the existence of a discredited administration."

Of course, Dufferin added as Macdonald took his leave, if he managed to retain a healthy majority in Parliament he could consider the letter null and void since it only discussed the contingency of his "pulling through with the skin of his teeth."

The interview had been more than merely painful; it had been perplexingly ambiguous. The truth was that the Governor General shrank from the idea of losing his charming and able first minister, in spite of the many embarrassments he had caused. It would be different if there was a stronger man to fall back on; in that case, if Macdonald's majority in the House was narrow, Dufferin would have no hesitation in asking him to resign. But he considered Mackenzie "a poor creature," completely under George Brown's thumb, likable enough but "cautious, small and narrow." As for his supporters, they were "an incompetent set of men" on whose advent to power, he said privately, he would look with great alarm.

For the whole of Tuesday, an uncertain Macdonald was closeted with his cabinet. Then a chastening message arrived for the Governor General from the Colonial Secretary and the impetuous Dufferin realized he had gone too far. It was up to Parliament, Lord Kimberley reminded him, to withdraw confidence in its own people. The Governor General hastened to tell the Prime Minister that his letter was "in some degree cancelled." The stage was set for the parliamentary struggle.

Parliament opened on Thursday, October 23, a raw, wet day with the smell of snow already in the air. Millards, on Sparks Street, was enthusiastically advertising "thick-soled, water-defying, slush-repelling, damp-excluding, snow-dispelling, cold-defying, heat-contracting boots." The roads and sidewalks were in their usual terrible condition, pocked by cavities and riven by cracks, which caused one lady, that day, to sprain an ankle. But this did not deter the crowds who congregated all along the principal streets early that morning. Tantalizing rumours were about. It was said that George McMullen was in town. It was said that Louis Riel, the Member for Provencher, was in town to take his seat in Parliament. It was said that the two brothers of Thomas Scott, Riel's victim, were in town to exact revenge. It was said that Macdonald was despondent over the criticisms of the British press. It was said that Macdonald was confident of a majority. It was said that Macdonald would retire into private life. In the cavernous stairwells of the Russell House, the famous hostelry which every visitor and parliamentarian of note made his headquarters, the whispers echoed as human eddies formed and parted and circulated and formed again to exchange gossip about the scandal.

By noon a river of people was flowing towards Parliament Hill. By two, the galleries and corridors of the House were so tightly packed that it was difficult to breathe. Never before had there been such a crush within those Gothic walls. Outside, a damp wind was cutting through the thickest overcoats; inside, the temperature had become oppressive.

On his way to Parliament, Lord Dufferin paused to open the new iron bridge across the Rideau Canal. The bridge – which was to bear his name – had been appropriated by the crowd and detectives were required to clear the structure, which had then to be barricaded to prevent the sports of the city from crossing ahead of the Governor General so that they could boast that they had performed the ceremony. Dufferin made one of his brief, graceful addresses and then, to the accompaniment of roaring cannon, moved on to the real business of the day.

Once more he found himself within the crimson chamber before that rustling flowerbed of silks and velvets, reading another man's speech in two languages – a speech that announced, among other things, that the report of the Royal Commission would be tabled in the House and that the Royal Charter for the Canadian Pacific Railway would be surrendered for lack of financial backing. The House adjourned. The preliminaries were over. After the weekend, the real contest would begin.

There had been one ironic moment: long established custom decreed that a resolution be moved declaring that the House would proceed with the utmost severity against all persons guilty of bribery and corrupt practices. When that rote issued from the Prime Minister's lips, it was greeted with derisive cheers and scornful laughter from the Opposition benches. The atmosphere was anything but genial; the air crackled with suppressed antagonism; the usual social amenities attendant on an opening – the easy banter and chaff, the mutual greetings – were absent.

At three that Monday afternoon the members of the Government and Opposition were in their places. Macdonald lounged at his desk to the Speaker's immediate right, presenting to the world a picture of jaunty indifference. Nearby, in Cartier's old place, squatted the rotund figure of Langevin, his new Quebec lieutenant, a shrewd and affable man, gentler than Cartier, but embattled now by virtue of his role in the scandal. It was a powerful front bench: Hincks, the aging Hyena, making his last appearance in Parliament, Tilley, the handsome New Brunswicker, untainted by any scandal, and, of course, Tupper, the doughty "Cumberland War Horse," perhaps the best tactician in the House, poised for the attack. Young George Ross of Middlesex, sitting in the Opposition back-benches and looking over the political heavyweights with a tyro's eyes, thought that Tupper even in repose looked "as if he had a blizzard secreted somewhere about his person." The "Fighting Doctor," as he was called in Nova Scotia, had inherited many of his abilities from his father – a man of dogged character and methodical thought who had been able to read the Old Testament in Hebrew and the New in Greek at the age of nineteen and who, at twenty-one, had become an evangelist with all the forensic powers that calling requires.

Directly across from Macdonald sat Alexander Mackenzie, perhaps the bleakest looking man in the House, whose features might have been carved out of the same granite he himself had fashioned in his days as a stonemason. His desk was piled high with references for the speech that he had been working on all weekend.

The Opposition had a formidable offensive team of its own: Mackenzie, himself, caustic and dry, an expert at invective; Edward Blake, the strongest man in the Grit party, a master of satire whose every word carried conviction, his scorn so withering that he could crush an opponent with a phrase; Cartwright, known as "the Rupert of Debate," his speeches models of classic purity and polished diction, a coiner of pungent, cutting phrases; the one-armed E. B. Wood,

127

known as "Big Thunder" because of his roaring speeches, which came freely garnished with scriptural references and resounding passages from the great orators and poets; and, of course, the eloquent, sonorous Huntington. They stared across the no-man's land of the Commons at their enemies, hungry for the kill.

Both sides were confident of success. Though the Opposition had the public on its side, the Government still had the votes. At this stage of political development, party lines were not yet tightly drawn and whips could not exert the kind of discipline that was eventually to prevail. The Opposition itself was a loose amalgam of Reformers and Clear Grits, working under the umbrella of the Liberal Party. Many of those who supported Macdonald called themselves Independents. In addition there were six members from the new province of Prince Edward Island, who had never sat in the House before. Nobody had a clear idea of how they would vote.

At the close of the Royal Commission hearings, Macdonald counted his supporters and estimated a majority of twenty-five. He held to this estimate through most of October. Lord Dufferin thought it overoptimistic; but he, too, believed the Government could easily weather a vote. Part of the parliamentary struggle, therefore, took place not on the floor of the House but behind the scenes, as one side struggled to hold its supporters and the other strove to capture them. Doubtful members found themselves besieged day and night with promises, cajolery, threats and even bribes. The Prince Edward Islanders were hotly pursued: Mackenzie had made a special trip to the Island before the session with Tupper right behind him, both intent on swaying these new unknown quantities. Amor de Cosmos, the mercurial Victoria member, was besieged by representatives of both sides as soon as he entered Ontario. He stepped off the train at London into the arms of Edward Blake and J. D. Edgar, the Liberal Party whip. When he left Toronto for Ottawa, Senator Alexander Campbell, Macdonald's old law partner, was practically in his berth. In Ottawa the whiskey flowed as freely as the waters of the Rideau and to such an extent that certain Government supporters, known for their conviviality, were kept under lock and key lest they, in the phrase of the day, be "spirited away" and persuaded to vote contrary to their expressed intentions.

By Monday, October 27, Macdonald could no longer be sure of his majority of twenty-five. The number had dropped to eighteen and then to sixteen; some thought it as low as thirteen. "There is no

128

country in the world, I imagine, where the rats leave the sinking ship so fast," Dufferin remarked acidly. But if Macdonald could hold the debate down to three or four days and make one of his powerful speeches early in the game, he could probably win the vote.

This was not to be. Everyone wanted to speak (forty managed to do so); and everyone was on hand. Such a crowded House had not been seen in the short political history of the Dominion. Every seat seemed occupied save one: the elusive Member from Provencher would not be heard from.

The battle was joined shortly after three, once the routine business was dispensed with. An address in reply to the Speech from the Throne was duly moved and seconded. The first clause was read and agreed to. The second was put; and then, as the cheers of the Opposition echoed from the vaulted walls, a grim Mackenzie rose to his feet. He spoke for almost three hours to the continual accompaniment of applause and cries of encouragement from his followers. It was a wickedly effective speech, in which Mackenzie told the House that it was being asked to vote that black was white – that Sir Hugh Allan had simply given his money as a good member of the Conservative Party, though the country had been told "very plainly by that gentleman that he had no party views at all." Mackenzie wound up with a motion of censure.

When Tupper rose to reply after the dinner recess, the galleries were jammed. The entire first row of the Speaker's Gallery was occupied by Lady Dufferin and her entourage. It was whispered that the Governor General himself was disguised in the audience. Actually, the eager Dufferin had pleaded with Macdonald "to arrange some little closet for me in the House . . . a 'Dionysius ear' no matter how dark or inconvenient." Macdonald was too wise to allow such a breach. The idea that a *Globe* reporter, or some sharp-eyed member, might uncover the person of the Queen's representative trespassing, like a secret agent, on the hallowed ground of the Commons at this moment of crisis, must have sent shivers down his spine. "If, as I believe, we defeat the Opposition . . . they will be sulky and savage and ready to wreak their vengeance on everybody and everything," he told the Governor General. Dufferin was forced to get his reports second-hand from his lady and from the press. He concluded that, though the speeches were "enormously long, most of them averaging three or four hours" and "characterized by a kind of rude vigour," none of them was really talented or brilliant. "It was in fact rather the encounter of blundering rustics trying to beat out each other's brains with bludgeons than that of trained lawyers wielding effectual weapons." It was well for Lord Dufferin that his confidential correspondence with Lord Kimberley did not suffer the same fate as that of Sir Hugh Allan's with George McMullen.

Tupper, certainly, was a master of the bludgeon. The robust Nova Scotia doctor with the hard, unblinking eyes and the creased, pugnacious face believed in one tactic in debate: attack with every weapon available; admit nothing; pound, hammer, swipe, thrust; if an opponent dares utter a word, batter him down.

He leaped to his feet, rejoicing that "the time has come when I and my colleagues are in a position to discuss this question in the presence of an independent Parliament." After that barefaced opening, he never let up: The country's prosperity was being affected. Canada's fair name was being tarnished. The real plan was to frustrate the building of the railway, nothing more. The sum Allan had contributed was "of an insignificant character." Public feeling was strongly with the Government. The charges were false and scandalous. All loyal people would regard the Opposition with suspicion. No intelligent person could fail to perceive that they had entirely abandoned their case.

This show of bravado put the House in a spirited mood and the Cumberland War Horse had to trample his way through a thicket of catcalls, derisive cheers and whoops of laughter. Totally undeterred, he galloped on for more than three hours and then gave way to the hero of the Opposition, Lucius Seth Huntington.

Huntington was a different kind of speaker; indeed, every parliamentarian in those days had his own style of address, which was as much his trademark as that of a popular singer in a later age; hence the political nicknames, all of which seemed to deal with this one aspect of parliamentary ability – "Big Thunder," "War Horse," "Hyena," "Rupert of Debate," "Bismarck" (the last for Peter Mitchell). The craft of public debate was a well-developed art in the Canada of the seventies. The rousing platform address, delivered outdoors at a picnic or a rally, or indoors in a closely packed meeting hall, was the chief means of communication and the prime form of entertainment. Major speeches were published verbatim in the press, as were the full proceedings of Parliament. The oratorical styles of various public figures were dissected and compared. Newspapers and periodicals reviewed the declamatory techniques of star speakers

130

much in the manner of drama critics. A politician's voice, like an opera singer's, had to carry like thunder in an age devoid of artificial aids; and, since it was the custom for speakers of opposing views to share the same platform like verbal gladiators, the aspiring public servant needed to be quick on his feet. He also had to be long on stamina. It was nothing for a man like Blake to speak for five hours (indeed, in Blake's case, anything less than five hours seemed trivial). The sophisticated Dufferin might find Canadian oratory rude and rustic, but it was directed at a rude and rustic audience, not a conclave of British peers. It was no accident that the most successful politicians were often the best speakers. It was this that made the spectacle of Parliament as exciting as Mr. Barnum's Circus and Menagerie, which had just completed a successful tour of Ontario.

A Huntington speech was honed and polished with great care and delivered in a voice rich in melody. There was more than a hint of the future novelist in his style. With the clock past eleven, Huntington plunged into a spirited defence of his own position and a sardonic attack upon his adversaries, among whom Charles Tupper led all the rest.

At one point, Huntington had the House roaring with laughter as he pounced on Allan's statement to General Cass that he had suborned twenty-seven of Cartier's phalanx of forty-five Parliamentary supporters:

"As a mere matter of curiosity, I should like to know who are the twenty-seven. (*Cheers and laughter.*) We have in this House a Sir Hugh Allan brigade consisting of twenty-seven members. We have it upon Sir Hugh Allan's authority that they were sent here to vote for the Government, and if any of the twenty-seven desire to stand up, I will sit down. (*Loud laughter.*) How delighted that brigade must have been, how their sore toes must have been relieved, when the hon. member for Cumberland in his eloquence wandered off . . . and when, by and by, in a few words he proceeded to assert that there was no evidence at all of corruption, how these twenty-seven must have *wilted*. (*Laughter.*) Why, they were the exhibits themselves of their corruption! They were twenty-seven of the thirty-one who had voted down the investigation which I attempted to obtain here. (*Cheers.*) Will the hon. gentleman tell us how many steamships Sir Hugh Allan has, and is there a man to each steamship? Sir Hugh was asked at the Commission how many ships he had, but they had no need to ask him how many members of Parliament he had, because they had incontestable evidence that Sir Hugh had twenty-seven here. . . ."

Huntington continued, in the same vein, to twit the Prime Minister for being on the bench, in the dock and prosecutor all at the same time. He wound up, at 1.30, with a glance at the wavering Government supporters, by declaring that "the time comes when they have to choose between fidelity to party and fidelity to country."

Thus, day after day, the debate see-sawed back and forth. On Wednesday night, a storm broke over Ottawa and the citizens awoke to find their city shrouded in the first snow of winter. But a more important question than the weather hung on every lip: what on earth was wrong with Macdonald? Why had he remained silent? His boasted majority was drifting away "like leaves in the Valley of Vallombrosa" (Dufferin's literary style again); and yet he had not joined in the debate. His friends were full of angry entreaties. He *must* speak; only he could stem the tide. Stubbornly, the Prime Minister refused.

He had started to drink again. By Friday, when he had an interview with the Governor General, he was clearly not himself. Haggard in appearance, he was weak with fatigue and ill with strain. It was assumed by many that he did not feel himself fit to take up the cudgels in his party's defence.

But this was not the case. Macdonald was waiting for Blake to speak for he was tolerably certain that the Opposition was holding some damning piece of evidence, some document of "a fatally compromising character," that Cartier had written. Or, perhaps, he himself had dispatched some damaging letter during the election; the appalling thing was that the Prime Minister could not be sure whether he had or not, he had been in his cups for so much of that period. The press had certainly been hinting that there was more to come. Abbott had told him the previous July that the Montreal papers were preparing further revelations. These had not appeared; was it because the Liberals were holding one devastating piece of evidence in reserve? He *must* have the last word. He could not afford to make his move and then have Blake follow him with such a *coup de grâce*.

It was only at the end of the week that the truth began to dawn upon him that, for once, he had been shamelessly outmanoeuvred. Blake was holding back on purpose, calculating that Macdonald's physical condition would deteriorate to the point where he could not speak at all. There would be no fresh revelations; the Liberals were waging a war of attrition.

It was dangerously late. Edgar, the Liberal whip, sat in his place in the House and tried to figure how a division would go. Without the new members from Prince Edward Island he could count, he thought, on 99 votes. He expected four more from the new province. That would give the Opposition 103 votes out of 206 – exactly fifty per cent. Three others were wavering; if they thought the Government would be defeated they would change sides. Edgar had been working mightily, buttonholing members, talking, cajoling and promising. At night, when the session ended, he sat on the edge of Mackenzie's bed, going over the day's strategy with his weary leader. His most recent trophy was David Glass, a black-bearded Irish criminal lawyer, who defected with a ringing speech in which he proclaimed that he had always treated the charges against Macdonald with contempt until the McMullen revelations hit him with full force. He drew cheers when he declared that it was better that "all who stand in the pathway of the country's honour be removed rather than that the country's honour should be removed." The speech cut deep. Glass was a highly respected public figure with a colourful background who had crossed the continent on horseback, flirted with death in Mexico and prospected for gold in California before returning to Canada to become mayor of London, Ontario. Later, he would be rewarded for his defection.

By this time, the public could not help but agree with the leonine E. B. Wood, "Big Thunder," who roared that "before many days the Government will have fallen like Lucifer, never to hope again."

"But we *shall* rise again," cried the imperturbable Tupper from across the floor.

"Rise again!" boomed Wood, "but that resurrection shall not be until the last trump shall sound – when the graves shall give up their dead and death and hell shall give up the dead that are in them!"

Macdonald resolved to enter the arena on Monday night. The preliminaries were not propitious. That very afternoon, Lord Dufferin noted that he was tipsy. And Robert Cunningham, the Manitoba journalist who represented Marquette, rose on a question of order to declare that an Ottawa alderman had offered him a government job in the North West and a bribe of up to five thousand pounds if he would cast his vote for the Government. At this point the Prime

Minister had to be dragged to his feet before he could reply. Yet in just three hours he would have to make the speech of a lifetime.

6

Macdonald versus Blake

Nine o'clock, Monday, November 3, 1873. On Parliament Hill the corridors are choked, for the report has been abroad since early afternoon that Macdonald will speak at last. Scores have forgone their dinners in order to hold their places in the packed galleries. Even the sacrosanct back-benches have been invaded by strangers. Hundreds more, holding useless tickets, stand outside, straining for a whisper of the proceedings within. People have poured into the capital anticipating the coming verbal duel between John A. Macdonald and his dour adversary, Edward Blake.

In the parliamentary restaurant, a few stragglers are finishing their coffee. Suddenly the word comes: "Sir John is up!" The cups scatter as the stragglers race to the floor.

Now every member is in his seat, save the exiled Louis Riel. The buzz of conversation has been cut off as cleanly as if a muffler were placed over the House. Macdonald has risen slowly to his feet, pale, nervous and haggard, "looking as if a feather would knock him down." Then, for the next five hours, he proceeds to electrify the House.

Those who were there would never forget it. Many felt it was the greatest speech Macdonald had ever made; some said it was the greatest they had ever heard. Even the vituperative *Globe* called it "extraordinary." Sick, dispirited and weary he might be; but somewhere within himself this homely, errant and strangely attractive political animal had tapped a hidden well of energy. Some said it was the straight gin, which Peter Mitchell insisted that alternate pageboys poured at regular intervals into the waterglasses at his elbow (each thought the other was pouring water); but Macdonald was driven by another, more powerful stimulation. He was fighting, with his back to the wall, for his career; only he could salvage it.

He began very slowly and in a low voice, but, bit by bit, he warmed to his audience. Gradually, tone and manner changed, the voice became louder, more strident: Macdonald began to fight. He

134

struck savagely at Huntington: the object of his resolution, he said, was "to kill the charter in England and to destroy it." (*Cheers and catcalls.*) He kept on. Huntington's course, cried Macdonald, was governed from behind the scenes by a "foreign and alien power." The Yankee-lover sat in the House "not only by alien money but by alien railway influence." Here, all of Macdonald's inbred distrust of the Americans was coming to the fore – the same dark apprehensions that would one day force a railway across a seven-hundred-mile ocean of rocky desert rather than see it diverted through a foreign land.

As the clock ticked its way past midnight, Macdonald continued to goad the Opposition: "They have spies and thieves and men of espionage who would pick your lock and steal your notebook." Why, Huntington had paid McMullen seventeen thousand dollars for the famous documents! Huntington was on his feet, in an instant, with a denial, amid cheers from the Opposition and calls of "Order!" from the Government benches.

"I challenge the Honourable gentleman to combat!" cried Huntington. "I dare him, Sir, on his responsibility to take a committee . . . I challenge him to stand up and take a committee!"

More cheering, more cries of "Order!"

"I dare him to do it!" Huntington kept shouting.

"It is very evident," said Macdonald, "I hit a sore spot."

Yes, he said; he would call a committee to investigate the whole matter of election expenses. He knew of one gentleman opposite who had spent twenty-six thousand dollars getting elected. Another had spent thirty thousand dollars. Others had spent from five to ten thousand dollars.

"Hear! Hear!" called a puckish voice from the opposite side of the House. It belonged to David Blain, a Scottish-born lawyer from West York who had married the sister of a wealthy and prominent Toronto hardware merchant.

Macdonald picked up the cry and turned it against his taunter. He would, he said, prove the payment of money to an elector to vote for Blain.

"Not a cent went out of my pocket!" cried the outraged Blain.

"Well, you know, if a man has not a pocket, his wife has," retorted Macdonald wickedly.

By now he had the Opposition benches in an uproar.

"How dare you make such a statement?" the aggrieved Blain was shouting above the cries of "Shame!" and "Order!" Macdonald's supporters were cheering him on. Blain was crying: "You ought to be ashamed of yourself!" The Speaker stepped in and the Prime Minister moved on to other subjects, reiterating, again and again, that there was no bargain, no contract, between his Government and Allan – and that Allan's contribution was merely an election subscription.

It was past 1.30. Not a soul had left the House. From her seat in the Speaker's Gallery, Lady Dufferin gazed down with admiration. What a tale she would have to tell at Rideau Hall! (It would take her at least two hours, with many gestures, to satisfy her husband's hunger for the details.)

Macdonald, roused now to a kind of fever pitch, intoxicated as much by the crowds and the cheers as by the glass in his hand, was reaching the climax of his address. No illegal expenditure had yet been proved before any legal tribunal against any Member of Parliament, he declared. He challenged the House, he challenged the country, he challenged the world to read the charter – to read it line by line and word by word to see if there was in it anything that derogated from the rights of Canada (*loud cheers*) or if there was in it "any preponderance of any one man of these thirteen [directors] over another" (*more cheers*).

"Sir, I commit myself, the Government commits itself, to the hands of this House, and far beyond this House, it commits itself to the country at large. (*Loud cheers.*) We have faithfully done our duty. We have fought the battle of Union. We have had Party strife setting Province against Province, and more than all, we have had in the greatest Province, the preponderating Province of the Dominion, every prejudice and sectional feeling that could be arrayed against us.

"I have been the victim of that conduct to a great extent; but I have fought the battle of Confederation, the battle of Union, the battle of the Dominion of Canada. I throw myself upon this House; I throw myself upon this country; I throw myself upon posterity, and I believe that I know, that, notwithstanding the many failings in my life, I shall have the voice of this country, and this House rallying round me. (*Cheers.*) And, Sir, if I am mistaken in that, I can confidently appeal to a higher Court, to the court of my own conscience, and to the court of posterity. (*Cheers.*)

"I leave it with this House with every confidence. I am equal to either fortune. I can see past the decision of this House either for or

136

against me, but whether it be against me or for me, I know, and it is no vain boast to say so, for even my enemies will admit that I am no boaster, that there does not exist in Canada a man who has given more of his time, more of his heart, more of his wealth, or more of his intellect and power, such as it may be, for the good of this Dominion of Canada."

It was over. He sat down, utterly exhausted, while his supporters, and even some of the Opposition, cheered him to the roof. Lady Dufferin, who had brought along Lord Rosebery, a future prime minister of England, as her guest, was already scurrying off to Rideau Hall. There, until five that morning, she would regale her husband with a spirited account of the proceedings and pen a graceful note to Lady Macdonald, congratulating her on the "splendid speech [which] grows upon one as one thinks over its various points." Maudlin it might have been, but it was, by all odds, a personal triumph for the Prime Minister, producing at Rideau Hall, as Dufferin reported to him, "a continuous chorus of admiration from all my English friends." More important, the speech had solidified Macdonald's hold upon his own party, a hold which had become increasingly weak and aimless. Without it he could scarcely have continued as leader.

In spite of the late hour, the House continued to sit. Now Edward Blake hoisted his big frame from his chair and stood, erect and commanding, peering sombrely through his small, silver-rimmed spectacles at his enemies across the floor. To this tousled and scholarly looking lawyer with the powerful build and the strange pallor the Liberal Party had entrusted its final volley. Blake was a nemesis to many, a friend to few and an enigma to all, a kind of political Hamlet who, seething inwardly with personal ambition, showed a strange distaste for those laurels that were dangled before him. Generally considered by his colleagues as the man most likely to succeed, he never quite succeeded. He had been Premier of Ontario for scarcely a year when he quit to enter the federal arena. He could have led the Liberal Party, instead of Mackenzie (Mackenzie had once served under him in Ontario), but he declined the opportunity. All his life he would dally over similar honours.

The key to this diffidence lay in Blake's extraordinary sensitivity; an imagined slight could cause him to burst into tears in public. He once astonished the Governor General by crying in his presence over a remark Macdonald had made about him. As a brilliant lawyer – perhaps the most brilliant of the century – he had been used to the deference of his judges and his peers. He could not accustom himself to the coarse invective and bitter imputations of personal motive that were a feature of the politics of his day. And this was singular because Blake himself, when in full voice, was perfectly capable of reducing an opponent to jelly. "I have seen men turn pale and press their knees with their hands as if restraining themselves from running away from that merciless shower of incisive invective," the Ottawa correspondent of the *Canadian Illustrated News* wrote that same year. The irony did not escape that perceptive observer John Willison, who wrote of Blake: "This man of whom giants might well be afraid let his soul be harried by insects and to gnats gave victories which belonged to the Gods."

The Liberal Party, seeking to cap the debate with climactic oratory, had chosen well. The speech that Blake was about to give was exactly the kind the situation called for and exactly the kind at which he excelled. It was Blake's strength that he built his speeches, brick by brick, on solid fact and hard evidence – and his weakness that he generally gave his listeners too much of both. He kept on talking until there was absolutely nothing left to be said, a quality that did not endear him to his associates; after all, they had speeches of their own to make. Blake took nothing for granted. He verified every statement by reference to the original documents and, long after he had proved his case conclusively, he kept piling it on and on, until, as a colleague remarked ruefully, "everyone became dizzy scaling the heights to which he was being lifted." No wonder Blake constantly appeared pale, nervous and exhausted. While others were relaxing in the smoking room, the Hamlet of the House was grubbing away in the parliamentary library.

The two speeches, Macdonald's and Blake's, laid side by side are mirrors of the two totally disparate men who made them. Where Macdonald had been hotly emotional, Blake was icily dispassionate. Where Macdonald had been witty, Blake was earnest. Where Macdonald had been personal and subjective, Blake was aloofly analytical.

He stood now, as the cheering died, left hand sunk characteristically deep into his side pocket, totally immobile – Blake the Avenger. He had neither the time nor the inclination for humour. Instead he cut right to the bone, scooping up Macdonald's closing plea and turning it against him: "It was not to these high and elevating sentiments that the right honourable gentleman appealed during the election, it was not upon the intelligent judgement of the people he relied, but upon Sir Hugh Allan's money!" This blunt beginning, James Young recalled, electrified the House. Blake kept on until 2.30 that morning, in his soft, resonant voice, and then for another four hours the following afternoon and evening, building his case, fact piled upon fact, every sentence deftly turned, the phrases all arranged in ringing parallels.

The ladies of the Dufferin household, who had slipped out immediately Macdonald took his seat the previous evening and returned the following afternoon to watch Blake worrying away at the evidence like a terrier, thought it all a bore. "Dull and uninteresting and not nearly so amusing and lively as Sir John's," was Dufferin's verdict on the speech. Then he added: "But it reads well." It read very well indeed in its pitiless logic – far better than Macdonald's impassioned and lachrymose remarks. And, to the faltering Members, Blake's very lack of histrionics – no arm-waving, no rising inflections – added weight to his words.

"I believe that this night or to-morrow night will be the end of twenty years of corruption. (*Cheers.*) This night or to-morrow night will see the dawn of a brighter and better day in the administration of public affairs in this country. . . . (*Continued cheering.*)

". . . We are here to set up once again the standard of public virtue. (*Cheers.*) We are here to restore once again the fair face of the country which has been tarnished; we are here to brighten, if we may, that fame; we are here to purge this country of the great scandal and calamity which those who are entrusted with the conduct of its affairs have inflicted upon it.

". . . I do not understand that Spartan virtue which deems a theft no crime so long as it is undiscovered. I do not understand that morality which will permit a crime unseen, but is deeply shocked and alarmed for the credit of the country should the crime become known. . . . Sir, you will not heal the festering sore by healing the skin above it. You must lance it and cleanse it.

". . . Let us not be carried away by the absurd notion that there is a distinction between the standards of public and private virtue; let us not be carried away by the notion that that may be done in secret which it is a shame to be known in public; let our transactions be open, and as the shame exists, as it has been discovered, as it has been conclusively established, as it has been confessed, let us by our vote – regretfully, it may be – give the perpetrators of it their just reward."

When Blake took his seat even some Government members rendered him the accolade of their applause as some Liberals had for Macdonald. Macdonald was not present. He lay upon a couch in a committee room, half conscious, ill with fatigue. Joseph Pope, who edited Macdonald's papers, recalled the "sense of extreme uneasiness" in the ministerial ranks, the "sound of going on the tops of the mulberry trees . . . a feeling of impending change everywhere abroad."

Yet still the vote was in doubt. How effective had Blake been? Had he managed to cancel out the morale-building effects of Macdonald's passionate appeal? The Liberals had still not been able to force a vote; every man was in his place, waiting hour after hour for the division that would not come. "It is a dreadful strain," James Edgar admitted in a letter to his wife, written at his desk in the Commons while speaker followed speaker in the debate.

After Blake was finished all eyes turned to the proud Scots face of David Laird, the leader of the new group of Islanders, founder of the Charlottetown *Patriot* and a man much respected for his moral and intellectual strength. Laird was a Liberal provincially but, in the past, many a provincial Liberal had followed the Conservative Party after his province entered Confederation. The Island leader rose timidly. It was the first time he had addressed such a gathering. "Was there ever a maiden speech so fraught with doom?" George Ross asked. Laird did not keep his listeners waiting long. In a calm voice, he declared his opposition to the Government and again the Liberal benches rang with cheers.

Now it was the turn of another independent member, Donald A. Smith of Selkirk riding, Manitoba, the tough former fur trader, who was becoming a power in the Hudson's Bay Company and the Bank of Montreal. Smith normally supported the Government; moreover, he had been a member of Allan's board of directors, but it was by no means certain how he would vote. Macdonald's supporters were hesitant about approaching this frosty and imperious man who managed, throughout his career, to remain constantly in the limelight without ever appearing to seek it. Finally, the Prime Minister was himself persuaded to talk to Smith. The meeting was not a success; when the Member was taken to Macdonald's office he found him drunk and belligerent. Smith was received with more curses than flattery. Nonetheless the feeling in the Government ranks was that Smith was on their side.

It was 1 a.m. when Smith rose to an expectant chamber. The future

Lord Strathcona was not unaware of the drama. His speech was brief but he managed to squeeze from it every possible ounce of suspense. His tone was bland, his manner inoffensive: he did not consider that the first minister took Allan's money with any corrupt motive. In fact he knew personally that Allan at one time had thought of giving up the charter. In every instance he knew the provisions were made more and more stringent against Sir Hugh.

The Government benches began to cheer. W. T. R. Preston, a long-time Liberal organizer, later claimed that some twenty Tories rushed to the parliamentary restaurant, popped open bottles of champagne, prepared to drink Smith's health and sang "Rule, Britannia!"

But Smith was not finished: he felt the leader of the Government was incapable of taking money from Allan for corrupt purposes. He would be most willing to vote for the Government – the cheers from the ministerial benches were now gleeful – *could he do so conscientiously.* . . .

Consternation on the Conservative side! Cheers and laughter from the Opposition.

. . . It was with great regret, Smith said, that he could not do so: there was no corruption but "a very grave impropriety."

In the parliamentary restaurant the champagne was left untasted. The Members skulked back to their seats as Smith sat down and the Speaker, with only the slightest tremor in his voice, adjourned the House. As the Commons broke up, there was a storm around Smith. The Members rushed towards him, cheering, hand-shaking, reviling, threatening. Smith remained, as always, totally imperturbable. He had been Macdonald's choice – a good one – to deal with the ticklish problem of Riel, during the Red River uprising; the Prime Minister had always admired him. Now he felt betrayed, for he had always held to the concept that party must come before principle. For most of the decade the name of Donald A. Smith was anathema to the Conservatives.

It was, of course, all over. In the Opposition smoking room, the handsome and dapper George Elliott Casey, at twenty-three the youngest member in the House, carolled to the tune of "Clementine" that "Sir John is dead and gone forever." In the lobbies and the downstairs restaurant there was a buzz of activity. Suddenly the atmosphere had changed; the vanquished took their defeat in good part, the conquerors refrained from being overjubilant.

Macdonald did not wait for the ignominy of a vote. He resigned the following day and went, remarkably cheerfully, into opposition. "I can only say that an awful sense of relief has come over me," the weary but triumphant Edgar scribbled to his wife as soon as the news broke. His colleagues showered him with applause for his exertions to the point where he felt "perfectly unnerved & ready to weep." The same feeling of relief spread among politicians of both parties as the country simmered down. "As is the case with this somewhat volatile people, the excitement . . . has disappeared," Lord Dufferin reported to England.

It was painful to lose his first minister. "It cut me to the heart," he wrote, "that a career so creditable to himself, and so serviceable to his country . . . should have ended in such humiliation."

Macdonald was not a man to wear his heart on his sleeve for long. After he announced his resignation, he moved the adjournment of the House and then went to his office to ask his secretary to pack up his papers.

When he arrived home, he went straight to his upstairs bedroom.

"Well, that's gone along with," he remarked casually to his wife.

"What do you mean?" she asked.

"Why, the Government has resigned," he replied. He slipped into his dressing gown and slippers, picked up two or three books from a nearby table and stretched out on the bed.

"It's a relief to be out of it," he said. Then he opened a volume and began to read. Characteristically, he never again alluded to the subject; it was as if, to preserve his equilibrium, he had dismissed it from his mind.

The new leaders of the country did not. For most of the decade they would, on every possible occasion, taunt their opponents with the memory of the Pacific Scandal. It would influence their policies and their actions as it would influence those of the Conservatives. When, years later, a contract was finally signed for the construction of the Canadian Pacific Railway, the terms of the agreement and the choice of the principals and, indeed, their later relations with the Government, would, in some degree, be affected by the events of 1873.

Macdonald's own role in these events was ambiguous. It is clear that an agreement was made between Cartier and Allan on July 30 and that this agreement remained in force in spite of Macdonald's telegram repudiating it. Allan thought he had bought and paid for the presidency of the Canadian Pacific railway; Cartier was certainly

142

party to that belief. Did Macdonald realize it? Perhaps; but he was, as Tupper had told Dufferin, "on the drink" at the time and could not be certain of exactly what had or had not been written or telegraphed. Some time later he told Dufferin that he was quite unaware of the extent to which Cartier had drawn on Allan and shocked when Cartier confirmed it.

On the other hand, Macdonald's curiously stubborn and continuing espousal of Allan as the only possible president of the new syndicate is harder to understand. He made a strong case before the Royal Commission of Allan's obvious qualifications for the job; but a month before negotiations with Macpherson were broken off, Macdonald had every reason to have his doubts about the Montrealer. Allan's deception regarding the American interest in his company ought to have been one warning signal. Allan's verbal indiscretions about his agreement with Cartier ought to have been another. By spring Macdonald himself was referring to Allan as a terrible negotiator. Did no tiny doubt ever cross his mind before that revealing New Year's Eve meeting with George McMullen? Could Macdonald, in his own mind, explain away Allan's enormous and unprecedented contributions to the Conservative campaign chest as he tried to explain them away to the Royal Commission?

It is true that he had made a promise to Allan in July; but it was not a promise that had to be kept unless it were tied, explicitly or implicitly, to Allan's cheque-book. It is more logical to suppose that Macdonald, suspecting both Allan and Cartier, but not knowing the details – and not wanting to know – rationalized to himself, and later to the country, his own actions. On being found out, he engaged in as much political manoeuvre as he dared, first to delay revelation and then to mute it. It did no good. In the end he was forced to admit that he had taken Allan's money and spent it illegally. It meant little that he was innocent of Huntington's other charges; the captive Royal Commissioners did not render a verdict but Parliament and, subsequently, the voters did. When Mackenzie went to the country early in 1874, he was returned in a landslide.

It was generally agreed that Macdonald was finished and that he would quickly resign and vanish from the political scene. The railway, it seemed, had been his nemesis. It had ruined his health, stained his honour and wrecked his career. George Ross remembered thinking that a Macdonald revival would be a greater miracle than the passage of the Israelites through the Red Sea.

As for Macdonald's *bête noire*, George W. McMullen, he never

143

again had anything to do with politicians. He outlived all the major figures in the Pacific Scandal, his active mind leaping from project to project, many of them promising but few of them profitable. His interests ran the gamut from woven-wire fences (he developed and manufactured them) to railroad ties (he invented a method of preserving them). Growing things seemed to fascinate him. He tried growing celery in a concrete building on top of a peat bog; it did not work out. He tried turning hard maple chips into maple syrup; that did not work out either. He farmed ginseng, which grew wild around Picton, and shipped it off to China where it was prized as an aphrodisiac; not much came of that. He experimented with sugar beets and then with Cuban sugar cane, forming a company to use the waste in the paper-making process; that, too, came to nothing. He backed a Chicago inventor in the development of a long-distance, high-powered gun; the U.S. army showed initial interest but abandoned it. He experimented in the attic of his rambling Picton home with a machine for evaporating fruit, vegetables and eggs; the machine was still there in 1970. For a time he and his brothers owned the Central Ontario Railway which they bought to connect with some iron mines they were developing. Everybody assumed that George McMullen was wealthy – after all, he was involved in so much – but when he died, aboard a railway train to Chicago in 1915, he left very little behind him except the memory of his role in the Pacific Scandal, several progeny (including one university professor and one artist) and several not too complimentary anecdotes. Old timers in the Picton area still talk of the time McMullen tumbled off the ferry from Belleville to Prince Edward County. He was hauled out by a fellow passenger whom he thanked profusely. "Good God," was the reply, "if I'd known it was you I'd have left you in." Nonetheless, when McMullen died, all business in his home town came to a stop to mark his passing.

From McMullen's one-time partner, Sir Hugh Allan, there was only silence in the years that followed the scandal. Taciturn and uncommunicative after his one terrible lapse, he left no memoir of his role in the affair, expressed no regret, delineated no hint of his emotions at the time. The closest he ever came to it was one night in his cavernous castle in Montreal when he was entertaining William Smith, a Deputy Minister of Marine and Fisheries. Warmed by Allan's hospitality and emboldened by Allan's brandy, Smith made bold to try to break through the crust of Allan's reticence.

144

"Sir Hugh," he ventured, "between ourselves, don't you think you made rather a mistake in mixing yourself up with John A. in that Pacific Scandal business?"

The shaggy knight of Ravenscrag stared into the fire. It was some time before he delivered himself of a definitive response. Finally . . .

"Mebbe," he replied.

Chapter Four

1
"Hurra! The jolly C.P.S.!"

2
The bitter tea of Walter Moberly

3
Ordeal in the mountains

4
"That old devil" Marcus Smith

1

All the time the political hurricane was gathering force in the settled East, hundreds of men were freezing, starving, sickening and sometimes dying in the unexplored crannies of the new Canada, as they tried to chart a route for the railway. On July 5, as Macdonald arrived in Toronto to launch the election campaign of 1872, a young man named George Hargreaves, deep in the rain forests of the Homathco, wrote in his diary that "there was more bad news from A Camp"; two more men had been drowned, making a total of five that summer. On August 7, the day on which Allan wrote his compromising letter to General Cass, seven men perished in a forest fire in the Nepigon country north of Lake Superior. On December 27, when George McMullen was dining in the Russell House with his fellow conspirator, Senator Asa B. Foster, another survey party found itself marooned in 50 below zero weather on Superior's frozen shores. On April 15 the following spring, when John Hillyard Cameron was preparing the Oaths Bill for the House, Robert Rylatt, in the Athabasca country, was scribbling in his diary that "the quantity of blood discharged somewhat alarms me"; he was suffering from acute scurvy.

No life was harsher than that suffered by members of the Canadian Pacific Survey crews. None was less rewarding. Underpaid, overworked, exiled from their families, deprived of their mail, sleeping in slime and snowdrifts, suffering from sunstroke, frostbite, scurvy, fatigue and the tensions that always rise to the surface when weary and dispirited men are thrown together for long periods of isolation, the surveyors kept on, year after year. They explored great sections of Canada. The first engineers scaled mountains that had never before been climbed, crossed lakes that had never known a white man's paddle and forded rivers that were not on any map. They walked with a uniform stride developed through years of habit, measuring the distances as they went, checking altitudes with an aneroid barometer slung around the neck and examining the land with a practised gaze, always seeing in the mind's eye the finished line of steel – curves, grades, valley crossings, bridges and trestles, tunnels, cuts and fills. In the first six years of the Canadian Pacific Survey, forty-six thousand miles of Canada were reconnoitred and blazed in this manner.

Twelve thousand of these miles were then laboriously charted, foot by foot, by scores of survey parties. Axemen, following the pathfinders' blazes, hacked the lines clear of brush. The chainmen

148

who followed meticulously divided the distances into hundred-foot sections, each marked by a stake. Behind the chainmen came the transit men, calculating the angle of each bend and estimating, by triangulation, those distances which could not be measured by a chain. Behind the transits, the rodmen and levellers worked, reckoning the altitudes and inscribing them on bench marks at half-mile intervals. By 1877 there were twenty-five thousand of these bench marks and more than six hundred thousand chainmen's stakes scattered across Canada from the Shield to the Pacific. At this point the surveys had cost three and one half million dollars and the lives of thirty-eight men by drowning, forest fire, exposure, illness and shipwreck.

Sandford Fleming, who took charge as Engineer-in-Chief in April, 1871, had by midsummer dispatched twenty-one survey parties, totalling eight hundred men, across the country. His task was not easy. A special kind of man was needed and, as Fleming reported after the first season, it was impossible to find enough of them: "Many of those we were obliged to take, subsequent events proved, were unequal to the very arduous labour they had to undergo, causing a very considerable delay and difficulty in pushing the work."

"The leveller in party S is physically unequal to the hard work that I shall unquestionably require from all my staff," Walter Moberly, the pioneer surveyor of British Columbia, scribbled in his journal when he reached the Athabasca country in November, 1872. "He is a capital man, nevertheless I *must* have strong men for my work."

But even if enough good men could have been found, it is doubtful if Fleming would have been able to employ them. Political considerations entered into the question: various sections of the country had to be considered, different nationalities and creeds had to be consulted. Then there was the problem of patronage; there was constant pressure on Fleming to appoint the friends or protégés of Members of Parliament or of Senators. As late as 1879, Charles Shaw, an experienced transit man, discovered he could not get a job on the prairie survey with his old chief because a son-in-law of Senator John Sutherland, a powerful Manitoba Conservative, had been given the post. Major C. F. Hanington, a civil engineer with considerable experience in British Columbia, found himself, after the election of 1874, working in the area of Rat Portage under a man named Lucas "who says he is the friend of the wife of the new Prime Minister, Mr. Mackenzie." A good many Conservative surveyors, indeed, lost their jobs after the new regime came to power.

Often appointments were made over Fleming's head at Cabinet

level. The chief engineer found he had people of whom he had never heard working for him; such appointees could not easily be fired for inefficiency. Fleming did not bother to protest. As he put it, "I knew that patronage had to be respected." Sometimes work had to be invented just to keep the political appointees busy, a phenomenon that a royal commission subsequently felt might help explain the incredible amount of unnecessary surveying that took place in British Columbia in those years. Fleming testified before it that the public interest had suffered because of patronage in the hands of the party in power.

One man Fleming was apparently forced to put up with for political reasons was the surly photographer-explorer Charles Horetzky, who was given his job as a result of the intervention of Sir Charles Tupper. Horetzky, after parting from Macoun at Fort St. James, had pushed on westward towards Port Simpson, "an irksome and hazardous journey." When he returned to Ottawa a fanatical advocate of the Pine Pass–Port Simpson route, which he had explored, Fleming dismissed him. Horetzky always insisted that Fleming acted out of pure jealousy: "I should have made no allusion to the Pine River route and should have known that opposition to the Chief Engineer's pet theory . . . was a signal for my dismissal." Fleming's version differed. "It was sometimes necessary to employ persons who were not adapted to the work or qualified to be chief engineers." Whatever the reasons, Horetzky ingratiated himself with the new administration and was soon back on the job again, exploring his favourite country along the northern British Columbia coast. There was nothing, apparently, that Fleming could do. In the summer of 1875, Marcus Smith, in charge of surveys in British Columbia and as irascible an engineer as ever existed, had a raging row with Horetzky at Waddington Depot near the head of Bute Inlet. Smith arrived to find that Horetzky had been there for ten days, contrary to instructions. When Smith inquired about this, "he flew at me like an enraged tiger, defied me in my instructions and said he was going home to Ottawa." Smith had several witnesses to the scene, but Horetzky kept his job until the administration changed in 1878.

After the first year of surveys, Fleming reported that it was impossible to obtain "the class of men required." That year two crews, working through the unexplored and impenetrable country between Ottawa and Fort Garry, simply gave up the ghost. One party had had enough by late summer; the second, on learning that they would be required to stay out all winter, "suffered a few days of cold and snow and then promptly trooped in to Fort Garry." There was a seller's market in survey labour and, like it or not, Fleming and his staff had to retain incompetents.

"I wish you would find out what Walter Dewdney is doing," Marcus Smith wrote to a subordinate, Joseph Hunter, in May of 1875. "I heard last week that [he] was seen on the wagon road blind drunk and making an ass of himself. I had told him his duty was to look after the transport but as he is evidently unfit for this duty he had better . . . go with the trains that are to follow Jarvis to Tête Jaune Cache." Since Dewdney's brother Edgar was Member for Yale and a strong political power in the province, the erring Walter could scarcely be dismissed.

The same year, Smith again wrote to Hunter, this time about the head of Party "N," H. P. Bell. "I find Bell utterly incompetent to manage the working of a party beyond the surveying position. He cannot calculate more than a child how much he can do in a fortnight or how much stuff he could take out of the country in a given time but acts entirely by impulse – and if left to himself would be certain to be snowed in. I have therefore told him that you will take full charge of the party when you arrive and he must work under you. This will be a disagreeable task for you – but it is necessary in order to close the surveys and save the packtrain. I think you had better let Bell attend entirely to the surveys and not interfere much about the line unless he does something very absurd which he is likely to do – for he is evidently more than half-crazy." Three days later, Smith decided that Bell could not even handle the survey party: "I find he is as incompetent as an engineer as in general management." And again: "I am almost afraid to trust him out of your sight as he is almost certain to do something desperate – some wild fancy."

The wonder was that anyone worked on the surveys at all. In spite of the difficulty of getting men each season, there was little long-term job security, even for experienced engineers. Crews were discharged at the end of the summer, left without winter work and re-engaged the following spring. When the work began to diminish towards the end of the decade, there was real hardship. "There is much distress among the engineers, etc., of the staff who were dismissed last spring," Marcus Smith, then Fleming's deputy, wrote in February 1878 to his chief, who was on leave in England. The men had been dismissed on a month's notice "and have not a shilling to maintain their families.

If all the surveying staff is now dismissed there will be wholesale distress."

It was a lonely, remote existence the surveyors led in the field, cut off from news of family, friends or the world at large, in a land where the native rites and customs were as foreign as those of an Oriental satrapy. In the spring of 1875, Henry Cambie, exploring the east branch of the Homathco, came upon Indians so removed from civilization that many of the women had never seen a beard "and would not believe that mine really grew on my chin." Jason Allard, one of Walter Moberly's men, unwittingly accepted an invitation to visit an Indian lodge on the Fiddle River and made the mistake of sitting on a bear rug next to a strapping maiden. Too late he realized that this was tantamount to an offer of marriage. In desperation he traded her back to her father for a handsome finger ring.

Yet out they went, year after year, men who were for the most part tough, intelligent and uncomplaining. They drank anything they could get: "Be it known and I say it without shame at all, all engineers in those days were accustomed to take what they felt like," one of them, Harry Armstrong recalled. When they drank, they sang their theme song to the tune of *"Les Deux Gendarmes"* – sang it from the ravelled coastline of British Columbia to the gloomy granites of northern Ontario – the song of the Canadian Pacific Survey:

> *Far away from those we love dearest,*
> *Who long and wish for home,*
> *The thought of whom each lone heart cheereth,*
> *As 'mid these North-west wilds we roam,*
> *Yet still each one performs his duty*
> *And gaily sings:*
> *Tra, la, la, la, la, la, la, la, la, la, la, la,*
> *Hurra! The jolly C.P.S.!*
> *They're at home upon Superior's shore,*
> *Hurra! we'll drink to them success,*
> *And a safe return once more.*

In 1872, it was a nightmare just to reach that "home upon Superior's shore." Charles Aeneas Shaw, who was with the Canadian Pacific Survey from the beginning until the last stake was driven, graphically recalled his initiation in November of that year. Shaw, a wiry eighteen-year-old at the time, "keen to learn and a hog for work," was hired as a packer under William Murdoch, seeking to locate a

152

line west from Prince Arthur's Landing. The trick was to try to reach the Landing before winter sealed off the lake. The group attempted it first in a cockleshell of a steamer, the *Mary Ward*. It foundered on a reef in a howling blizzard, drowning three of the party. The survivors returned to Toronto, picked up new kits and set off again. Murdoch made his way overland to Duluth, where he offered to pay as much as twenty-five hundred dollars for a tugboat to take his men up the lake. Conditions were so desperate that no seasoned skipper would attempt the crossing. Notwithstanding, the party bought a small fishing boat and started off in mid-December, rowing and sailing to their destination. The temperature sank to 52 below zero − so cold that each crewman had to chip from the blades of his oars a ball of ice the size of a man's head. They crept along the shoreline, sleeping in the snow at night, existing on frozen pork and hardtack and even surviving a full-force gale. When the lake froze on New Year's Day, they finally abandoned the boat, built toboggans out of strips handsawn from frozen birch logs and hiked with their supplies the last fifty miles to Prince Arthur's Landing.

Such hardships were commonplace. Fleming's friend J. H. E. Secretan, a man who liked his food, was reduced to eating rose haws washed down with swamp water during a survey near Lake Nepigon in 1871. In the same year seven members of a survey supply party were lost near Jackfish River as the result of a forest fire so hot that the very soil was burned away. Only one body was found. Of the remainder there was no trace, save for six holes scratched out of a nearby swamp and apparently abandoned when the smoke grew too thick.

In the same area north of Lake Superior, the problem of supplies resulted in costly delays and bitter recriminations. Henry Carre, in charge of a party working out of Lac des Isles in the Thunder Bay area, found himself in country through which no white man had ever been. He would have finished his survey had he been properly supplied but had to turn back to Prince Arthur's Landing, otherwise "I verily believe the whole party would have been starved to death." William Kirkpatrick, working near Long Lake north of Superior the same year, had to take his party off surveying to pick blueberries to save their lives. For a week the group had nothing else to eat. In 1875, Kirkpatrick headed a party of more than thirty men locating the line from Wabigoon. Winter set in but no toboggans, tents, clothing or footwear arrived. The resourceful Kirkpatrick made forty pairs of snowshoes and thirty toboggans with his own hands, fashioned a tent out of canvas and scrounged another one, made of skins, from the Indians.

In the Thompson River country of central British Columbia, forty miles out of Kamloops, Roderick McLennan's survey party lost almost all of its pack animals in the winter of 1871. Eighty-six of them, McLennan reported to Fleming, died from cold, hunger or overwork.

An even worse winter expedition was the exploration launched in 1875 by E. W. Jarvis, who was charged with examining the Smoky River Pass in the Rockies. Fleming had already settled on the Yellow Head as the ideal pass for the railway, but this did not prevent him from carefully examining half a dozen others, just in case. Jarvis set off in January from Fort George with his assistant, C. F. Hanington, Alec Macdonald in charge of dog trains, six Indians and twenty dogs.

Both Jarvis and Hanington left graphic accounts of the ordeal, illuminated by uncanny episodes: the spectral figure of Macdonald knocking on the door of their shack in 49 below zero weather, sheathed in ice from head to toe; the lead dog who made a feeble effort to rise, gave one spasmodic wag of his tail and rolled over dead, his legs frozen stiff to the shoulders; and the auditory hallucinations experienced one night by the entire party – the distinct but ghostly sound of a tree being felled just two hundred yards away but no sign of snowshoes or axemanship the following morning.

The party travelled light with only two blankets per man and a single piece of light cotton sheeting for a tent. They moved through a land that had never been mapped. A good deal of the time they had no idea where they were. They camped out in temperatures that dropped to 53 below zero. They fell through thin ice and had to clamber out, soaked to the skin, their snowshoes still fastened to their feet. They stumbled down box canyons and found the way blocked by frozen waterfalls, two hundred feet high. They suffered from *mal de raquette*, a kind of lameness brought on by the constant need to wear snowshoes. One day they experienced a formidable change of temperature – from 42 below zero to 40 above – and this produced a strange exhaustion, as if they were suddenly plunged into the tropics. One morning, while mushing down a frozen river, they turned a corner and saw an abyss yawning before them: the entire party, dogs and men, were perched on the ice ledge of a frozen waterfall, two hundred and ten feet high; the projection itself was no more than

154

two feet thick. One evening they made camp below a blue glacier when, without warning, great chunks of it gave way; above them they beheld "masses of ice and rock chasing one another and leaping from point to point as if playing some weird, gigantic game." A chunk of limestone, ten feet thick, scudded past them, tearing a tunnel through the trees before it plunged into the river.

By this time it was March. Dogs were dying daily. Even the Indians were "in a mournful state of despair, declaring that they . . . would never see their homes again and weeping bitterly."

On March 15 Hanington described Jarvis as "very thin, very white and very much subdued." When they had reached the Smoky Pass, some time before, Jarvis had entertained grave doubts about proceeding further, but Hanington had said he would rather starve than turn back. It began to look as if he would:

"I have been thinking of 'the dearest spot on earth to me' – of our Mother and Father and all my brothers and sisters and friends – of the happy days at home – of all the good deeds I have left undone and all the bad ones committed. If ever our bones will be discovered, when and by whom. If our friends will mourn long for us or do as is often done, forget us as soon as possible. In short, I have been looking death in the face. . . ."

Jarvis described "the curious sensation of numbness, which began to take hold of our limbs," as they pushed slowly forward on their snowshoes, giving the impression of men marking time in slow motion. Yet they made it. Hanington had lost 33 pounds; Jarvis was down to a bony 125. The food given them when they finally reached Edmonton produced spasms of dysentery and vomiting. Still they kept on, setting off once more across the blizzard-swept prairie for Fort Garry. All told, they spent 116 days on the trail, travelling 1,887 miles, 932 of those miles on snowshoes and 332 of them with all their goods on their backs, the dogs being dead.

Why did they do it? Why did any of them do it? Not for profit, certainly, there was little enough of that; nor for adventure, there was too much of that. The answer seems clear from their actions and their words: each man did it for glory, spurred on by the slender but ever-present hope that someday his name would be enshrined on a mountain peak or a river or an inlet, or – glory of glories – would go into the history books as the one who had bested all others and located the route for the great railway.

2

One man who thought he had the route and who spent the twilight of his life recalling, with increasing bitterness but not always with great accuracy, the attempts to "humbug" the route away from him, was Walter Moberly.

Moberly was working in Salt Lake City in 1871 when the news came of the pact with British Columbia. He went immediately to Ottawa where his enemy, Alfred Waddington, was already trying to promote a railway company. Moberly hated Waddington – the verb is not too strong – for the same reason he hated anyone who tried to promote a railway route to the Pacific that did not agree with his own conception. Waddington was a fanatic on the subject of Bute Inlet as a terminus for the railway. It was "his" inlet; he had explored it. Moberly was equally fanatical on the subject of the Eagle Pass, the Fraser River and Burrard Inlet. That was *his* inlet; he had trudged along its shores before any white man had settled there. He apparently viewed the massacre of Waddington's survey party as a salutary act, for he was incensed when some of the murderers were hanged.

Surveyors tended to fall in love with the virgin territory they explored. Moberly had fallen in love with the Eagle Pass, which he had discovered and named in the summer of 1865 as a result of watching a flight of eagles winging their way through the mountains. Moberly knew that eagles generally follow a stream or make for an opening in the alpine wall. Eventually he followed the route of the birds and discovered the pass he was seeking through the Gold Range. According to his own romantic account, he finally left his companions, after a sleepless night, and made his way down into the valley of the Eagle River, where he hacked out a blaze on a tree and wrote the prescient announcement: "This is the Pass for the Overland Railway."

Moberly had gone to school in Barrie with a tawny-haired, angular girl named Susan Agnes Bernard. In Ottawa, Susan Agnes, now Lady Macdonald, invited her former schoolmate to lunch at Earnscliffe, the many-turreted residence on the Ottawa River. Here, the weathered surveyor with the long, ragged beard and the burning eyes pressed his particular vision of the railroad on the Prime Minister of Canada. He insisted, with superb confidence, that he could tell Macdonald exactly where to locate the line from the prairies to the seacoast. Not only that but "you can commence construction of the line six weeks after I get back to British Columbia."

156

"Of course," Moberly added, "I don't know how many millions you have, but it is going to cost you money to get through those canyons."

Macdonald was impressed. Moberly was a fighter who came from a family of fighters. He was half Polish: his maternal grandfather had been in command of the Russian artillery at Borodino. His father was a Royal Navy captain. As a young engineer working on the Northern Railway, Moberly was fired by tales of the frontier which he heard first hand from Paul Kane, the noted painter of Indians. The Fraser gold rush of 1858 lured him west. It was Moberly who helped lay out the city of New Westminster in 1859. It was Moberly, too, who located, surveyed and constructed part of the historic corduroy road from Yale to the Cariboo gold-fields. He was a better surveyor than a businessman. The project left him with debts that took eight years to pay off. Moberly, like so many surveyors of that day, was also in politics, but he resigned his seat in the colonial legislature to take the post of assistant surveyor general for British Columbia. It was in this role that he discovered the Eagle Pass in the Gold Range, later called the Monashees.

When he returned to the province, with the Prime Minister's blessing, as district engineer in charge of the region between Shuswap Lake and the eastern foothills of the Rockies, he was in his fortieth year, supple as a willow and tough as steel. There was no better axeman in the country. His staying power was legendary: he had a passion for dancing and when he emerged from the wilderness would dance the night out in Victoria. He loved to drink and he loved to sing but, as his friend Noel Robinson recalled, "no amount of relaxation and conviviality would impair his staying power when he plunged into the wilds again."

He was as lithe as a cat and had as many lives, as his subsequent adventures proved. Once, while on horseback in the Athabasca country, he was swept into a river and carried two hundred feet downstream. He seized an overhanging tree, hoisted himself from the saddle and clambered to safety. On a cold January day he fell through the ice of Shuswap Lake and very nearly drowned, for the surface was so rotten it broke under his grasping hands. Nearly exhausted from his struggle in the icy water, Moberly managed to pull the snowshoes from his feet, one in each hand, and by spreading out his arms on the ice, climb to safety. Once, on the Columbia River, he gave chase, in a sprucebark canoe, to a bear, cornered it against a river bank, put an old military pistol against its ear and shot it dead, seizing it by the

157

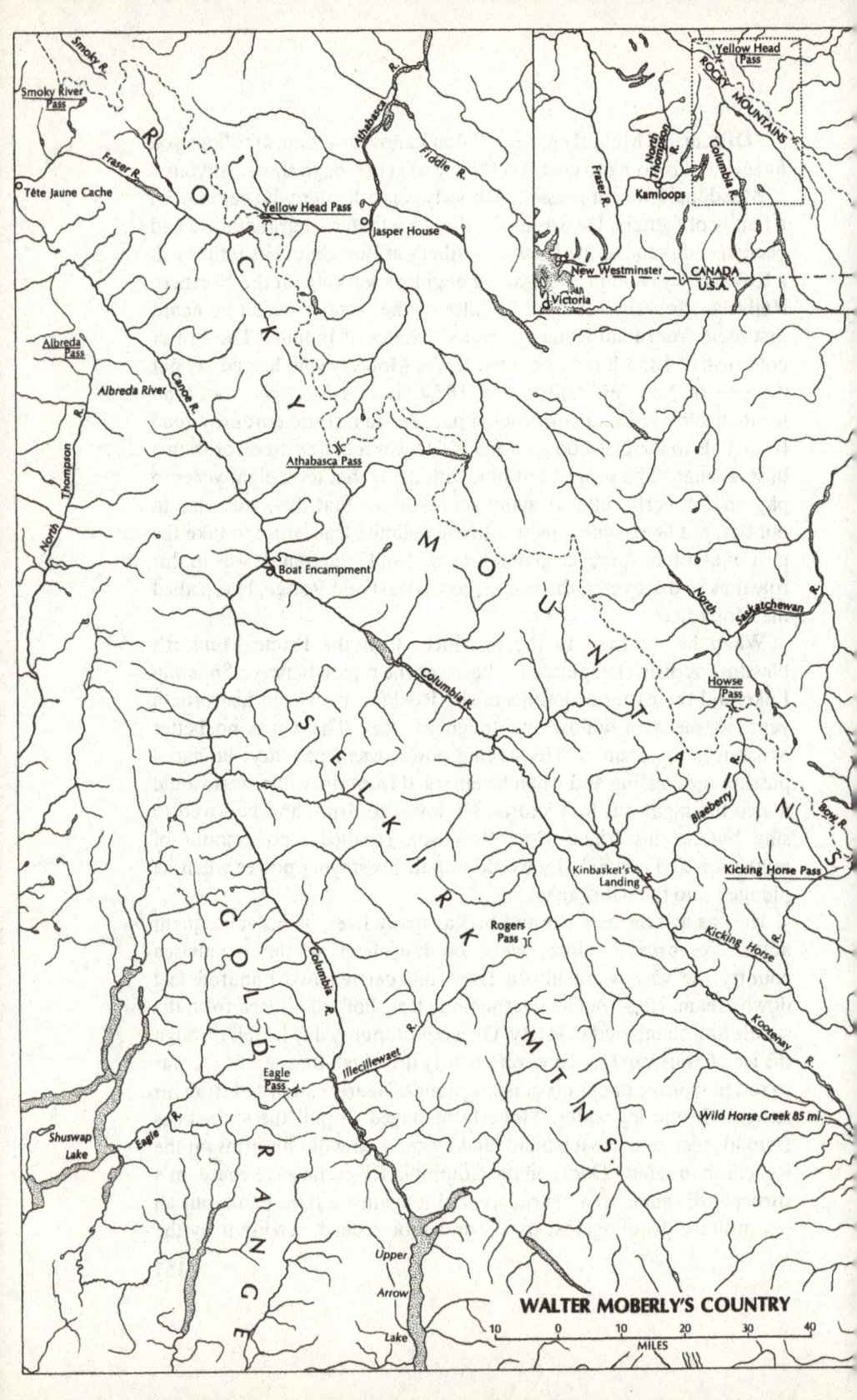

WALTER MOBERLY'S COUNTRY

10   0   10   20   30   40
MILES

hind legs before it sank – all to the considerable risk and apprehension of his companions in the frail craft.

Moberly, in short, was a character: egotistical, impulsive, stubborn and independent of spirit. He could not work with anyone he disagreed with; and he disagreed with anyone who believed there was any other railway route to the Pacific than the one that had been developing in his mind for years. Moberly had been thinking about the railway longer than most of his colleagues, ever since his explorations in 1858. Now, thirteen years later, he set out to confirm his findings. He began his explorations on July 20, 1871, the very day the new province entered Confederation.

Moberly took personal charge of his favourite area bounded by the Eagle Pass of the Gold Range and the Howse Pass in the Rockies, just north of the Kicking Horse. Between these two mountain chains lay an island of formidable peaks – the apparently impassable Selkirks. It was in the hairpin-shaped trench around this barrier that the Columbia flowed, first northwest, then southeast again, until it passed within a few miles of its source. It was Moberly's theory that the railway would cut through the notch of the Howse Pass, circumvent the Selkirks by following the Columbia valley, and then thread through the Gold Range by way of the Eagle Pass, which led to Kamloops and the canyons of the Fraser.

Moberly spent the next eight months in the mountains and trenches of British Columbia. He travelled down the olive-green Columbia with a crazy flotilla of leaky boats, burned-out logs and bark canoes, patched with old rags and bacon grease. He trudged up and down the sides of mountains, clinging to the reins of pack horses, accompanied always by a faithful company of Indians for whom he sometimes showed a greater respect than he did for white men. ("The Indian," he wrote, "... when properly handled and made to feel that confidence and trust is reposed in him, will work in all kinds of weather, and should supplies run short, on little or no food, without a murmur; not so the generality of white men.")

When winter set in, he set off on snowshoes for New Westminster, a distance of more than four hundred miles, as casually as if he were heading off on a pleasant Sunday hike. He went straight over the top of the glacier-capped Selkirks, seeking a practical pass, and was almost buried by an avalanche en route. New Year's Day, 1872, found him all alone, in an abandoned trapper's hut, scrawling in his diary: "I think it . . . one of the most wretched and dreary places I ever saw ... this was the most wretched New Year's Day I ever spent." But he did not find what he was seeking: "I found there was not any practicable pass through the Selkirk Range," he reported to Sandford Fleming.

When Moberly emerged from the mountains, he had so convinced himself that his route was the only conceivable one that he determined to take it upon himself to push forward immediately locating the actual line through the Howse Pass. He would get permission later – he "never doubted for a moment" that Fleming would see it his way; going to Ottawa to discuss the matter would only be "a useless waste of time."

He did, indeed, have some communication with his superior, but in his single-mindedness, he misread it. Fleming agreed that a trial line should be run through the Howse Pass, to see if it were at all practicable for a railway. Moberly had already planned something far more ambitious: "a careful location survey," which is the detailed kind that engineers make when they have finally, through exploration and trial lines, decided on the eventual route. Moberly, who had made the most cursory investigation of the pass from its summit to the Columbia, was hopelessly seduced. He seized on Fleming's telegram, "which led me to infer that the line I had taken so many years to explore and discover, and which I was quite confident would be the best to adopt for the proposed transcontinental railroad, would be adopted." He set about hiring extra men, engaging trains of pack animals and buying thousands of dollars worth of supplies, great quantities of which he had cached at Eagle Pass since he reckoned his men would spend two seasons locating the line and would stay out all winter.

Four hours before Moberly and his party were scheduled to leave Victoria for the hinterland, he received a staggering blow. The Lieutenant-Governor, Joseph W. Trutch, whose brother John was a colleague of Moberly's, had a telegram for him. It was literally the eleventh hour, since Moberly's boat was scheduled to leave at 3 a.m. Moberly hurried to Carey Castle and tore open the message. His head must have reeled: it was from Fleming, announcing that the Yellow Head Pass had officially been adopted for the route of the Canadian Pacific Railway and that the Howse Pass survey was to be abandoned. He was to move his survey parties north by way of the Athabasca Pass and then take charge of and make a survey through the Yellow Head. All of Moberly's dreams dissolved at that moment. "His" route was not to be *the* route, after all.

160

Bitterly disappointed, the surveyor rushed to Portland, Oregon, where he tried to buy his way out of his costly contracts. But most of the supplies had already been dispatched to remote mountain areas where they could never be used. Seven thousand dollars worth were abandoned forever at the Eagle Pass.

There was another problem: Moberly needed to hire pack trains to move men and supplies from the Columbia north to the Athabasca country. It was late in the season; most trains were engaged far in advance when there was a buyer's market in renting pack animals. If the packers knew of his dilemma they would charge extortionate rates. Moberly would have to outflank the packers, who were moving toward Kinbasket's Landing at the foot of the Howse Pass, race ahead of them, intercept them and re-engage the horses for the Yellow Head survey before their owners learned about the official change of plans.

He set off, first through Oregon by stagecoach (which broke down) and by steamboat (which sank), and then up through the state of Washington on horseback. He re-entered British Columbia in the Kootenay country, successfully intercepted the packers on the way, hired them all, together with four hundred horses, and then, hacking a trail as he went, reached the Columbia. With a heavy heart, he began moving his survey parties north to the Athabasca country and the despised Yellow Head Pass where Fleming had arranged to meet him on his trip with Grant from ocean to ocean. "Move" is scarcely an adequate verb to describe Moberly's transit: the pack trail had to be carved, foot by foot, out of the tangle of fallen cedars that barred the way up through the cavernous valleys of the Columbia, Thompson and Albreda rivers.

By early September (election day had come and gone in Canada; Allan had made the fatal pact with Cartier) Moberly had reached the Yellow Head. One day, a few miles west of Jasper House, he came upon some fresh tracks, which the Indians sneered at as those of *Moneasses* – "men of the east." A short time later, he ran into the Reverend Dr. Grant, "a long stick in his hand, driving some worn-out and very dilapidated pack animals."

In Grant's *Ocean to Ocean* there is no hint of the disagreeable encounter that took place that week between the Engineer-in-Chief and his errant British Columbia deputy. Moberly's "was the first face we had seen since leaving St. Ann's," Grant wrote. "To meet him was like re-opening communication with the world. . . . How welcome he was, we need not say!" That evening Fleming treated the group to a glass of punch and a cigar. Toasts were drunk to Queen and country and Moberly put Grant in a high good humour because he had some oatmeal and the minister could, for the first time in many days, enjoy a Sunday breakfast of porridge.

Fleming waited until after the Sunday service before his interview with Moberly. The twenty-one men from both sides of the mountains – English, Scots, Irish and Indians – representing every one of the six Canadian provinces, joined in singing Old Hundred. Grant preached a sermon, "not very short, on the plea that the majority of the congregation had not heard a sermon for six months." Then Moberly made his report to his chief.

The interview must have been a painful one. Fleming was taken aback at the slow progress made on the surveys and by Moberly's reckless spending. Tons of supplies left forever at Eagle Pass! "It seemed to me as if some country store had been bought out when I first saw the account," Fleming later recalled. And four hundred pack horses! The chief engineer could not understand the need for so many. At that point his impulse was to fire Moberly. He could not afford to: somebody had to take charge at the Yellow Head and push the surveys forward. But Fleming made no secret of his dissatisfaction.

Moberly's attitude to Fleming's verbal spanking was one of disgust, not with himself but with Fleming for his own "unpatriotic action" in abandoning his pet line. To Moberly, the decision to use the other pass was little short of treason. By his own account, he was on the point of leaving the service, "which I should have done there and then had I not known the very critical position my men and animals were in on their way via the Athabasca Pass and how much they relied on me to see them safely through."

A decade later, the embittered Moberly came very close to suggesting, publicly, that his chief had tried to starve him to death in the Yellow Head by ordering all purchases stopped. "Had such an order ever reached me I should simply not have gone to the Yellow Head Pass, for I would not have taken a number of men into the mountains to starve to death when winter set in."

As Moberly took his leave of the Fleming party, he was himself plagued by worry over the slow progress of the surveys under his command. Ill fortune seemed to dog his footsteps; the survey parties were taking an unconscionable time to arrive from the Howse Pass. Actually, with Moberly so long gone they had simply settled down to wait out the winter. Moberly got them moving again: it would be

162

touch and go if they could get through the high Athabasca Pass before the blizzards blocked it and cut them off from their work at the Yellow Head.

Another party, under a veteran British Columbia surveyor, Edward Mohun, had lost six precious weeks because its supplies had unaccountably failed to reach him from Victoria. The men, reduced to a diet of bread and tea, refused to work; the party became disorganized and spent a month and a half hunting game, at a cost of nearly eighty dollars a day in wages. "I can only say," Moberly wrote in his diary, "there has been some shameful mismanagement somewhere." Fleming, on discovering the situation, packed Mohun and his men off to Victoria. It later turned out that the purveyor and accountant there – another political appointee – was incompetent. There were drafts on the department for $130,000 and vouchers for less than one-fifth of that amount. Moberly, as the man in charge, took most of the blame.

By this time Fleming had lost all confidence in Moberly. He sent him a message by Indian runner ordering him back to Kamloops. He had changed his mind, he said, about the surveys of the line: Moberly was to place the supplies and pack animals in the charge of another man in whom Moberly later related he had no confidence. Fleming was convinced that this raw tactic would force Moberly to quit the service but his stubborn deputy decided simply to ignore the order and press on with the survey of the Yellow Head come hell or blizzard. His later explanation was that "the instructions conveyed in the letter were too childish to be followed." He would carry on the work according to his own best judgement and would obey orders "when I could see they were sensible but not otherwise . . . I went on the survey for business, not to be made a fool of."

Fleming tried again after the new year. In another message, delivered by half-breed runner, he informed Moberly that Marcus Smith had superseded him and would be in charge of all exploratory surveys in British Columbia. To Moberly "this was joyful news . . . for I saw the way clear to get out of the distasteful occupation of making useless surveys." He did some further work for Marcus Smith, who wanted to see if there was a suitable pass up the North Thompson. Moberly reported (one suspects with a certain amount of glee) "an impenetrable wall of rock, snow and ice." Then he quit the service and left for Ottawa where he was "very coldly received by the Engineer-in-Chief." He lingered in the capital waiting for Fleming

163

to sign his expense accounts. Fleming rejected the first audit and passed the accounts on to a second auditor who went over them again. They were passed at last, but not until the frustrated Moberly had been forced to borrow money to pay for his room and board.

Disheartened by his experience, Moberly moved to Winnipeg where, presently, he busied himself at the comparatively prosaic job of building the city's first sewers. For all of his life he complained bitterly about the treatment he had received at the hands of Fleming. Eventually the railway did go south, as he said it should, but to Moberly's disgust the railway builders discarded the Howse Pass in favour of the Kicking Horse.

As the years went by Moberly began to insist that he and not the American engineer Major A. B. Rogers had discovered the pass in the Selkirks that bears the latter's name. But his journal entries, written on the spot in 1865 and 1866, are explicit: neither he nor any of his party saw or explored the Rogers Pass. Still, it became an enduring legend among Canadian engineers, repeated in print as late as 1970, that the damned Yankee had cheated one of their number out of his rightful accolade. Moberly's vituperation against Rogers grew fiercer as his memory grew dimmer. In 1915 he went so far as to tell his biographer, Noel Robinson, that Rogers had not even gone over the pass until after the railway was built. But it was Moberly who first saw the Rogers Pass from a train window.

There was one triumph, however, of which he could not be deprived. Twenty years after he discovered the Eagle Pass, the last spike of the CPR was driven at Craigellachie, almost on the very spot where Moberly, in a moment of clairvoyance, had chalked on a blazed tree his prophecy that the overland railway would have to come that way.

3

Ordeal in the mountains For Moberly, a surveyor's life might have been disappointing but it was at least stimulating. For the men under him – axemen, packers, chainmen, levellers, rodmen – it could be pitiless.

One such man, who left a record of his feelings, was Robert M. Rylatt, a former sergeant with the Royal Engineers, who had been hired by Moberly to take charge of the commissariat and pack train

164

for Party "S" to survey the Howse Pass in the Rockies in the summer of 1871.

Rylatt had won three medals fighting with the Turkish army under Omar Pasha on the Danube and later in the battle of Inkerman during the Crimean war. He arrived in Canada as part of the engineering detachment under Col. R. C. Moody, who laid out New Westminster, the first capital of the new colony of British Columbia. For all of his five years in Canada his wife had been a hopeless invalid and Rylatt badly needed money. Not without misgivings, he signed on for the ordeal of his life.

He was to be gone a year and his description of "the painful hour of parting" is heart-rending: how his wife Jane, rising from her pillow, cried, "Oh, Bob, I shall never see you again"; how he hastened away "fearing each step to hear her cries"; and how, on the steamboat, "as every stroke of the paddles bore me further from her, I felt as if I had ruthlessly abandoned her."

If Rylatt had known what lay ahead he would never have signed a contract with the Canadian Pacific Survey; but there was no way in which he could quit once he began. He was virtually a prisoner, walled off by a five-hundred-mile barrier of mountain and forest which few men could dare to penetrate alone. The job, he thought, would take a year but Rylatt, who left New Westminster in July of 1871, did not return until June of 1873.

Party "S" was under the charge of E. C. Gillette, an American engineer of good reputation whom Moberly had known for many years. It consisted of four officers, who were surveyors, and sixteen men – mainly axemen – together with eight Mexican and Indian packers and one hunter. The forty-five pack animals carried almost seven tons of food and equipment.

To reach the Rockies, the party had to struggle over hills choked with loose boulders and through mudholes so deep the horses were mired to the girth. Over and over again Rylatt had to go through the laborious business of unloading each animal, hauling him out of the mud and reloading him again. Some had to be left to their fate:

"How worried would be any member of the Humane society, could he see the treatment animals in a Pack Train receive, where the animals themselves are only a secondary consideration, the open sores on their backs, from hard and incessant packing, angry and running with humour, over which the Packer, too often, if not closely watched, without washing throws the heavy *apparajos* or Pack saddle, and as the sinch [*sic*] is tightened . . . the poor beast groans, rears and plunges and not unfrequently sinks down under the pain, only to be whipped again into position."

Ahead of the horses moved the axemen, hacking their way through the massive network of prostrate cedars, cutting tunnels in a green tangle as thick as any Borneo jungle and laying down patches of corduroy for the animals to cross.

The party pushed straight across the Selkirk Mountains into the Kootenay country and did not reach the upper Columbia until late in September. They started down it on rafts and in small canoes, watching with growing alarm as it swelled in size with every mile. On the third day, the raft on which Rylatt was travelling hit a submerged log in the rapids and was sucked under. The five men on the raft leaped for the shore; one, James Malloy, fell short. The current pulled him under with the raft and he was never seen again.

At the mouth of the Blaeberry River, which flows down from the summit of the Howse Pass to join the Columbia, the axemen were faced with a Herculean task. They must cut a pathway to the top through forests untrodden since Palliser's associate, Hector, had passed that way a dozen years before. The fall winds had already reduced the country to a mire so thick that one mule could not be pulled from the gumbo; Rylatt was forced to shoot him in his swampy prison.

Yet there were moments of great beauty and mystery here among the silent peaks and Rylatt, who was a sensitive man, was not unmoved. On his first Sunday in the mountains he found himself alone – the others were working five miles farther up the pass. It was his first such experience in the wilderness and he made the most of it. He watched the sun dropping down behind the glaciers on the mountain tops, tipping the snows with a gold that turned to red while, in the shadowed gorges, the ice could be seen in long streaks of transparent blue. He watched the glow leave the peaks and the gloom fill up the valleys. He watched velvet night follow ghostly twilight and saw the pale rays of the aurora compete with the stars to cast "softening hallows [*sic*] of light around these ever-lasting snows." Suddenly, he began to shiver and a sense of irreconcilable loneliness overcame him. It was the silence – the uncanny and overpowering silence of the Canadian wilderness: "Not a leaf stirred; not the hum of an insect; not even the noise of the water in the creek – this being too distant. . . . I listened for a sound but did not hear even the rustle of a falling leaf. . . ."

He made a fire, as much to hear the crackling of the wood as for the warmth. It came to him that no one who had not experienced what he was going through could ever really understand what it was like to be truly alone:

"Your sense of being alone in the heart of a city, or even in a village, or within easy distance of fellow beings . . . gives you no claim to use the term 'alone.' You may have the feeling peculiar to being alone – that is all. Listen sometime when you think you are alone. . . . Can you hear a footfall; a door slam in the distance; a carriage go by? Or the rumble of one . . . ? Can you hear a dog bark? Have you a cricket on the hearth or even the ticking of a clock . . . ?"

Rylatt realized that the tiniest of sounds can give a feeling of relief – "the sense of knowing your species are at no great distance" – but here, in the solitude of the Rockies, there was only silence.

The sense of isolation was increased by the onset of winter and the absence of mail. Goaded by Walter Moberly, who had rejoined the party, Gillette and his men began chopping their pathway to the summit of the pass. By the time the trail was opened, on October 26, the snow was already falling. The following day, with eight inches blanketing the mountainside, the surveyors gathered at the summit, ready at last to start work, but the instruments were so full of water they were useless and the slopes so slippery with wet snow that no man could maintain a footing. The following day another foot of snow fell, the engineers realized that nothing could be done, and the party settled down for the long winter. It would be May before the mountain trails would be passable again and for those sections that ran through the canyons it would be considerably later. It was not really safe to travel with loaded pack horses before June; even then the mountain torrents could be crossed only with difficulty, being swollen with melting snow from above. The twenty-nine members of the party, including two ex-convicts, were faced with each other's company for six or seven months.

At the very outset the party was beset by worries over mail and pay. It was months before they saw a pay-cheque. A government official in Victoria – another political appointee – had withheld the money, banked it and appropriated the interest to himself. Nor was the mail forwarded. It lay for months in various post offices because

167

no arrangements had been made to handle it. One of the packers set off in late November for Wild Horse Creek, a five-hundred-mile journey on snowshoes, and returned with a few letters, but nothing for Rylatt, who was beside himself with anxiety over his wife's condition.

"Poor wife, are you dead or alive?" he confided to his diary. "Have the two deposits of money I sent reached her? It may easily be understood in my case how hard it is to receive no word, no sign, and altogether I am very miserable."

On December 4, Walter Moberly, accompanied by his Indian guides, left the camp on his long trek across the Selkirks. He took with him one of the party, a Frenchman named Verdier who had just learned that his wife had eloped leaving their five children alone. "He was like a crazy man," Rylatt observed; he sent a note with some money to his own wife with Verdier, knowing there would be no further communication with the world until the following May or June.

A few days later he cut his thumb and opened a small roll of bandage material his wife had stowed in his kit. "When I saw scraps of oiled silk, fingers of old gloves, and the softest of lint, how tenderly I felt towards her, but when a slip of paper came to light, on which were the words 'God bless you, Bob,' it made me feel wretched. . . ."

On Christmas Day, the thermometer dropped to 34 below zero and the following day the mercury in it froze solid. Though Christmas dinner was served piping hot, the food was frozen to the plates before the men could consume it.

By New Year's Eve, 1871, Rylatt felt he had reached the bottom. He and four others sat in their cabin, seeing the old year out and trying to keep warm. Though a rousing fire had been lit it was necessary for each man to change position constantly as the side of the body away from the heat became numbed with cold.

"We talked of our wives, adventures, etc.; but there was no mirth; and when the New Year was announced by the watch, we crept into our blankets. I was quite a time before I slept, my brain being busy with past remembrances. This was the first time the anniversary of the New Year had not been kept in the company of my wife."

Ahead of the party stretched four more months of this prison-like existence. The tensions, which had been simmering beneath the surface, began to burst out more frequently. Already Rylatt and the chief surveyor, Gillette, were speaking to each other only when necessary. Earlier in the season they had had an altercation in which Gillette had thrown a grouse bone in Rylatt's face. Rylatt had responded with a cup of hot coffee and Gillette had threatened to shoot him. By February Rylatt had conceived a deadly hatred for the surveyor, who he was convinced was going crazy. This raging antipathy was returned in kind. "That man, Gillette, is not only a fool but an unmanly cur, deserving the sympathy of none, and the power that pitchforked such a being into even our rough society, and placed him pro tem at the head of it, ought to be blackballed," Rylatt wrote in his diary. Gillette, on his part, promised Rylatt he would drill a hole in him before they parted.

"The men are growing rusty for want of activity and biliousness has soured their tempers," Rylatt recorded on February 25. Two weeks later he noted in his diary that "the roughs of the party are in open mutiny. Growling at their food, cursing me for being out of sugar; all this I care little for . . . but my pent up feelings have found vent today, and the leader of the roughs will carry my mark to his grave. I have passed through a somewhat exciting scene and don't care to have it repeated."

Seven of the most mutinous of the party had gathered at the cookhouse door, intent on rushing it and seizing the food including the non-existent sugar, which they believed Rylatt was secretly hiding. In the altercation that followed, Rylatt was threatened by Roberts, the ringleader, an Australian ex-convict. Rylatt snatched up a hatchet and when Roberts made a move, chopped off three of his fingers. This drove off the mob but they returned again in an hour, armed with axes. Rylatt held them off with his Henry rifle and stayed on guard until the threat diminished and the camp returned to a state of sullen tension.

As the sun grew warmer in April and the river ice showed signs of breaking up, much of the ill-humour disappeared. Some mail arrived in May, but still Rylatt had no word of his wife; the white man who had undertaken to carry letters from Wild Horse Creek to Hope on the Fraser the previous fall had perished in the snows, his body discovered in the spring with the mailbag beside it. "I cannot understand why no line has reached me from my wife," Rylatt wrote. "Is she dead? . . . this suspense is terrible . . . surely some one of our many acquaintances would have let me know. . . . Generally people are ready to signal bad news. My chum Jack had some bad news;

his house being burned down. His wife it would appear was enjoying herself at a Ball. . . . He lost everything. . . ."

May 6: "I have somehow got it into my head my wife is not dead, but out of her mind – this thought haunts me."

On May 15, Walter Moberly arrived with the news that the Howse Pass route had been abandoned and that the party must quit its quarters on the Columbia and move north. In his pocket he carried a letter from Rylatt's wife. It had been on his person so long that the cover had been worn away. It was dated October 9, 1871.

Moberly dealt swiftly with the mutineers and with Gillette, who had surreptitiously countenanced the attack on Rylatt: "If Gillette has sown the seed of this discontent, damn him, he shall reap the harvest." Four of the malcontents were dismissed; Gillette was suspended and his assistant, Ashdowne Green, put in charge of the party.

"I cannot forget the look of hatred on Roberts' face as, upon my leaving in the boat, he held up to my sight his mutilated hand and exclaimed: 'You see this; it will help me to remember you!' "

Gillette tried to carry out his threat to shoot Rylatt but as his hand reached for the Smith and Wesson on his belt, Rylatt staggered him with a heavy blow and another member of the party pinioned his arms.

Guided by Kinbasket, the Chief of the Kootenays, a "daring little shrivelled up old fellow," the party started on the long journey northward, breaking trail for the pack horses as they moved through dense clouds of mosquitoes. "I have smothered my face with mosquito muslin, smeared my hands with bacon grease, but bah! nothing keeps them off, and the heat only melts the grease and sends it beneath my clothing," Rylatt wrote in disgust.

In mid-August Chief Kinbasket came to grief when a grizzly bear attacked him. "The old chief had barely time to raise the axe and aim a blow . . . 'ere the weapon was dashed aside like a flash and he was in the embrace of the monster; the huge forepaws around him, the immense claws dug into his back, the bear held him up. Then fastening the poor chief's shoulders in his iron jaws, he raised one of his hind feet, and tore a fearful gash, commencing at the abdomen, and cutting through to the bowels, he fairly stripped the flesh and muscles from one of his thighs, a bloody, hanging mass of rent flesh and clothing." Kinbasket was not found until the following morning. Miraculously, he was still alive; more miraculously, he survived; but the party had lost its trailblazer.

In late September, the party reached the Boat Encampment at the Big Bend of the Columbia River. The route now took a right angle towards the Rockies and the foot of the Athabasca Pass. It seemed impossible to reach the Yellow Head before winter set in. The party hesitated. And here, in the shadow of the glowering peaks, with the brooding forest hanging over them and the moon glistening on the great, rustling river they indulged in a weird charade. On September 28, they held a Grand Ball.

"Think of it," Rylatt wrote in his diary, "a dance – and an enjoyable dance at that."

The "orchestra" consisted of the best whistler in the party, a man who knew all the latest dance tunes ("Little Brown Jug," "The Man on the Flying Trapeze" and "Shoo, Fly, Don't Bother Me" were all popular during the early years of the decade). "He puckered his mouth, beat loud time on an empty soap box with a stick, and the graceful forms began to whirl."

The dancers were deadly serious. Some were assigned the role of lady partner – and later allowed to change about. Rylatt described his assistant, the bespectacled Dick White, dancing with one such "lady" – a great six-footer, hairy-faced and with a fist like a sledge, pants tucked carelessly into boots still covered with river mud, "while Dick, with eyeglasses adjusted, held the huge hand gingerly, and by the tips of his fingers, then circling the waist of this delicate creature with the gentleness due to modesty and the fair sex, his lovely partner occasionally letting out a yell of hilarity, would roll the quid of tobacco to the other cheek of the sweet face, discharging the juice beneath the feet of the dancers."

The dancing grew wilder as the full moon shed its eerie light over the scene. Whenever the whistler gave out the dancers themselves supplied the music, shouting the tunes aloud. The entire crew, "panting like pressure engines," seemed to have forgotten where they were and saw themselves in some vast, chandeliered ballroom, far from the dripping forests, the mires and the deadfalls.

"They were now in the last dance, and appeared to have gone mad, and when at last the orchestra stopped, and Dick White doffed his cap with the indispensable flourish, and the moon shone on his bald scalp as he offered his arm to the fair one at his side, preparatory to leading her to a seat on a log, I fairly screamed with laughter, and then to see that modest young lady suddenly throw out one of her number eleven

171

boots, and sledge hammer arm, and place Dick in an instant on his back and to observe the lady dancing a jig around him, yelling at the same time that made the distant hills echo, was glorious fun."

Thus did Party "S" by temporary madness save itself from a larger insanity.

The following day, Rylatt received three letters from his wife, the last written by a neighbour, she being too ill to hold a pen. It ended with an earnest appeal: "Oh, Bob, come home, I can't bear it!"

He could not go home; Moberly had already refused to release him from his two-year contract. As the fall rains began, pouring down in such sheets that it was impossible to cook a meal, the party, reduced in numbers, moved north again, spurred on by Moberly who had returned from his interview with Fleming at the Yellow Head to find them settling in for the winter.

"The whole valley is like a lake," Rylatt noted. "Thus, under the present state of affairs, I exist. My drenched clothing is taken off at night, wrung out, and I turn in to my equally wet blankets. When resuming my clothing in the morning, I shiver all over, my teeth chatter, as I dolefully reflect how difficult it will be to prepare a meal."

There were no more warm breakfasts for the wet, shivering crew, only flapjacks larded over with bacon grease and a muddy coffee made from beans placed in a piece of canvas and bruised between two rocks.

With winter setting in and their goods far behind them, they found themselves in the heart of the Rockies, sixty-five hundred feet above sea level, fifty miles still from their wintering place, "where no trail exists nor ever has existed . . . wholly unexplored . . . every mile to be contended with, swamps to be crossed, heavy timber to be hacked through, dense undergrowth to be levelled for our animals."

For weeks no scrap of news seeped through. Two thousand miles away a series of events not unconnected with their own toil was taking shape. Macdonald was in the midst of his futile negotiations with Macpherson. Allan was moving gingerly to dump his American associates. Rumours were beginning to reach Liberal ears of a damaging agreement signed by Cartier. But the men in the Athabasca Pass were cut off from the world. At last, on October 19, a pack train arrived and Rylatt was handed a slip of paper on which was scribbled the message he had been dreading:

"Dear Rylatt – The papers state your wife has passed beyond the stream of time. Don't be too cut up, dear old fellow."

There were no particulars. Three days later, while brooding in his tent, he was startled by a strange cry. His dog Nip, a faithful companion during all his hardships, who shared his blankets and his food, had broken through the shore ice and was struggling vainly in the river. Rylatt did his best to save him but failed. " 'Oh, God,' I cried in my distress, 'must everything be taken from me?' "

By the following April, near the Fiddle River, Rylatt was nearly dead himself of scurvy:

"My mouth is in a dreadful state, the gums being black, the teeth loose, and when pressed against any substance they prick at the roots like needles. At times the gums swell, almost covering the teeth. To chew food is out of the question and so have to bolt it without mastication. My legs also becoming black below the knee. . . . My breath is somewhat offensive and I am troubled with a dry cough. In fact I feel like an old man. . . ."

At length, Rylatt persuaded the reluctant Moberly to allow him to quit the service and go home. He said his good-byes on the evening of May 13, 1873, and this leave-taking was warm and fervent. Suddenly he "felt a pang of regret at having to turn my back on such comrades." They crowded around him with warm hand-shakes and clumsy words of Godspeed. The cook appeared with some doughnuts, especially made for the occasion. In the two years together these men had come to know one another as men can only under conditions of hardship and stress. Rylatt and a burly Scots companion, Henry Baird, took three horses and set off south towards Kamloops through unknown country, trudging through soaking moss "so deep that an animal could be buried overhead and suffocate," swimming and re-swimming the ice-cold rivers – packs, horses and all – crawling on their hands and knees over the fallen timber, stamping out a trail through the crust of the melting snow-fields, foundering in the rapids of the treacherous watercourses, slashing away at the impeding underbrush, flogging their animals unmercifully as they struggled on in search of feed.

A month later they were still on the trail, provisions lost, matches almost gone, sugar used up, a single sack of flour between them and starvation. About one hundred and fifty miles out of Kamloops, they happened upon a meadow where the horses could graze. They made a fire, dried their clothing and cooked some flapjacks in a pan. Then, stretched before the blaze, in the closest thing to comfort they had known for many weeks, the two exhausted and weather-beaten men fell to "cogitating on the possibilities and probabilities of the Canadian Pacific Railroad."

"In the mind's eye we pictured a train of cars sweeping along over this flat, over the fierce streams we had passed, puffing and snorting up the mountains in gentle curves and windings, shrieking wildly as some denizen of the forest, scared at the strange monster . . . is hurrying off. . . ."

They talked about "the weary looks in the eyes of the passengers, longing for the end of the route." They could almost see them settle back in their corners, yawn, complain of fatigue and "doze away the terrible hours of idleness." Then their thoughts turned to the dining car and, with watering mouths, the two men began to enumerate the kind of dinner that might be served on such a train in the future: ". . . hot joints, mealy potatoes, pies, cheese, etc., and wine to be had for the paying for."

The fantasy grew more graphic. The two began to conjecture that the imaginary passengers on the imaginary train were gazing out on *them* and remarking: "Those two fellows yonder seem to have it pretty much to themselves, as they toast their skins . . . and are doubtless happier and more at freedom than we. . . ."

At length, the train of imagination rolled on beyond the forested horizon. Rylatt and Baird roused themselves and counted their matches: there would not be many more hot meals. They still had a long way to go but the end of that long sentence on the Canadian Pacific Survey was at last in sight. They cooked some more flapjacks on what was left of the fire to eat cold on the morrow. They saved what little tea and tobacco was left for an emergency. Then, wearily, they shouldered their loads, gathered up their grazing horses and, with that strange vision of the future still fresh in their minds, set off once again into reality.

4

"That old devil" Marcus Smith Marcus Smith, the man who took over all surveys in British Columbia in the spring of 1873, was without doubt the most controversial figure that the Canadian Pacific Survey produced. No two men in the service seemed to agree about him. Moberly liked him. C. F.

Hanington wrote that "he was a wonderful man to my mind." Thomas Henry White, another colleague, talked rather ambiguously about "the fire and sparkle of Marcus Smith's genius." Harry Armstrong, who worked first in Smith's drafting room in Ottawa and became his friend, described him as "a very crabbed and impatient man, though withal very kind of heart." Later, Armstrong, a full-fledged engineer, ran into him on Lake Superior and recalled that he was "still the same, brusque, irritable man." Some of the men who worked under Smith used harsher terms. Rylatt, when he was at a low point on the Columbia, wrote in a fury that Smith was "a hard, unjust and arbitrary wretch." In the summer of 1872, a young rodman named Edgar Fawcett, toiling in the Homathco country, called him "an old devil" and wrote in his diary that "I did not come here to be blackguarded by Mr. Smith for $45 a month." And when Smith announced he was leaving the party and moving on, another member wrote in *his* diary that it was "the best news we have heard since we left Victoria."

Smith was a pretty good hater himself. He referred to one of Roderick McLennan's travelling companions, a man named Wright, as "a Yankee sneak." Henry J. Cambie was also a sneak and, in addition, "a little toady," as was James Rowan, Fleming's assistant, and, by inference, Fleming himself. Fleming's successor, Collingwood Schreiber, was "mean and inferior" and a conniver, to boot, Major A. B. Rogers was "a thorough fraud" and Charles Horetzky was "a crazy, conceited fellow." Smith was suspicious of all politicians: Alexander Mackenzie was dishonest, in his view; the Governor General, of all people, he suspected of railway land speculation; and John A. Macdonald would "sacrifice anything or anybody to smooth down difficulties."

Smith reserved his choicest epithets and his most withering contempt for those who dared to oppose the route to the Pacific in which he had come, by 1877, to believe. This route led from the Pine Pass southwest through Fort George, across the Chilcoten Plains to the headwaters of the Homathco and thence down that turbulent river to its mouth at Bute Inlet. Smith quarrelled bitterly with anyone who favoured any other line for the railway. He fought with Fleming because Fleming continued a strong advocate of the Yellow Head Pass–Fraser River–Burrard Inlet route. He fought with Cambie because Cambie sent back favourable reports on both the Fraser River route and the northern alternative from the Yellow Head to Port Simpson. He was angered by Horetzky, who also wanted the railway to keep to the north and come out to the mouth of the Kitlope. He became such a monomaniac on the subject of "his" route that, when he took Sandford Fleming's place during the latter's leave of absence, Mackenzie, who was both Prime Minister and Minister of Public Works, refused to talk to him.

Smith employed every device he knew to force the government to accept the Pine Pass–Bute Inlet route. He wrote to Members of Parliament, dispatched secret surveys into the north, arranged for letters and articles in the newspapers and bombarded everybody, including two prime ministers, with his views. He was darkly suspicious of conspiracies, which he believed were being mounted against him, and he accused Fleming of suppressing his reports (as did Horetzky) out of jealousy. Fleming bore it all with remarkable equanimity, at least in public, but he did his best to get rid of Smith. At one point he thought he *had* fired him. Smith stuck around. Fleming acted as if he didn't exist. Smith may have been erratic but he was a good engineer and he was a born survivor; long after Fleming himself had been eased out of the service, he was still part of the Canadian Pacific Survey, though his position was less exalted.

In 1872, when Smith first entered the long fiord of Bute Inlet, and then made his way up the Homathco – "a scene of gloomy grandeur, probably not met with in any other part of the world" – it was love at first sight, as it had been with Moberly and Horetzky and all the other enthusiasts who championed a line of route, including, indeed, the chief engineer himself. Surveyor's diaries are seldom gems of literary art. A tired man, squatting on the edge of a river bank, scribbling with a pencil stub in a greasy notebook, is anything but poetic; but Smith, who had a habit of noting the curious trivia around him – the character of Indian communities, for instance, or the sight of a young native girl throwing off her shift coquettishly and bathing in the river – waxed positively lyrical about the region:

"Scene awfully grand – the river rushing and foaming in a narrow chain between walls of rock, a frowning cliff overhanging all and the snow capped mountains piercing the clouds and hidden by curtains of glaciers glittering blue and cold in the sunlight."

Later, he wrote for an official government report an equally eloquent description of the Chilcoten meadows – "the silence of the plains only broken by the silent tread of the Indian or the sad wail of the solitary loon" – and of the Homathco canyon, "where the awful grandeur of the mountains, the roar of the waters, and the constant sense of danger kept the nerves strong and the mind active."

His description of the "charming" mile-wide valleys of the Chilcoten and Chilanko rivers had the ring of a hopelessly infatuated suitor composing a paean to his intended. He wrote of the bottom lands, ripe and mellow with bunch growth, with the clear streams meandering through them in graceful curves, of the pale, greyish green of the grasses "in agreeable harmony with the dark foliage of the spruce," and of the "picturesque irregularity of the evergreens," the whole "forming a scene of pristine beauty rarely to be met with." Compared with the spare, routine prose of some of his colleagues, Smith's, on occasion, seemed almost sensual.

Smith had just turned fifty-six – a stubby man with a barrel chest, tough as shaganappi and bristly as a warthog – when he first clambered up the dripping cliffs of the Homathco. His hooded eyes, drooping moustache and grizzled beard gave him a querulous, almost dour look. Topley, the Ottawa photographer who managed to make most of his subjects look as if they had been stuffed and mounted, did not quite succeed with Marcus Smith. There remains upon that sturdy but weather-ravaged face a fleeting expression of slight distaste. One can almost see the subject shifting impatiently in the prop studio chair and blurting out: "Look ye [a favourite expression] does it have to take so damned *long*?"

He was a Northumberland man who had been a land surveyor all his life, first in England and Wales, then in South Africa and, since 1850, in Canada. He had worked for Fleming on the Intercolonial, as had so many of the men on the c.p.s.; and like so many of the others – men accustomed to fend for themselves in wild and inhospitable climes – he was totally self-confident and more than a little proud. "I have no claim for genius," he wrote at the close of his career (he lived to be 89), "but a strong love of my profession, an aptitude and energy for carrying out great works, and a determination for honesty and accuracy which I have so far carried out, that in a long practice there has never been a dollar lost to any of my employers from any blunder of mine."

He was a hard drinker. On the prairie surveys, where prohibition reigned, his keg of "lime juice" contained straight whiskey. On the Homathco, he and his subordinate, W. O. Tiedeman, broke open a case of brandy and fought and drank an afternoon away. "They would keep having a drink and a row, turn and turn about," one of the party noted. He was not an easy man to work under for he did not suffer incompetence, fatigue or any kind of human frailty. Young Edgar Fawcett, the rodman on the Bute-Homathco survey, was toiling up a steep, rock-strewn hill in June, 1872, when an enormous boulder, bouncing down the slope, struck him a blow that knocked him insensible. Smith took personal affront at the mishap. He could not have children working for him, he said. "That boy who could not keep out of the way of stones would have to be sent home."

Anything that interfered with the progress of the survey distressed him and this impatience seems to have rubbed off on his subordinates. Tiedeman, who was in charge of the Bute Inlet survey under Smith's over-all supervision, insisted on moving camp at the end of October even though it meant leaving one lost man to die in the wilderness. Anyone who got lost, Tiedeman said, in his thick German accent, deserved to die. Some other members of the party remonstrated with him and he finally consented to send out search parties. Eventually, the missing man was found: he had been wandering around in circles for two days and nights without sleep or food and was so far gone he did not recognize the comrade who eventually located him. Tiedeman's reaction was an echo of Smith's: "You shall have four more days' work for losing those two days."

"Sunday morning and no one sorry for it except perhaps Old Smith who I think would like to keep everyone at work night and day and then growl and snap at anyone he came near or happened to speak to him," George Hargreaves, the leveller on the party, confided to his diary that June.

Three days later he wrote that "Old Smith came to camp about 7.30 and boiled over, accusing us of putting obstacles in his way and saying he would carry through with the survey if he had to send 5,000 miles for men."

Six days later: "Had a row with Old Smith for not bringing the levels through before stopping work. . . . Says he, 'what did you mean by saying you was through, you must be an idiot.'"

Two days later: "It appears Smith had a big row with two or three of the men and also with Bristow, the Transit. Called him a Gd. dmd. fool and Idiot, who said he would not have such language used to him that he would go home to Canada if he continued to use it, and also told Smith he was stopping the work by carrying on so. Smith told him to go back to his instrument or he would give him the Gd. damdist daming ever he had dam'd. . . ."

178

"It was most awful the way that old devil swore and went on generally," young Fawcett wrote of Smith in his own diary a week after the incident with the boulder. "He swore at me for the most ordinary things and kept us from dinner till half-past two."

Yet, Fawcett admitted, he was treated no worse than the others, for Smith made no distinctions. He barked at Tiedeman, the head of the party, and barked at transit men, levellers, axemen and Indian packers with a fine democracy. The Indians, who could afford the luxury of independence, calmly unloaded their canoes and prepared to head off into the wilderness. Smith called in Hargreaves and asked him who had authorized the Indians to leave. Hargreaves replied that Indians didn't require any authorization to do anything, a remark that seemed to astonish Smith. "He said we must talk about that, only while he was talking about it, they were going, which put him in a flutter rather." Smith asked what the Indians wanted. The Indians replied they didn't want to work for Smith. Hargreaves prevented a wholesale desertion by apologizing for Smith and agreeing to pay the Indians in cash at the time of every trip.

But if Smith was hard on others, he was equally hard on himself. When he was sixty years of age, he travelled for one thousand miles through the Lake Superior country by canoe, all in a single summer, making two hundred portages that varied from a few yards to four miles.

He must have seemed a superman albeit a satanic one, to the young chainmen and rodmen who, at the end of each day, found themselves so exhausted they were ready to throw in the sponge. Some of their diary excerpts from the Bute Inlet survey of 1872, when Smith was driving them without mercy, tell the story:

"So tired I could hardly drag myself along. After one of the hardest, hottest and longest days I had ever experienced in my life, we arrived at 'W' camp. I was so far done in I could not get up and sat down to rest."

"Yesterday I really thought I should have to give in I felt so the loss of having eaten nothing all day but a bit of bread and fat pork in 12 hours. If this is surveying, I have had my bellyfull of it."

"I am heartily sick of the whole business and feel like turning tail."

". . . legs and feet all benumbed and aching fearfully. I felt like giving up and leaving it many times but knowing it had to be done

179

sometime, and if we left it today would have to go again tomorrow, managed to get through. . . ."

Yet here was the demonic Smith, a man twice their age, driving hard late into the evening, scaling the rocks and forging through the glacial waters with enough breath left in his barrel chest to shower curses and imprecations upon the stragglers.

The truth was that he was as exhausted as any. "Felt terribly used up," he wrote in his journal on July 9, 1872 – it is a phrase that keeps recurring on those cramped pages. But he would not give up that night until he had worked out the calculations of his travels across the mountains. Four days later, when he boarded the boat to Victoria (to the immense relief of his men), he was near collapse. "Fatigue set in after a month of excessive labour and anxiety and I lay and dozed the hours away, totally unfit for anything."

Sick or not, Smith was back in the upper Homathco country a month later. He was tortured by pains and cramps in his hip and left leg and by August 11 was so ill he could not rise until noon. But rise he did, saddled a horse and headed off across a swamp. The swamp was so bad that Smith had to leave it and make his way up the side of a hill, still on horseback. After this detour, Smith plunged into a second swamp. The horse became mired. Smith tried to spur it on. The saddle slipped off and Smith tumbled into the morass. He was too weak to re-saddle the horse but he managed to crawl all the way to the head of a lake where he found two Indians who cared for him.

He was still at it, in the same country, in the summer of 1875. He was then in his sixtieth year and he confided to Joseph Hunter, one of his surveyors, that he had "less heart for this journey than any I have undertaken. I am far from well and very weak and the mountain torrents are very high."

When he wrote that letter, Smith was planning to force his way from the Chilcoten plains through the Cascade Mountains by way of the Homathco Pass and move down to Bute Inlet. Tiedeman and Horetzky had started at the inlet and were on their way to meet him, opening up a trail and bridging the streams as they went.

Smith set off on foot with five Lillooet Indians and a Chilcoten guide, struggling for two and a half days along the dripping, perpendicular cliffs of the canyons. Sometimes it took several hours to move a few yards since they had to climb as high as fifteen hundred feet and descend again to circumnavigate the spurs of rock that jutted

180

from the canyon face. At one point, unable to bridge a torrent (six of the largest trees, thrown across the chasm, had been swept away like chips), they were forced to detour by way of a glacier, fifteen miles long, whose sharp ridges they crossed on their hands and knees.

It was not the kind of summer excursion a doctor would prescribe for an ailing man in his sixtieth year. En route to the coast Smith discovered that Tiedeman's bridges had been swept away by the mountain torrents. It took him and his men seven hours to construct an Indian fly bridge over the Grand Canyon of the Homathco. It "looked like a fishing rod and line hanging over the torrent, the butt end resting on the ground and loaded with boulders." Smith crept gingerly over this precarious filament, dropped heavily to the rocks below and then spent six hours scrambling over tangled creepers, huge deadfalls and masses of detached rocks before reaching the camp of division "X."

Smith's love-hate relationship with this strangely compelling land of grim canyons and smiling meadows had, to borrow his own phrase, used him up. Would all this travail be in vain? Survey parties were crawling over the rumpled face of British Columbia and probing the ragged fiords of the coastline, seeking a feasible method of reaching the Pacific. Sandford Fleming was contemplating no less than eleven different routes leading down from the mountain spine to salt water. Only two led through Smith's country. What if another route should be chosen? What if all those ghastly days in the numbing bogs and among the brooding crags should end in defeat? Marcus Smith was not a man to contemplate defeat; and he had not yet begun to fight.

Chapter Five

1
Lord Carnarvon intervenes

2
"The horrid B.C. business"

3
The Battle of the Routes

1

*Lord
Carnarvon
intervenes* "I will leave the Pacific Railway as a heritage to my adopted country," Alexander Mackenzie is said to have declared in his dry, Gaelic accent, when Donald A. Smith, the Member for Selkirk, tried to argue the merits of using a private company to build the line. Smith, nonetheless, remained in Mackenzie's camp. "He is a noble man," Smith said of him and the voters, who returned him with a landslide early in 1874, seemed to agree.

They wanted a noble man and they got one: a high-principled Scot with honest eyes of piercing blue, clear as ice, which seemed to bore right through an adversary. Though he was in no sense immune to the pressures of nepotism and patronage, he appeared to be a man of probity. The public had reduced Macdonald's following in the House to a corporal's guard, as he ruefully remarked, and placed his antithesis on the pedestal. With his graven features, his metallic voice, his rigid attitudes, his Baptist teetotalism and his blunt manner, Mackenzie was in every possible sense, except for his Scottish heritage, the exact opposite of the rounded, soft-spoken, tolerant and indulgent politician whom he replaced.

As Prime Minister he lacked Macdonald's conciliatory gifts and in debate he tended to continue as if he were in opposition, striking down his opponents with the blunt bullets of his words. He "shot to kill," George W. Ross said of him, "and he rarely failed." Sometimes, it seemed, he tried too hard. He took, said Ross, "a strange delight in making his opponents feel he was their master." Mackenzie could never quite let well enough alone and his tendency to want to rub his adversaries' noses in their mistakes, or imagined mistakes, was to affect his railway policy.

He was a bear for work and never allowed an early adjournment of the Commons if there was business to fill up the time; but he sometimes worked unnecessarily hard, for he found it difficult to separate small details from over-all plans – a stonemason's trait, perhaps. He had the body of a man who has worked hard with his hands all his life – lithe and well-proportioned without a spare ounce of flesh and not a fold of surplus tissue on his drawn face. As a stonemason he had created fortifications, canals and court houses. When the Martello towers were built at Fort Henry, in Kingston, he was the foreman on the job. He built well: the towers were a major

184

tourist attraction a century later. One day when he was at work on the bomb-proof arch at the fort, a huge piece of cut stone weighing more than a ton fell upon the lower part of his foot. He allowed no cry of agony to escape from his thin lips. For all of his political career he masked his inner tortures. He was not one to cry out in public; but then he was not one to chuckle, either.

Goldwin Smith remarked, wickedly, that while his strong point as a political leader consisted in his having been a stonemason, his weak point consisted in his being one still. This was not quite fair. The Governor General, who still yearned secretly for Macdonald, came to revise his opinion of Mackenzie. "By no means a man of genius," he wrote, "but he is industrious, conscientious and exact." Dufferin had once thought of him as terribly narrow but he was not so narrow in his interests. In his early days in Kingston he had owned a telescope with which he used to gaze at the night sky from his log shanty. He was a lover of poetry and English literature; his speeches were seasoned with quotations from the classics. He had not had much formal schooling – and he was sensitive about that – but he had managed to read everything to which his better-educated peers had been exposed and seemed to remember far more of it. Though he had, in his younger days, been an incorrigible practical joker, his public image was one of uncompromising sobriety. Strong drink had never passed his lips and it is difficult to imagine anything but the bleakest of smiles illuminating those chiselled features. The church, to Mackenzie, was the rock on which civilization rested; scarcely a day went by on which he did not read his Bible and fall on his knees to ask his God for forgiveness and guidance.

Though the new Prime Minister had no natural gaiety, his speeches and his private conversation could be marked by a dry and often cutting wit. There was the story of his remark to William Paterson of Brantford, a fierce-faced man with a bull's voice, which was seldom restrained. Paterson, after his maiden speech, was desperate for his leader's approval. "Do you think they heard me?" he asked Mackenzie. "Aye," was the Prime Minister's only comment, "they heard you at the Russell Hoose."

As a Liberal, he stood for a retrenchment of government spending. He could not stomach the grandiose schemes of the Conservatives which all too often seemed to him to be designed as much for profit and patronage as for empire building. He had been a persistent critic of the Grand Trunk railway project and had fought an attempt to

185

merge the Great Western with it because, he felt, the measure was designed to give leading Tories more contracts. For similar reasons, he and his followers opposed Macdonald's plan to build the Canadian Pacific; to them it was precipitate, rash and spendthrift. The Tories, with their big business connections, were temperamentally attuned to taking chances; but Mackenzie had neither the imagination nor the gambling instincts of the successful entrepreneur. His political base was in the sober farming districts and small towns of Ontario.

During Mackenzie's term of office, only a few miles of the CPR were built; but it is arguable that Macdonald, in those lean years, could not have done much better, though he might have handled matters with greater finesse. Mackenzie committed the worst of all political crimes: he was unlucky. Macdonald had made his rash promises when the country was caught up in a mood of extravagant optimism. It was Mackenzie's misfortune to take office just as the bubble was bursting. For the whole of his term the country was in the grip of a serious continental depression.

Like so much else, the depression was imported from the United States. Ironically, it was touched off by the spectacular failure of Jay Cooke's Northern Pacific, the same company which, through a series of happenstances, had been the trigger that catapulted Mackenzie into office. But the Cooke failure was only the end product of a variety of catastrophes as ill-assorted as the Chicago Fire and the Franco-Prussian War. It really marked the end of the great period of railway empire building which saw the United States double its transportation machinery in eight years, exceeding for decades to come its real needs and sinking an enormous amount of capital into frozen assets. In short, there was no ready money, and though Cooke continued to feel "an unfailing confidence in God," the deity on this occasion proved fickle. On September 17, at the very moment the Royal Commission was considering the implications of Cooke's secret deal with Allan, the great financial house closed its doors and the white-bearded Tycoon wept freely in public. Five thousand commercial houses followed Cooke and his allied brokers and banks into failure; railroad stocks tumbled; by midwinter, thousands of Americans were starving.

The tidal wave of the great crash washed over all of settled Canada and continued past 1878. The collapse of grain prices in Britain hit Ontario farmers hard. The Canadian foreign shipping trade almost ceased; the three-masters floated forlornly at anchor in the harbours

186

of Quebec City and Halifax. With the collapse of the United States market, the lumber industry, which had undergone a rapid expansion during the years of prosperity, suffered a slump. What little industry there was began to stagnate as American manufacturers dumped their surplus goods at cut-rate prices on the Canadian market. "Let no mechanics come to Canada," warned one disgruntled immigrant in a letter to *The Times* of London. "There are no factories here to employ them."

The farmers, fleeing from the land, were moving into village trade with disastrous results. The *Monetary Times* decried "the craze for storekeeping" and quoted a correspondent in western Ontario who reported that "every village has twice as many struggling for trade as can live; and failures are a weekly occurrence. . . . The tendency to crowd into towns has huddled up in them a fourth of our population." By 1875 business failures were running at the rate of six for every working day; each was said to represent an average loss of fifteen thousand dollars in unpaid debts. The rate of failure in Canada that year – one for every twenty-eight businesses – was three times that of the United States. During the Mackenzie regime almost ten thousand businesses, including two major Montreal banks, closed their doors. All of this had an adverse effect on business morals and ethics, which were never very high by later standards. Business men, the *Monetary Times* reported, had "lost faith in others and even faltered in their loyalty to themselves."

It was an accident of economic history that the depression of the seventies – the Great Depression, it came to be called – neatly bracketed the Mackenzie regime. At the very end of the stonemason's term of office Dufferin was still bemoaning it. "It is to be hoped," he wrote to Whitehall, "that this terrible commercial depression will not continue much longer – if it does I do not know what will become of us. Our lumber trade has utterly ceased to exist – there is scarcely a lumber merchant at Ottawa who is not almost or quite bankrupt and from the window at which I am writing there are not half a dozen ships to be seen in the port of Quebec." The Canadian treasury itself was in trouble; to have entered upon an ambitious railway project could easily have bankrupted the country.

That was the cross Mackenzie had to bear; he was shackled financially. On the other hand, it is doubtful that, given prosperity, he would have accomplished any more than he did. He could gaze upon the universe with his telescope, but he did not see his country as a great transcontinental nation, settled for all of its length from sea to sea. Canada, to Mackenzie, lay east of the Shield; far off were two small islands in the Canadian archipelago: the Red River settlement and British Columbia. These were necessary nuisances.

In addition, Mackenzie seemed to be plagued with a compulsion to slash his rival's railway policy to shreds. On the hustings in 1874 and later in his public speeches he could not refrain from the kind of wild remark that filled British Columbians with dismay and goaded them into retaliation. As late as 1877 he was still using the word "insane" to describe the pact with the Pacific province. The men who perpetrated that treaty, he declared, deserved "the everlasting political execration of the country." It was this kind of thing that turned Victoria, in Lord Dufferin's on-the-spot description, into a "nest of hornets."

Clearly his predecessor had saddled Mackenzie with an impossible burden. The policy was scarcely insane, but some of the terms were certainly foolhardy. A decade later George Grant recalled for *Scribner's Monthly* that in 1870 "it had come to be considered that a railway could be flung across the Rocky Mountains as easily as across a hayfield." In those roseate moments Macdonald had blithely promised the British Columbians that he would commence construction of the line in two years. *Two years!* In the spring of 1873, with the surveyors bogged down in the bewildering mountain labyrinth, Macdonald realized he must pay lip service to his incautious pledge. A few days before the deadline he recklessly picked Esquimalt, the naval harbour on the outskirts of Victoria, as the terminus of the Canadian Pacific Railway.

In practical terms, this meant that the railway would run to Bute Inlet on the mainland; it would then thread its way down for fifty miles from the head of the inlet through the sheer, granite cliffs of the coastline and leap the Strait of Georgia, a distance of twenty-nine miles, to Nanaimo on Vancouver Island and follow the east coast of the island to Esquimalt. The work, as Fleming reported, would be "of a most formidable character." It would require eight miles of tunnelling and untold rock cuts just for the right of way to negotiate those sea-torn precipices. Then the track must hop from island to island over six deep intervening channels through which the rip tide sometimes tore at nine knots; that would require eight thousand feet of bridging and in two instances the spans would have to be thirteen hundred feet in length. That was greater than any arch then existing anywhere in the world.

But Macdonald at that moment had not been concerned with engineering. The votes were in Victoria; and Victoria, whose merchants were heavily involved in real-estate speculation, needed an economic boost. On July 19, 1873, exactly two years less a day after British Columbia's admission into Confederation, a group of dignitaries took part in the cynical fiction of turning a sod near the Esquimalt naval base. In the ensuing debate over the Pacific Scandal, Macdonald had the grateful support of the island members.

This, then, was the *fait accompli* Mackenzie faced: a deadline determined, a sod turned, a terminus established and a province militant. In this fertile ground were sown the seeds for the uneasy relationship between the Pacific province and central Canada that was to be maintained into the nation's second century. Right from the beginning, the British Columbians viewed "the East" with suspicion: the East was reneging on its promises; the East did not care about the world beyond the Rockies; the East wanted to hog everything: even the patronage plums were being awarded to men from Ontario and Quebec. On its part, the East – for Mackenzie unquestionably had the support of the public at large outside British Columbia – saw the new province as greedy, shrill and bumptious, prepared to wreck the economy of the nation for the sake of petty provincialism and real estate profits.

The Liberals had grudgingly gone along in 1871 with the fiction that British Columbia had a population of sixty thousand. It did, but only if one counted the Indians and the Chinese, who outnumbered the whites four to one. This was a special concession made to the Pacific province to help lure it into Confederation; no other province was allowed to count either natives or Orientals when it came to enjoying federal grants or popular representation. British Columbia was receiving Ottawa largesse and sending members to Parliament at a rate out of all proportion to the rest of the country. The rest of the country resented it.

Each side accused the other of bad faith. British Columbia was incensed by Mackenzie's declaration during the election campaign that the pact of 1871 was "a bargain made to be broken." The Government, on the other hand, was equally aggrieved when it was discovered that the province had completely forgotten the promise made by its chief delegate, Joseph Trutch, that British Columbia would not insist on the literal fulfilment of the bargain.

During the election Mackenzie had been at pains to water down Macdonald's impossible dream. He talked about a land and water route across the nation, with the rail line being built piecemeal. This, in effect, became Liberal policy, although the administration, beginning in 1874, made continuing attempts to entice private entrepreneurs to build the entire line by offering a subsidy of ten thousand dollars and twenty thousand acres per mile. Although that offer was considerably more generous than Macdonald's, there was no real hope of attracting private capital during the depression. If the railway was to be commenced, it would have to be built in sections as a public work. There would be an easterly link – a subsidized extension of the Canada Central from Pembroke to Lake Nipissing – and two westerly links: first, a line from Lake Superior to the Red River to replace the Dawson Route and, secondly, a branch line from Selkirk to Pembina on the United States border which, it was hoped, would give the Red River its long desired connection with the outside world. After that, as funds were available, other sections would be built – but scarcely within ten years.

This was not good enough for British Columbia. Its premier. who was a federal M.P. to boot, was an eccentric but canny creature. He had been born plain Bill Smith in Windsor, Nova Scotia, but had legally changed his name to Amor de Cosmos, a mixture of Latin, French and Greek, so that he could get his mail in the California mining camps, which were crawling with Smiths. De Cosmos had started as a photographer in Victoria, established the *British Colonist*, and gained a reputation for a vitriolic pen and certain idiosyncrasies of character which became more pronounced as the years went by (it was whispered, among other things, that he dyed his hair and beard!). His attempts to make a pragmatic deal with Ottawa over the railway pact brought about his downfall. His plan was to trade away some of the original terms in return for Mackenzie's pledge to build a drydock at Esquimalt. The Victorians would not hear of it. In February, 1874, eight hundred of them attacked the crimson, pagoda-shaped buildings in which the legislature met – the Bird Cages, they were called – drove the Speaker from his chair and the Lover of the World from the room and right out of provincial politics. (He retained his federal seat but relinquished the premiership.) They created, on the spot, a Terms of Union Preservation League and made it clear that they wanted the terms of the "insane act" fulfilled to the letter. "The terms, the whole terms and nothing but the terms" became a Victorian rallying cry for most of the decade.

Out to British Columbia, post-haste, went the former Liberal

190

Party whip, James David Edgar, commissioned by Mackenzie to bring about some feasible arrangement with the British Columbians who were "setting at defiance all the rest of the Dominion and the laws of nature." Edgar's job, as Mackenzie saw it, was to explain the truth behind the Conservative seductions. The reason Macdonald had promised them so much was "because the administration here sought additional means of procuring patronage before the general election and saw in coming contracts the means of carrying the elections." As Edgar was to discover, such an explanation would scarcely appease the British Columbians who were themselves as hungry for patronage and for contracts as the greediest eastern favour-seeker.

Edgar, who had worked so hard and so effectively for his party during the debate on the Pacific Scandal, seemed the ideal negotiator: handsome by the standards of the day with his fierce Dundreary whiskers of jet black, his waxed moustache, his scholar's brow and his hard, muscular body. He was a poet of some stature – he won a prize that year for some "spirited lyrics" – and he was to have considerable influence on the country's literary future: Canada owes her first copyright laws to Edgar. His two-year-old son, Pelham, would become the most discerning literary critic in the country.

But he was also "Edgar the Unlucky," a nickname he was in the process of earning for a run of adversity at the polls: he lost five elections in a row. In Victoria, it was his misfortune to batter his head against the unyielding barrier of George Walkem's intransigence. The two and a half months he spent in British Columbia must have been frustrating ones to Edgar. Walkem, the new premier, drove him into a state of helpless rage.

"Not, I imagine, a person of any great consequence," wrote the lofty Lord Dufferin of De Cosmos's successor. "He is a lawyer in a small village and the son of a clerk in the Dominion Militia Department, so that in one's intercourse with him, one has to be on one's guard against the intellectual frailties engendered by his professional antecedents."

The man the Governor General thus dismissed was short of stature, robust of physique and – with his eyeglasses, drooping moustache and thin, wispy cowlick – Kiplingesque of feature. He may have suffered from intellectual frailties, but there was a streak of brilliance in his family and a broad stripe of political shrewdness in his make-up. All of his brothers – he came from a family of ten – had achieved

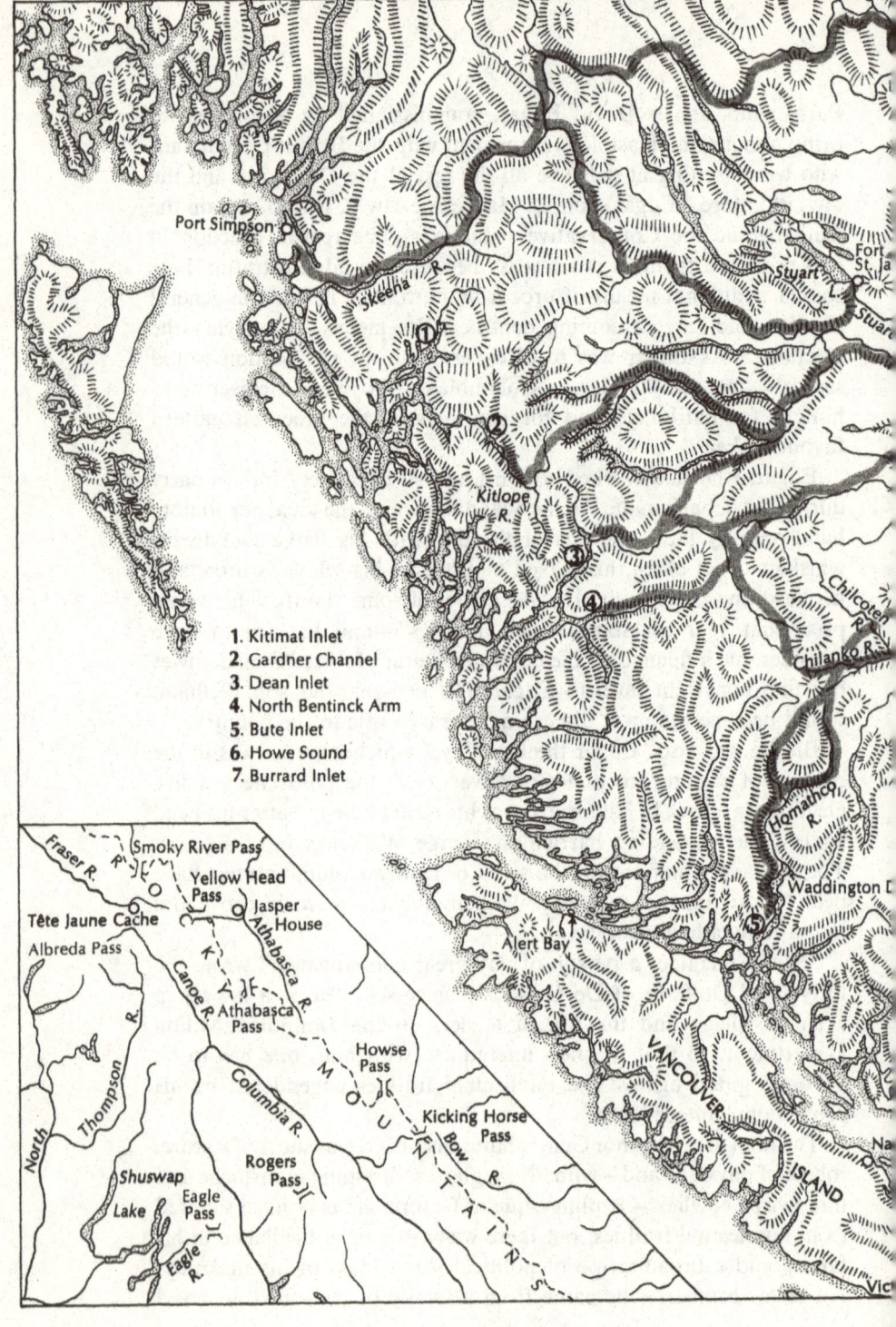

1. Kitimat Inlet
2. Gardner Channel
3. Dean Inlet
4. North Bentinck Arm
5. Bute Inlet
6. Howe Sound
7. Burrard Inlet

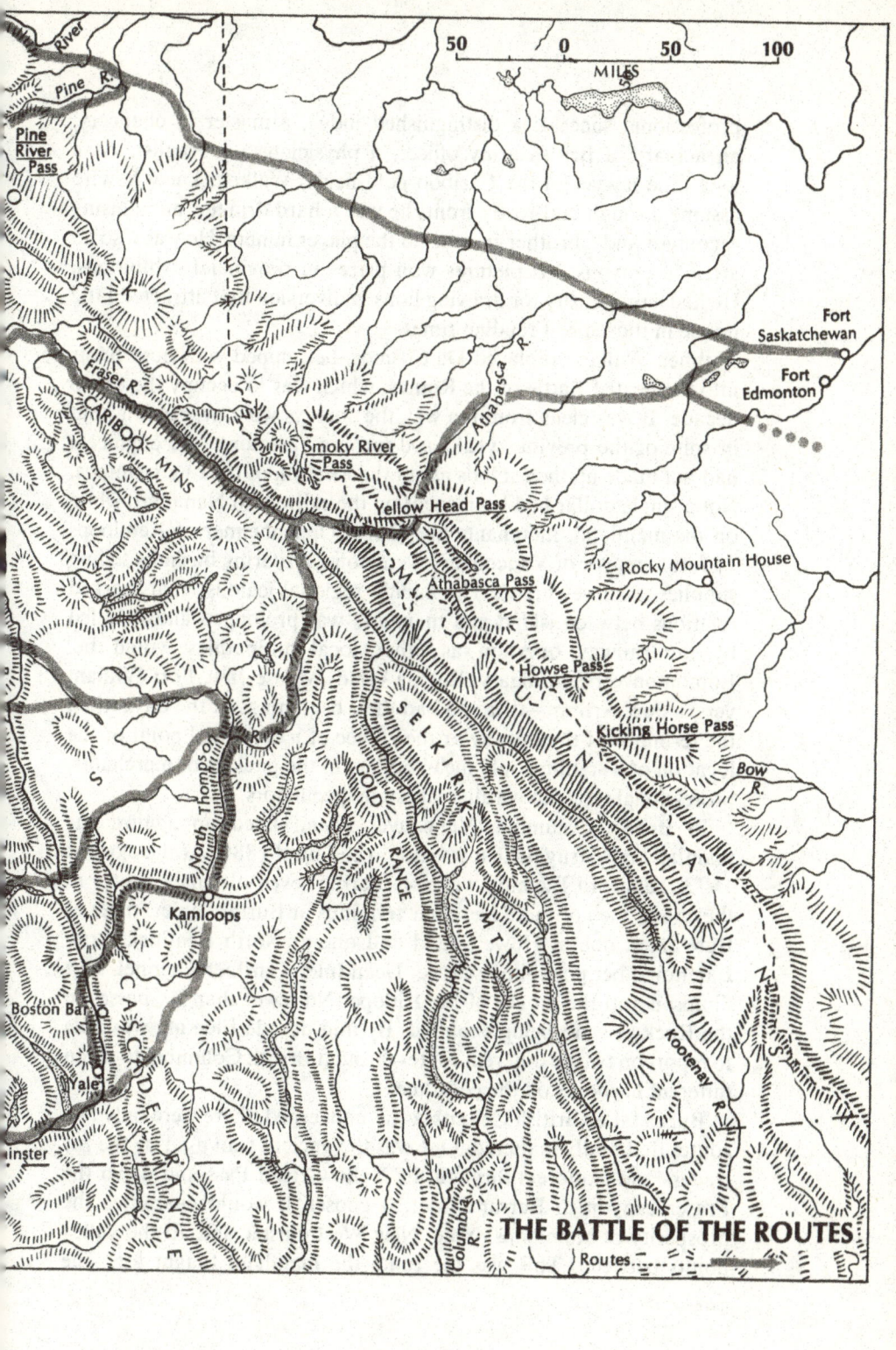

THE BATTLE OF THE ROUTES

Routes ....

Pine River Pass

Pine R.

River

Fraser R.

CARIBOO MTNS

Smoky River Pass

Yellow Head Pass

Athabasca R.

Fort Saskatchewan

Fort Edmonton

Rocky Mountain House

Athabasca Pass

Howse Pass

Kicking Horse Pass

Bow R.

SELKIRK MTNS

GOLD RANGE

North Thompson R.

Kamloops

CASCADE RANGE

Boston Bar

Yale

minster

Kootenay R.

Columbia R.

MILES
50   0   50   100

professional success: a distinguished judge, a master in chancery, an actuary, a British army officer, a physician, a journalist. As a long-time lawyer in the Cariboo gold-fields, Walkem knew how to assume a rough-and-ready front; he was a hard drinker, an amusing raconteur and a brother-in-arms to the placer miners. He was also an artist in crayons; his pictures won prizes in provincial exhibitions. He had a propensity for drawing lions, a diversion that attracted little notice in those pre-Freudian times.

When Walkem replaced De Cosmos, he jumped with both boots into the heated Battle of the Routes, which was to occupy the entire decade. It was clear from the way the surveys were proceeding that in spite of the previous year's sod-turning ceremony, the engineers had not made up their minds about the location of the CPR terminus. Not a single dollar had been spent on the railway to Nanaimo; while on the mainland, merchants like David Oppenheimer of Kamloops (a future mayor of Vancouver) were doing a roaring business selling supplies to survey crews. The intense regional jealousy that marked relations between island and mainland was prolonged and refueled by the railway question as other local antipathies would be. Edmonton versus Calgary, Regina versus Moose Jaw, Fort William versus Port Arthur – these all had their beginnings in the days when the terminus of the railway or the choice of a divisional point or the location of a station could mean dollars in the pockets of merchants, professionals and, above all, real estate speculators.

In British Columbia, Vancouver Island lined up against the mainland in a struggle that was not to end until 1880. At the close of 1873, Sandford Fleming was considering seven alternate routes to the coast. Two of these had their terminus at Burrard Inlet, three at Bute Inlet, one at Howe Sound and one at North Bentinck Arm. Later on other possibilities arose: Dean Inlet, Gardner Channel, Port Simpson and the mouth of the Kitlope. No fewer than six passes in the Rockies were being explored. By mid-decade Fleming was able to report on twelve different routes through British Columbia to seven different harbours on the coastline.

But as far as British Columbia was concerned, there were only two routes that really mattered. One was the ancient trail used by the fur traders and explorers through the Yellow Head Pass and down the Fraser canyon to Burrard Inlet; if chosen it would guarantee the prosperity of Kamloops, Yale, New Westminster and all the valley points between. This was the route the mainland fought for. The

194

other would lead probably from the Yellow Head Pass through the Cariboo country and the Chilcoten plains to the Homathco River and Bute Inlet, then leap the straits to Nanaimo and thence to Victoria; it would guarantee the prosperity of the dying gold region and the island. Walkem, a Cariboo man who knew a political issue when he saw one, opted instinctively for the Bute Inlet route.

From March 9 to May 18, 1874, Edgar did his best to negotiate with Walkem: the government could not build the railway immediately but it would prosecute the surveys energetically; it would spend an annual million and a half dollars on railway construction in the province, once the surveys were completed; and, in the meantime, it was prepared to build a wagon road and telegraph line across British Columbia. Early in April, Edgar added a sweetener: the government was also prepared to commence at once the construction of a line from Esquimalt to Nanaimo.

This pleased nobody. The islanders suspected a plot to make their line a purely local one. What was to prevent the government from scrapping both the Bute route and the causeway across the straits? The jealous mainlanders, on the other hand, felt the island was being outrageously favoured. In April, Edgar reported that "it was now quite apparent that the Local Ministers were determined to be obstructive." In May, Walkem wriggled out of the entire matter by calling Edgar's credentials into question. What authority did he have, anyway, to act as a government agent? The exasperated Edgar expostulated that Walkem and his colleagues had "recognized me as such agent almost every day for two months." It did no good. Walkem blandly stuck to his point that he had no proof that Edgar was specially accredited. This "extraordinary treatment" sent Edgar back to the East in a huff.

With Edgar thus disposed of, Walkem meant to go over Mackenzie's head to the Crown itself. He prepared to set off, memorial in hand, to see Lord Carnarvon, the delicate-featured colonial secretary, whom Disraeli called "Twitters," because he had difficulty coming to a decision. In this instance, Carnarvon was uncharacteristically expeditious. Briefed in advance by British Columbia's agent-general in London, he did not bother to wait for Walkem. He telegraphed to Ottawa on June 17 that he was prepared personally to arbitrate the dispute between British Columbia and the Canadian government.

The time was not far off when the very whisper of the Colonial Office interfering in the domestic affairs of an independent dominion would raise the hackles of the least sensitive of politicians. Certainly Mackenzie's immediate instinct was to reject the offer. He telegraphed a rebuff of "the curtest description," in Carnarvon's pained phrase. Dufferin, who was on a fishing trip at the time, after being "cooped up for nine consecutive months," apologized for the stonemason's characteristic bluntness; had he been in Ottawa, he hastened to assure Carnarvon, his first minister's reply "would have been couched in different terms."

These ruffled feelings were scarcely soothed when Walkem appeared on the horizon, like Cogeia's comet, which was that month clearly visible in the sky. He saw Mackenzie and there was a cursory attempt to reach an agreement. When the Prime Minister asked Walkem to put his proposals on paper, the British Columbia premier replied with "a very hostile memorandum," and that was that. Walkem steamed off to London where Carnarvon, briefed by his prolific vice-regal correspondent in Ottawa regarding the Premier's "intellectual frailties," saw him in early August and renewed his offer of arbitration.

"I am having a terrible fight with my government," Dufferin informed him a month later. The Governor General wanted Mackenzie to accept Carnarvon's offer but he was meeting resistance. In Parliament, the Prime Minister's supporters were blaming him because the Edgar offer was too liberal. Dufferin, who liked to have a finger in every political pie, kept on with his terrible fight. In all the long negotiations with British Columbia over the railway one gets the impression that Dufferin, in spite of his protests, his letters of exasperation ("People lie so much in this country," he complained in July) and his knockdown battles with his ministry, was enjoying himself hugely. He was a dynamic and positive man, a veteran of twenty years of public service. He had been under-secretary for India and under-secretary for war in the Conservative cabinet. Now he had a role which certainly flattered his social position (though he would have much preferred to have been Viceroy of India) but frustrated his desire for direct action. A governor general had a little more leeway in those days than in later years and Dufferin took all the leeway he was allowed to – more than any other vice-regal appointee; but when it came to decision-making, he could only advise, he could not command.

In the end, the harassed Mackenzie, to his later regret, gave in and with the greatest reluctance accepted Lord Carnarvon's offer of arbitration. "From what I hear," Lord Dufferin wrote, "Mr. Walkem will make no difficulties, and will hurry back to British Columbia across the bridge of gold we have built for him with the greatest expedition." The "Carnarvon Terms," which were to become a rallying cry in British Columbia, were remarkably similar to those proposed by Edgar: the island line would be built, the surveys would be pushed, and when the CPR began the government promised to spend at least two millions a year on its construction. In return, the province accepted an extension of the deadline to December 31, 1890.

Now the stoic stonemason, who had forborne to cry out under physical pressure, began to suffer under the crushing millstone of office. He was plagued with intestinal inflammation and insomnia, both the products of political tensions. "I am being driven mad with work – contractors, deputations and so on," he told Edgar early in 1874. "Last night I was in my office until I was so used up I was unable to sleep." A year later he was still driving himself: "The machine won't stop . . . I'll drive it whatever may betide if it should cost me my life. . . ." By 1876 the crunch of office caused him to cry out in a letter to Luther Holton about "a burden of care, the terrible weight of which presses me to the earth." The railway – the terrible railway – a dream not of his invention, a nightmare by now, threatened to be his undoing. On one side he felt the pull of the upstart province on the Pacific, holding him to another man's bargain – a bargain which his honour told him he must make an honest stab at fulfilling. On the other, he felt the tug of the implacable Blake, the rallying point for the anti-British Columbia sentiment and a popular alternative as Prime Minister.

Among the flaming maples of Aurora, north of Toronto, that October of 1874, the rebellious Blake, who had left the Cabinet on the eve of Edgar's mission, delivered himself of the decade's most discussed public speech. In a section devoted to railway policy he dismissed British Columbia as "a sea of mountains," charged that it would cost thirty-six million dollars to blast a railway through it and declared the annual maintenance would be so costly that "I doubt much if that section can be kept open after it is built."

He met the growing threats of separation from across the mountains head on: "If under all the circumstances, the Columbians should say – you must go on and finish this railway according to the terms or take the alternative of releasing us from the Confederation, I would take the alternative!"

That was exactly what the audience of hard-pressed farmers wanted to hear. They cheered him to the skies.

"They won't secede," Blake continued, sardonically. "They know better. Should they leave the Confederation, the Confederation would survive and they would lose their money."

A ripple of laughter at the expense of the greedy British Columbians rolled up from the crowd. But on the far side of the divisive mountain rampart, the name of Blake became anathema – the symbol of the unfeeling East.

It was, of course, as illogical that Blake should be out of the Cabinet as it was dangerous; Mackenzie knew he must be lured back. Blake was willing but he had a price. A constitutional purist, he was totally incapable of the kind of political legerdemain which, in 1871, had caused a fictitious population explosion in British Columbia. In Aurora, he had made it clear that the Edgar proposals were the extreme limit; it was that or separation. But, under the Carnarvon Terms, the government was raising the stakes by an annual half million! This was too much; Mackenzie would have to backtrack. Mackenzie did: he added a hedge to the terms; they would be carried out *only* if that could be done without increasing taxes.

Macdonald, as Mackenzie liked to remind the House, had made a similar pledge at the outset. But Macdonald's plan at that time had been to build the line in one single effort and pay for it through the sale and subsidy of the prairie lands, which he believed would be quickly taken up. Mackenzie was forced to build the railroad piecemeal as a public work through a series of tendered contracts for which the government would foot the bill in cash. If this was to be done without raising taxes, the pace of construction was certain to be sluggish.

In March, 1875, Mackenzie introduced a bill to provide for the construction of the Esquimalt-Nanaimo line, making it clear that it was not an integral part of the CPR but a compensation for extending the time limit. The following month the Senate threw the measure out and the Carnarvon Terms lay in shreds. His opponents saw in this the fine hand of Edward Blake, two of whose supporters in the Senate had, in a close vote, opposed the bill. An alarmed Edgar informed Blake of the reaction from British Columbia: Dewdney had reported that "annexation to the U.S. is talked on all sides."

Edgar was one of several prominent Liberals whom Mackenzie asked to reason with Blake. Finally, with the "no taxation" pledge made, the moody lawyer re-entered the Cabinet in May as Minister of Justice. Together, he and the Prime Minister worked out a compromise offer to British Columbia. In lieu of the island railway, the government was prepared to pay the province $750,000. But the order-in-council was not worded that way. The money was to be advanced, it said, "for any delays which may take place in the construction of the Canadian Pacific Railway." There was that word again – *delays*! British Columbia had had nothing but delays and now the government was practically promising more and offering hush money to boot. It was not money Victoria wanted: it would have to share that with the rest of the province. The island railway, on the other hand, would keep all the prosperity on the western side of the Strait of Georgia. The railway must be built. Early in 1876, the province rejected the offer and threatened secession.

Public opinion in the rest of Canada had by this time swung solidly behind Blake and Mackenzie. Dufferin wrote to London that "John Macdonald himself and his friends are of the same way of thinking." The general attitude was best reflected later that year by J. W. Bengough's cartoon in the *Canadian Illustrated News*, entitled "British Columbia in a Pet." It showed Mackenzie ("Uncle Aleck") promising a frowning lady ("Miss B. Columbia") that "you'll have your railway by and by," to which the lady replies: "I want it now. You promised I should have it, and if I don't, I'll complain to Ma."

An order-in-council, dated March 13, 1876, defended the Government's position. Mackenzie could not refrain from adding a few intemperate phrases. The order contained references to "the appalling obligations" to which the country was committed and talked about "avoiding disaster from a premature announcement and a reckless prosecution of the Pacific Railway." These inflammatory statements fed the fires of secession in British Columbia.

In April, Parliament embodied in its act of supply the taxation declaration that Blake insisted upon and it was a measure of its popularity that it passed by a vote of 149 to 10. Only the island members, headed by that "dogmatic dog," De Cosmos, voted against it.

The Government of Canada had resolved to go its own way in the matter of the railway and to stop trying to conciliate British Columbia. If that meant separation, so be it.

2

"The horrid B.C. business" Frederick Temple Blackwood, Viscount Clandeboye and Earl of Dufferin, was once again chafing with inactivity. Life in Ottawa he found so irksome that he filled his evenings reading his way through Plutarch's *Lives* in the original tongue. He longed to get away, not on a fishing trip this time, but on a voyage of conciliation for which he felt his undoubted gifts as a diplomat superbly qualified him. In short, he wanted to go out to British Columbia to soothe ruffled feelings – and in a double capacity, as both a spokesman of the federal government and an agent for the Colonial Secretary.

Mackenzie, Blake and Cartwright, the Liberal Minister of Finance, greeted His Excellency's proposal with something akin to terror – at least that was the word the Governor General used. The idea of the Queen's representative, especially *this* Queen's representative, plunging into the most delicate problem in Canadian dominion politics did not make them rest easily. The British Columbia government had already shown a propensity to grasp at straws. What straws would Dufferin unwittingly offer them? He loved making speeches; he made them on every possible occasion. He would undoubtedly make speeches all over British Columbia. His speeches were full of Irish blarney and could be calculated to butter up his listeners to the point of embarrassment. Macdonald, on first acquaintance, had found the new Governor General "rather too gushing for my taste." He could, said Macdonald, stand a good deal of flattery, "but he lays it on rather too thick." Would that flattery unwittingly inflate the expectations of the people to the point where a revival of understanding would be more impossible than ever? The three called on the Governor General on May 26 and "there ensued a long and very disagreeable discussion." Finally, it was agreed that Dufferin would make a state visit to British Columbia but would maintain the traditional vice-regal attitude of strict neutrality.

The Governor General and his handsome countess went by rail to San Francisco and there embarked by naval vessel for the "nest of hornets." Her Ladyship kept a journal, which was subsequently published, complete with sketches by her husband. They debarked from H.M.S. *Amethyst* at Esquimalt harbour on August 16, 1876, and drove through the streets of Victoria, cheered on by the entire populace – canoe-loads of Indians, Chinese in pigtails, Cariboo miners, scores of little girls in private-school uniforms, old Hudson's Bay hands and, most of all, hundreds of loyal English men and women – retired army officers, former civil servants, newly arrived immigrants. A company of archers, magnificently attired in green, rode out of an adjacent wood and acted as escort. They were shortly joined by a band of horsemen, red ribbons across their breasts, and then another company of green-clad soldiers and several bands and various detachments of militia and an army of small boys, each carrying a brightly coloured flag, and three hundred Indians selected from twelve tribes. All these and more accompanied the long train of carriages which conveyed the Governor General, his entourage and the leading citizens on a two and a half hour parade through the centre of town towards Government House, where one hundred young ladies were waiting to strew the ground with flowers.

The noble figure in the carriage, acknowledging the cheers that engulfed him, had just turned fifty and was still devilishly handsome. Such was his profile that, save for the short, dark beard on his chin, he might have posed, in a later era, for an Arrow Collar ad. There was a certain haughtiness to the tilt of his head for he was not without vanity. Long before the applause meter was invented he had devised a literary method of achieving the same effect: he used to send out verbatim reports of his speeches to the press, with bracketed phrases, such as "Prolonged applause," "Great laughter," "Cries of Hear! Hear!" inserted in the appropriate places. When reading a Dufferin speech, one gets an impression of near pandemonium. But they were good speeches for all of that, the sentences nicely turned, the local allusions graceful. Dufferin, after all, came from the best literary stock. His mother – hers was the Sheridan side of his family – wrote ballads; his aunt was a poet and singer. He himself had produced an amusing book of travel. A product of the British class system, Eton and Oxford educated, he knew all the titled families of England, but he also hobnobbed with Tennyson, Browning and Dickens.

Coming as a stranger to the new nation, he was able to see Canada whole and not as a loose collection of self-centred and often antagonistic communities. The petty provincialism of the Canadians bothered him and he tried, throughout his term and not unsuccessfully, to encourage in them a feeling of national pride. It is to Lord Dufferin that Canada owes two great national tourist attractions. Thanks to him, the city of Quebec was persuaded to retain its ancient walls; the terrace that bears his name is one result. And it was he who made the first suggestion that the area around Niagara Falls be preserved as a national park and not a sideshow.

In Victoria, Dufferin, the instant nationalist, was dismayed to find no flicker of national feeling. The island town was in every sense a little bit of Old England, a condition that might one day be a tourist asset but was, in the situation of 1876, a threat to Confederation. Most of the residents had been born in Britain and "like all middle class Englishmen, have a vulgar contempt for everything that is not English." The mentality was still that of a Crown Colony. The Victorians sent their wages home to the old country, referred to themselves as "English" and spoke of "Canadians" as if they came from a foreign land. Indeed, it had been their custom, at least until Confederation, to allude to Canadians as "white Chinamen" – aliens or adventurers. Dufferin discovered that officers of the Dominion sent across the mountains were seen in the same light as the carpetbaggers in the American South. The bitterness against the East was all-embracing: "The perfidy with which they consider themselves to have been treated has filled the entire community with a sentiment of genuine contempt for everything and everybody East of the Rocky Mountains," the Governor General noted.

Not only did Victoria consider itself separate and distinct from Canada, but it also considered itself apart from the rest of the province. A secret society, the Carnarvon Club, was forming; one of its members was the son of Sir James Douglas, first governor of the colony. The club, in effect, advocated total separation from the mainland since the only alternative it would accept was the total fulfilment of the Carnarvon Terms. The mainland had no intention of consenting to those since it would mean adoption of the Bute Inlet route.

During Dufferin's triumphal tour through the streets of Victoria, the vice-regal carriage approached an arch on which the motto "Carnarvon Terms or Separation" was inscribed. Dufferin would have preferred to ignore it but the handsome new lieutenant-governor, Albert Norton Richards, insisted on pointing it out, much to the Governor General's dismay. Richards, an Upper Canadian, who had been only five years in British Columbia, was a strong nationalist and as such was reviled and execrated in the capital city. "An obscure wire puller" the *Daily Standard* had called him on his appointment the previous month. Dufferin was chagrined to discover that he had to struggle to get the townspeople to accord to Richards the precedence his position demanded. "His appointment is bitterly resented as a social insult and he himself is denounced as a carpetbagger," Dufferin remarked. He himself did not think too highly of the new lieutenant-governor, whose brother was Chief Justice of Canada. This man was "far inferior to him in every respect," faulty in both his manner and his personal appearance. And now his gaucheries were about to force an embarrassing incident, on the very first day!

Dufferin, sighing inwardly, ordered the carriage to a halt, called for the reception committee and proceeded to make one of his ingenious little diplomatic speeches: "Gentlemen, I will go under your beautiful arch on one condition. I won't ask you to do much; I beg but a trifling favour. I only ask that you allow me to suggest a slight change in the phrase you have set up. I merely ask you to alter one letter in your motto. Turn the S into an R – make it 'Carnarvon Terms or Reparation' and I'll gladly pass under it."

It was a measure of the popular feeling that the stubborn Victorians refused. There was, indeed, an attempt made to force the carriage forward under the arch but it wheeled around in the nick of time, whereupon, as Lady Dufferin confided to her journal, one man "jumped about as if he were mad, and when he met us above the arch he jumped again and shrieked, 'Three groans for Mackenzie.' "

There were other arches – at least twenty in Victoria alone – for this was a period of arches and processions in Canada. There were Roman arches and Gothic arches and parabolic arches, arches made entirely of evergreens (Johnson Street was a veritable avenue of verdure) and arches of sturdy Douglas fir. The Chinese had erected three arches in the shape of pagodas, one of which bore the wistful legend "British Laws Are Just"; not far away another arch read "Chinese Must Go," erected by those who wanted to ban all Orientals from the province, just laws or no. Under this arch, too, Dufferin refused to travel. But most of the arches on that sparkling August day dealt with the question of the moment: "Our Railway Iron Rusts" . . . "Confederated without Confederation" . . . "Railroad, the Bond of Union" . . . "The Iron Horse, the Civilizer of the World" . . . "Carnarvon Terms" . . . "United without Union." The Governor General could scarcely avoid getting the message. One of the first things that met his eye was a huge inscription: "Welcome to Our Sea of Mountains."* Everywhere, the references to Blake were pointed and vituperative.

*Though the British Columbians blamed Blake for this smear, it was actually the *British Colonist* that first spoke of the route through which the railway would run as "a sea of mountains."

Dufferin's preconceived notions about the greed of British Columbians ("we may take it for granted, I think, that the spending of money in their neighbourhood and not the Railway is the real thing to which the British Columbia people look") were largely confirmed in the remarkable week that followed. Day after day, beginning at nine in the morning and continuing without interruption until seven that night, the representative of the Queen found himself receiving delegation after delegation to discuss the most controversial question in the country. There had never been anything quite like it before and there could never be anything like it again. He saw, in his own words, "every single soul in the place." He saw the little ex-premier, Walkem, who had gone down to defeat ("he and all his family have a worldwide reputation for lying"); and he saw the new premier, A. C. Elliott, "a Dublin lawyer, respectable, but I should say of no more than respectable ability, a perfect gentleman, moderate and anxious to go as far as he dare in composing the dispute with Canada, but as he is member for Victoria he cannot afford to be behind his opponents in fighting for Victorian interests."

At night there were social functions without let up; whist with the gigantic chief justice, Matthew Baillie Begbie, serenades by choruses of young girls, a "drawing-room" at the Legislative Buildings, garden parties, dinners, concerts, theatre, canoe races. By the end of the week, the Governor General was beside himself. He had not even had time to attend to his personal dispatches. His private secretary, the Hon. E. G. D. Littledon, handled them for him. "Lord Dufferin," he wrote, in a postscript to a letter to Mackenzie, "bids me add that he finds great difficulty in keeping his temper with these foolish people." It was understandable. At that point, the Governor General had spent seven days, ten full hours a day, "listening to the same old story, abuse of Mackenzie, of Canada, of Sir John Macdonald and the absolute necessity of bringing the Pacific Railway via Bute Inlet to Esquimalt."

But then, Victoria was literally fighting for its life. The depression had dealt the community a blow more staggering than that which the rest of the country had suffered. The economy, which had been based largely on the wild spending of the Cariboo gold miners, was grinding slowly to a halt, yet the cost of living remained astronomical since all the provender from Europe and eastern America had to be shipped around the Horn and up the long western coastline of two continents.

Now this isolated English village with a total population of 5,000 – and only 950 voters – saw its chance, and its only remaining chance, to rival San Francisco as the great port of the Pacific. The superb naval harbour, the mooted drydock at Esquimalt, the rich Nanaimo coal-fields, the shorter distance to the Orient – all these could be bound together into one enormous asset if only the railway could be made to span the channels of the strait. But without the terminus Victoria could never become the major metropolis of British Columbia.

"In Victoria," Lord Dufferin reported to Lord Carnarvon, "the one idea of every human being is to get the railway to Esquimalt. It is upon this chance that the little town must depend for its future . . . most of its inhabitants have wildly speculated in town lots. . . . You can therefore imagine the phrensied [sic] eagerness with which Victoria grasps at every chance of making itself the terminus of the great transcontinental railway."

When he reached the mainland, it was the same story. "The location of the Canadian Pacific Railway, and its terminus along such a line, and on such a spot as may enhance the value of his own individual town lot, or in some other way may put money into his pocket, by passing as near as possible to where he lives, is the common preoccupation of every Columbian citizen."

Again in New Westminster it was arches all the way; the messages pushed for the Fraser Valley route. "Speed the Railway," one arch read, and above, a little model train tooted back and forth. At Yale, Dufferin's gaze rested on a horse whose blanket bore the inscription: "Good But Not Iron."

"Here also," he wrote, "the same intense longing to become the terminus of the railway possesses the people." The entire population along the Fraser and North and South Thompson rivers shared the same desire; only the Cariboo miners remained indifferent. But the merchants who lived among them, ex-Victorians all, were entirely partisan. Though the large majority of the mainland population was anti-Victorian, the Nanaimo–Victoria–Cariboo alliance gave the Victoria interests a parliamentary majority of something like fifteen to ten.

Dufferin was given the grand tour of British Columbia: the fantastic corduroy road to the Cariboo, perched on the rim of the Fraser canyon; the Indians scooping salmon out of the frothing gorge from rickety platforms; the old diggings at Boston Bar; the curious native houses; the great trees, twelve feet thick, severed by axemen; the goggle-eyed totem poles at Alert Bay – he and his countess were introduced to all these wonders. The Governor General took the trouble to visit Bute Inlet about which he had heard so much. He was dismayed by the precipices which rose from the ocean and by the bad anchorage at Waddington Harbour. He did not respond with any greater enthusiasm to two other fiords, farther to the north, also being considered as possible termini: Dean Inlet and the Gardner Channel. The mouths of both, he learned, would probably be stuffed with ice all winter.

He had found much less bitterness on the mainland: very little abuse of the government, though some denunciation of the island railway. When he returned to Victoria he was privately convinced that the Fraser Valley route offered many advantages over the island's choice – an opinion he was to push at Ottawa. Actually, he could see no reason for anything more than a cheap local line for years to come, on a route which would make use of water as well as rail transportation. But he did not say that in his farewell speech on the island. In a highly successful address that occupied two and a quarter hours, interrupted by much applause, he soothed the Victorians as best he could, pointing out that the passes in the Rockies were not yet fully surveyed, that the railway could not be started until the engineers had done their work, and that construction would soon commence. He even spoke favourably of the Bute Inlet route. Then, with the cheers of his audience still ringing in his ears, His Excellency took his leave.

In spite of the constant pressure upon him, he returned to Ottawa with considerable sympathy for the British Columbians. He had the feeling – he expressed it before his departure – that Mackenzie, pushed by Blake and Cartwright, was trying to wriggle out of his commitments. On his return that feeling was reinforced. There is a revealing tale about his arrival in the capital: at the Ottawa railway station he was presented with an address of welcome by the Mayor and Council and here, in the presence of some of his ministers (it was said), he went so far as to make a speech which some thought reflected on Government policy. Within a few hours the word that the Cabinet had been repudiated by the Governor General was all over Ottawa. There was only one verbatim report of His Excellency's remarks – so the story has it – and George Holland, an able reporter, was rapidly transcribing it in the office of the Ottawa *Citizen*. In the midst of his labour, Holland received a message: the Governor General would be interested in having a copy of his speech. Holland cheerfully obliged. At Government House, an affable Dufferin asked casually what system of shorthand Holland used; he explained that he himself read shorthand fairly well. Flattered, the reporter produced his notes. Dufferin looked them over carefully, made a pretty compliment about the clarity of their style and then pocketed both the original notes and the transcribed speech. The matter, said Dufferin gravely, was too important to be settled hastily; would the journalist join him for lunch the following day? Between the two of them they could put the speech into shape for publication. Holland agreed, but asked for his notebook back. Ah, said His Excellency, that would be impossible; he was not accustomed to exerting himself so soon after a long journey. The journalist left empty handed. The next day, the Governor General, still in possession of the notes, persuaded him to publish an innocuous report without reference to his objectionable remarks. Thus was a political crisis nipped in the bud.

There was another crisis to come. In November, the "horrid B.C. business," as Lord Dufferin was to call it, touched off an extraordinary scene at Rideau Hall. Here, for the first and only time in Canadian history, a governor general and his two chief advisers came perilously close to fisticuffs.

Dufferin had returned from the West convinced that Lord Carnarvon should re-enter the picture. Why not have a representative of each government meet in London under the Colonial Secretary's auspices and make a decision about the island railway, which Victoria continued to claim was part of the main line of the CPR and which Mackenzie insisted was a local project divorced from the transcontinental route? Later, Dufferin suggested raising the $750,000 offered in lieu of the line to an even million: "I don't think it would be ill-spent in getting this troublesome matter out of the way." Any reasonable sacrifice was worth while, if Confederation was at stake.

On Saturday, November 18, Dufferin met with Blake and Mackenzie at Rideau Hall. Both men were obdurate. Mackenzie obviously regretted that he had ever consented to the British colonial office's interference in Canada's domestic affairs. Blake was immovable. Carnarvon, he said, had written a dispatch approving $750,000 as a fair and legitimate offer; the payment was to be made on the understanding that British Columbia accepted the qualification about no tax increases. This was not strictly true and now Dufferin completely lost his temper "and told them both in very harsh language

what I thought of their principle of interpreting public documents."
The interview, he reported to Carnarvon, was stormy and disagreeable. They "nearly came to blows ... Mackenzie's aspect was simply
pitiable and Blake was on the point of crying as he very readily does
when he is excited."

The day after this extraordinary encounter, everybody cooled
off. Dufferin agreed not to send the 180-page dispatch he had so
laboriously composed for Lord Carnarvon though he could not quite
bring himself to consign it to the fire. There were expressions of regret
and mutual respect all round and a kind of face-saving formula was
evolved in which the matter was hoisted for eighteen months until the
surveys could be completed and a route fixed; failing that, Mackenzie
cautiously agreed to some sort of London meeting under Carnarvon's
auspices.

With that, the importunate Dufferin had to be content. He had
pushed his ministers as hard as any governor general could or ever
would; he undoubtedly felt he had been successful; but the hard fact
was that he had battered his noble head against an unyielding wall
of granite.

3

The By 1877, the Battle of the Routes had reached the stage of a pamphlet
Battle of war – that tried and true propaganda technique of the Victorian Age.
the Routes Print and paper were cheap and pamphlets could be issued as swiftly
as a newspaper. Advocates of burning causes duelled with tracts as
they had, in earlier times, duelled with swords. In the Battle of the
Routes, the adversaries attacked each other with blizzards of paper.

One of the pamphleteers was the federal member for Yale, British
Columbia, Edgar Dewdney, a massive surveyor with flaring side
whiskers who liked to appear in public in fringed buckskin. Dewdney
was perhaps the most powerful advocate of the Fraser River–Burrard
Inlet route. It was he who at a public meeting charged that the
Burrard route had been abandoned because Marcus Smith was
caught in a blizzard in the Fraser canyon in 1874 and had to trudge
forty miles through the snow on foot. In a letter to Mackenzie, read
at the meeting, Dewdney urged the Prime Minister "not to be guided
by a single circumstance of this kind."

Early in 1877, a New Westminster writer signing himself "Old Settler" wrote to *The Times* of London attacking the "bitterness and selfishness of Victorians" for trying to appropriate the terminus "so that their lands and town lots and speculative purchases may be made to return $20. for $1.00." This produced an immediate answer in the form of a pamphlet titled *A British North American Reply to a Letter of "Old Settler."* Then Fraser Tolmie, a member of the provincial legislature for Victoria, wrote an interminable series of letters to the *Colonist* dealing with harbours and anchorages. All of these were subsequently churned out on the paper's steam presses in pamphlet form. The pamphlet, which one suspects was preaching to the converted, attacked both Dewdney and Old Settler and advocated the Bute Inlet route for scientific reasons. Even the British Columbia government joined the pamphlet war with a publication of all the correspondence relating to the controversy.

And still Fleming had not settled on a final choice for a pass through the Rockies or a terminus along the coastline or a route in between. Some of this apparent dallying had to do with the nature of the country itself, but much of it was clearly political procrastination. In the late fall of 1875, Richard Cartwright, the Minister of Finance, had written Mackenzie a pointed letter regarding the restive Carnarvon's doubts about the Government's flexible interpretation of his arbitration award. "But," said Cartwright, "he is willing to hold his peace until he is driven into a ·corner and we had better leave the matter so for the present especially as the contingency is not likely to arise unless your surveys were *very promptly* closed indeed." The italics are Cartwright's and the inference is clear: it was in the Government's interest to keep the surveys going.

Sandford Fleming's own opinions in his massive report of 1877 are clouded in ambiguity. By 1875 there was a general understanding that Bute Inlet would probably be the terminus rather than Burrard. Engineering interest in the latter harbour cooled. Then, in November of 1876, it occurred to Fleming, rather tardily, that the Admiralty might be asked its opinion of the various harbours along the coast. Fleming sent along twenty-eight questions about eight different harbours on the mainland. The answers varied somewhat but the overwhelming opinion of the seamen was in favour of Burrard Inlet. Admiral de Horsey, the naval commandant at Esquimalt, who favoured Bute Inlet was, Lord Dufferin suspected, "very much under the influence of Mr. Marcus Smith."

Fleming still could not make up his mind. A discussion of the anchorage at Bute Inlet was, he said, irrelevant since the real terminus would be on the island. On the other hand, the cost of bridging the channel was "unprecedented in magnitude." On the *other* hand, Fleming rationalized, British Columbia would some day be a rich province. "The exigencies of the future may render a continuous line of railway to the outer shore of Vancouver [Island] indispensable at any cost."

Fleming was treading on eggshells. His appreciation of Burrard Inlet as a terminus was equally vacillating. On the one hand, it was more expensive to build than the Bute Inlet route. On the other hand, it was "the route of the greatest advantage to the population." On the *other* hand, on a cost-of-transportation basis, it stood fifth on the list of projected lines.

Summing up, Fleming wrote that the Bute Inlet route was the only one open for selection "if it be considered of paramount importance to carry an unbroken line of railway to . . . Vancouver Island.

"If, on the other hand, the object be to reach the navigable waters of the Pacific simply by the most eligible line," then the Fraser Valley–Burrard Inlet route was preferable.

Fleming was scarcely telling the politicians anything they did not already know. What he was really saying was that the decision was now theirs to make. In case they could not make up their minds, he had a suggestion. There was another, perhaps better, choice at the mouth of the Skeena River, a harbour five hundred miles closer to the Orient than the other two. The Admiralty's experts had dismissed it but "their opinions are expressed guardedly, for the reason that no proper or laudable surveys have been made there as yet." Curiously, the one naval objection to Burrard Inlet also applied to the harbour at the Skeena's mouth: both were very nearly within cannon shot of United States territory, Burrard being in the shadow of San Juan Island and the northerly harbour nudging the Alaska panhandle. But the latter demurral did not seem to occur to anybody.

Even after Admiral de Horsey, the following October, dismissed the Skeena harbour as "totally unfit for the Ocean Terminus," Fleming in his cautious way refused to eliminate the northern route: "The Government should, I think, have something more, if possible, than an opinion, however strongly expressed . . . it would be desirable to have on the record data sufficient to enable anyone to judge . . . the propriety of completely rejecting a northern terminus. . . ." In short, more surveys – and more surveys there were.

Fleming, at this time, was an absentee engineer-in-chief. He was a robust man who thought nothing of warding off a bear with an umbrella or unrolling his blankets in two feet of snow, as he had done on his twenty-fourth birthday, but by 1876, in his fiftieth year, he was exhausted. A Fifeshire Calvinist, who prayed aloud on the tops of mountain peaks, he had as a boy copied out a maxim from *Poor Richard's Almanack*: "Dost thou love life? Then do not squander time, for that is the stuff life is made of." Fleming loved life; he held gay parties in Ottawa and was perfectly prepared to join in an Indian dance in the wilds, a wolfskin draped over his head; he was fond of champagne and kept it by the case in his office; he loved rich food – oysters were a favourite; and he certainly did not believe in squandering time. Between 1871 and 1876 he held down two man-killing jobs: he was chief engineer of both the Intercolonial and the Canadian Pacific. Thus he could devote only half of his working day to the transcontinental line. He had taken the second job reluctantly and at no extra pay, because that would have meant a total salary higher than that received by the cabinet minister over him. "I . . . felt the weight of responsibilities that were thrown upon me and I laboured day and night in a manner that will never be known," he told Charles Tupper. After all, Poor Richard had said: ". . . the sleeping fox catches no poultry . . . there will be sleeping enough in the grave." The boy Fleming had written that down, too.

When the Intercolonial was completed in 1876, Fleming's doctors ordered a complete rest. He had suffered two accidents, one of which nearly killed him, and he was worn out. He was granted a twelve-month leave of absence and went off to England but was twice recalled by the Government, once to write the monumental 1876 report and again as a result of a hurry-up call to deal with his deputy, the bristly Marcus Smith. The leave stretched out over a two-year period.

For nineteen months, between the spring of 1876 and 1878, Fleming was absent and Marcus Smith was in his place. Smith had the job but he did not, apparently, have the authority, nor – as he bitterly complained – the salary. During his visits back to Canada, Fleming would countermand his deputy's instructions or disagree with his views. The personality clashes within the department seemed to be continual. More and more, as the months went by, Fleming and Smith failed to see eye to eye. Much of this was due to Smith's furious championing of a single railway route through British Columbia from the Pine Pass to Bute Inlet. But Smith was never an easy man to get along with. Some of Fleming's personal appointees, now working under Smith, clashed with him. James Rowan, who had been Fleming's chief assistant before Smith took over, ignored for eighteen months the letters that Smith sent out to him on the north shore of Lake Superior.

"I was obliged to detail [to the Minister] his most ungentlemanly conduct and language to me," Rowan later testified, adding that "other members of the staff have been treated in the same brutal manner in my presence."

Fleming himself said, when he finally returned in 1880, "I found my staff demoralized and many things had been allowed to drift into a state of confusion."

Smith would not give up on Bute Inlet. The obvious impracticality of a causeway across the strait had not cooled his ardour for "his" route. "I feel confident that a steamboat properly constructed could take a railway train on board and pass safely all seasons of the year from any convenient point on Bute Inlet to a good landing on Vancouver's Island, near Seymour Narrows," he wrote in an appendix to the report of 1875. Originally he had thought of the railway running to Bute Inlet through the Yellow Head Pass, which his absent chief favoured, but by 1877 there had taken shape, in the back of that mysterious mind, a preference for the Pine Pass, which Horetzky had first explored. In April of 1877, he wrote to Mackenzie, in his capacity of Minister of Public Works, asking permission to probe the pass with three survey parties; he added that he himself would like to go along. Smith pointed out that the land on both sides of the Yellow Head "is a dreary barren waste," while the Peace River country adjacent to the Pine Pass was much more promising. Mackenzie, who was trying to slash expenses in his department, turned him down, whereupon the irrepressible Smith determined to go ahead secretly without authority.

He wrote to Henry Cambie, who had replaced him as chief of surveys in British Columbia, to send Joseph Hunter to the Pine River country with two or three men and some packers. The trip was to be completely confidential: "You will understand . . . that we are not pretending to favour this route but simply extending the northern exploration from River Skeena to get a geographical knowledge of the country." Cambie was put on his guard, especially against John Robson, the former *Colonist* editor who had been appointed paymaster and chief of commissariat for the c.p.s. in British Columbia.

212

Robson "rushes everything into the *Colonist*," Smith pointed out. If Robson snooped, Cambie was simply to say that Hunter was extending his explorations of the Skeena country.

Meanwhile Smith went himself out to British Columbia and returned full of enthusiasm for the Peace River country. In October he warned Hunter, from Victoria, to continue to keep his mouth shut: "I have simply to ask you to give no opinion about your work to anybody but bluff them off with *chaff*." Smith's tour of British Columbia took on some of the aspects of a political campaign. Two years later, Robson told Mackenzie that one reason he had lost votes in the province was "the insolence of Marcus Smith, who in passing through the district in the fall of 1877 everywhere and most industriously spoke of your railway policy as shuffling, bumbling, declaring that you had really not the slightest intention of going on with the work in British Columbia and predicting very positively the return to power of the Conservatives, the only men, he said, from whom Columbia could hope for a railway – statements which coming from such a source were *bound* to have considerable influence. . . ."

Smith now accelerated his behind-the-scenes manoeuvres to get "his" route approved. On December 7, he wrote to Hunter that Mackenzie and Dufferin were "moving Heaven and Earth" to get the Fraser River–Burrard Inlet route adopted. He instructed Hunter that the time had arrived for him to leak some information to the press about his Pine Pass explorations *"but not official information on my authority."* Hunter was to allow himself to be pumped into describing the country which he had explored, but was not to give an opinion about the route. With this letter, Smith enclosed a release marked "For the press" and headed "PACIFIC RAILWAY ROUTE." It began: "Notwithstanding that the matter has been kept very quiet, it has leaked out that the explorations of the acting Engineer-in-Chief, Marcus Smith, from the East, and Mr. Hunter, from the West, last summer have been most successful." The press release went on to say that the Fertile Belt continued right to the foot of the Pine Pass, that the pass itself was shorter and lower than the Yellow Head and that it would connect most favourably with Bute Inlet.

The same day Smith wrote to Dr. John Sebastian Helmcken, a prominent Victoria politician, son-in-law of Sir James Douglas and one of the original British Columbia delegates to Ottawa during confederation negotiations. Helmcken, like everyone else, had been speculating in land and was a strong advocate of the Bute Inlet route. Smith warned him against raising a public clamour for an immediate start on the railway; if he did, the Burrard Inlet route would certainly be accepted, but if matters could be delayed, Smith was sure his own views would prevail. After all, Admiral de Horsey had approved the Bute Inlet route. "Mackenzie and Dufferin are furious and wish to prevent the Report reaching the British Government" – Mackenzie, indeed, had thrown it away in a rage – but he, Marcus Smith, would send a report of his own and then "I feel certain that no company under the sun will construct a line by the Yellow Head Pass and Fraser and that none dare attempt it without incurring certain destruction." In closing, Smith suggested that Helmcken also let the press know about Hunter's explorations.

An accomplished intriguer himself, Smith was a man who saw dark plots and sinister motives everywhere he went. He lived in a cloak-and-dagger world of the mind in which he imagined himself desperately staving off, at great personal and financial risk, the sombre forces or treason and corruption.

"I see now that the storm is going to burst as regards myself," he wrote to Fleming on December 7, 1877 (it was his third letter on the subject that day). "At Victoria, I found out about this Burrard Inlet mania, which is a huge land job in which the Minister and his friends are concerned – the latter certainly are from the Lieutenant Governor downwards. It was first started by Lord Dufferin in 1876 while you were in England and I was away north of Lake Superior. His Excellency was much amazed at not succeeding in gaining the leading men of Victoria over to his views – that is to abandon the Railway and leave its carrying out to the good faith of the Canadian Government. . . ."

In Smith's dark view, the Governor General, cheated of a victory that "would help him much in his diplomatic career," promised the Burrard terminus to the mainland as an act of revenge.

Meanwhile, Henry Cambie in British Columbia had been caught up in the intrigue. Mackenzie, unable to budge Smith, had gone around him and wired direct to Cambie, a friend of Dewdney's, to commence the survey of the Fraser, which the Governor General had so urgently recommended on his return. Cambie, who was an advocate of the Fraser route to Burrard Inlet – "*crazy* about it," in Smith's contemptuous words – uneasily complied. When Smith returned from the West, he found himself snubbed by Mackenzie, who was closeted with Cambie, "pumping him, flattering him and getting him to show off his opinions."

At length, Mackenzie asked Cambie for a written report on the

Fraser. This put Cambie in a dilemma. Properly, reports should go to the Engineer-in-Chief, who would read and assess them all and then write a report of his own. Cambie was being asked to go over Smith's head. He brought his plight to the crusty Smith who gave him a fierce reception: after all, Cambie was a Burrard Inlet man and therefore the enemy. Cambie said he would much prefer to give his report to Smith but could not very well quarrel with the Minister "on account of his bread and butter." He would like to send the report through to Smith so that Smith could put his remarks on it. "I told him I would not look at it until I had a report from all my subordinates and then I would give them a dressing all round," Smith reported to Helmcken.

Smith also reported to Fleming. "I told him [Cambie] that I had been all along aware of the endeavour to favour that route to advance his own 'interests' – but I also have bread and butter to provide and I think I know how to defend myself. Of course I know the Minister can and will dismiss me and he is trying to do so at a month's notice – but I am determined *to die hard* and shall expose his tricks. The whole thing is a trick to get votes and enrich his friends."

The strange spectacle of a Cabinet minister (and Prime Minister to boot) trying to circumvent his own department head in order to obtain information from a subordinate continued all that month. Mackenzie continued to ignore Smith and meet secretly with Cambie. For the wretched Cambie, the squeeze was getting tighter. He was a bearded Tipperary Irishman, with a craggy hawk's face and a touch of brogue in his speech, privately witty, publicly grave, a pillar of the Anglican Church and an experienced engineer who had worked on both the Grand Trunk and the Intercolonial. As a Canadian Pacific surveyor he had trekked over most of British Columbia from the Homathco to the Skeena. He had been in some tight fixes in his time. Just that summer he had taken a leaky boat, caulked only with leaves, for 150 miles down the rivers of the Rocky Mountain Trench, one man bailing furiously all the way. But never had he encountered a situation fraught with such tension. Cambie kept putting off his written report to Mackenzie. Mackenzie kept demanding it. He did not, however, ask for any special report from Marcus Smith. "He shall get one nevertheless whether he likes it or no," Smith remarked, grimly.

Smith firmly believed that Cambie was being used as a tool by Fraser Valley speculators to push the Burrard route. Cambie, cross-examined by Smith, admitted that he had expressed a preference for the route but said he thought he ought to have a right to his opinions. Smith replied, with some truth, that Cambie should not be expressing opinions in public; if he had any, he should express them to his immediate superior, Smith. (Smith, of course, did not always follow his own advice.)

A few days after this confrontation, Mackenzie asked Cambie to give his written opinion of the several lines surveyed in British Columbia. Smith reported to Fleming that Cambie was in "great tribulation." All the Minister was entitled to, he told Cambie, was a brief report of the previous season's work – with *no* opinions. Smith would supply the opinions.

"I have made up my mind to take the bull by the horns and am prepared to resign my post rather than truckle to the whims or political necessities of the Government against my better judgement," Smith declared.

Cambie complied with Smith's instructions and ventured no opinion on the relative merits of the various routes proposed through British Columbia. Smith sent the report along to Mackenzie with a laconic note stating that it was "about as full and accurate as it could be in the present unfinished state of the plans." He added that he was in no position yet to make a comparative judgement on the various routes. But Mackenzie had other sources. Smith complained to Fleming that he "continues to get information secretly from private interested and irresponsible persons while he refuses to receive or suppresses all information laboriously and disinterestedly obtained by myself."

Quite clearly, the Prime Minister had settled on the Burrard route. In the *Globe*, his old mentor George Brown faithfully reflected these views. There were many reasons for Mackenzie's decision: the Admiralty report (De Horsey's demurral notwithstanding); the skilful advocacy of the mainland Members of Parliament led by Edgar Dewdney and Lieutenant-Governor Richards, which was far more temperate than the shrill carping of the islanders; Lord Dufferin's own opinion; the new surveys by Cambie; and, finally, Smith's bull-headed intransigence. The acting chief engineer had got his minister's back up. By March, 1878, Mackenzie had ceased to consult him or even speak to him.

On March 29, Smith sent in his own official report, as acting chief, on the progress of the surveys of the previous year. Predictably, he advocated the Pine Pass–Bute Inlet route, but suggested another year's delay to settle the final location of the line.

"It has apparently fallen like a thunderbolt," Smith wrote gleefully to Helmcken a month later. "It has been repeatedly asked for both in the House and Senate but kept on one excuse or another."

Smith's report presented Mackenzie with a new dilemma. He could scarcely settle on Burrard Inlet in the face of the direct and public opposition of his acting chief engineer. The islanders would pounce on that and cry foul. There was only one thing to do: without telling Marcus Smith, he sent for Fleming who, for the second time, found his sick leave in England interrupted.

Fleming returned to find his department in an uproar. Rowan complained of Smith's language and treatment of him. There were also reports that Smith had stated in public that some of the department engineers were working in collusion with railway contractors – a charge designed to infuriate the members of that proud service. Rowan reported that in Winnipeg, Smith had spent more time collecting data to be used against Fleming and Mackenzie than he had on the knotty problems connected with his own department. Smith was totally unabashed by these charges.

"He spoke to me in a way in which I had never been spoken to before by a gentleman, on several occasions," Fleming later told the public accounts committee of the House. Mackenzie determined that Smith must go. He told Fleming that he no longer had confidence in him and that he, Fleming, must no longer consider Smith an officer of the department. This resulted in a curious situation: there was the peppery Smith, still fuming away in his office, still, apparently, on the staff, but stripped of his powers.

"He did not receive his dismissal but he was as good as dismissed," Fleming later recounted, "and I was not at liberty to consult him any longer, inasmuch as he was no longer a public officer." No doubt Fleming expected Smith to resign, as he had once expected Moberly to resign, but Smith hung on stubbornly, as he had once hung on to the slippery crags of the Homathco canyon. He was more than a little paranoid by this time. He explored, in a letter to Helmcken, the possibility that Lord Dufferin had an interest in Fraser Valley land – hence his motives in "moving Heaven and Earth" in favour of the Burrard route. Smith added that Dufferin wanted another term of office as Governor General and thus would do "any dirty work for the Canadian Government if they will use their influence to get it for him."

While Smith busied himself with his correspondence – he had nothing else to do – Fleming set about writing his own report. In this he was finally forced to a conclusion: if engineering decisions alone were to govern the selection of a route, and if that selection could not be postponed further, then the Bute Inlet route should be rejected and the Burrard Inlet route selected. He left the question of a pass open. He thought there should be more extensive surveys in the region of the Peace River Pass in case it proved to be less expensive than the Yellow Head.

Fleming included Smith's report as an appendix to his own. He did not, however, reproduce Smith's map, which purported to show the comparative richness of the country surrounding the Peace. This was to become a minor *cause célèbre* and political football. "The map which formed the most valuable part of my report was cunningly suppressed so that the report was not intelligible to any but those who had some knowledge of the country," Smith later charged. To this Fleming replied that Smith was neither a botanist nor an agronomist but a surveyor; the map, showing soils and fertility, was the work of a layman and not a professional and hence had no place in the report.

On July 12, 1878, the government settled officially on the Fraser River–Burrard Inlet route and prepared to call for tenders for the construction of the railway through the dismal canyon of the Fraser. That seemed to be the end of the horrid B.C. business. It was not. Party lines had already been drawn around the opposing routes. The Pine Pass–Bute Inlet route, thanks in part to Marcus Smith's importuning, had become something of a Tory route. The Burrard route had become a Grit route. As for Smith, he was still around. Two years later, in a new job and under a new administration, he would still be, in his own eyes at least, "the *Bête Noir* of the Govt."

Chapter Six

1

The On the morning of October 9, 1877, the citizens of Winnipeg were
first awakened by an unaccustomed fanfare – the shriek of a locomotive
locomotive whistle. For the generation to follow, this would become the authentic
sound of the prairie, more familiar, more haunting, more nostalgic
than the laugh of the loon or the whine of the wind in the wolf willow.
But on this crisp October day, with the sere leaves of birch and aspen
yellowing the ground, it was something totally new. There were many
there that day who had never heard a train whistle in their lives and
for some of these, the Indians and Métis, it was as symbolic in its sad-
ness as it was for the white community in its promise.

George Ham, the western editor and raconteur who was there that
day, recalled the scene:

"A lone, blanketed Indian standing on the upper bank of the river
looked down rather disdainfully upon the strange iron thing and the
interested crowd of spectators who hailed its coming. He evinced no
enthusiasm but stoically gazed at the novel scene. What did it por-
tend? To him it might be the dread thought of the passing of the old
life of his race, the alienation of the stamping grounds of his fore-
fathers, the early extinction of their God given provider, the buffalo,
which for generations past had furnished the red man with all the
necessities of life . . . whatever he may have thought, this iron horse
actually meant that the wild, free, unrestrained life of the Indian was
nearing its end."

She was a Baldwin engine, built especially for the job, and she
bore a noble name, *The Countess of Dufferin*. She came complete
with six flat cars and a van; but she could not arrive under her own
steam. She had to be floated down the river on a flag-decked barge,
pushed by the stern-wheeler *Selkirk*, because the railway to the
boundary, which Mackenzie had been promising since 1873, was
not finished. Even if it had been, there was nothing yet on the other
side of the American border with which it could connect.

But a locomotive, even without a railway, was still a marvel and
the entire town was streaming to the dock with whistles, bells,
banners and bunting to inspect it. They gave three cheers for the
massive contractor, Joseph Whitehead, who was in charge; as a boy,
he had worked on railways in the old country when they were drawn

by horses. Then, as the barge touched the bank, they crowded aboard and began to crawl over the little black engine with the huge smokestack. Two hours later, the *Selkirk* steamed to a location below Douglas Point where a piece of track had been laid to the water's edge and here the crowds watched in awe as the little train puffed its way off the barge and ran under full steam up the bank and into St. Boniface. Whitehead, who was laying track on the line between St. Boniface and Selkirk, had imported her as a work engine. For the white community, at least, she was a promise of things to come, an end to the maddening isolation of half a century and a tangible response to the pleas for a railway, which had been issuing from the Red River since the beginning of the decade.

This isolation was real and terrible and could be translated into concrete terms. At the beginning of the decade a keg of nails, if nails were available at all, cost at least ten times as much at Red River as in Ontario – a fact of life which helps explain why Red River carts were held together with shaganappi. And it cost six shillings — more than a farmhand earned in a day – to send a letter to the old country.

The steamboats, which began to arrive on the river in the late sixties, did not appreciably lower prices save during those brief, adventurous periods when rival lines fought for control. The Hudson's Bay Company held a monopoly of the Red River traffic with its rickety *International* until one spring day in 1871 when a strange vessel loaded with 125 passengers and 115 tons of freight steamed into Fort Garry. This was the *Selkirk*, operated by James Jerome Hill, a one-eyed ex-Canadian with a razor-sharp mind now operating out of St. Paul. Hill, an omniverous reader, had discovered an old United States law which held that all goods crossing the international border from American territories into Canadian ports must be bonded. He quietly built the *Selkirk*, had her bonded and persuaded the customs officials at Pembina on the border to hold up all unbonded vessels plying the river. The *International*, in short, was legally beached and Hill had a transportation monopoly of the Red River Valley. It was said that he paid off the entire cost of constructing his new steam-boat with the profits of that first voyage.

Jim Hill had had the audacity to challenge the monopoly rule of the Hudson's Bay Company, which for two centuries had enjoyed the mastery of the North West. Donald A. Smith, the chief commissioner of the company, lost no time in fighting back. He had the *International* bonded by assigning the steamer to Norman Kittson, the respected Minnesota fur trader who was the Hudson's Bay agent in St. Paul. Then he leaped into battle with Hill.

They were evenly matched adversaries and, in many respects, remarkably alike – short, fierce-eyed, muscled men, all bone and gristle, with backgrounds crammed with adventure and romance. They knew and respected one another, having met quite by accident in exacting circumstances on the bald, snowswept prairie in February of 1870.

This scene, which took place near the Elm River, north of the United States border, was a memorable one for it marked the beginning of an association which would eventually launch the Canadian Pacific Railway company. Hill, en route to Fort Garry to investigate at first hand the Red River troubles, had made a truly terrible journey from St. Paul. First, the stage out of Breckenridge, on which he was travelling, had fought its way through gigantic drifts, the passengers shovelling out the route themselves and sleeping in the snow. Hill left the stage, hired a dog team and pushed north through the blizzard. When his Métis guide became surly, Hill drove him away at revolver point and plunged on alone. The situation grew more serious: he was sleeping out by night, running behind the dogs by day, existing on a pocketful of pemmican and tea made from melted snow. He travelled this way for eighty miles until he reached Pembina. Here he hired another guide and pressed on towards Fort Garry. On his way across the white wastes of the southern Manitoba prairie he suddenly beheld, emerging from the curtain of swirling snow, the vague outline of another dog team coming south. Its passenger was Donald A. Smith, en route to eastern Canada by way of St. Paul, to report to Ottawa on his successful mediation in the Red River Rebellion; he had, among other things, bribed Louis Riel into exile with three thousand dollars of his own money and one thousand of the government's.

The scene deserves to be preserved on a broad canvas or re-enacted on a wide screen: the two diminutive figures, muffled in furs, blurred by the drifting snow and dwarfed by that chill desert which stretched off for one hundred and forty miles, unmarked by a single human habitation. There they stopped and shared a frozen meal together – Hill, the young dreamer, his lively mind already crammed with visions of a transportation empire of steel, and Smith, the old Labrador hand, who had clawed his way up the slippery ladder of the fur trade. Hill was thirty-two, Smith, fifty; within a decade both of

222

them would be multimillionaires as the result of a mutual association. A quarter of a century later, Smith would recall that bleak scene and say: "I liked him then and I have never had reason to change my opinion."

These were the two adversaries who, in 1871, found themselves locked in a cutthroat battle to control the Red River traffic between Minnesota and Fort Garry, where the nearby village of Winnipeg was slowly rising out of the prairie mud. Since it was axiomatic that neither would give quarter to the other, the two at last agreed to join forces in secret. On the face of it, both the Hudson's Bay Company and Jim Hill retired from the steamboat business and left the trade in the hands of Norman Kittson's Red River Transportation Company. In actual fact, the Kittson Line, as it was called, was a joint venture of Hill, Kittson and the Hudson's Bay Company. The company's shares were in Smith's name, but he agreed in advance to transfer them to whoever succeeded him as chief commissioner. The Kittson Line gave the Hudson's Bay Company a one-third discount on all river freight, and thus a commanding edge on its competitors. That, too, was part of the secret.

No sooner was this clandestine arrangement completed than the freight rates shot skyward. In the winter of 1874-75 a group of Winnipeg and Minnesota merchants, incensed at the monopoly, launched a steamboat line of their own – the Merchants' International. They built two large steamboats, the *Minnesota* and the *Manitoba*, and when the first of these, the *Manitoba*, steamed into Winnipeg on Friday morning, May 14, 1875, an impromptu saturnalia took place on her decks. Champagne flowed all that day, all that night and again the following morning by which time the merrymakers had broken a fair share of the vessel's glass and crockery and thrown all their hats overboard in celebration of their release from "the dreaded monopoly."

That summer there were seven stern-wheelers plying the Red and another battle was in progress. Norman Kittson, who had once fought the Hudson's Bay as a free trader in Pembina, now fought on the Company's side and without giving quarter. He launched a rate war, bringing his own prices down below cost. Through friends in the Pembina customs depot, he arranged that the *Manitoba* be held indefinitely at the border. When it was finally released in July, Kittson charged it broadside with his *International*, rammed it and sank it with its entire cargo. The Merchants' Line raised the battered craft

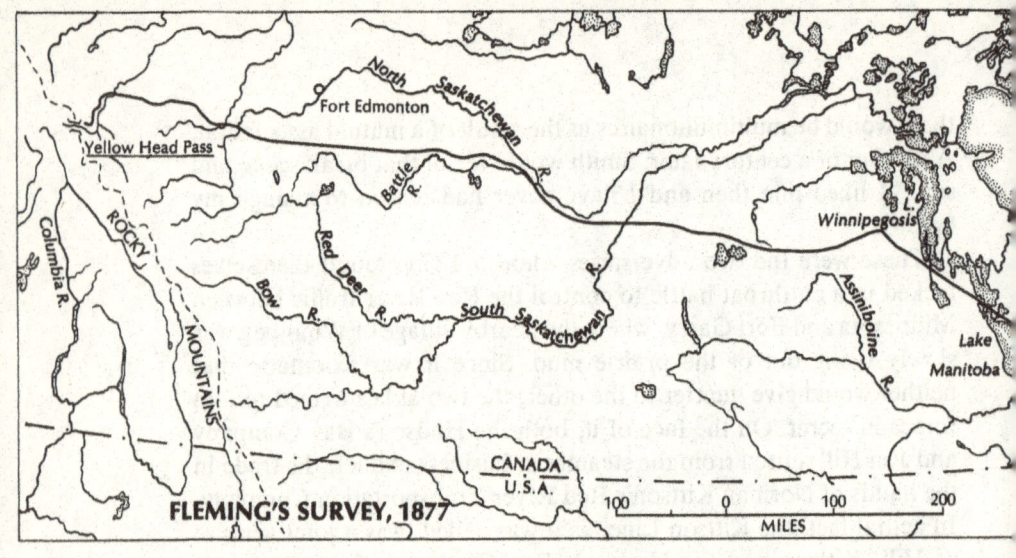

FLEMING'S SURVEY, 1877

and repaired it at staggering cost. No sooner was it back in service than it was seized for a trifling debt. The same fate awaited its sister ship, south of the border. Reeling from this series of blows, the merchants sold out to Kittson in September. Up went the rates again, as Kittson and his colleagues shared a dividend of eighty per cent and the rising wrath of the Red River community. The tousled John Christian Schultz, Conservative member for Lisgar, Manitoba – he had been Riel's prisoner and leading opponent in 1871 – claimed that wheat could be sent the whole length of the Mississippi for half the cost of the three hundred miles of slack water covered by Kittson's steamboats.

There was good reason for this fevered strife. The trickle of newcomers into the Red River Valley was rapidly becoming a torrent. They arrived, in Schultz's words, "huddled like sheep and treated like hogs in the lower decks" of the "notorious monopoly." By the midseventies, the immigrant sheds on the banks of the Red near its confluence with the Assiniboine were bursting with new arrivals who spilled out into a periphery of scattered tents and board shacks. Obviously, whoever controlled transportation into the newly incorporated town of Winnipeg would reap rich profits.

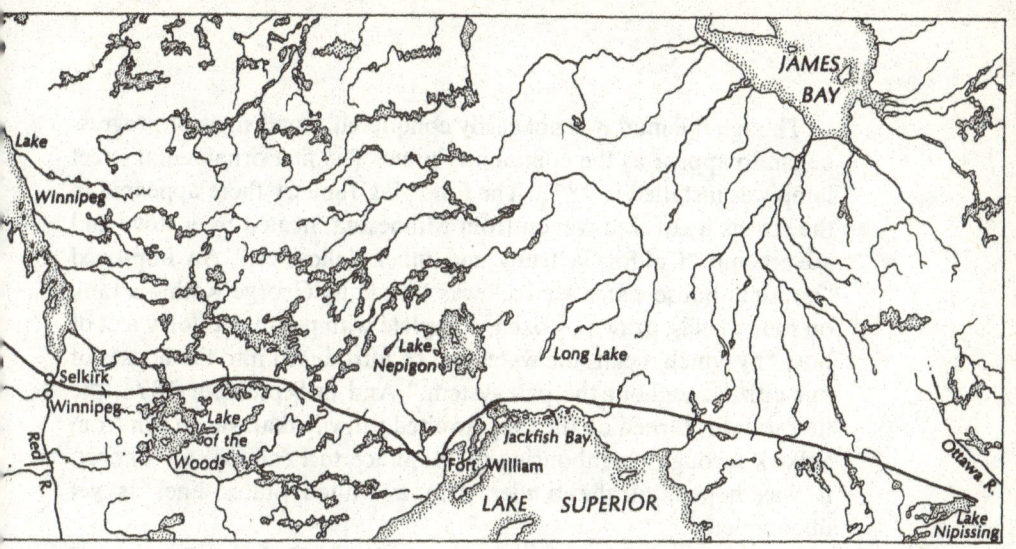

At the time of its incorporation in 1873, Winnipeg was still, in George Ham's description, "a muddy, disreputable village," sprawled between Main Street and the river. It had no sidewalks, no water-works, no sewerage, no pavement; but it had gumbo of such a glutinous consistency that for more than a decade every traveller who described the town devoted several vituperative sentences to it. "It is a mud which no person who has not seen it can appreciate," wrote one English parliamentarian. "A mixture of putty and bird-lime would perhaps most nearly describe it." Baked hard by the sun it looked innocent enough; but the first rainstorm turned it into a tenacious adhesive which clung stubbornly to boots and clothes and made foot travel a nightmare. Only the most perceptive of the old timers saw that the mud was wealth. Father Lacombe, the itinerant prairie Oblate, once happened upon a party of immigrants so totally discouraged by Winnipeg's mud that they were planning to return to the East. Lacombe gave them a tongue-lashing: "Then go back, since you have not any more sense than to judge a country before you have looked into it. If there is deep mud here it is only because the soil is fat – the richest in America. But go back to your Massachusetts, if you want, where the soil is all pebbles, and work again in the factories."

Though the mud was not easily conquered, small signs of progress began to appear as the community grew. The first ornamental street lamp was installed in 1873. The following January there appeared in the streets a covered wagon from Minnesota, heated by a stove and advertising "California fruits and other delicacies." An improved "house to house water service" was started by George Rath – a tank on four wheels, drawn by oxen, complete with pump and forty feet of hose "by which means the water can be introduced into the houses of our citizens without the pail system." And in September 1874, the first sod was turned on the long-awaited railway that was to run from Selkirk through neighbouring St. Boniface to Pembina, to connect, it was hoped, at the border with a United States line, as yet uncompleted.

Winnipeg had already outdistanced the old Hudson's Bay post of Fort Garry in size but, to its growing chagrin, it was not on the main line of the CPR. The route being planned from the head of Lake Superior was to go through Selkirk some twenty miles to the northeast. After that, it was intended that it should swing sharply north and across the pinched midriff of Lake Manitoba at The Narrows before following the general line of the Fertile Belt to Edmonton. Under this scheme of things the road would ignore the two major settlements in the new Manitoba – Winnipeg and Portage la Prairie. In spite of the obvious political inexpediency of such a route, Sandford Fleming continued to cling to it, to the repeated howls of the Winnipeggers. "A tough subject with an election at hand," Marcus Smith wrote to Fleming late in 1877. "I fear politics will be a more powerful consideration than reason." A month later he advised Fleming to tone down his condemnation of a proposed deviation, which would take the railroad south of the lake, and suggested that the whole matter be postponed until after the 1878 election by the old device of resurveying. "The result of the survey," Smith concluded, "will probably be to keep the present line."

The pull of population would soon outweigh engineering considerations and Winnipeg would eventually force a change in the main line. By 1877, southern Manitoba had become, in the words of one government pamphlet, "the most inviting field for immigration in the world." In the early days there had been only one hotel in Winnipeg but by the mid decade rival after rival was springing up: the Grand Central, the International, and then the Merchants' and finally the Queen's, the most ostentatious caravanserai in the North West. Rents were astronomical. A six-room house could not be had for less than fifty dollars a month – four or five times as much as a similar dwelling in Toronto. In 1876, Walter Moberly and his former surveying colleague Roderick McLennan built the first wooden sewer down Main Street – the first, indeed, in all the North West. Another ex-surveyor, Edward Jarvis, the man who had almost starved to death the previous year exploring the Smoky River Pass, was doing a roaring business in lumber and starving no more. Winnipeg could no longer be ignored.

The construction of the Pembina Branch proceeded at an unbelievably leaden pace. After the grading was completed work stopped. There was, after all, no point in building a railroad to nowhere – and there was as yet no connecting American line to be seen on the horizon. The contract for laying steel was not let for another three years until it became clear that the moribund St. Paul and Pacific, reorganized and renamed the St. Paul and Manitoba, was actually going to reach the border (as it did late in 1878).

The last spike in the Pembina Branch was finally driven in November, 1878. By this time the population of Winnipeg had risen to six thousand and a gala excursion load of citizens was taken by train to Rousseau for the ceremony. Here a gap, 125 yards long, still lay incomplete. Two teams of workers set about finishing the line, cheered on by the gleeful throng. It was decided that one of the ladies should have the honour of driving the final spike, but no one could decide which one. Finally, the silver-haired United States consul, James Wickes Taylor, who had, ironically, worked secretly for years for the annexation of the Canadian North West by Jay Cooke and his forces, made the diplomatic suggestion that *all* the ladies present should be allowed a whack. Each in her turn hammered away, with little success, until Taylor called over Mary Sullivan, the strapping daughter of an Irish section boss. With a single blow, the buxom Miss Sullivan drove the spike home, to the cheers of the assembly.

The cheers did not last long. The rails had been laid, but to describe the Pembina Branch as a railway was to indulge in the wildest kind of hyperbole. Under the terms of the contract, the builders had until November 1879 to complete the job and turn the finished line over to the government. They determined, in the meantime, to squeeze the maximum possible profit out of it by running it themselves while they continued to build the necessary sidings, station houses, water towers and all the requisite paraphernalia that is part of a properly run railway.

In the months that followed, the Pembina line became the most cursed length of track on the continent. Since there was only one water tank on the whole sixty-three miles, it was the practice of the engineer, when his boiler ran out of steam, to halt beside the closest stream and replenish his water supply. There was no shred of telegraph line along the entire right of way and so the train dispatching had to be accomplished by using human runners. There were, of course, no repair shops nor were there any fences, which meant the train must make frequent stops to allow cattle to cross the tracks. The only fuel was green poplar, which was piled along the track at intervals. It gave off enormous and encouraging clouds of dense smoke but supplied little energy. Under such conditions it was not easy to build up a head of steam: the passengers were often compelled to wait at a station while the unmoving locomotive, wheezing and puffing away, finally gathered enough motive power to falter off to the next one. The trip to Winnipeg was best described – and in an understatement – as "leisurely." Passengers were in the habit of alighting to watch the perspiring crew hurling poplar logs aboard the tender. Sometimes they would wander into the woods and go to sleep in the shade. On each of these stops it became necessary to make a head count and beat the bushes, literally, for missing ticket holders. An even more ludicrous spectacle was caused by the lack of a turntable at St. Boniface. When the engine reached that point, it could not turn about but had to make the entire trip back to the border tender foremost.

To travel the Pembina line in those days required nerves of steel, a stomach of iron and a spirit of high adventure. Each time a bridge was crossed, the entire structure, foundations and all, swayed and rocked in a dismaying fashion. The road was improperly ballasted so that even at eleven miles an hour, the cars pitched and tumbled about. In many places mud spurted over the tops of the sleepers. A man from *The Times* of London, surely accustomed to the derring-do of Victorian journalism, reported that he and his party were more seasick on the Pembina Branch than they had been crossing the stormy Atlantic. One of the company, so *The Times*'s man said, had not really said his prayers in a long, long time but was so shattered by the experience that he reformed on the spot, took to praying incessantly and, through sheer terror, managed to scare up some extra prayers that had lain forgotten in the dim recesses of his mind since childhood; the Pembina railroad shook them loose.

A retired British army officer, bent on settling his sons in the North

West, arrived at St. Vincent, the border point, with twenty pieces of luggage, several of which contained china and other fragile articles. He made bold to ask the station manager to treat his possessions as gently as possible. "His reply . . . to which was ordering me, in tones of Imperial importance, to 'stand back' and hurling the luggage with all his force from one end of the car to the other."

The subsequent journey was "a miserable apology for railway travelling" but the travellers did not complain too much. They counted themselves lucky that the train did not run off the track, "a misadventure that at this period was happening almost daily."

In Winnipeg, the citizenry could only wait and hold their breath and listen to the faint sounds of activity in the East where, piece by piece, the railway was being built on Canadian soil from the head of Lake Superior.

2

On the afternoon of June 1, 1875, a spirited little ceremony took place on the left bank of the Kaministiquia River, about four miles from its mouth on Thunder Bay, Lake Superior, in the sprawling township of Shumiah. Here was turned the first sod of the main line of the Canadian Pacific Railway. The affair was sponsored by the firm of Sifton and Ward, which had secured the contract to grade the first thirty-two miles of roadbed for a line that the government intended to build in sections between Fort William and Selkirk. *Adam Oliver's favourite game*

Like so many contractors in those days, John Wright Sifton and his brother Henry were up to their sideburns in politics. It was more than merely useful to have a friend in high places; for a contractor it was virtually mandatory. The Siftons came from Petrolia, near Sarnia, in Alexander Mackenzie's federal riding of Lambton. J. W. Sifton had served as reeve of the municipality and as a member of the Lambton County council. His other partner, Frank Ward, was an American, but he and his brother were, as Josiah Burr Plumb took care to point out in the House of Commons, "ardent supporters and close friends of the hon. gentleman in his constituency of Lambton." J. W. Sifton's decision to seek contracts along the route of the CPR (he and his brother were awarded several) not only changed his personal life pattern but also had a considerable effect on the political future of the country. He himself went on to become Speaker of the Manitoba legislature but it was his sons, both of whom were in their teens at the time of the sod-turning, who would make history. The elder, Arthur, would rise to become Premier of Alberta and later a federal cabinet minister. The younger, Clifford, would become Minister of the Interior in the Laurier cabinet, and would also found the best-known and most powerful newspaper dynasty in Canada. Such were the ever-widening ripples set in motion by the brief June ceremony of 1875.

By two that afternoon, two steamers, "loaded with the beauty and fashion of the neighbourhood," had arrived from Prince Arthur's Landing, a few miles away. With a crowd of five hundred in attendance, Judge Delevan Van Norman gained the platform.

"We have met today," he said, "for no other purpose than to inaugurate the beginning of the actual construction of the Canadian Pacific Railway."

The Judge confessed his utter inability to do even a measure of justice to the occasion, but he tried manfully nonetheless, pointing out that an immigrant with his family "seeking a new home in this new world, but still under the old flag, may with celerity, safety and certainty examine the country from Cape Breton in Nova Scotia to Vancouver's Island in British Columbia, in the meantime passing over a space as vast as the great ocean that divides and separates the old world from the new."

Then Judge Van Norman told his listeners what they really wanted to hear: Buffalo had once been no larger than Prince Arthur's Landing, Chicago no bigger than Fort William!

"I verily believe," the Judge said, "that history is about to repeat itself."

Adam Oliver rose as the applause died. He was a bulky man with shrewd, narrow eyes and a small billy goat's beard, who hailed from Oxford County in southwestern Ontario, which he represented in the local legislature. He was known as an impassioned player of euchre, then the most popular family game on the continent. Euchre has several variations including "Railroad Euchre" and "Cutthroat Euchre"; Oliver, as events were to prove, certainly knew something about the cutthroat aspects of the railroad game. He and his partners owned forty thousand acres of good timber in the Fort William area together with considerable property and a lumber mill. They already had one government contract, to build the telegraph line accompanying the railroad to the Red River, and were about to sign another for the construction of an engine house. Oliver, too, was a prominent Liberal.

Amid loud cheers, Oliver pointed to a pile of five hundred wheelbarrows and a thousand shovels lying ready for use.

"Looking farther still up the line you can see hundreds of men clearing the way," he cried, "while the magnificent wharf along the side of the river is rapidly approaching completion. The place on which you are now standing is destined in no distant day to form one of the most important cities in your great Dominion."

In the crowd applauding those remarks were: Peter Johnson Brown, one of Oliver's partners and a former reeve of Shumiah Township, which harboured both communities; Thomas Marks, the pioneer merchant at the Landing and the incumbent reeve; and Peter Mc-Kellar, an old Fort William settler and council member. Working together, these men, with Oliver's political help, had succeeded in wrestling the official lake terminus from the rival port of Nepigon, farther to the east. Now they were united in a moment of common triumph. It was the last that they would share together.

Originally the controversy had been between Thunder Bay and Nepigon. Nepigon won the railhead by default after a fire in the engineering department, early in 1874, destroyed all the evidence in favour of Thunder Bay. When the Thunder Bay merchants learned of this from Adam Oliver they mustered a delegation from the twin communities to reassemble the original arguments and lay the evidence before Sandford Fleming. An aggressive paper battle was mounted as well. The Thunder Bay delegation made sure that every Member of Parliament received a pamphlet trumpeting the advantages of the westerly terminus and hinting at dark and sinister plotting on the part of the Nepigon boosters who, it charged, were land speculators.

Nepigon fought back with a pamphlet of its own, pointing out that the land around the harbour had always been the property of the Crown. Each pamphlet indulged in an orgy of statistics designed to prove that the rival harbour was choked with ice at a time when the other was open. The Thunder Bay pamphlet, for instance, contained an affidavit from one James McKay, a Hudson's Bay Company trader at Nepigon, who swore that the harbour was never open before June 1. To which the author of the Nepigon pamphlet, *another* Hudson's

Bay trader at Nepigon, replied: "Poor McKay! Into what designing hands hast thou fallen? Poor fellow! I fear the best excuse for you would be that you were drunk when you swore to such a tissue of lies."

Nevertheless, the government changed its mind and awarded the terminus to Thunder Bay. This prompted a third pamphlet from James Beaty, editor of the Toronto *Leader*, entitled *The History of the Lake Superior Ring*. The pamphlet promised more than it delivered since it carried on its cover the jaw-breaking subtitle: "An account of the rise and progress of the YANKEE COMBINATION, headed by HON. ALEXANDER MACKENZIE, premier of Canada and THE BROWNS for the purpose of selling their interest and political power to enrich Jay Cooke & Co. and other AMERICAN SPECULATORS, changing the route of the Canada Pacific Railway, with a view to breaking up our great Dominion, and severing our connection with the British Empire. THOROUGH EXPOSÉ of Mackenzie's and Brown's TREACHERY TO THEIR COUNTRY."

There was only one piece of hard evidence in Beaty's shrill tract. He was able to show that, late in 1873, when Mackenzie was contemplating the change of route to bring the railway close to Lake Superior, two mining companies had been incorporated to buy and develop lands in the same general area. Four of the six principals were Mackenzie, George Brown of the *Globe*, his brother Gordon, and the American consul in Toronto, Col. Albert D. Shaw.

The impropriety of the Prime Minister of Canada speculating in real estate along the line of a proposed government railway scarcely fazed the voters of that day who were inured to far more blatant instances of political jobbery. It was an era in which plots and counterplots, sinister "rings" and cabals, intrigues and conspiracies of all kinds, fancied or real, were part of the standard political and economic weaponry. People of standing were conditioned to believe – sometimes with good reason – that secret forces were working just beneath the surface. Almost forty years later, Peter McKellar of Fort William, who had helped compose the pamphlet attacking the wicked Nepigon "interests," recalled that he had believed the affair was "a culpably deep laid scheme." In his old age he confessed, "I have changed my mind."

Early in 1874 Fleming settled on a point two miles from the old Hudson's Bay post of Fort William, on the Kaministiquia River, as the terminus for the Fort Garry–Thunder Bay line. After the first flush of victory, the people at Prince Arthur's Landing, which was seven miles away, began to experience a sense of discrimination. The rivalry between the two communities had actually begun the winter before with the appearance of two opposing newspapers, both produced on foolscap and hand written in ink. Peter McKellar was the mainstay of the Fort William *Perambulator*, George T. Marks (Thomas Marks's nephew) of the Landing's *Thunderbolt*. Each condemned the other in the most violent and abusive language on the only subject that counted: the exact location of the terminus. In describing the future of their respective villages, each paper always portrayed the rival community as being wiped out of existence.

The two newspapers vanished with the ice on the lake, but early in the fall the Landing got a journalistic champion in the person of an itinerant and volatile Irishman named Michael Hagan. With the backing of the Marks family, Hagan founded the Thunder Bay *Sentinel* and immediately began to reflect the popular opinion that the choice of Fort William as the terminus was part of a scheming conspiracy. In one of its earliest issues, the newspaper hit out at the Toronto *Mail*, which was supporting Fort William and attacking the Landing. What was this "tirade of abuse," Hagan asked. Then he began to fuel the fires of suspicion:

"Some would have it that a certain excursion to Silver Lake with persons well known hereabouts, together with Fort William Hudson Bay rum, cooked the job. Others would have it that [it was a] certain unpleasantness at the Queen's Hotel, where a little amusement was had at the expense of a would-be 'expert' from Toronto; and another class think there is a lady in the case, and jilting don't go down with high blood."

By October, the bitterness between the communities was so great that Fort William, led by Oliver and his two business partners, Joseph Davidson and Peter Johnson Brown – started a movement to separate from Prince Arthur's Landing. The *Sentinel* rushed into print on November 4 with the inside story of why the "Fort William clique" or "this little band of schemers," as it called them, was trying to engineer the schism. The Landing interests wanted to finance, with municipal help, a railway to hook up with the CPR terminus. Fort William wanted no part of this. In order to save paying taxes to build the line and also to protect their own real-estate holdings at the town plot of Fort William, the Oliver interests were trying to opt out of the township of Shumiah.

The two communities were quite different in character and in history. Fort William was by far the older of the two; it had been a fur-trading post for almost two centuries and the venerable Hudson's Bay fort guarded by twin cannon was its oldest building. The new town was to be built on a plot of land surveyed some two miles distant, not far from Adam Oliver's sawmill – "the nucleus of a second Chicago," as one visitor wrote of it.

The Landing had been the taking-off point for the Gladman-Hind-Dawson expedition of 1858, for Wolseley's military trek across the Shield and for the ill-fated Dawson road. It was now the end of steam transportation from Ontario. Silver discoveries had caused it to boom in the sixties and by the time of the sod-turning ceremony it was by far the larger of the twin settlements, a prosperous mining town and lake port of more than one thousand souls, with several churches, hotels and lodges and four lines of steamboats, both side-wheelers and screw-driven, making use of its dock facilities. It had the characteristics of a silver town: a love of easy money, a propensity for speculation, a get-rich-quick philosophy and a cynical attitude regarding human nature.

"The very streets show veins of silver, prospecting being the prevalent topic," James Trow wrote of it in 1874. "Speculation often runs wild. Mineral locations are sold for fabulous sums and resold repeatedly. One victim wants to victimize another."

Now the entire community thought itself victimized. "There is no disguising the fact," wrote one journalist, "that the recent location of the terminus of the railroad seven miles distant has cast a cloud over this place." The leading citizens of the town formed a company to build the railroad to hook up with the main line and managed to get municipal backing – but not before a bitter struggle, since Fort William interests were also involved.

There were public meetings in which charges and countercharges flew between the two groups like poisoned arrows. Oliver, Davidson and Brown, the three partners who stood to make the most money out of the Fort William terminus, attacked the whole idea of a connecting railroad to the Landing. Simon J. Dawson, now a member of the provincial legislature for the district, retorted that all three were absentee landowners, who wanted to get rich at the expense of the community. Brown replied by charging that the Landing had twenty-two liquor outlets and all the members of its council were selling liquor in direct contravention of the law. The Fort William group

234

were attacked as "vile slanderers." At last the by-law was passed and the little railway was built but the Mackenzie government refused to link it with the CPR. The citizens of the Landing responded in another pamphlet, in which they charged that the refusal had been brought about "at the instigation of parties interested in crushing their settlement and building up a town on the Kaministiquia" and that "through the sinister influence of these parties, they have been subjected to the most cruel persecution."

Fort William needed a propaganda arm. With the help of Adam Oliver, a new newspaper, the Fort William *Day Book*, was established at the town plot. Hagan and the *Sentinel* engaged the upstart journal in a battle which was fought without mercy. Week after week both papers published interminable accounts of the deficiencies of the rival community. The *Sentinel* marshalled columns of scientific evidence to show that the Kaministiquia River was too shallow for lake traffic. The *Day Book* published equally impressive evidence to prove that the harbour at the Landing was so exposed as to be virtually useless. An early settler in Fort William later recalled that "so keen was the interest in the exciting squabble between the two villages that almost the entire population would go into the office to watch the interesting process of getting the paper to press."

The *Day Book*'s apprentice delivered the paper, with some misgivings, to twenty-seven subscribers at the hated Landing, travelling there by tugboat. He was allowed just twenty-five cents in expense money, that being the exact one-way fare. This meant he had to walk home, carefully making his route through the back streets to avoid being mobbed by boys from the Landing who were as interested in the rivalry as their elders.

The *Day Book* had scarcely begun publication in the summer of 1877 when Hagan of the *Sentinel* with the help of the Toronto *Mail* got hold of some powerful ammunition: the carpetbagger Oliver and his Liberal friends had apparently been selling land to the government at fancy mark-ups. Worse than that, they had actually put up part of a building on land already appropriated for the railway and had managed to sell it to the Crown at an inflated price.

This was the famous Neebing Hotel case, which became a popular scandal in the big city papers and finally prompted a Senate inquiry. The Senate committee, after hearing the evidence, came to the conclusion that the charges were correct.

It was an unblushing piece of jobbery, even for those days. Oliver,

Davidson and Brown were all implicated. Lots purchased by Oliver and his partners for between sixty and ninety dollars were sold two years later to the government for as much as three hundred. And who was acting as an official government evaluator? Brown! He had one hundred thousand dollars invested in Fort William lands. In one instance the partners had purchased 136 acres for one thousand dollars and laid out a paper town. They sold eight acres of this non-existent community to the government for four thousand dollars. The valuation was Brown's.

The Opposition press charged that the former Liberal M.P.P., Oliver, had inside information on which lands the government would buy and pointed out that he also just happened to own land on which the Ontario government was then planning to build a mental institution. Oliver was no longer in the Legislature; he had been unseated for "bribery and corruption" (his own phrase). His partner Davidson had, witnesses testified, been seen with a plan of the Fort William town plot showing the lots the government would need marked in colour as far back as November 1874 – before anyone else had that information. The map appeared to be a tracing taken from the public works department. There was evidence, denied vehemently by Davidson, that he had the information direct from Mackenzie. Certainly Mackenzie's role in the matter was suspect; at best he was shown to have a terrible memory. It was he who had asked the Department of Justice to appoint Brown to act with the government evaluators. He did not know, Mackenzie swore, that Brown was a member of the Oliver, Davidson firm. Yet Brown's name appeared with that of Oliver and Davidson on a document – it was the contract for the telegraph line – that Mackenzie himself signed in February, 1875.

The Senate committee was certain that Oliver and his partners had inside information. "After having heard and weighed the evidence . . . your Committee find it difficult to believe that the persons who enriched themselves at the expense of the people of Canada had not in some way ascertained, in advance of the public, that the Government had determined to locate the terminus of the Canadian Pacific Railway on the town plot of Fort William."

In addition, the committee concluded that there was no real reason for the railway to go through the Oliver townsite at all. There were better locations available for a terminus before the town plot was reached where the land would have been cheaper and easier to

236

assemble. And the government seemed to have waited a suspiciously long time before buying *any* land. Fleming had personally urged Mackenzie to buy up the land for the terminus in 1874, when the lots could be had at a quarter of the price eventually paid. Mackenzie ignored him.

In the case of the Neebing Hotel, Oliver and his partners certainly knew in advance what was happening. He and Davidson, having been notified of the position of the line of track and having sold the property to the government for ten thousand dollars, began the hasty construction of a "hotel" on the same piece of ground. The Neebing Hotel, as the Toronto *Mail* reported gleefully, was "the only structure of its kind in the world, an imaginary hostelry in an imaginary city. For this shell, unfinished, rudely and hastily thrown together, composed of refuse slabs, with not even a chimney, $5,029 was paid." Testimony before the Senate committee showed that the builder was paid only thirteen hundred dollars to construct the hotel; but then the books were shamelessly padded – five hundred dollars, for instance, for non-existent "damages," another item of five hundred dollars charged twice, discrepancies between accounts and vouchers, and so on. The Senate committee, which thought that the price of all real estate sold to the government at Fort William was "exceedingly and unaccountably extravagant," reported that in the case of the Neebing Hotel the government had been "grossly overcharged" and confirmed that the building had been erected long after the owners knew it would be on railway property. They "were not entitled to payment or compensation of any kind."

The case became nationally notorious. During the campaign of 1878, John A. Macdonald never failed to draw a laugh when he declared solemnly that the only punishment he wished for the Government, if they were defeated, was that they be compelled to board for the next two years at the Neebing Hotel.

Just how much political muscle Adam Oliver had with the Mackenzie administration came to light two years later when a royal commission began investigating various contracts awarded along the north shore of Lake Superior. The circumstances under which Oliver, Davidson and Company secured a quarter-million-dollar contract to build the telegraph line from Thunder Bay to Winnipeg were as astonishing as they were suspicious.

Tenders for the line were opened in August, 1874, but the actual contract was not awarded until the following February. The intervening months were spent in what a later century was to brand as "wheeling and dealing." The lowest bid was passed over in a fashion that the Royal Commission described as "peremptory": the bidders, when they asked for a little time to complete their security, did not even receive the courtesy of an answer. The next two lowest bids were both entered, in effect, by one Robert Twiss Sutton of Brantford and it became clear from subsequent testimony that he had no intention of fulfilling the contract but had simply entered the contest in order to be bought off by his competitors, a fairly common practice in those days. In December, Adam Oliver arrived in Ottawa to do the buying off.

The lower of the two Sutton bids was twenty-five thousand dollars higher than the rejected tender. It was in the name of Sutton and Thirtkell. The other Sutton bid was twenty-eight thousand dollars higher still. It was in the name of Sutton and Thompson. Both W. J. Thirtkell, a Lindsay druggist, and William Thompson, of Brantford, were mere front men, brought in for a price to lend the weight of their names to the tender. Sutton was, in fact, used to buying Thompson's name for this purpose.

Oliver arrived in Ottawa expecting to be able to buy up the lower of the two Sutton bids. But once in the capital he discovered for mysterious and unexplained reasons that he could actually be awarded the higher one. Oliver promised Sutton a quarter of the profits; Sutton paid off his silent partner, Thompson, with a cheque for eight hundred dollars; and Oliver's firm ended up with the coveted contract. It was fifty-three thousand dollars fatter than it would have been had the lowest tender been accepted.

Apart from the cavalier treatment of the lowest bidder, there was never any explanation of how the higher of the two Sutton bids came to be accepted, rather than the lower one. But one thing did develop from the testimony. It was Mackenzie himself, Smith's "noble man," who handled the entire business and not one of his underlings, as was the general practice. And all the dealings with the Minister were in the hands, not of Robert Sutton, the official tenderer, but of Adam Oliver. To achieve the kind of financial miracle that Oliver managed required a detailed knowledge of all the tenders for the contract – information that was supposed to be secret. But then, at the same time, Oliver's partner Davidson was brandishing the map of the town plot full of supposedly secret information from Mackenzie's department.

In Adam Oliver's favourite game, the maker's side must win at least three tricks to avoid being euchred. Oliver had won them all: he had got the terminus moved to Fort William, he had sold property to the government at extortionate prices and he had gained a telegraph contract at a bonus rate. He was not quite as successful as a builder. The complaints about the state of the line were continual. Poles, badly anchored, kept toppling. Wires stretched over trees in lieu of poles strangled and killed them; the roots decayed, and the trees fell over, taking the wires with them. Sometimes it took a message as long as a month to reach Winnipeg on Adam Oliver's expensive telegraph line.

By this time the two rival communities at the lakehead had stubbornly gone their separate ways. The apartheid was formalized in 1881 when a new municipality was chopped out of the old one to accommodate the settlement of Fort William. The twin villages grew to towns and the towns to cities until it was difficult to tell where one began and the other ended. But so deep were the ancient animosities that each developed its own bus line, police force, fire department, power commission, newspaper and service clubs. It was not until 1969, ninety-four years after the sod-turning ceremony on the banks of the twisting Kaministiquia, that the rusty hatchets were finally buried and the twin cities became one.

3

The strains of office were beginning to tell on Mackenzie's temper and health; it was the railway that was chiefly to blame. Not only was he Prime Minister, but he had also chosen to assume the burden of the Ministry of Public Works, the most sensitive of cabinet posts in that era of railway contracts. In the spring of 1877, the ex-stonemason revealed a little of his feelings when he exploded in the House that "it is impossible for any man in this country to conduct public affairs without being subjected to the grossest political abuse. Let a political friend get a contract and it is stated at once that [it] is because he is a political friend. Let a political opponent get a contract and we are charged with trying to buy him over to the Government."

Nonetheless more friends than opponents were awarded contracts on the various sections of the rail and telegraph lines being built along

The stonemason's friends

the granites of Superior and the muskegs of Manitoba. The Mackenzie government awarded eleven contracts west of Lake Superior,
between 1874 and 1878, for grading, track laying and telegraph
lines. The total amount paid, as of June 30, 1880, was $5,257,336.
Eight of the largest contracts – amounting to a total of $4,986,659 –
went to prominent Liberal wheel-horses, men who in every case were
members of a federal or provincial parliament, past, present or future.
These included J. W. Sifton, Adam Oliver, Joseph Whitehead,
Patrick Purcell, James Conmee, and David Glass. Glass's was one of
several names prominent on the Liberal side in the Pacific Scandal
which popped up subsequently in the railway contracting business.
Another was that of Senator Asa B. Foster, who secured a contract
for the eighty-five mile "Georgian Bay branch," which was never
built because it subsequently developed that the grades were impossibly steep. But Senator Foster, the man who paid off McMullen,
received forty-one thousand dollars for his work on the contract
before it was annulled.

"The Mackenzie government," wrote John Willison, a journalist
of the period, "like all other governments in Canada, had greedy
mercenaries hanging upon its skirts, bent upon pillage and crafty
beyond the wit of man in devising means to get at the treasury by
devious contracts or skilful alienation of the public resources."

Mackenzie poured out his own feelings on the matter to a fellow
Liberal: "Friends expect to be benefited by offices they are unfit for,
by contracts they are not entitled to, by advances not earned. Enemies
ally themselves with friends and push their whims to the front. Some
attempt to storm the office. Some dig trenches at a distance and
approach in regular siege form. I feel like the besieged, lying on my
arms night and day. I have offended at least 20 parliamentary friends
by defence of the Citadel. A weak minister here would ruin the party
in a month and the country very soon."

Yet it is arguable how strong the stonemason himself was. Mackenzie took over the Department of Public Works with the memory
of the Pacific Scandal haunting him and, before that, distasteful
recollections of the Grand Trunk–Conservative marriage and allied
railway schemes. He determined to establish an inflexible method of
handling tenders on public contracts: the lowest bidder *must* be given
the job. On the face of it this was designed to prevent favouritism. In
practice it turned the department into a broker's office.

It did not matter who the low bidder was, or how outrageous his tender. He could be an incompetent, a bankrupt or – as generally developed – a man interested in peddling contracts. Theoretically a deposit accompanied each bid which was to be forfeited if the bid was not successful, but these deposits were too small to deter anyone; besides, they were invariably returned to the unsuccessful bidders after the tenders were opened.

The new regulations relieved the government of all responsibility in choosing contractors. But they also made it possible for bogus contractors to flourish – men who had no intention of grading a mile of line, whose only purpose was to enter a bid so low it must be accepted, and then to sell the contract for a profit. Of the seventy-two contracts awarded for the construction of the Canadian Pacific Railway during the seventies, there were ten major ones from which the successful low bidders withdrew. The increases involved in awarding these contracts to higher tenderers totalled more than one million dollars. Some of the low bids were entered by men who had no intention of doing the job, others by *bona fide* contractors who saw a chance to make a bigger profit by pretending to drop out while actually joining forces with a higher bidder and splitting the difference between the bids. In addition, many large contracting firms who paid substantial sums to buy up a contract expected to recoup their losses by charging later for "extras," not included in the original specifications. Apart from this cost, the unwieldy system slowed down the awarding of contracts sometimes by several weeks at critical seasons of the year. A few weeks' delay in the spring, for example, could mean the loss of a full season of work.

In 1880, a royal commission began to inquire into government spending on the CPR. It sat for more than a year and took sworn testimony from scores of witnesses – contractors, surveyors, politicians, journalists. Its exhaustive three-volume report gives a comprehensive picture of the way in which the government sections of the railway were surveyed and constructed, under both Liberal and Conservative regimes. Both were found wanting.

One leading contractor, A. P. MacDonald, himself a former Conservative member, painted an unpleasant picture of corruption in the public works offices. "You do everything in your power to find out where your tender is. You offer inducements to clerks to do things that they would not [normally] do . . . you offer them bribes to get at things that are dangerous. . . . You take a clerk that gets $1,000 a year salary, and offer him $2,000 to get certain information in his

241

office, and there is a temptation for him to break a lock and get it. . . ." Some people, MacDonald added, thought everyone in the department was corrupt.

Once a contractor secured the coveted information, he would do his best to prevent the man below him from getting the contract. One method was to try to thwart him from putting up the substantial cash security that was required once a tender was accepted. Men who supplied such surety were generally paid off by the successful tenderers with a cut of the profits, but their rivals often spread the word that the bid was impossibly low and future profits illusory. Unable to raise security money, the low bidder would have to relinquish the contract. Under this system a man who could command large sums of money tended to get the job, no matter what the original bids had been. As MacDonald pointed out, such men "can obtain more favours, etc., than the ordinary contractor could."

Political friends could also obtain special favours. For them, in instance after instance, the department found a way to depart from its rigid policy of accepting the lowest bids. One such firm was Sifton, Glass and Company, which managed, in 1874, to acquire a lucrative contract for telegraph construction west from Fort Garry along the proposed right of way. The active partner in this firm was Mackenzie's friend and fellow Liberal, John Wright Sifton. The front man, who did the talking in Ottawa, was David Glass.

Glass was not a contractor at all, and certainly knew very little about building telegraph lines. He was a trial lawyer in London, and a good one, known especially for his abilities in murder cases. A swarthy Ulsterman, he had been elected as a Conservative, only to turn against Macdonald in the Pacific Scandal debate of 1873 – the first public defection in the Tory ranks. Now he was a Liberal with a special claim to Mackenzie's gratitude.

That gratitude was not long in appearing. The complicated methods by which Sifton and Glass obtained a contract worth more than one hundred thousand dollars, in spite of the presence of lower tenders, astonished and nettled the Royal Commission. To put the matter simply, the firm entered a tender that was so ambiguous that Mackenzie, Fleming and other members of the department appeared to misunderstand it – though the commissioners did not believe there was really a misunderstanding. They not only passed over a better offer, but they also allowed Sifton and Glass to renegotiate the original tender on their own terms, without challenge and to their considerable financial advantage.

242

It took the commissioners some seventy-five hundred words to explain the curious series of steps involved in this political legerdemain. The partners tendered on the basis of the entire line but were awarded the contract for only part of it – the easy part; yet they were allowed to charge for the work as if they were building the difficult parts as well. In short, they were paid an inflated price. Theirs was by no means the lowest bid: two lower bidders mysteriously dropped out and a third firm was passed over on the flimsy excuse that they had already been awarded a section of the line which "would require all their energies to complete." Normally it required an order in council to pass over a low bidder but Sifton and Glass got the contract without any such authority, even though the department's law clerk pointed out the omission to Mackenzie himself.

The resultant telegraph line, which the contractors were supposed to maintain for five years, was, like Adam Oliver's, almost totally unsatisfactory. The poles were badly set, so that they often fell into the swamps and muskegs, and – since they were made of short-lived poplar (the cheapest available wood) – quickly rotted and fell away. The contractors, however, pocketed a sizable profit, having received, in the commission's words "that to which they were not entitled." Why such favourable terms were granted to John Sifton and David Glass the commission was unable to say, though it did refer to Sandford Fleming's somewhat vague testimony that Glass "pressed his own views very strongly" in frequent meetings in his office. But a political debt was a political debt and David Glass could not say that his bold support of the party in 1873 had not been recognized in the contract of 1874.

Another political friend was Joseph Whitehead, former mayor of Clinton, Ontario, and a Liberal member of Parliament from 1867 to 1872. He was an enormous Yorkshireman with a great, bald dome of a head, a vast, patriarchal beard and a big, fleshy nose. He had been a railwayman since the very beginning; as a boy, he had helped drive teams of horses which pulled coaches along wooden rails before the days of steam. At the age of eleven, he had been the fireman on Stephenson's first experimental locomotive, which pulled history's first public passenger train on the Stockton and Darlington Railway in England.

Whitehead, said the pioneer Manitoba paper *Nor'wester*, in a tribute to him while he was grading the line to Pembina, was "a plain working man, [who] knows what work is. . . . He is no kid-gloved, silk-stockinged, patent type of leather-booted, speculating, job-finessing

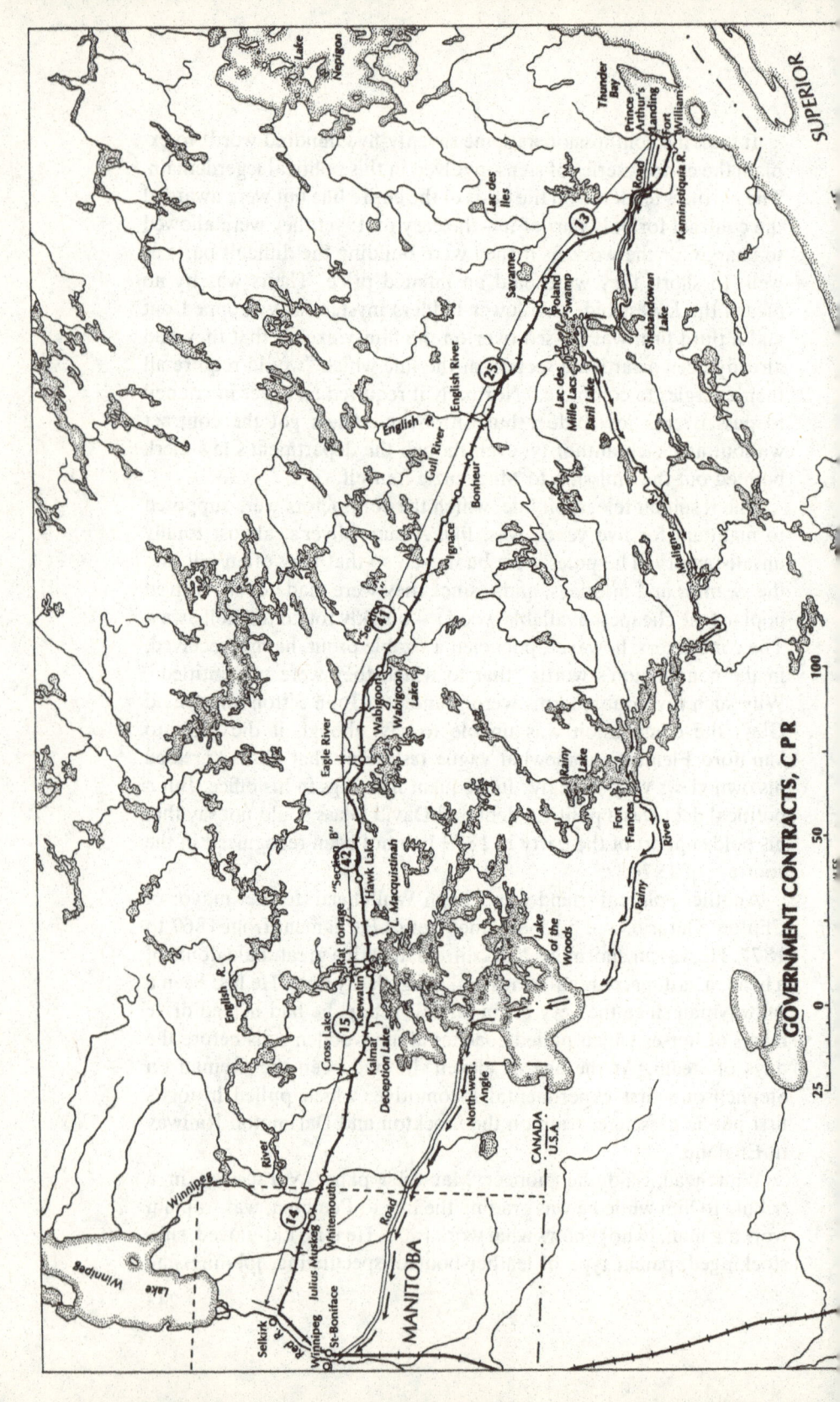

GOVERNMENT CONTRACTS, C P R

contractor." But as an old railway hand, Whitehead knew enough to be an old political hand, too; in the seventies the two vocations were all but inseparable. He knew how to buy his way into newspapers or the goodwill of newspapermen, how to peddle influence, how to purchase contracts and how to deal with politicians. The commission came to the conclusion that "he had a strong belief in the corruptibility of public men." The machinations by which he secured the contract for Section Fifteen of the Thunder Bay–Selkirk line give an insight into the relationship between politics and business in the Mackenzie era.

Section Fifteen was a thirty-seven mile stretch of right of way that ran through muskeg country between Cross Lake and Rat Portage, near the border between Ontario and Manitoba. Whitehead tendered on the contract for grading and laying track, but when the bids were opened on September 20, 1876, his was certainly not the lowest. As the law required, the lowest tender was awarded the contract; the bidder declined to take it up because, he claimed, his prices had been based on the early completion of an adjoining piece of the line, which was well behind schedule. Accordingly the next lowest bidder, a firm called Martin and Charlton, was awarded the contract.

Whitehead immediately wrote to Mackenzie that it would be a mistake to give this company the contract since Charlton, an American from New York, was simply a jobber. ". . . it is well known that [he] says that he never intended to put a spade into the contract of Section 15; he only wanted to make some money out of it, the same way he did out of the Grenville Canal when he sold out to Cooke & Jones, and got six thousand dollars." The pressure was already on Mackenzie to give the contract to Whitehead. On his desk was another letter, this one from a long-time Liberal stalwart, M. C. Cameron, urging that "our old mutual friend from Clinton" be awarded the job.

In the matter of Section Fifteen, Whitehead knew exactly who had bid and how much had been bid. Indeed, as he later testified, everybody in Ottawa knew as soon as the tenders came in: "I know things that have not been in that department more than a couple of hours before they are known on the street." It was understandable: the sealed bids were simply shoved into an old desk drawer.

Whitehead, then, knew whom to pay off. He had no funds of his own but he did have his brother-in-law, Senator Donald McDonald, a one-time surveyor for the Canada Company and a prominent Liberal. Senator McDonald offered to buy off Charlton, the successful bidder, for twenty thousand dollars. Whitehead was never sure whether or not McDonald actually paid that much but he found himself paying ten per cent interest on the sum. Charlton withdrew, pleading "dissension from within and extraordinary pressure from without." His partner protested that he was personally prepared to deposit the security as required but the government ignored him. Mackenzie awarded the contract to the next highest bidder, Sutton and Thompson.

This firm, which had no security at all, was one of those that made a practice of bidding low purposely in order to be bought out – a technique that had worked very well for it in the case of Adam Oliver's telegraph line. To achieve this end, Sutton and Thompson now engaged with Whitehead in a little game of make-believe. As successful bidders they pretended that Whitehead had joined their firm, even going through the motions of a legal paper association. Senator McDonald supplied the required security of eighty thousand dollars and again charged Whitehead ten per cent — a nice transaction for the Senator, who put up real estate instead of hard cash.

At this point a newspaper story appeared charging that either McDonald or Whitehead had, on behalf of Sutton and Thompson, paid Charlton to withdraw his bid. Without turning a hair, the Senator denied it. Mackenzie's department queried Sutton and Thompson. They denied it too. Mackenzie accepted the denials. Sutton and Thompson were awarded the contract and the Senator gave *them* ten thousand dollars to dissociate themselves from Whitehead and leave him with the contract. The government, however, continued to pretend that the partnership was alive.

In return for his aid, and in addition to his ten per cent, McDonald asked for and was given an equal partnership in the firm. Since he was a Senator he could not officially be involved in railway construction and so the industry was treated to the odd spectacle of the Senator's son Mitchell, a bankrupt who knew nothing about railways, apparently working in tandem with the veteran Whitehead.

It had been a neat gambit on Whitehead's part. He had secured a contract worth a million and a half dollars. But this, he figured, would be only the beginning; the area through which Section Fifteen would run had been subjected to the skimpiest of surveys; there would be unavoidable extra charges, not subject to competitive bidding, for which he could bill the government. Before Whitehead was through,

246

these extras, none of them officially authorized by the department, had come to $930,000. When Whitehead secured the contract he had estimated his eventual net profit at close to $200,000. He might easily have made that much had it not been for the muskegs of Cross Lake, which eventually forced him to abandon the work.

Whitehead obtained another lucrative contract from the Mackenzie government through political pull. In 1874 he had been awarded the grading of the Pembina Branch from Winnipeg to the border. In May, 1877, shortly after obtaining the contract for Section Fifteen, he was given a so-called "supplementary contract" to extend the branch north from Winnipeg to Selkirk where it was expected to join the main line of the CPR. This plum, worth $161,000, was handed to Whitehead without any tendering on the pretext that it was part of the original Pembina Branch contract. It was, however, a totally different piece of work, involving much more than grading. It became clear from subsequent evidence that the government paid a higher price for this piece of railway than it was worth and much more than it need have, had the work been let by tender. Whitehead himself admitted that, though he had charged almost twenty-five thousand dollars for off-take ditches, the job could have been done profitably for half the price.

Another firm that obtained extraordinary favours in the fall of 1874 was Cooper, Fairman and Company, a hardware company in Montreal. The Department of Public Works showed an astonishing preference for this concern in its purchases of steel rails, nuts, bolts and fishplates.

Here the department departed from its tendering policy and awarded a contract for steel rails worth $265,000 to Cooper and Fairman even though, two days before, another company had offered to supply the rails at ten shillings a ton less. The price the Government paid was demonstrably higher than the going price that fall.

In another instance, where the government did stick to its usual policy, the tendering was so complicated and confusing that again Cooper and Fairman were able to obtain what the commissioners described as "an undue advantage."

In three other contracts – for nuts and bolts, for rail transport and for the construction of an engineer's house – the same firm was given special treatment, other firms with lower prices and lower bids being passed over in their favour. Clearly Cooper and Fairman had an inside track with Mackenzie's department. As the commissioners reported, "it appears that an understanding existed from time to time between this firm and the Department of Public Works, beyond that which is conveyed by letters or papers on record."

What was Cooper and Fairman's secret? In the winter of 1874-75, the Conservative press began to leak some of the story. The silent partner of the firm was a Sarnia hardware merchant named Charles Mackenzie. He was the Prime Minister's brother. In 1873 he had put fifteen thousand dollars into the firm – more than the other two partners combined. He was to receive a third of all profits in return. There were no profits and, indeed, no losses – no business, in truth – until the government contracts began to roll in. Mackenzie left the firm officially in May, 1875. In his testimony, long after the fact, he said he had really quit earlier – around the time the contracts came in; but he could not remember the exact date – "my memory is very poor for dates" – and his testimony and that of his former partners was so vague that it was clear to the commissioners and everybody else that he was very much a part of the firm for at least a portion of the period when his brother's department was granting them extra-ordinary public favours.

In the end, it developed that not all the steel rails were really needed. They had been purchased prematurely – fifty thousand tons of them – apparently because both Fleming and Mackenzie believed they were getting a bargain, or so Fleming testified. He had thought the price was at rock bottom in 1874; besides, he said, he hoped that the presence of the actual steel in the country might speed the construction of the line.

The rails purchase was a disaster for all but Cooper, Fairman and Company. At most, twenty thousand tons were needed for the work in progress. But having purchased that amount, Mackenzie ordered an additional thirty thousand tons, even though the price was higher. Half of this extra order was supplied by Cooper and Fairman at double the going rate. After that, to everyone's discomfiture, the bottom dropped out of the market. The rails rusted for years, unused, while the price of new rails went lower and lower and the interest mounted on the original investment. It was beginning to be apparent to the country at large that the government's venture into the railway business was as disastrous as that of Sir Hugh Allan.

From his poplar-shaded mansion of Silver Heights, high above the *"Mean,* serpentine Assiniboine, Donald A. Smith was contemplating with *treacherous* more than passing interest the future of the Pembina Branch line. In *coward!"* 1875, as a Member of Parliament, he had been part of a delegation that had lobbied for the line to be built "irrespective of the action of the Minnesota railway companies." By 1878, his interest was personal as well as political. He was a member of a syndicate which was establishing rail connection from St. Paul to Pembina on the border. If the same group could lease the government line into the Red River Valley they would have a through line to Winnipeg. It was left to Smith to handle the matter politically.

As the man who had laid the last straw on the camel's back in the Pacific Scandal debacle of 1873, Smith had considerable political power. This was demonstrated in the case of one of the shipments of rails in 1875 – those same rails that were to return to haunt Mackenzie during the Royal Commission hearings of 1880-81. A quantity of rails could have been moved up the river by the Canadian firm of Fuller and Milne, who were that summer competitors of the Kittson Line in which the Hudson's Bay Company, through Smith, was a silent partner. The government appeared to be about to accept the Canadian firm's quoted price when James J. Hill, Smith's associate in the line, appeared in Ottawa and was closeted with Mackenzie. The $214,000 contract was then given to the Kittson Line without tender. The commissioners reported that Kittson had charged $44,000 more than the Canadian firm had offered and even then did not complete the contract. Such was Smith's influence with the Mackenzie government.

There was something a little frightening about Donald A. Smith. Perhaps it was the eyebrows – those bristling, tangled tufts that jutted out to mask the cold, uncommunicative grey eyes and provide their owner with a perpetual frown. At fifty-eight, his face leathered by the hard glare of the Labrador snows, his sandy locks and flowing beard frosted by the years, Smith had the look of a Biblical patriarch.

He was a stoic; nothing could touch him; the Company had seen to that. There is a particularly telling story about Smith's service within the Hudson's Bay Company that underlines the Spartan aspects of his character. Years before, in the heart of Labrador, he had suf-

249

fered an appalling attack of snow-blindness, an affliction that turns the whole world crimson and makes the victim feel as if his eyeballs are being scoured with burning grit. Accompanied by two half-breed guides, the sufferer set off from his post at Mingan, which lies on the northern coast of the St. Lawrence Gulf, on a fearful snowshoe journey to Montreal, five hundred and fifty-five miles distant by crow's flight. Arriving at his destination, Smith hammered on the door of Sir George Simpson, the "Little Emperor," who ran the company with a hand of iron. Simpson was not remotely concerned about Smith's plight; rather he was enraged that a servant of the company should have deserted his post. He gave the victim a tongue lashing: "If it's a question between your eyes and your service in the Hudson's Bay Company, you'll take my advice and return this instant." Then, after a peremptory medical examination, he turned him face-about into the snows. The return journey was so harsh that the guides died before reaching their destination. Smith stumbled the remainder of the way, half dead from exhaustion, fear and hunger. Years later when asked to describe that ghastly journey he could not bring himself to recall it. "No, no, I can't," he told an interviewer. "It is too terrible to think about."

There is no doubt that this incident, and others like it in that bleak land which Jacques Cartier said belonged to Cain, had left its mark upon him. For all of his life he never complained and he never explained; that was the Company way. Few public men had more vitriol heaped upon them than Smith in his long lifetime; he bore it all without blinking as he had borne the Little Emperor's abuse. In the election of 1874, Macdonald's supporters, incensed beyond reason by his defection from their ranks, had pelted him with raw eggs until he was unrecognizable. He did not flinch. Wintry of temperament, courtly of manner, he wrapped himself in a screen of suavity which masked the inner fires, bitter furies and the hard resolution of his soul. He was unshakable in crisis and this, one future day, would stand the CPR in good stead. It was impossible to panic Smith; he invested in stocks and debentures with great Scottish prudence but once he bought a stock, so legend had it, he never sold it. The market could bounce around like a tumbleweed; Smith did not turn a hair. Once, late in life, when he had achieved a baronetcy, he was discussing with a friend the merits of a certain security. "Your Lordship has some of it," the friend insisted. The old man did not believe him but finally got out his long investment list and there, sure enough, was the forgotten stock, purchased many years before and greatly increased in value.

It was this quality of unruffled repose – a kind of patrician self-confidence derived from the old fur-trading days when orders were unquestioned and a chief factor was a minor liege lord – that made Smith so formidable in negotiation. He did not suffer from false modesty. "It is said of the Scotch that they have a good opinion of themselves," he was wont to remark. "Well you know that, in reason, is a good thing. You know the Scotchman's prayer, 'Lord, gae us a guid conceit o' oursels.' That prayer has been abundantly answered."

In Winnipeg he was admired, hated, feared, respected but scarcely loved. On his first visit to the North West as Macdonald's envoy in the Riel uprising, he had shown courage, tact and diplomacy. His name was mentioned as a possible lieutenant-governor of Manitoba. Smith preferred the hurly-burly of political life. His active support came from the fur traders, many of whom were shunted across constituency lines at Company expense on election day. Being disciplined Hudson's Bay Company men, they knew what to do.

For all of his days in Winnipeg, Donald A., as he was called, was a figure of controversy. Seldom quoted in the newspapers, he was constantly attacked in them, especially after he shifted his political loyalties in 1873. The *Nor'wester* attacked him. The *Times*, which believed – probably correctly – that he had a financial interest in the rival *Free Press*, hit out at him month after month. Later, the *Free Press* attacked him as well. The laird of Silver Heights remained imperturbable, travelling daily by coach the six miles to and from his office, living his Spartan life – two meals a day, no spirits – sitting around the fire at night with visitors, recalling the old days in Labrador. His stays in Winnipeg were solitary enough, for his wife refused to join him in the barbarous North West. She was a child of Labrador and the hub of her existence had always been the fur-traders' capital, Montreal. She sprang from the Hardisty dynasty of Hudson's Bay traders. Smith had married her, in the custom of the trade, by "the rites of Labrador," i.e., without benefit of clergy, there being none available in those days. Years later, when he was about to become Lord Strathcona, it was revealed that he had no marriage certificate. This would never do: with his title in the balance, Smith agreed to a hasty wedding in the British Embassy in Paris. He was seventy-seven at the time.

The rail line to the border, which Smith and his partners coveted, was officially a branch of the almost non-existent CPR. Early in 1878, before the branch line was completed, Smith's cousin George Stephen made several trips from Montreal to arrange with Alexander Mackenzie for a ten-year lease of the government line to the syndicate, which was building the connecting line to the border from St. Paul. This would require an amendment to the Canadian Pacific Railway Act of 1874. On March 18, Mackenzie rose in the House to introduce a bill which would empower Parliament to lease the Pembina Branch to unspecified parties. The House would have to approve the principle first, Mackenzie pointed out, before going into the details of any contract. No mention was made of Donald A. Smith's interest; in fact, one month before, Mackenzie had firmly denied in Parliament that he had had any discussion about such an arrangement with Smith and his friends. This was, to put the very best construction on it, a not-very-white lie. On February 10, George Stephen had written to Jim Hill that he was on his way to Ottawa to see Mackenzie "to come to a definite and written understanding as to the terms of our arrangement with them for the Pembina branch. . . ."

On March 8, the *Globe* reprinted an earlier dispatch from the St. Paul *Pioneer Press*, which gave Donald Smith and his partners cause for alarm since it named them as having already secured the lease on the Pembina Branch of the CPR. "Antagonistic parties"— which meant the Northern Pacific – were warned not to waste their time trying to secure something which was already locked up. Mackenzie was queried about this in the House and again he was careful in his reply not to mention the interest of Donald A. Smith. "The Government know nothing about who all the parties are who are connected with the road; but Mr. Stephens [*sic*] has been in communication with the Government. . . ."

Of course the Prime Minister knew all about Smith's interest in the Pembina Branch. Why was he at such pains to conceal it from the House and the public? Simply because Smith's name was an abomination to the Conservative opposition; they would fight like mad dogs any scheme in which he had an interest. On this occasion Smith's personal interest was identical with that of his employer, the Hudson's Bay Company, and also with that of his Manitoba constituents. It was clearly advisable to get control of the much-abused line from Pembina into the hands of a group that could run it efficiently. But Smith had made some bitter enemies in 1873 and one of them was Macdonald, a political leader famous for the retort that he did not

252

want men who would stick by him when he was right, he wanted men who would stick by him when he was wrong. Smith had not stuck by him. If, in 1878, the Member for Selkirk had risen in the House to support motherhood, it is conceivable that Macdonald and his followers would have been strongly tempted to opt for matricide. They were out for Smith's blood. At a political picnic in Orangeville the previous summer, Tupper had launched a vicious attack on Smith, who, he charged, was really at outs with Macdonald because as Prime Minister he had once refused certain favours to the Hudson's Bay Company. Then he had "sat on the fence and watched the course, certainly not in the interests of the country, because he did not want to jump too soon and find he had jumped into a ditch. But when he came to the conclusion that the Government was going out, he made a bolt and he [Tupper] had no doubt that he had a great deal of reason since for having congratulated himself on having jumped as he did."

When the debate began on the Canadian Pacific Railway Act Amendment Bill, at the time of its second reading on April 4, 1878, Macdonald and his followers were ready with sharpened claws. It had scarcely been launched when George Kirkpatrick, a locomotive manufacturer who was Member for Frontenac, pointed out that the group seeking the lease were proprietors of the reviled Kittson Line of steamboats which "had ground down the people of Manitoba." A railway to Winnipeg, Kirkpatrick pointed out, would simply increase their monopoly. But the real opening guns were fired by Riel's old adversary, Dr. John Christian Schultz. Schultz came armed with facts and figures. He revealed the Kittson Line's interest in the newly organized St. Paul railroad and showed how Smith and his partners had acquired a huge land grant in Minnesota. Then he referred to repeated reports in the St. Paul *Pioneer Press* that the Pembina lease was a *fait accompli*. If the Prime Minister was right, he said, and no deal had been made, then Smith and his partners "must be using the grossest falsehoods" to strangle competition. If they succeeded, "Manitoba may expect no mercy in the way of reduced freight."

Another M.P. (and a future prime minister), Mackenzie Bowell, pressed the attack on Smith when he warned the Government that there might be persons connected with the St. Paul line "who had political influence which they used to their own advantage and to the detriment of this country."

In the acrimonious set-to which followed, Smith never at any time admitted to his own substantial interest in the company, even when pressed and taunted by the Opposition – though it was clear to all that he was deeply and personally involved. He spoke as one who had inside knowledge: "Some gentlemen of enterprise and means were at length induced to look into the matter and he believed they had been able to make arrangements by which they would be prepared to open up communication with the North West." He did not believe that they would charge rates higher than if there were competition. They were prepared to act "in the most fair way possible to the people of the North West." As for the Kittson Line, "not having been in any way personally interested in that company, even to the extent of sixpence, he had no right to have any knowledge of its internal affairs." This was, strictly speaking, true. Smith's shares, held by Kittson, had belonged to the Hudson's Bay Company and he had turned them over to his successor when he retired from the commissionership in 1874 to take another post. But whether he had the right or not, he was certainly intimately informed about the line's affairs, especially as the firm was about to merge all its assets with the newly purchased St. Paul railway, in which Smith was a major partner.

Schultz returned to the attack. Smith had made repeated references to "certain persons" and "parties" involved in the St. Paul line.

"Who are they?" Schultz asked.

"The hon. gentleman says he has the authority of certain persons for making a statement and, when asked, he will not say who they are," Macdonald broke in.

"I do not think it necessary to do so," Smith replied.

The debate grew warmer and more personal. Mackenzie Bowell put his finger on Smith's tenderest spot when, referring to the St. Paul report, he declared that if what was stated in the paragraph was a matter of fact then the House was witnessing "the extraordinary spectacle of the champion of this proposed lease using his power and influence as a very humble and obedient supporter of the Government to secure to himself and his partners in this transaction the advantage of a lease." Smith, Bowell continued, had but one object: ". . . to secure the lease which the Government ask power to grant this company, thereby benefiting himself individually." He did not believe the line should be leased; running rights should be granted over it to any line which the government could control. There should be no monopoly.

J. J. C. Abbott, when he was both a Member of Parliament and solicitor for Sir Hugh Allan's Canada Pacific company, had been careful to absent himself from all debates dealing with the railway – a practice he followed again when he became solicitor for the CPR in 1880. But Smith gave no indication that, as a Member of Parliament, he was involved in a clear conflict of interest. He replied obliquely to Bowell's taunts. He felt "humble, so very humble, under the correction of the hon. member"; but all that was being discussed was the government's power to lease the line; when a specific agreement came before the House, as it must, they could approve it or not. He had no desire to use any influence one way or another.

Now it was Macdonald's turn to unleash a cutting attack on his old enemy:

"There was seen the indecent spectacle of an honourable gentleman coming into the House as an advocate and pressing this lease in his own interest . . . he advocated more warmly and strongly this Bill, which was in his own interest, and which would put money in his own pocket, than the Minister who introduced it. The hon. gentleman admitted he was a partner in this concern, and the House should know something about it."

"I have admitted no such thing," Smith retorted; but Macdonald pointed out that he had not denied it, "and there is no doubt that, if he could have done so, he would."

So great was Macdonald's antipathy to Smith at this time that in the course of the debate he actually appeared to champion the cause of the Northern Pacific, as an alternative to or competitor of the St. Paul line, on the Pembina Branch. This was the same Northern Pacific, reorganized after the Jay Cooke debacle, whose attempts to move into Canada by this very route he had once so stoutly resisted.

It was inevitable that the bill should pass; the Government's majority saw to that. But it was a different story in the appointed Senate, where the Tories still had a preponderance of votes. The Senate, in effect, threw the bill out and there is no doubt it did so because of Smith's involvement.

On May 9, the day before the end of the session, Mackenzie took occasion to reprimand the Senate for its actions. This allowed Macdonald to return to the attack. The Senate's action, he said, put a stop to the Government's bargain with Smith "to make him a rich man, and to pay for his servile support."

Macdonald's sally provoked, in the closing moments of what

turned out to be the final session of the Mackenzie parliament, the most explosive and perhaps the most harrowing scene in the history of the House of Commons.

Smith was not in the House on May 9 but he read an account of Macdonald's attack in the press. The following day the House was scheduled to dissolve. The members were in their seats at 3 p.m., awaiting the traditional knock of the Gentleman Usher of the Black Rod when Smith, brandishing the Ottawa *Free Press* in his hand, arose on a question of privilege.

He denied that he had ever admitted being a member of the St. Paul syndicate.

"Even had I done so, I think that hon. gentleman had no right to speak of me as he did on that occasion. Whatever I have done in this respect I have done in the most open manner possible."

Smith said that as a Member from Manitoba, he had laboured earnestly for a railway connection for two or three years; now that it had become possible, the Opposition was putting every obstacle in its way. He declared that he had never asked the Macdonald government for a favour, that he had never "received a sixpence of public money . . . either for myself or any other persons connected with me." Then he went on to discuss Tupper's attack on him at Orangeville.

"I think it was at what is called the Orangeville picnic. I know very little of these picnics, I have not followed them closely, nor indeed have I followed them at all. I was otherwise, I trust, honestly and more properly occupied in the pursuit of my duties."

Macdonald broke in: "More profitably engaged, no doubt!"

"I trust so," said Smith smoothly. "More profitably and more properly." He began his reference to Tupper again; but Tupper, seeing Black Rod at the door, realized that in a few moments Smith would have had his say and he would have no opportunity to answer. The Cumberland War Horse had no intention of allowing that. He rose at once on a point of order, forced Smith to his seat and asked the Speaker if it were not an abuse of the rights of Parliament to bring up an old matter, since Smith had had three months during the session to refer to it. Tupper charged that Smith's tactics were "to shelter himself from the answer he would otherwise get."

"And the punishment he would otherwise get," Macdonald threw in.

"I had no opportunity," Smith protested.

But Tupper was warming to his task: "And a more cowardly thing I have never seen ventured in this House," he cried.

256

Smith began again. Again Tupper interrupted: "Anything more cowardly I never heard of . . . I have sat here for three months and no reference has been made to this by the honourable gentleman or anybody else."

The murmurs on both sides of the House became an uproar as members shouted for order.

Tupper continued to speak, but Smith interrupted: "The charge of being a coward I throw back at the honourable gentleman."

"Let the poor man go on," Macdonald advised his colleague. Smith then read the account of Tupper's attack upon him into the record and made a positive denial of the charge that he had "held back and sat on the fence." Both parties had approached him, Smith said, and he had made it very clear what his conscience dictated at the time of the Pacific debate.

Tupper was now bellowing across the floor in the face of repeated cries of "Order!" that Smith had telegraphed his support of the Government back in 1873. Smith denied it. "I do deny it. I never telegraphed I would be here and support the Government. Never. Never."

Now Macdonald tried to break in and, over more cries, shouted that Smith did not dare listen to an explanation. Smith kept going. He had, he said, expected a different amendment – one in which the Government frankly confessed its faults and took the issue to the country. That he would have voted for.

More bedlam! Tupper managed to call out: "That is not what you telegraphed." He had to repeat himself to be heard, for the Liberal benches were in full cry. "It was a sight to make sluggish blood tingle!" one eyewitness recalled.

The argument continued. Smith entered the name of Peter Mitchell, one of Macdonald's former cabinet, who, he claimed, "has got up in many an assembly where I have been and said I was perfectly justified in doing what I did."

This drove both Macdonald and Tupper into a fury and created near anarchy in the House as both men dared Smith to name "one single meeting where Mr. Mitchell ever made such a statement anywhere." The Opposition began to chant, "Name! Name!" The vain knocking of Black Rod could be heard faintly at the Commons door behind the uproar; the Speaker tried in vain to answer – then, with resignation, resumed his seat.

Smith continued to speak and with each new declaration the verbal contest grew more heated. As the Opposition cried "Order!" and the

Government benches shouted "Hear! Hear!" he declared: "The right honourable gentleman . . . spoke of Selkirk [Smith's riding] . . . as being a rotten borough, an Old Sarum, but in speaking of me, as he did, on the evening of November 4 [1873], he must have counted on the whole of Ontario being one great rotten borough, a veritable Old Sarum, as he said that if he appealed to it he would have Ontario to a man with him."

Macdonald was on his feet in an instant: "There is not a single word of truth in that statement – not one single word of truth. The honourable gentleman is now stating what is a falsehood."

"How much did the other side offer you?" cried a voice from the Opposition benches to Smith.

Smith ignored it as he twisted the knife into Macdonald, remembering perhaps that last evening before his speech of 1873, when the Prime Minister had received him with drunken abuse: "The honourable gentleman says he did not say so; certainly the spirit within him said it; for the words came out of the honourable gentleman's mouth."

This reference to Macdonald's drinking was too much. The situation became more confused as Macdonald engaged Smith in a shouting match.

But Smith managed yet another dig: Tupper, he said, had told him that very night that Macdonald was not capable of knowing what he said.

Now Tupper was on his feet, demanding of the Speaker whether it was "competent for a man to detail private conversations while falsifying them."

Through the hail of shouts and catcalls, Tupper cried that he had never witnessed such "cowardly abuse."

Smith was allowed to continue. Over repeated protests and interruptions he asked if Tupper would deny "that he said to me that so soon as it was possible to make that right honourable gentleman [Macdonald] to understand right from wrong, or to that effect . . ."

More interruptions: Tupper, determined to turn the course of the debate into a less embarrassing channel, cried that he was prepared to prove that Smith's statement that he had never sought a favour from the Government was "as false a statement as ever issued from the mouth of any man, and he has continued with a tissue . . ." Tupper was unable to finish the sentence because of the cries for order.

Smith, diverted from his intriguing account of Tupper's remarks about Macdonald, retorted that he had "never asked, prayed for, desired or got a favour from the Government."

258

But Tupper was on the attack and over the shouts and catcalls managed to declare that "the honourable gentleman begged of me to implore the leader of the Government to make him a member of the Privy Council of Canada. That is what he asked for and he was refused; and it was the want of that position, and that refusal, which, to a large extent, has placed him where he is today."

It was now Smith who was on the defensive. "The hon. gentleman knows that he states what is totally untrue, and, driven to his wit's end, is now going back to a journey he and I made to the North West in 1869, and I give the most positive denial to any assertion by him, or any other person, that I asked for or desired any favour from the Government."

At this point, with the House at a fever pitch, the Sergeant-at-arms managed to announce "a message from the Governor General."

As Smith continued to speak and the House continued in disorder and the Speaker tried to say that he had "very much pleasure in informing the House it now becomes my duty to receive the Messenger," Tupper's powerful voice was heard, over all, bellowing, "Coward! Coward!" at the imperturbable Smith.

Smith held his place.

"Coward! Coward! Coward!" Tupper boomed.

"You are the coward," replied Smith, evenly. Then he tried to squeeze in a final blow. Two members of the Government, he said, had come to him on the eve of the vote of 1873 and offered to get rid of both Macdonald and Langevin if Smith would agree to support the ministry.

This produced a chorus of rage from the Opposition. Tupper was beside himself. "Mean, treacherous coward!" he shouted.

"Who is the coward?" Smith retorted. "The House will decide – it is yourself."

"Coward!" shouted Tupper once again. "Treacherous . . ."

Smith began to speak again, but the harried Speaker interrupted him and asked that Black Rod be admitted.

It was Macdonald who got in the last word, surely the most unparliamentary expression ever to appear in Hansard.

"That fellow Smith," he cried, "is the biggest liar I ever met!"

The Gentleman Usher was admitted, performed his graceful triple bow, the Sergeant-at-arms shouldered the mace and the Speaker descended from his chair, followed by "as excited a mob as ever disgraced the floor of a Parliamentary chamber." Tupper and Macdonald and several other Tories, enraged beyond endurance, rushed at Smith, bent on physical assault. Several tried to strike him. The Speaker, without naming them, called for their arrest. Macdonald had to be pulled away from Smith, crying that he "could lick him quicker than hell could scorch a feather." The disorder was so great that the Speaker could not at once leave the House because of the throng at the door. Finally he was allowed to proceed to the Senate chamber, followed by the dishevelled crowd. Thus did the Mackenzie regime come to an end, not with a whimper but a bang. It could not accommodate Donald A. Smith and his colleagues with an exclusive lease of the Pembina Branch but it could grant running rights for ten years over the line and it did just that in August. That was one of its last official acts.

Chapter Seven

1

September 17, 1878, was the day of a political miracle in Canada. True to Charles Tupper's forecast, made in the dark days of '73, the party had risen again. Long before the election was called, it was clear that the Conservatives were on the rise; but nobody could be sure of the results. When they began to come in few could give them credence.

In the election, the Liberals found themselves on the defensive, with their railway policy trenchantly supported and vehemently attacked in rival political pamphlets, some of which, it turned out, were written by the same scriveners. There is a story about Edward Farrer, of the *Mail*, walking around Parliament Hill in a brown study after a sleepless night.

"What are you doing up at this hour?" asked a friend, who encountered him.

"Thinking over my paper in defence of the Government's railway policy," Farrer told him.

"Well, are you satisfied with your work?"

"Satisfied, yes. I am so damn well satisfied that I don't see how I'm going to answer it and that's what's keeping me up." He had undertaken to write a similar campaign sheet for the Tories.

But the political battle was not fought entirely on a philosophical level. Young Joseph Pope, who had been seconded to the giant Senator Macpherson in Toronto, recalled a singular scene at the height of the campaign. Into Macpherson's office strode a man named Piper from St. John's ward, wearing a black top hat and a light-coloured tweed suit.

"The boys in the ward are waiting to be fixed," said Piper to Macpherson in a hoarse whisper.

"Fixed?" exclaimed Macpherson. "What an extraordinary expression. Good gracious, Mr. Piper, what do you mean?"

Piper replied in a surly tone that "those chaps have got to be looked after or there'll be trouble," and left it at that. A day or so later he returned, leaned over Pope's desk and told him confidentially that "the boys in the ward are all right. Harry was down there last night and attended to them." Harry was the Senator's brother and *he* knew what "fixed" meant. It was apparent that the example of the Pacific Scandal, which did bring about some changes in electoral laws and practice, had not entirely eliminated tried and true methods of vote-gathering.

Fixes or no fixes, the country was on Macdonald's side more strongly than even he suspected. Macdonald was not a man to share his innermost thoughts with anyone; even his wife had no idea how he thought the vote might go. Towards the end of July it became a necessity for her to gain some inkling, since a Conservative win would mean a move back to the capital from Toronto where the Opposition leader had been practising law. She prodded her husband to give her a hint until, at last, he spoke: "If we do well, we shall have a majority of sixty; if badly, thirty." As it turned out, he did better than his most optimistic forecast.

Election day dawned in Ontario bright and crisp. Before the sun was up tens of thousands of canvassers from both parties were scouring the incredibly rutted and hilly concession roads for doubtful voters. The political uncertainties were compounded by the fact that this was to be the first federal secret ballot in history. This time no one could count noses or threaten wavering electors. Each man marked his X on the ballot paper, secure in the knowledge that prying eyes could not identify him if he changed his allegiance.

The night that followed was exciting and memorable. The polls closed at five and by seven it was clear that Macdonald had suffered personal defeat in Kingston. But this news was superseded by indications of massive Conservative gains. By nine, it was apparent that the Mackenzie administration had fallen, by eleven, that Macdonald and his party had scored a landslide of unprecedented proportions. In the session just past, the Liberals had held 133 seats to the Conservatives' 73. In the new Parliament, the Conservatives would have 137 seats to the Liberals' 69. Both Blake and Cartwright had gone down to defeat. For Macdonald, who would soon win a by-election in Victoria, B.C., revenge was sweet.

He was overwhelmed by the magnitude of his victory. The elections, Lord Dufferin reported to London, had "taken the entire political world by surprise." A week later both parties were still in a state of shock: "Sir John himself was as much astonished by the sweep as anybody." As for Mackenzie, he wrote a friend that "nothing has happened in my time so astonishing."

Mackenzie's railway policy had cost him the West. He had made an election eve gesture of moving rails from Esquimalt to Yale, in the interior of British Columbia, at a cost of thirty-two thousand dollars.

But this hint that the railway might at last be commenced along the canyons of the Fraser did not help him.

Worse, Mackenzie had also lost Ontario. By election day he was an exhausted man, teetering on the edge of a long decline, made irritable by the tensions and travails of office. Macdonald had the ability to bounce back after defeat. Part of the secret of his long tenure of office was his refusal to worry – the gift of putting things from his mind once events had taken their course. Unlike Mackenzie, he had the ability to delegate authority. Mackenzie attempted personally to handle the smallest details of his department and when his subordinates disappointed him by being unable to meet his standards, he broke under the strain. He would not lead his party for long for, truth to tell, he was already "a dry shell of what he had been." One day on the steps of Parliament Mackenzie spoke of his depressed spirits to Macdonald, who replied: "Mackenzie, you should not distress yourself over these things. When I fell in 1874, I made up my mind to cease to worry and think no more about [it]." To which Mackenzie made the candid and illuminating reply: "Ah, but I have not that happy frame of mind."

For two years after his defeat, the Tory chieftain had kept his peace while the Liberal press continued to announce his imminent retirement. In his first two years as Leader of the Opposition, he rarely divided the House for he "saw no advantage in publishing to the world every morning that we numbered only a handful." During that time the unquenchable Tupper spoke more often for his party than did his leader. Then, during the session of 1876, Macdonald revived and the country became familiar with the phrase "National Policy," on which the election of 1878 was fought.

It was not a new term. Tupper had used the phrase as early as 1870 when he talked of a national fiscal policy to make Canadians masters of their own economic affairs. The slogan was not a popular one and it was quietly dropped. By 1876, however, the industrial situation had become critical. United States manufacturers, protected in their own markets by heavy duties, were dumping their surplus products into the Canadian "slaughter market" at cut-rate prices. On occasion they even sent their own travellers to follow in the wake of Canadian drummers and offer to cut any of their rates. Industry after industry was forced to the wall and still Mackenzie, the traditional free trader, made no move towards protection.

The Tories were convinced he would raise the tariff and seize it as an election issue. In 1876, Tupper actually had two speeches ready –

one in each pocket – since he had no way of knowing what policy Mackenzie would announce. One was an eloquent, all-out attack on the tariff; the other was an equally impassioned defence of it. To his considerable relief, he was able to use the second one. The Macdonald administration was never overburdened by anything as consistent as a political philosophy. The leader himself was totally pragmatic. At one time he had avoided protection like the pox. "You needn't think I am going to get into that hole," he remarked. Just two months later he was prepared to embrace it. "Yes, protection has done so much for me that I must do something for protection," he jested, in justification.

In 1876 and again in 1877 and 1878, Macdonald called for a National Policy in the form of a series of resolutions before the House. In brief, he proposed to readjust tariffs so as to support local manufactures, mining and agriculture, to restore prosperity to the struggling native industries, to stop the flow of Canadians across the border to the United States and to protect Canadian interests from unfair competition. He did not use the word "protection," which the free-trading Grits had made so unpopular. ("There is no policy more consistent with what we call the Dark Ages of the world," Mackenzie had said.) Instead, at a series of political picnics, which became an established feature of the Canadian scene in the late seventies, he talked of prosperity and "Canada for the Canadians." In a depression-ridden nation it was an attractive slogan.

The National Policy was an aspect of Macdonald's instinctive anti-Yankee philosophy, and his speeches on the subject set the pattern for political rhetoric for another century. "We will not be trampled upon and ridden over, as we have [been] in the past, by the capitalists of a foreign country," he told an audience in the Eastern Townships of Quebec in 1877. Mackenzie was all for making everything "as cheap as the state of the revenue will permit," through free and unfettered trade, but Macdonald sensed the mood of the country more accurately. The movement from the farms to the cities had already begun but there was no work in the cities – hence the leakage across the border of those who did not wish to farm. By offering protection for urban manufacturing firms, Macdonald convinced the country that he was widening the opportunities for employment in Canada – "a fair day's wage for a fair day's work," as he put it. He was also reinforcing the traditional Conservative alliance with vested business interests and laying the basis for the introduction of American branch plants into Canada.

In 1878, the National Policy was nothing more than a euphemism for a protective tariff but in later years it was seen as one leg of a three-cornered foundation on which the superstructure of the transcontinental nation rested. The other two legs were the encouragement of western settlement and the construction of the Pacific railway. The railway was the key; without it western settlement would be difficult; with it there would be more substantial markets for the protected industries. Macdonald himself saw this. "Until this great work is completed, our Dominion is little more than a 'geographical expression,' " he told Sir Stafford Northcote, the Governor of the Hudson's Bay Company. "We have as much interest in British Columbia as in Australia, and no more. The railway once finished, we become one great united country with a large interprovincial trade and a common interest."

The National Policy, which won Macdonald his stunning victory in 1878 and which helped to keep his party in office for almost twenty years, was to become the policy of the country. The future would extend it to include a variety of awkward, expensive and contentious Canadian devices which, like the railway, would continue the horizontal development of the nation that Macdonald began.

Though the two parties differed on the tariff, there was not much difference, in 1878, between the new government's railway policy and that of its predecessor. Mackenzie had long since abandoned his original idea of a land-and-water route (a mixture which, Macdonald quipped, "generally produces mud") and clearly wanted to get rid of the piecemeal method of construction, which was causing so much trouble west of Lake Superior. His excuse for not proceeding faster and linking the two main sections under construction in that area was that he wanted the whole undertaking to be in the hands of a single private company.

That was Macdonald's hope, too. But in the absence of any offers from private capitalists, his administration was forced to continue Mackenzie's policy of building the line in instalments: the 171-mile gap in the Lake Superior area would be completed; an additional two hundred miles would be contracted for, to run west of the Red River. It would be accomplished without raising taxes. As Tupper, the new Minister of Railways, announced in May, 1879, the line would be paid for by selling the uncultivated land of the western plains. "We believe," said Tupper, "that we have there the garden of the world. We believe we have something like 180 million acres of land which, in regard to the fertility and grain-bearing qualities, are equal to any on the face of the globe."

266

These figures were largely the result of John Macoun's enthusiastic, and sometimes overenthusiastic, reports of 1877. Macoun flatly contradicted the findings of Palliser and Hind, who had talked of an "arid belt" on the southern plains, which they believed to be an extension of the Great American Desert.

"I wrote as much truth about the country as I dared," Macoun recalled in his autobiography, "for I saw that my best friends believed me rather wild on the 'illimitable possibilities' of the country. When summing up the various areas, I reached the enormous figure of 200 million acres and recoiled from making public this number on the ground that the very immensity would deny that amount of credence I desired, so, as a salve to my conscience, I kept the large number of 200 million but said there were 79,920,400 acres of arable land and 120,400,000 acres of pastures, swamps and lakes. . . . My statements appeared as those of a crack-brained enthusiast and little attention was paid to them."

Tupper, however, had somewhat hesitantly decided to accept Macoun's estimate for this and subsequent statements of public policy ("Macoun . . . for God's sake, do not draw on your imagination"). In his 1879 resolution, which urged that the railway be built "with all practical speed," he asked that one hundred million acres of land be chosen, appropriated and sold at two dollars an acre, the proceeds to be used to pay for the line.

He also announced several changes of route. In order to achieve speed, railway construction and colonization would have to proceed hand in hand and, therefore, the line must go through the prairie country that afforded the best attraction for newcomers; hence the route would be lengthened to pass south of Lake Manitoba. Moreover, Tupper continued, the selection of Burrard Inlet as the Pacific terminus was premature. The government wanted more time to make more surveys, including surveys of the Pine and Peace River passes and of Port Simpson on the coast. Marcus Smith's furious efforts had obviously not been in vain.

On the other hand there were "the excited feelings of British Columbia in consequence of long delays." Because of these, the government felt compelled to let contracts that year for 125 miles of railway. Tupper could not say where that railway might be built but, by coincidence, that was the distance between Yale, in the Fraser canyon, and Kamloops. This was a curious business: on the one hand the government was going to survey Port Simpson again and was talking of a possible choice between it and the Bute or the Burrard termini; on the other it appeared to be preparing to build the most expensive portion of the Burrard route.

Mackenzie, in his reply to Tupper, declared that Macdonald had been elected in Victoria for the purpose of bringing the route through Bute Inlet to that city and this was probably the politics behind the paradox. Nevertheless, the surveys continued.

Characteristically, Tupper had decided to attack the most difficult section of the British Columbia line first. His reason was that "its early completion meant the breaking of the backbone of the undertaking." The contracts were let in four sections. The successful tender for two of these sections, totalling almost five million dollars, was from a syndicate larded with the names of prominent Conservatives: A. P. MacDonald, ex-mayor of Toronto and ex-member for Middlesex; Duncan McDonald, sitting member for Victoria, Nova Scotia; and one of the Shanly family of Montreal, leading Tory politicians as well as railroad engineers.

One of the bidders on all four sections, though by no means the lowest, was a young American named Andrew Onderdonk, the courtly, sophisticated scion of a prominent Hudson River family of Dutch ancestry. Onderdonk arrived in Ottawa in November, 1879, at the time the tenders were opened, his pockets stuffed with letters of recommendation from Canadian bankers and United States railway-men. His backing was impressive: he had almost unlimited means behind him. There was H. B. Laidlaw, a New York banker, L. P. Morton of the great New York banking firm of Morton, Bliss and Company, S. G. Reed, president of the Oregon Railway of Portland, and last, but certainly not least, the legendary San Francisco financier, Darius O. Mills, who was at that very moment constructing the world's most palatial office building – nine stories high! – on New York's Broad Street.

Onderdonk, who had just finished constructing a sea-wall at San Francisco, went straight to see Tupper and Tupper was impressed. In the muskeg country west of Lake Superior, Canadian contractors were running into difficulties. Joseph Whitehead was teetering on the edge of financial ruin. Some of the low bidders on the four British Columbia sections looked alarmingly shaky. One of them had already had an internal falling out and could not raise the required security. Obviously, a man of experience backed by solid capital could build all four sections more cheaply and efficiently than four under-financed contractors working independently. Onderdonk was allowed to purchase all the contracts. He paid a total of $215,000 for the privilege, arrived at Yale on April 22, 1880, to a salute of thirteen guns, and by May was ready to begin construction. None of Macdonald's followers appeared to grasp the irony of a Conservative government awarding an important section of the railway to a Yankee contractor.

Meanwhile, Marcus Smith, who had been pronounced dead by both Fleming and Mackenzie, refused to lie down on the subject of the Pine Pass–Bute Inlet route. Indeed, he seems to have gained a new lease on life with the advent of the new administration – an administration in which Fleming's position was becoming increasingly insecure.

There is something madly magnificent about Smith's furious windmill-tilting at this late date. He simply refused to give up, even when the odds were against him. On January 20, 1879, he sent Tupper a confidential memorandum detailing his differences with Fleming, whose reports he categorized as "an apology for a course predetermined by the Minister"; he also revealed that his map of the Peace River country had been "cunningly suppressed." He followed this up with another long memo to Tupper. In it he charged that Mackenzie, who was writing articles for the *Globe* advocating the Burrard route, "was nervously anxious about it for he is well aware that it is not only a blunder but a *political fraud* connected with a land job before which that of the Kaministiquia [at Fort William] pales into insignificance." Smith wanted Tupper to give him charge of a two-year survey of the Pine Pass section of the Bute Inlet route – scarcely a feasible suggestion in view of the clamour from British Columbia. In May he wrote to Macdonald asking him to intercede on his behalf to reinstate him as Engineer of the British Columbia division, the job he had held before becoming Fleming's deputy. Fleming, he complained, was advising the Minister of Public Works, Langevin, to "suppress all information adverse to [Smith's] views." A week or so later he shot off a private letter to the editor of the Toronto *Mail*, all about the missing map.

In the meantime, Henry Cambie had taken a distinguished party of surveyors and scientists right across the uncivilized hinterland of northern British Columbia. They started at Port Simpson, "one of the finest harbours on the Pacific Coast," worked their way up the Skeena, and then followed a succession of rivers, canyons and mountain trails on foot and packsaddle and by canoe, raft, and leaky boat until they reached the Peace River country on the far side of the mountains. In all that journey they did not encounter a single human being. Cambie returned on his own with a pack train and reached the top of the Pine Pass in a raging blizzard. He made his way back to civilization down the fast-freezing Fraser, shooting the rapids of the canyon himself, without a pilot. "Sham surveys" Smith called them, in a letter to Brydges, when Cambie returned; but on the strength of his report the government, in October 1879, finally gave up on the Bute Inlet route and announced that Burrard Inlet would be the official terminus after all. The Yellow Head, apparently, would be the pass through the Rockies.

Still Marcus Smith would not admit defeat. He wrote immediately to Senator David Macpherson, attacking the whole decision, predicting that there would never be any through traffic on the route and urging that it be considered a local line only, to be built at one-third the estimated cost. Then he allied himself with General Butt Hewson,* an American engineer resident in Canada, who was preparing a pamphlet advocating that the Fraser contracts be cancelled and that either Bute or Dean Inlet be named as the terminus and the Pine Pass substituted for the Yellow Head. Smith supplied Hewson with a good deal of material for his critical pamphlet but balked at a cash donation.

The Battle of the Routes continued all that winter, with Smith firing off letters to A. P. MacDonald, the Tory contractor, to Langevin, to Brydges and to Dr. Helmcken in Victoria, all peppered with the bitterest accusations against Macdonald, Tupper, Cambie, Trutch, Dewdney, Onderdonk, Fleming, all of the British Columbia mainland members and everyone else in the growing army of critics of the Bute Inlet route. As the months wore on the battle grew more confused with Smith still advocating Bute Inlet, General Hewson wavering between Bute and Dean inlets and Charles Horetzky entering the fray with a pamphlet melodramatically entitled *Startling Facts*, urging Kitimat Inlet as the railway terminus. These three strangely assorted propagandists had one thing in common: they all insisted that the Pine Pass was a better choice than the Yellow Head.

*Hewson was wrangling with Macdonald over the fee supposedly owed him for some newspaper work he had done for the Conservatives. When the party demurred at paying, the General threatened to horsewhip the Prime Minister on Parliament Square. He eventually settled, however, for "a neat pile of Bank of Montreal bills, clean and crisp," to quote the Ottawa *Free Press*.

Horetzky's pamphlet was by far the most intemperate published. In it, he too claimed that Fleming had suppressed one of his reports – that written in 1874 as a result of his exploration of Kitimat Inlet and the Kitlope River. Ironically, Fleming had edited the report on Marcus Smith's advice. Smith had pointed out that Horetzky was not an engineer and that as long as he confined himself to descriptions of what he saw he was serviceable enough, but not when he gave engineering opinions, descriptions of grades, tunnels and curvatures: "You will have to explain this to Mr. Horetzky for he is such a crazy, conceited fellow, he will think (and publish) that his genius is being repressed, if he has not his say, although, I may inform you that, except for his photographs, his work is altogether worthless and can't be laid down on a general map."

Six years later Smith was proven right: Horetzky was having his say, laying about him with a verbal scythe, attacking George Grant, John Macoun, Henry Cambie and Fleming and charging that his findings had been mutilated for sinister reasons. "Nobody in his senses can believe any such nonsense as this," wrote the *Canadian Illustrated News*; but a good deal of what Horetzky wrote was believed and used for political purposes.

All this pressure undoubtedly had some effect on public policy. On February 16, 1880, Tupper told the House that he still wanted more information on the Pine River–Peace River country before finally making up his mind about the choice of a pass through the Rockies. It was now the ninth year of the Canadian Pacific Survey in British Columbia and it seemed by this time that every notch in each of the mountain ranges and all the intervening trenches had been combed as carefully as a Japanese sand garden. Gillette and his party had toiled up the slopes of the Howse, Jarvis had almost starved at the Smoky, Cambie and Horetzky had struggled over the Pine and the Peace, Roderick McLennan had lost all his horses probing the Athabasca, Moberly had braved the avalanches in the Selkirks and scoured the Gold Range, while Fleming himself, not to mention a score of others, had come through the Yellow Head.

Every pass had been checked with transit, level and aneroid, again and again; every pass had been argued over, reported on, discarded or, sometimes, resurveyed – every pass, that is, except the Kicking Horse, which lay to the south, neglected and unsurveyed, waiting to be chosen.

2

Sandford Fleming's days as Engineer-in-Chief were numbered. The dissensions within his own department, as symbolized by the intractable Marcus Smith, the total identification with Mackenzie's sluggish and sometimes inept railway policies, the bills coming in from Lake Superior, far in excess of estimates, the expensive surveys in British Columbia – all these were laid at his door. In the spring of 1879 he had been given a hard time as a witness before the Commons Public Accounts Committee and it was clear that more investigations were to follow.

"I have the conviction that you will neither obtain speedy nor economical construction under Fleming's management," that old railway hand Alexander Galt wrote to Macdonald after his election victory. It was not an entirely disinterested comment; Galt wanted the job himself, or one like it, which he called "railway commissioner." He urged Macdonald to "get rid of Fleming and all his copious paraphernalia" and in a later letter added that "Fleming seems incapable of grasping the idea of what the country wants and what its resources enable it to do and I must say with a frankness I trust you will pardon that his continuance on the direction of the Pacific Railway will defeat all our plans for the development of our country."

Galt then suggested that the change might be effected through the appointment of a commission to report on the whole subject, with himself, Charles Brydges and Sir Casimir Gzowski – all experienced railway builders – as commissioners.

Macdonald had other plans for the ambitious Galt. He would shortly be appointed Canada's first high commissioner to London. He did, however, intend to appoint a royal commission to look into the entire operation of the railway, though not with the personnel Galt suggested. He intended that Fleming should go, but not as a result of the commission's findings. Senator Macpherson had also been urging the move upon him, perhaps partly as a result of Marcus Smith's importuning; and there were other murmurings. Fleming had made substantial profits as a contractor on a section of the Intercolonial Railway and his opponents were insinuating that his friend Tupper had shared in these. (The *Globe* rarely mentioned Tupper without referring, somehow, to corruption.) This was never proved, though Fleming certainly contributed to Tupper's campaign funds, but somebody had to be sacrificed and it could not be Tupper. After nine years of service Fleming would go with as much honour as possible and with the government's blessing; one never knew when he might be needed again.

Clearly, Fleming was not the man to prosecute Macdonald's aggressive railway policy. He could be maddening in his caution yet wild in his extravagances. He had, for instance, insisted on a great many instrumental surveys in British Columbia when simple exploratory surveys would have done, for the routes were later abandoned as too expensive, too difficult or too unwieldy. An exploratory survey involves one or two men; an instrumental survey involves a painstaking, foot-by-foot measurement by a large, heavily supplied party. Even Fleming was to admit that the expense in British Columbia "was simply enormous." In British Columbia, between 1874 and 1876, there were twenty-nine instrumental surveys and only eight exploratory surveys. The former cost an average of thirty thousand dollars apiece, the latter less than nine.

Even when the explorations revealed little chance of a practical route – as they did in the case of Gardner Channel – the overcautious Fleming ordered an instrumental survey anyway. It is true that such a criticism, which was levelled at the time, was made from hindsight as Fleming himself was quick to point out – after all, the map of northern British Columbia was absolutely blank for more than two hundred miles. But it was also true that Fleming had settled on the Yellow Head Pass and rejected Moberly's choice of the Howse on the basis of simple surveys.

Everybody acknowledged Fleming's genius; yet at times he could be singularly blind. Why, for instance, did he wait five years before consulting the Admiralty about the usefulness of the various harbours at the head of the inlets his men were examining? A great deal of money could have been saved if these reports had been in his hands at the outset, for they made it clear that Burrard Inlet was the only really satisfactory terminus on the mainland.

Fleming, of course, had to take the blame for all the manifold political sins of the day. The surveys had to be kept going while the Government tried to arbitrate between warring factions. Untrained and incompetent employees were forced upon him. Sometimes he had to invent work where no work existed. Often he was late getting his men into the field in the spring because he was forced to wait for the estimates to come down in Parliament before he could know how much money he had to spend. He was also unlucky: a disastrous fire in the engineering offices on January 26, 1874, destroyed most of the work of the previous two years which meant that all the hardships suffered by the men on the unfriendly shores of Lake Superior, in the canyons of the Homathco and Fraser and in the passes of the Rockies had been in vain; it had to be repeated. But Fleming also tried to do too much. When he was on the job he could give only half of his working day, admittedly a long one, to the Pacific railway; and, after 1876, when the Intercolonial was completed, he spent a great deal of time away from the job on doctor's orders, working on his concept of standard time, visiting Thomas Carlyle, hob-nobbing with the Prince of Wales in Paris. Even in Ottawa a great deal of his time was taken up with preparing for and testifying before parliamentary committees of inquiry.

Overly scrupulous in the Far West, he appeared to have been unduly hasty in his eastern surveys. Here there were terrible delays and extraordinary added charges because the engineers on the job had made only cursory examinations of the ground. In every case between 1875 and 1878, the contractors arrived on the job before their work was fully laid out. In one instance, J. W. Sifton turned up with sixty teams of horses and twelve hundred men all of whom had to be kept idle because the surveyors had not yet adopted a final location. Contracts were let on the basis of profile plans only, so that the estimates of the quantities of rock and earth to be removed or filled were nothing more than guesses and expensive adjustments had to be made after the fact. The disputes between the government and the contractors, as a result, seemed endless and many of them went to court. On four contracts tendered at a total cost of $3,587,096 the government paid extras amounting to $1,804,830. The surveyors apparently had no idea of the kind of ground the railway builders would be working. They did not know, for instance, how deep the marshes and muskegs would go; and, because they had not studied the nature of muskeg, huge prices were paid for fill materials. Muskeg is so spongy that when it is taken from an embankment and dried out it loses about half its size. Yet the removal of muskeg, and its employment as fill, was charged for as if it were ordinary earth. On one contract, the loss from this oversight amounted to $350,000.

Often enough, Fleming, the thrifty Scot, was penny wise and pound foolish. The cost of running the railway through the gorges of the Thompson and the Fraser to Burrard Inlet seemed so high that

274

he continued to search, diligently but vainly, for a cheaper route. Eventually even the Pine Pass was abandoned and, in 1880, Fleming's original route of 1871 was selected. On the other hand, the cost of probing the muskegs in advance seemed to Fleming so great that he decided he could not afford it; in that instance, further exploration would have paid off. The price of steel rails seemed so low in 1874 that he ordered far more than he needed, only to see the price go even lower – at a loss to the public of some two million dollars – while the unused rails rusted away. In all of this expensive penny-pinching, Mackenzie was Fleming's partner, but there is no evidence that the Engineer-in-Chief ever resisted the Minister or even argued with him. For a good deal of the time he simply was not available and his deputy, Marcus Smith, was not on speaking terms with his political master. These displays of temperament were costly and confusing. In November 1877, for instance, Joseph Whitehead wanted to change the work on certain portions of his contract from temporary trestlework to permanent earth and sand embankments (which were more costly and, of course, more profitable to Whitehead). The district engineer, James Rowan, endorsed the change, which was approved by Fleming who then left for England. Mackenzie, meanwhile, decided not to accept Fleming's recommendation but he did not inform Smith. The work proceeded on its own momentum without authority.

Political expediency, as Fleming himself admitted, forced the premature start of construction between Fort William and Selkirk in 1875. The Red River community was clamouring for it; so were the commercial interests of Thunder Bay. Mackenzie rose in the House that year to insist that "a most elaborate survey had been made" of Section Fifteen. "It would be impossible," he said, "to have a more careful survey, a closer examination or a more careful calculation than had been made on these thirty-seven miles."

But the surveyor himself, Henry Carre, later gave the lie to that statement: "We just ran through, using the men that packed the provisions, on days when we were not moving the camp, to chop out a line which I ran with my eye and a pocket compass; then as soon as the transit men came along they ran the transit level over it and plotted it; then I put down the location line, and the location men ran that line. If the profile showed a practicable line, then I was satisfied. I never went back over it again, so that I never actually saw the country after the line was located. . . . I never gave the estimate as an actual estimate of the cost. If I had been asked to estimate the actual cost of the work, I would have refused point blank to pretend to give it. No mortal man could give it."

Yet mortal men did give estimates on those perfunctory surveys and other mortals tendered on the basis of those estimates. Mackenzie, during the election, had boasted that "under our wise and economical system of contracts" the total cost of the Thunder Bay–Red River section would amount to $24,535 a mile, or about half the cost of the Intercolonial. But by the time the Government changed, the estimates had risen to $38,092.

The Royal Commission put most of the blame on Fleming's shoulders. It was not all warranted. Horetzky was one of the witnesses the commissioners paid attention to. His testimony was venomous: "Mr. Fleming stands convicted of deliberate and malicious falsehood. His malevolence has been directed against me ever since I brought the Pine Pass under his notice. In doing so I unconsciously wounded his vanity, which could not brook the idea of any one but himself proposing a route."

Only a few months before giving this testimony, Horetzky had written to Fleming offering his friendship while attacking Tupper, whose protégé he had been in 1872 ("I have it in for Tupper and will follow him to the last. I shall never forget in a hurry his insulting language to my wife. . . ."). Fleming received "three extraordinary letters in which he volunteered to pledge me his lasting friendship provided I would assist in getting him the money he demanded from the Government, at the same time vowing vengeance if I failed to recommend payment."

Horetzky, who was not an engineer, thought he ought to be paid as one and this was one of the bones of contention between him and his former chief. Fleming's method of handling Horetzky was, to put it mildly, oblique. He refused to do battle with him. Horetzky would write, demanding his money. Fleming would reply with great courtesy that it was not in his power to grant the raise – the matter was up to the Minister. Horetzky would write Tupper, who would reply with equal courtesy that the government had no power to pay except on a certificate from the Engineer-in-Chief. Fleming had no intention of certifying a larger amount for Horetzky, but he did not make this clear to him. Horetzky managed to get the matter raised in the House, where he heard himself praised by Simon J. Dawson as "a very capable and energetic officer"; but he did not get his money.

Fleming's lack of confidence in Horetzky cost the public money. When Marcus Smith, in 1874, on the strength of Horetzky's explorations decided that a further examination of the Kitlope valley would be a waste of funds, Fleming sent along a second and much more expensive expedition anyway. It was a decision that enraged the temperamental Horetzky. As for Smith, Fleming blamed him for much of the extra cost on the contracted work west of Lake Superior, which, he pointed out, was done in his absence. It was, he said, "startling . . . alarming . . . unaccountable . . . incomprehensible." Smith, who arrived on the scene from British Columbia after some of the locations were established and the contracts let, blamed Fleming. Often enough, he claimed, when he tried to adjust matters during Fleming's absences, the men under him would insist that they were following the chief engineer's instructions: "I had on several occasions to complain to the responsible members of the staff of a want on their part of systematic and intelligent direction of the works and their leaving too much to juniors. But all these gentlemen were high in their esteem of the Engineer-in-Chief, and specially appointed by him to the important positions they held. This may account in some measure for their neglect in reporting to me as often as I wished."

Fleming was eased out of office in February, 1880, before the Royal Commission commenced its hearings. The government provided for him handsomely. Since the Minister of Public Works was paid five thousand dollars a year and Fleming, as chief engineer of the Intercolonial, was already receiving forty-eight hundred, it had been considered impolitic to raise his salary when he assumed the double burden. But the government sent him on his way with an additional thirty thousand. It also offered him a titular post with the railway, but this Fleming declined; he did not care to be a figurehead.

When the Royal Commission finally made its report it came down very hard on the former engineer-in-chief but by then the construction of the railway was proceeding apace. Fleming went off to the International Geographical Congress in Venice to ride in gondolas and deliver a paper entitled "The Adoption of a Prime Meridian." Greater glories followed. His biography, when it was published, did not mention the petty jealousies, the bursts of temperament, the political jockeying, the caution, the waste and the near anarchy that were commonplace in the engineering offices of the public works department under his rule. He survived it all and strode into the history books without a scar. The story of his term as Engineer-in-

Chief is tangled and confused, neither black nor white, since it involved neither villains nor saints but a hastily recruited group of very human and often brilliant men faced with superhuman problems, not the least of which was the spectre of the Unknown, and subjected to more than ordinary tensions including the insistent tug of their own ambitions.

If there is a verdict on Fleming it is an indirect one. When the railway was finally organized as a private company, most of his surveys were discarded and an entirely new line was mapped out across the Shield, north of Lake Superior, through the southern prairies and across three mountain ranges. The matter was handled with dispatch, certainty and even foolhardiness. William Cornelius Van Horne boldly drove his steel across the prairies and straight at the mountain wall before his engineers were even certain that a pass in the Selkirks existed. He hustled his surveyors on, following their line of location so swiftly that they were hard pressed to stay ahead of him. It was madness, perhaps, but it got the entire job done in exactly half the time it took Fleming and his political colleagues to make up their minds about a route through British Columbia.

But, then, the times were different; the circumstances were different; the economics were different; and the men were different, too.

3

The
Strange Case
of Contract
Forty-two

The influence peddling, the bribery and the brokerage in contracts did not cease in the Department of Public Works under the Macdonald government. If the Strange Case of Contract Forty-two is any indication, it grew worse. Of all the unconscionable manoeuvres connected with the awarding of work on the government road, this was the most labyrinthine. It helps explain why the government was so anxious to get out of the railroad business and turn the task over to a private company.

Mackenzie's government had built the railway westward from the head of Lake Superior and eastward from the Red River, but there remained a gap of 181 miles between the two railheads. The new administration decided to let contracts on this section immediately, in order to give the Red River community access to the East through Canadian territory as swiftly as possible. There were two contracts,

278

numbered Forty-one and Forty-two. Contract Forty-one, for Section A of the railroad, ran from English River to Eagle River, a distance of 114 miles; Contract Forty-two (Section B) ran for 67 miles through more difficult country from Eagle River to Keewatin.

Tenders were called in the fall of 1878 and were due to be opened the following January 30 in order that the successful bidder could make an early start in the spring. Number Forty-two was a lucrative contract, running to an estimated four million dollars. The bidding was expected to be highly competitive.

Early in January, George D. Morse, a Toronto cattle exporter, and three partners decided to bid for the contract. None of them knew much about railways but they did know something about political influence. They intended to buy that from Patrick Close, a Toronto merchant and politician who was an intimate friend of leading Conservatives and a staunch contributor to party funds. Morse offered Close two per cent of the total amount of the contract if he could use his political influence to get it for him. Close agreed; two per cent would mean about eighty thousand dollars in his pocket. He, in turn, brought in a Conservative party fixer named John Shields; the two planned to split the commission.

Shields was a leading railway contractor whose services to the party would be many and varied. When the voters of Bracebridge needed to be lubricated, it was John Shields who arrived at a local hotel with five trunks full of whiskey to do the lubricating. When General Butt Hewson sued John A. Macdonald for a party debt, it was Shields who arranged to pay him off quietly, thus establishing, in the sardonic words of the Ottawa *Free Press*, "another claim to the good will and gratitude of the poor, persecuted Premier."

Shields advised Morse to make his tender as low as possible so that it would have to be accepted. He explained that Morse could make up the difference later by having friendly engineers on the ground authorize extra charges. Morse took the suggestion to heart. He set the price absurdly low and, at the last moment, lowered it still further.

He did not know that his adviser was playing a double game. Shields's own contracting firm – all its members were powerful Conservatives – was also bidding on the contract.

Morse's firm had the lowest bid. Marcus Smith ran his keen and always sceptical engineer's eye over the tender and reported at once that it was excessively low and inconsistent with a knowledge of the country. Nor did he believe that the second lowest bidder, Andrews,

Jones and Company, an American firm, could carry out the work without losing money. Fleming agreed with Smith and advised the department that the two low tenders should be passed over. A fortnight's delay ensued while Fleming was asked to make further inquiries. Thus at a critical time of the year two valuable weeks were lost; the Department of Public Works was not able to do what any private company would have done – adopt the report of its engineers and accept promptly the lowest offer of any firm believed capable of doing the job.

In spite of the engineers' objections, Morse was given the contract. He decided to relinquish it. His plan was to form a secret partnership with the second lowest bidder, the American firm of Andrews, Jones, and let them be awarded the job by default – at a bid almost half a million dollars higher than his own. The department now believed it was dealing with Andrews, Jones who promptly informed it that the required security of two hundred thousand dollars would be deposited at once. This was a bald lie. Neither the Americans nor their silent partners had a dollar. What they had was an influence peddler in the person of another American, Colonel J. N. Smith, the agent in Canada of a New York banking house. Smith was persuaded – in return for an interest in the contract – to play a double game and urge his New York employers to put up the security.

At this point John Shields, whose bid was fourth lowest, decided to join forces with the third lowest bidder, a Nova Scotian firm. The object of the new combination was to remove the two lowest tenderers from the scene and gain the contract for themselves. Patrick Close was also playing a double game. He was supposed to be helping Morse by raising security money. Shields bribed him out of the Morse camp by offering him a one-twenty-fourth interest in the contract – about twice the amount Morse had promised.

The scene now shifts to the Russell House at Sparks and Elgin Streets, the great listening-post of Ottawa and for half a century its leading hotel. Beneath the giant chandeliers of its vast dining hall, in the whispering galleries of its stairwells and corridors, or among the overstuffed settees of its drawing room, half the deals in the capital were worked out. Every politician of stature stayed at this deceptively plain, three-storey colonial Georgian inn. So did every gilded visitor, every prominent businessman and every major contractor, "manipulating some scheme or organizing some enterprise" as that literate traveller Peter O'Leary remarked in 1877. Its halls, one visitor noted, were "a thorough Parliamentary lobby" and its bar derived "a particularly brisk custom from convivial legislators." Here William Kersteman had spotted George McMullen dining with Senator Asa B. Foster in Christmas week of 1872 and wondered what kind of deal was afoot (Foster was dickering with McMullen for the Allan correspondence). Here some years later a chance encounter between Senator Frank Smith and a despondent George Stephen would help save the CPR from bankruptcy. And here John Shields's partner, John J. McDonald, had dinner with Samuel St-Onge Chapleau, his secret pipeline into the Department of Public Works.

Chapleau had been meeting daily with McDonald for months and these meetings had been highly profitable for both, for Chapleau was correspondence clerk in the department and, being in charge of the record room, was privy to all its secrets. His appointment was obviously a political one; he was the brother of Joseph Adolphe Chapleau, the Conservative premier of Quebec. Chapleau *frère* knew a good thing when it was handed to him. One of his "arrangements" was with George M. Mowbray, the pioneer manufacturer of nitro-glycerine. Mowbray paid Chapleau between thirty and forty dollars a month to keep him informed concerning contracts on rock work. That sum was alone was roughly equal to fifty per cent of Chapleau's government salary.

At one of the Russell House's long, glittering tables, where the fare was diverse and virtually unending – a multi-course meal could be had for about fifty cents – Chapleau brought his friend up to date on the details of the contract which would be awarded officially to Andrews, Jones once the security was deposited. It developed that Chapleau was a close personal friend of Colonel Smith, who was then on his way to New York to arrange financing for the successful bidder. McDonald offered Chapleau four thousand dollars to go to New York and give Smith's principals a bad report and thus prevent the American contractors from getting the job.

Shortly after this Andrews, Jones, unable to raise any security in New York, decided to throw in the sponge. However, Morse, their secret partner, wanted to hang on; it was his task to prevent the department from knowing that the successful tenderer was out of the picture. If he and his associates could continue that pretense and raise enough security, they could grab the contract for themselves in the Andrews, Jones name. They actually raised one hundred thousand dollars, which they deposited, forging the name of Andrews,

Jones to the necessary documents. Morse expected to get the rest through his friend Close, not knowing that Close had been bought off. When no further security arrived, the department gave the contract to the third lowest bidder – the Nova Scotians. Nobody yet knew – at least officially – that this firm had made a secret arrangement with Shields.

That was not quite the end of the negotiations and delays on Contract Forty-two. The whole of the following summer was wasted in quarrels between the Shields group in Toronto and their Nova Scotian partners, the Toronto members doing their best to oust the Maritimers but, as the Winnipeg *Times* put it, "finding great difficulty in raising the amount which had been advanced by these gentlemen, and also paying them what they considered a just consideration by their retirement."

Finally, in September, more than seven months after the tenders were opened on the contract for Section B, Shields and his partners bought out the interests of the Nova Scotians for $52,500. To raise the money they had to bring in three other contractors as partners. Only then could they get on with the business of building a railroad.

4

Bogs "We began the work of construction of Canada's great highway at a
without dead end," wrote Harry William Dudley Armstrong, a resident engi-
bottom neer along the half-completed Fort William–Selkirk line in the mid seventies. It was true. One chunk of railway was begun at the Red River and run hesitantly eastward towards the muskegs on the Ontario-Manitoba border. Another was built westward from Fort William, literally to nowhere. These two pieces were useless because they did not connect. The railway builders were at work in the empty heart of Canada without rail transportation to supply them, in a country scarcely explored; they were forced to rely on steamers, flat boats, canoes and barges to haul in supplies and construction materials. Four years later, when other contractors began to fill in the 181-mile gap between, every pound of supplies had to be taken in over the lakes by canoe and portage because the end of steel was still a good hundred miles from the water route. Steam shovels, horses, even locomotives and flatcars had to be hauled by sleigh in the winter-

282

time over the frozen lakes, the ice-sheathed granites and the snow-shrouded muskegs. Joseph Whitehead had a quarter-million dollars worth of machinery – steam drills, boilers and the like – which had to be transported in this manner at prodigious cost. Indeed, some of it could not be got into the Cross Lake country at all until the road was in a condition to carry traffic; it lay along the line of railway out of Winnipeg for months, eating up interest charges. On Section B (Contract Forty-two), eighty thousand dollars were spent just moving in supplies before a foot of road was graded or a single rail laid.

The distance between Fort William and Selkirk was only 435 miles as the surveyors plotted the line. But no one, not surveyors, not contractors, and certainly not politicians, knew the problems that lay ahead. It took seven years before through rail communication was completed from the lakehead to the Red River.

Armstrong, in a private memoir, wrote of those early days when his nearest neighbour was nine miles away, when he walked as far as fifteen miles to work and back again each day, when in the absence of any doctor he acted as midwife at the birth of his first child. Like almost everybody else who recalled those times he remembered the mosquitoes and blackflies rising from the stinking, half-frozen swamps in clouds that blotted out the sun. On one occasion, wading between the stumps of a spruce and tamarack swamps, the water four feet deep, the frozen bottom covered by a foot-thick sponge of moss, Armstrong, who was carrying a level on his shoulder, looked at the forefinger of his left hand, curled around the tripod. There were on the second joint alone no fewer than nine mosquitoes "with their bills sunk to the hilt on that space and they were equally thick on any exposed part of face or hands."

The land that the railway builders set out to conquer was beautiful in its very bleakness. At the western end of Lake Superior it was almost all rock – the old, cracked rock of the Canadian Shield, grey and russet, striped by strata, blurred by pink lichens, garlanded by the dark vines and red berries of kinnikinnick and sparkling, sometimes, with the yellow pinpoints of cinquefoil. From the edges of the dun-coloured lakes that lay in the grey hollows there protruded the spiky points of the spruce, jet black against the green clouds of birch and poplar. Sometimes there were tiger lilies, blue vetch, briar rose and oxeye daisies to relieve the sombre panorama; but in the winter the land was an almost unendurable monochrome of grey.

As the line moved west, the land changed and began to sparkle.

Between the spiny ridges lay sinuous lakes and lesser ponds of bright blue or olive green from which the yellow flowers of the spatterdock glittered. The lakes became more numerous towards the west, the bright sheets of water winding in chains between the broken, tree-covered vertebrae of granite, with here and there a chartreuse meadow of tall, rank grass. This lake country, smiling in the sunshine, gloomy in the frequent, slashing rains, would one day become a tourist mecca; but in the seventies it was a hellhole for the railway builders who saw their fortunes sink forever in the seemingly bottomless slime of the great muskegs.

The muskegs came in every size. There were the notorious sinkholes – little lakes over which a thick crust of vegetable matter had formed and into which the line might tumble at any time. There was one sinkhole near Savanne, north of Fort William, so legend has it, where an entire train with a thousand feet of track was swallowed whole. Sometimes new sinkholes would appear in land thought to be as solid as Gibraltar. This was partly due to an imperfect knowledge of frost conditions. During the winter the railway builders would construct enormous fills – work that looked as if it would last forever. But this would cause the frozen muskeg beneath to melt and the entire foundations would begin to heave and totter. Time and again these new holes would be filled only to reappear once more.

Worse than the sinkholes were the giant muskegs, like the Poland Swamp or the incredible Julius Muskeg, the most infamous bog of all – a vast bed of peat six miles across, depth unknown, sufficient, it was said, to supply the entire North West with fuel. From these deceptively level, moss-covered stretches the naked trunks of dead tamaracks protruded, their roots weaving a kind of blanket over a concealed jelly of mud and slime. Across these seemingly impassable barriers the road was carried forward on log mattresses floated on top of the heaving bog – unwieldy contraptions of long, interlaced timbers, which would sometimes run for eight hundred feet. Later on the muskegs were filled in.

Then there were the apparently placid lakes that seemed so shallow, whose bottoms consisted of solid, unfathomable muskeg – muskeg that swallowed up tons of earth and gravel fill, month after month. The problem was that there seemed to be a bottom where there was no bottom at all. The real lake bottoms were concealed by a false blanket of silt which had never been properly probed during the hasty surveys. On Section B, Lake Macquistananah devoured

284

250,000 yards of earth fill. Farther up the line a second lake swallowed two hundred thousand yards. On Section Fifteen the hapless Joseph Whitehead saw his dreamed-of profits slowly pouring into the notorious Cross Lake in the form of 220,000 yards of gravel at a cost of eighty thousand dollars. And still the line continued to sink.

Cross Lake was to prove Whitehead's undoing. The contractor began work on it in 1879 and was still pouring gravel into it when, with his capital used up, the government relieved him of his contract in March, 1880. It seemed a simple matter to run a line of railway across the narrows – just a shallow expanse of water through which an embankment could easily be made. Yet ton after ton of sand and gravel vanished into that black and monstrous gulf without appreciable results. Sometimes the embankment would be built up five or six feet above the water; then suddenly the lake would take a gulp and the entire mass of stone, gravel and earth would vanish beneath the waves.

At Lake Deception – eloquent name! – James Ross's huge force of horses and freight cars moved gravel into the water, using the first steam shovel to operate on the CPR, working at top speed, but the banks slid away faster than the gravel could be poured in. Ross built massive retaining walls with rock blasted out of one of his tunnels. One day in the space of a few minutes the banks settled some twenty-five feet, pushing the protective bulwarks of rock out into the lake for almost one hundred feet "as if they had been straws," and so swiftly that the men and horses barely had time to jump clear and save themselves. Ross tried hammering pilings deep into the lake bottom, building a trestle above them, and filling in the trestle with gravel and rock. One June day, just after a work train had rumbled across the causeway, the pilings sank fifty feet. There seemed no end to the depth of these incredible swamps. In one muskeg, piles were driven ninety-six feet below the surface before any bedrock was found.

A mile from Bonheur, a construction crew believed it had filled a muskeg hole when the entire track suddenly vanished into the black mud. Trainload after trainload of gravel was dumped into that apparently bottomless pit while men sweated with timbers to shore it up. Finally a track was laid and a locomotive was able to venture across. As the engine moved, the wobbly line behind it slowly rose while the ballast beneath squeezed out on both sides like pitch from a pot. A pole driven down showed there was thirty feet of quivering muskeg directly beneath the track, which was acting as a kind of pontoon bridge floating on a sea of slime. Of the gravel there was no trace.

Even after the muskegs were conquered, the rails anchored and through traffic established, the roadbed tended to creep forward with every passing train. When a heavy engine, hauling thirty-five cars, passed over the track, the rails crept about two feet in the direction the train was moving. As a result track bolts broke almost daily. An actual series of waves, five or six inches deep, rippled along the track and was observable from the caboose.

Temporary trestles were filled by dragging giant ploughs along a line of gravel-filled cars, by means of a cable powered from the detached locomotive. From each side of the bow of the plough there descended cataracts of sand but the track was often so uneven that the plough would catch onto the end of the car, stand on end for an instant and then topple thirty feet to the ground below. From there it would have to be dragged back by the cable to the far end of the trestle and up the bank, ready to be loaded again onto a car.

The most effective plough was the "wing plough" designed on the spot by Michael J. Haney, the colourful Galway Irishman who took over the running of Section Fifteen for the government after White-head's downfall. A lean, hard man with high cheekbones, cowlick and drooping moustache, Haney was described by Harry Armstrong, the pioneer engineer, as "a rushing devil-may-care chap who did things just as he chose without regard to authority." Haney almost lost the little *Countess of Dufferin* locomotive and his own life by displaying too much daring. He had drained a lake near Kalmar, about twenty-five miles from Cross Lake, and laid a mattress of timbers across the mud bottom to carry the track over it. But when the rails were laid and the cars backed onto them, the whole heaving mass began to sink. Jack Anderson, the engineer on the *Countess*, refused point-blank to take her out onto the quivering track so Haney boldly announced he would do it himself. With the cars uncoupled he began pushing them very slowly out along the track with the locomotive. The mattress began to subside; the engine tilted wildly until it looked to bystanders as if a ten-pound weight would pull her right over and into twenty feet of ooze. Haney, realizing his predicament, started to back up gingerly towards solid ground. It was nip and tuck, since the mattress had sunk so deep he was forced to propel the locomotive up an incline that rapidly grew steeper and steeper. By using sand on the rails and all the steam he could muster he managed to reach the top

286

of the bank, but by then the incline was so steep that the pilot scraping against the rails was torn from the frame. Haney astonished everybody by admitting that the move was damn foolishness. It was the only occasion in forty years' acquaintanceship, Armstrong recalled, that he had known Haney "to admit anything he did wasn't right."

Haney, though accident-prone to an almost unbelievable degree, had as many lives as a cat. At one point he was pitched off his horse and badly injured. On another occasion he caught his foot in some wire attached to the rails and a train ran over his toes. On July 18, 1880, he was riding an engine out of Cross Lake when the tender jumped the track and the locomotive with Haney in it rolled over a twenty-foot embankment. Clouds of scalding steam poured out of the wreck but Haney, who was in the fireman's seat, emerged without a scratch. Two months later he had another close call en route from Lake Deception to Cross Lake. He had just stepped out of the fireman's seat to get a drink of water and was raising it to his lips when the engine rounded a steep curve. Haney was knocked off balance and thrown, head foremost, into a rock cut. The train was travelling at twenty miles an hour and everyone assumed Haney was dead; he escaped with a flesh wound in the forehead.

Haney's particular brand of derring-do was hard on him physically – after two years on Section Fifteen he was a sick man and his doctor ordered a complete rest – but it certainly got results. When Whitehead finally withdrew in February, 1880, matters were in a dreadful snarl. The men had not been paid and another in what had been a series of ugly strikes was in progress. The men were in a black mood when Haney arrived, called them together and told them that they would all receive their money as soon as pay sheets could be made up. Some decided to stay on the job, others to strike. Haney warned the strikers that the loyalists would be paid first. Then he set off for Winnipeg to get the needed funds. There he was besieged at his hotel by some of the strikers, demanding their money at once.

Haney was adamant: "I told you what I'd do and I'm going to do it. I told you the men who stayed would be paid first and you can bet your last dollar that they'll all be paid before any of you get a cent."

The leader of the group swore that Haney would not be allowed out of Winnipeg with a penny until the strikers got their money. Haney boldly told him that he intended to row across the river to St. Boniface, pick up an engine there at midnight and steam back to the job. "You can do whatever you please about it," he said bluntly. He was as good as his word. With forty thousand dollars in cash on his person he set off down the track in the dead of night. It was a measure of the man that, in spite of all the threats, none dared stop him.

Back on the job Haney found himself faced with a series of dilemmas. Whitehead's caches were bare of provisions and yet Haney must keep four thousand men working without cessation. He and Collingwood Schreiber, Fleming's replacement, estimated that one thousand tons would be needed – and this amount had to be distributed immediately over some of the roughest country in Canada. It was March 1. Spring was on its way. In a very short time the trails would be so rutted that a wagon would be shaken to pieces in less than ten miles. Hauling could be done only over roads made of hard-packed snow. But teams were in short supply, too. There simply were not enough horses or wagons. Schreiber figured it was impossible but Haney was not a man to cry surrender. Off he set on a voyage of importunity, moving from farmhouse to farmhouse, browbeating, cajoling, pleading and promising. Within a few days he had hired every team in the country, and by March 15 he had accomplished the impossible.

Haney's ability to scrounge material became legendary. He was not a believer in proper channels or in red tape. When he wanted something he took it. On one occasion when Section Fifteen ran short of spikes Haney made up his mind to seize two carloads that were, he knew, sitting on the sidings in Winnipeg destined for another section. He knew the car numbers, so, on one dark night, he took a light engine with a regular crew and conductor into the yards. Haney located the cars, after a considerable search, untangled them from the array in the yard and spirited them away behind his train. There followed a wild night ride during which the spikes were unloaded at strategic points and the cars slipped back into the Winnipeg yards without anyone being the wiser. The incident baffled Schreiber more than anything else that occurred that year. The cars had been checked into the yards loaded and, after Haney's secret expedition, were checked out loaded; yet the spikes never reached their destination. Schreiber spent most of the summer tracing the two cars all over the continent. He finally caught up with one in Georgia and the other in Texas, but of course there was no hint of where the spikes had gone. The matter continued to prey on Schreiber's mind: how could two loads of railroad spikes suddenly dissolve out of two freight cars? The matter became so nagging that it dominated his conversation.

288

"What I can't make out is what became of those spikes," he said one day in Haney's hearing.

"Why didn't you ask me about it?" Haney asked.

"What in the devil would you know about it?" Schreiber exploded. "Didn't I tell you they were checked in and out of the Winnipeg yards?"

"Well," said Haney, "if you care to walk back a mile or so along the track I think I can show you every one of those spikes."

Schreiber's undoubtedly explosive retort has not been recorded but it was probably tempered with understanding. Haney's methods were unorthodox but they produced indisputable results. When he took over Section Fifteen there was a deficit on the books of almost four hundred thousand dollars. Under his management this was cleared up and a balance of $83,000 appeared on the black side of the ledger. Haney, of course, was a salaried man. The $83,000 was paid by the government to Joseph Whitehead.

5

Sodom-on-the-Lake

In the dismal land west of Lake Superior, nature seemed to have gone to extremes to thwart the railway builders. When they were not laying track across the soft porridge of the muskegs they were blasting it through some of the hardest rock in the world – rock that rolled endlessly on, ridge after spiky ridge, like waves in a sullen ocean.

Dynamite, patented in the year of Confederation, was as new as the steam shovel and, though the papers were full of stories of "dynamiters" using Alfred Nobel's new invention for revolutionary purposes, the major explosive was dynamite's parent, nitro-glycerine. This awesomely unstable liquid had been developed almost thirty years before the first sod was turned on the CPR but was only now beginning to replace the weaker blasting powder, being ten times more expensive not to mention more dangerous. It had been in regular use as a railway-building explosive only since George M. Mowbray in 1866 demonstrated its efficiency in the building of the Hoosac Tunnel – the successful results there having sprung largely from the development of a new kind of detonator, electrically fired. It had never before been used as extensively as it was west of the lakehead in the late seventies.

Here the technique was to pour the explosive into holes drilled often by hand but sometimes with the newly developed Burleigh rock drill, worked by compressed air. The liquid was then poured into the holes, each about seven feet deep, and set off by a fuse. In less than two years some three hundred thousand dollars was spent on nitro-glycerine on Section Fifteen, often with disastrous results. There was among the workmen an almost cavalier attitude to the explosive. Cans of nitro-glycerine with fuses attached were strewn carelessly along the roadbed in contravention of all safety regulations, or carried about with such recklessness that the fluid splashed upon the rocks. Whole gangs were sometimes blown to bits in the resultant explosions, especially in the cold weather, because the chemical was notoriously dangerous when frozen; the slightest jar could touch it off. Under such conditions it was kept under hot water and at as uniform a temperature as possible.

It could not be transported by wagon; the jarring along those corrugated trails would have made short work of the first drover foolhardy enough to risk it. It had to be carried in ten-gallon tins on men's backs. The half-breed packers and the Irish navvies remained contemptuous of it. Armstrong, the engineer, saw one packer casually repairing a leak in a tin by scraping mud over it with his knife, oblivious of the fact that the tiniest bit of grit or the smallest amount of friction would blast him heavenwards. Sometimes the packers would lay their tins down on a smooth rock and a few drops would be left behind from a leak. The engineers travelling up and down the line watched the portage trails with hawk's eyes seeking to avoid those telltale black specks which could easily blow a man's leg off. On one occasion a teamster took his horse to water at just such a spot. The horse's iron shoe touched a pool of nitro-glycerine and the resulting blast tore the shoe from his foot and drove it through his belly, killing him and stunning the teamster.

In drilling holes for the explosive, it was the practice to fill them first with water and then pour in the heavier liquid; the water then floated to the top and acted as tamping. Often, however, some of the explosive ran out, causing secondary explosions later on when the cut was trimmed. The number of men killed or maimed by accidental explosions was truly staggering. In one fifty-mile stretch of Section B, Sandford Fleming counted thirty graves, all the result of the careless handling of nitro-glycerine. Mary Fitzgibbon, on her way to homestead in Manitoba, watched in awe as a long train of Irish packers tripped gaily down a hill, each with a can of liquid explosive on his back, making wry, funereal comments all the while:

"It's a warm day."

"That's so but maybe ye'll be warmer before ye camp tonight."

"That's so, d'ye want any work taken to the Divil?"

"Where are ye bound for, Jack?"

"To hell, I guess."

"Take the other train and keep a berth for me, man!"

"Is it ye're coffin ye're carrying, Pat?"

"Faith ye're right; and the coroner's inquest to the bargain, Jim."

Mrs. Fitzgibbon wrote that in spite of the banter "the wretched expression of these very men proved that they felt the bitterness of death to be in their chests."

There were, indeed, some terrible accidents. A youth climbing a hill with a can of explosive stumbled and fell; all that was ever found of him was his foot in a tree, one hundred yards away. A workman in a rock cut handed a can to one of the drillers and as he did so his foot slipped: four men died, three more were maimed. One workman brushed past a rock where some explosive had been spilled; he lost his arm and his sight in an instant. At Prince Arthur's Landing, an entire nitro-glycerine factory blew up in the night, hurling chunks of frozen earth for a quarter of a mile and leaving a gaping hole twenty feet deep and fifty feet across. And then there was the case of Patrick Crowley, an over-moral Irishman, who objected so strenuously to Josie Brush's bawdy-house at Hawk Lake that he blew it up, and himself into the bargain.

Under such conditions the only real respite was alcohol. As Michael Haney recalled, "there was not an engineer, contractor or traveller who were not hard drinkers. Practically every transaction was consummated with a glass." The same was true of the navvies, and, in order to keep the work moving, herculean efforts were made to keep the camps dry. These were not too successful. Prohibition was in effect all along the line, but this did not stop the whiskey peddlers who had kegs of liquor cached at points along the entire right of way. "The knowing ones can obtain a bottle of a villainous article called whiskey by following certain trails into the recesses of the dismal swamps," the Thunder Bay *Sentinel's* railway correspondent reported from up the line in the summer of 1877. He added that there were many raids on the peddlers but these were "not altogether made in the cause of temperance. Not all the whiskey was spilled on the ground."

Since a gallon of alcohol, which was sold in the cities of the East for as low as fifty cents, could, when properly diluted, return forty-five dollars to an enterprising peddler on the line, business continued brisk in spite of the vigilance of the police. The peddlers hid out in the bush or on the islands that dotted the swampy lakes, moving into the work camps in swift canoes of birchbark and darting away again at the approach of the law. If caught, the peddler generally escaped with a fine since fines were the chief source of income for the struggling towns and villages that were springing up at the end of steel.

A few years later, when the railroad was finished, a *Globe* reporter on a visit to Rat Portage dug up some fascinating background on the good old days when, it was said, whiskey peddling was one of the chief industries:

". . . it is more than hinted that of the enormous amounts collected here in fines and costs, the Dominion Government received only a very small share, while some of the officials would have been rich men ere this had it not been for the large sums they have squandered on profligacy and dissipation. It is also stated on good authority that in some cases whiskey peddlers secured a certain immunity from the severe penalties by contributing regular stated sums, destined to appease the cravings for justice in the breasts of the officers of the Court."

Harry Armstrong, in his unpublished memoirs, has set down a spirited account of one whiskey trial held in the winter of 1877-78 in which he acted as clerk of the court. The trial was held at Inver on Section Fifteen. A man named Shay was arrested with a toboggan-load of whiskey and placed in charge of the local blacksmith. He was duly arraigned before two Justices of the Peace, one of whom was the government's divisional engineer, Henry Carre, and the other the contractor's engineer. It was their first case on the bench – the bench being literally a bench since the court was held in the company mess hall.

"Produce the prisoner," called Carre, and the blacksmith entered, holding Shay by the coat sleeve and pulling at his own forelock as he announced: "The prisoner, Your Honour."

The first witness was being questioned when Charles Whitehead, the son of the contractor, acting in his role of prosecutor, "wildly suggested to the bench that it was probably in order to swear the witness." It took some time to find a Bible but one was eventually located and the case proceeded. A further delay occurred when it was noticed that Armstrong, as clerk, was taking down the evidence in pencil. With difficulty, pen and ink were found, the evidence retranscribed and the case continued. Without much more ceremony, the prisoner was found guilty. He had formerly been employed as one of Carre's axemen and was well known to him. Obviously he had come up in the world financially, being attired in a fine suit with a fur collar – "the most distinguished looking man in the room."

"Shay," said Carre gravely, "I am very sorry to see you in this position."

"So am I, Mr. Carre," replied the convicted man with disturbing nonchalance.

"The decision of the court is that you pay a fine of twenty-five dollars."

"Well, I won't pay it. I'll appeal."

This was a disconcerting turn of events. There was no jail closer than Winnipeg and no funds to send the prisoner there, and so, after a few days of well-fed comfort in the bunkhouse, the miscreant was allowed to depart without his whiskey.

When Haney took over Section Fifteen his methods of handling the alcohol problem were characteristically his own. He made no attempt to curb the traffic himself but when the men were put on three round-the-clock shifts, whiskey tended to slow down the work. At such times it was Haney's practice to round up the peddlers and secure from them a promise that they would not sell whiskey as long as the 24-hour shift-work prevailed. Generally this *sub rosa* agreement worked but on one occasion the presence of five hundred thirsty men was too much for the entrepreneurs. Haney came to work one morning to find the whole camp roaring drunk. Work would be tied up for a week. Haney moved with his usual brusqueness. There were four officials working on the section who were technically known as "whiskey detectives." He called them before him and told them that unless all whiskey peddlers were brought before him by noon, all four would be fired. The peddlers were produced in an hour and haled immediately before a magistrate who was clearly taking his orders from Haney. The law provided increased fines for each recurring offence and the option of jail on a third offence. Haney saw that the maximum fines – a total of thirty-six hundred dollars – were levelled. The prison sentences were remitted but all peddlers were packed off to Winnipeg with the warning that if they returned they would be jailed. None of them ever came back.

When whiskey was unavailable on the spot the thirstiest of the workmen tried to escape to the fleshpots of Winnipeg. Haney's best foreman was one of these: every two or three weeks he would be missing. Haney handled this matter with considerable psychology. He kept *forcing* the man to go to Winnipeg As the compulsory trips became more frequent and the foreman grew the worse for wear, Haney continued to insist that he return. Soon the man was coming back, cold sober, on the return train, pleading to be allowed to work. As Haney later explained: "It's one thing to steal away for a few days of quiet dissipation but it's quite another to have someone else thrusting these days upon you. He didn't like anyone deciding that he should get drunk any more than he would have appreciated their efforts to prevent him from becoming so, and as long as we were on that work he was never away another day."

By the time Haney arrived on the scene, at the decade's end, the solemn, unknown land through which Harry Armstrong had trudged on his fifteen-mile treks to the job site, had come alive with thousands of navvies – Swedes, Norwegians, Finns and Icelanders, French Canadians and Prince Edward Islanders, Irish, Scots, English, Americans, even Mennonites, all strung out over nearly five hundred miles in clustered, brawling, hard-drinking communities, most of which were as impermanent as the end of track.

Armstrong recalled, not without nostalgia, the days when "life along the railway construction . . . was like one large family. There was hospitality, helpfulness, gentle friendship, good nature and contentedness all about." He described Christmas Eve, 1876, spent in a log cabin on the right of way, with a fiddler playing for dancing couples in a room which also contained a kitchen stove and an immense bed. Everything went fine, he remembered, until someone unwittingly sat on the bed and realized that there was a baby somewhere beneath the sheets.

His account contrasts sharply with that of the postmaster of Whitemouth, a railroad community midway between Winnipeg and Rat River, also describing Christmas Eve, just four years later.

"The demon of strong drink made a bedlam of this place, fighting, stabbing and breaking; some lay out freezing till life was almost

294

extinct. The Post Office was besieged at the hours of crowded business by outrageous, bleeding, drunken, fighting men, mad with Forty-Rod, so that respectable people could not come in for their mail. . . . It is only a few days since in one of these frenzies a man had his jugular nearly severed by a man with a razor."

The very impermanence of the construction towns made any kind of municipal organization difficult. In July, 1880, when the end of track moved beyond Gull River, Ignace became the capital of Section A. All the inhabitants of Gull River moved – stores, houses, boarding houses, a jewellery shop, a hotel, a telegraph office, a "temperance saloon," a shoemaker and a blacksmith shop. Often, though communities changed geographical location and names, they re-elected the same public officials to govern them. When Rush Lake City sprang up as the capital of Patrick Purcell and Hugh Ryan's Contract Twenty-five, Joseph Ettershank, who had been the mayor of two previous communities, once again offered himself to the shifting electorate. The election was typical of those times: he was beaten by a Liberal but immediately contested the result, charging his opponent with the usual bribery and corruption. The opponent was duly unseated and Ettershank won a moral victory. But he refused on principle to assume office and Rush Lake City found itself without a chief magistrate.

The one really permanent town along the half-constructed line and by far the largest was Rat Portage on Lake of the Woods. With true chamber of commerce fervour it called itself "The Future Saratoga of America." A less subjective description was provided by a correspondent of the Winnipeg *Times* in the summer of 1880:

"For sometime now the railway works in the vicinity of Rat Portage have been besieged by a lot of scoundrels whose only avocation seems to be gambling and trading in illicit whiskey and the state of degradation was, if anything, intensified by the appearance, in the wake of these blacklegs, of a number of the *demi-monde* with whom these numerous desperadoes held high carnival at all hours of the day or night."

The town itself, in the words of one observer, seemed to have been "laid out on designs made by a colony of muskrats." Shanties and tents were built or pitched wherever the owners fancied and without reference to streets or roadways. As a result, the streets were run

295

between the houses as an afterthought so that there was nothing resembling a straight thoroughfare in town "but simply a lot of crooked, winding trails that appeared to go nowhere in particular, but to aimlessly wander about in and out of shanties, tents and clumps of brush in such a confused and irregular manner as was extremely difficult for the stranger to find his way from one given point to another, even though they might not be over 150 yards apart."

Rat Portage, with a floating population sometimes bordering on three thousand, was the headquarters for Section B – the famous Contract Forty-two – under the control of Manning, Shields, McDonald and Company. The expense of the administration was borne by the contractors, who built the jail and organized the police force. All fines, however, went to the government. Between April and November of 1880, six thousand dollars were collected in fines. The convictions – highway robbery, larceny, burglary, assault, selling illicit whiskey and prostitution – give a fair picture of Rat Portage as a frontier town.

With both the contractors and the government in the law business, a state of near anarchy prevailed. At one point the company constable, a man named O'Keefe, seized four barrels of illicit liquor but instead of destroying it took it back to his rooms and proceeded to treat his many friends. He was haled before the stipendiary magistrate who fined him for having intoxicating liquor in his possession. O'Keefe paid the fine and then as soon as the magistrate left the bench arrested *him* for having liquor in his possession, an act he was perfectly entitled to perform since he was himself a policeman. He popped the protesting magistrate in jail and when that official asked for an immediate hearing O'Keefe denied it to him, declaring that he meant to keep him behind bars for twenty-four hours because the magistrate "had treated him like a dog and now it was his turn." With the only magistrate in jail another had to be appointed to act in his place; when this was done the hearing was held and the new magistrate fined the old magistrate one hundred dollars. In the end the local government remitted both fines.

The situation grew more complicated when Manitoba's boundaries were extended in 1881 and a dispute arose between that province and Ontario over the jurisdiction in which Rat Portage lay. Both provinces built jails and appointed magistrates and constables; so did the federal government. For a time it was more dangerous to be a policeman than a law breaker. Since there were several sets of liquor laws, the policemen began arresting each other until both jails were full of opposing lawmen. Ontario constables were kidnapped and shipped to Winnipeg. The Manitoba jail was set on fire. Anyone who wished could become a constable, and free whiskey and special pay were offered to those who dared to take the job. For a time Rat Portage witnessed the spectacle of some of its toughest characters – men who bore such nicknames as Black Jim Reddy of Montana, Charlie Bull-Pup, Boston O'Brien the Slugger, Mulligan the Hardest Case – actually acting as upholders of the law, or their version of the law. The situation came to a head in 1883 when both provinces called elections on the same day and two premiers campaigned in Rat Portage with such persistence that the Premier of Manitoba actually got more votes than there were registered voters. The confusion did not end until 1884 when Rat Portage was officially declared to be part of Ontario.

By then, with the government line finished, Rat Portage had settled down to become a mild and relatively law-abiding community, but in 1880 it was the roughest town in Canada, the headquarters of the illegal liquor industry with eight hundred gallons pouring into town every month, hidden in oatmeal and bean sacks or disguised as barrels of coal oil. It was figured that there was a whiskey peddler for every thirty residents, so profitable was the business. "Forty-Rod" – so called because it was claimed it could fell a man at that distance – sold for the same price as champagne in Winnipeg from the illegal saloons operating on the islands that speckled the Lake of the Woods.

Here on a smaller and more primitive scale was foreshadowed all the anarchy of a later Prohibition period in the United States – the same gun-toting mobsters, corrupt officials and harassed police. One bloody incident in the summer of 1880, involving two whiskey traders named Dan Harrington and Jim Mitchell, had all the elements of a western gun battle.

Harrington and Mitchell had in 1878 worked on a steam drill for Joseph Whitehead but they soon abandoned that toil for the more lucrative trade. In the winter of 1879-80, a warrant was issued for their arrest at Cross Lake, but when the constable tried to serve it, the two beat him brutally and escaped to Rat Portage where the stipendiary magistrate, F. W. Bent, was in their pay. The two men gave themselves up to Bent who fined them a token fifty dollars and then gave them a written discharge to prevent further interference from officials at Cross Lake. The magistrate also returned to Harrington a revolver that had been confiscated.

The two started east with fifty gallons of whiskey, heading for the turbulent little community of Hawk Lake where the railroad navvies had just received their pay. They were spotted, en route, by one of the contracting partnership, John J. McDonald (the same man who had once bribed Chapleau, the public works clerk). McDonald realized at once what fifty gallons of whiskey would do to his work force. He and the company's constable, Ross, went straight to Rat Portage, got a warrant and doubled back for Hawk Lake.

They found Harrington and Mitchell in front of Millie Watson's bawdy tent. Mitchell fled into the woods but Harrington boldly announced he'd sell whiskey in spite of contractors and police. The two men wrested his gun from him and placed him under arrest. Harrington then asked and was given permission to go inside the tent and wash up. Here a crony, bedded with a prostitute, handed him a brace of loaded seven-shot revolvers. Harrington cocked the weapons and emerged from the tent with both of them pointed at the constable. Ross was a fast draw; as Harrington's finger curled around the trigger the policeman shot him above the heart. Harrington dropped to the ground, vainly trying to retrieve his guns. A second constable, McKenna, told Ross not to bother to fire again: the first bullet had taken effect.

"You're damned right it has taken effect," Harrington snarled, "but I'd sooner be shot than fined." Those were his final words.

Magistrate Bent was removed from the bench the following week and the Winnipeg *Times* reported that "he is now actively engaged in the illicit traffic of selling crooked whiskey himself. He has now become an active ally [with] those whom he was at one time supposed to be at variance in a legal sense, whose pernicious vices he was expected to exterminate but did not."

It was these reports, seeping back to Winnipeg, that persuaded Archbishop Taché of St. Boniface that the construction workers needed a permanent chaplain; after all, a third of them were French-Canadian Catholics from Manitoba. He selected for the task the most notable of all the voyageur priests, Father Albert Lacombe, a nomadic Oblate who had spent most of his adult life among the Cree and Blackfoot of the Far West. In November, 1880, Lacombe set out reluctantly for his new parish.

Father Lacombe was a homely man whose long silver locks never seemed to be combed; but benevolence shone from his features. He did not want to be a railway chaplain. He would much rather have stayed among his beloved Indians than have entered the Sodom of Rat Portage, but he went where his church directed. On the very first day of his new assignment he was scandalized by the language of the navvies. His first sermon, preached in a boxcar chapel, was an attack on blasphemy.

"It seems to me what I have said is of a nature to bring reflection to these terrible blasphemers, who have a vile language all their own – with a dictionary and grammar which belongs to no one but themselves," he confided to his diary. "This habit of theirs is – diabolical!"

But there was worse to come: two weeks after he arrived in Rat Portage there was "a disorderly and scandalous ball" and all night long the sounds of drunken revelry dinned into the ears of the unworldly priest from the plains. Lacombe even tried to reason with the woman who sponsored the dances. He was rewarded with jeers and insults.

"My God," he wrote in his diary, "have pity on this little village where so many crimes are committed every day." He realized that he was helpless to stop all the evil that met his eyes and so settled at last for prayer "to arrest the divine anger."

As he moved up and down the line, covering thirty different camps, eating beans off tin plates in the mess halls, preaching sermons as he went, celebrating mass in the mornings, talking and smoking with the navvies in the evenings and recording on every page of his small, tattered black notebooks a list of sins far worse than he had experienced among the followers of Chief Crowfoot, the wretched priest was overcome by a sense of torment and frustration. The heathen Indians had been so easy to convert! But these navvies – nominal Christians all – listened to him respectfully, talked to him intimately, confessed their sins religiously and then went on their drunken, brawling, blaspheming, whoring way totally unashamed.

Ill with pleurisy, forced to travel the track on an open handcar in the bitterest weather, his ears ringing with obscene phrases which he had never before heard, his eyes affronted by spectacles he did not believe possible, the tortured priest could only cry to his diary, "My God, I offer you my sufferings." Hard as frozen pemmican, toughened by the harshness of prairie travel and the discomfort of Indian tepees, tempered by blizzard and blazing prairie sun, the pious Lacombe all but met his match in the rock and muskeg country of Section B.

"Please God, send me back to my missions," he wrote, but it was not until the final spike was driven that his prayers were answered. He had not changed many lives, perhaps, but he had made more friends than he knew. When it was learned that he was going, the workmen of Section B took up a large collection and presented him with a generous assortment of gifts: a horse, a buggy, a complete harness, a new saddle, a tent and an entire camping outfit to make his days on the plains more comfortable. Perhaps, as he took his leave, he reasoned that his tortured mission to the godless had not been entirely in vain.

Chapter Eight

1

Jim On one of those early trips to the Canadian North West in 1870, when
Hill's he was planning his steamboat war against the Hudson's Bay Com-
Folly pany, James Jerome Hill's single eye fastened upon the rich soil of
the Red River country and marked the rank grass that sprang up in
the ruts tilled by the squeaking wagon wheels. It was the blackest
loam he had ever seen and he filed the memory of it carefully away in
the pigeonholes of his complicated and active mind, to bring it out and
caress it, time and again, and contemplate its significance. Soil like
that meant settlers, tens of thousands of them. Settlers would need a
railway. With Donald Smith's help, Jim Hill meant to give them one.

There was a railway of sorts, leading out of St. Paul in 1870. It was
supposed to reach to the Canadian border but it had not made it that
far. One of its branches ended at Breckenridge on the Red River,
where it connected with the Kittson line of steamboats. Another
headed off northwest to St. Cloud at the end of the Red River trail.
An extension faltered north towards Brainerd, where it was supposed
to connect with the main line of the Northern Pacific. But neither
branch nor extension could properly be called a railroad. They had
been built in a piecemeal fashion out of the cheapest materials – iron
rails rather than steel, and fifteen distinct patterns of iron at that.
Bridge materials, stacks of railway ties and other bric-a-brac littered
the right of way. Nobody quite knew who owned what but the farmers
along the line were helping themselves to whatever they needed to
improve fences, barns and houses. As for the rolling stock, it was best
described as primitive, the engines ancient and creaky, the cars
battered and rusty.

The story of the St. Paul and Pacific Railroad is a case history in
railway looting in the mid-nineteenth century, when anybody who
promised to build a line of steel could get almost anything he asked.
In four years of railway madness between 1853 and 1857, no fewer
than twenty-seven railroad companies were chartered in the United
States. One of these was the St. Paul line, first known as the Minnesota
and Pacific. Its subsequent history is one of legislative corruption and
corporate fraud, and the complicated story of its financing has few
equals in railroad annals.

The villain in the piece was Russell Sage, the shadowy robber
baron from Troy, New York, who with a hand-picked group of

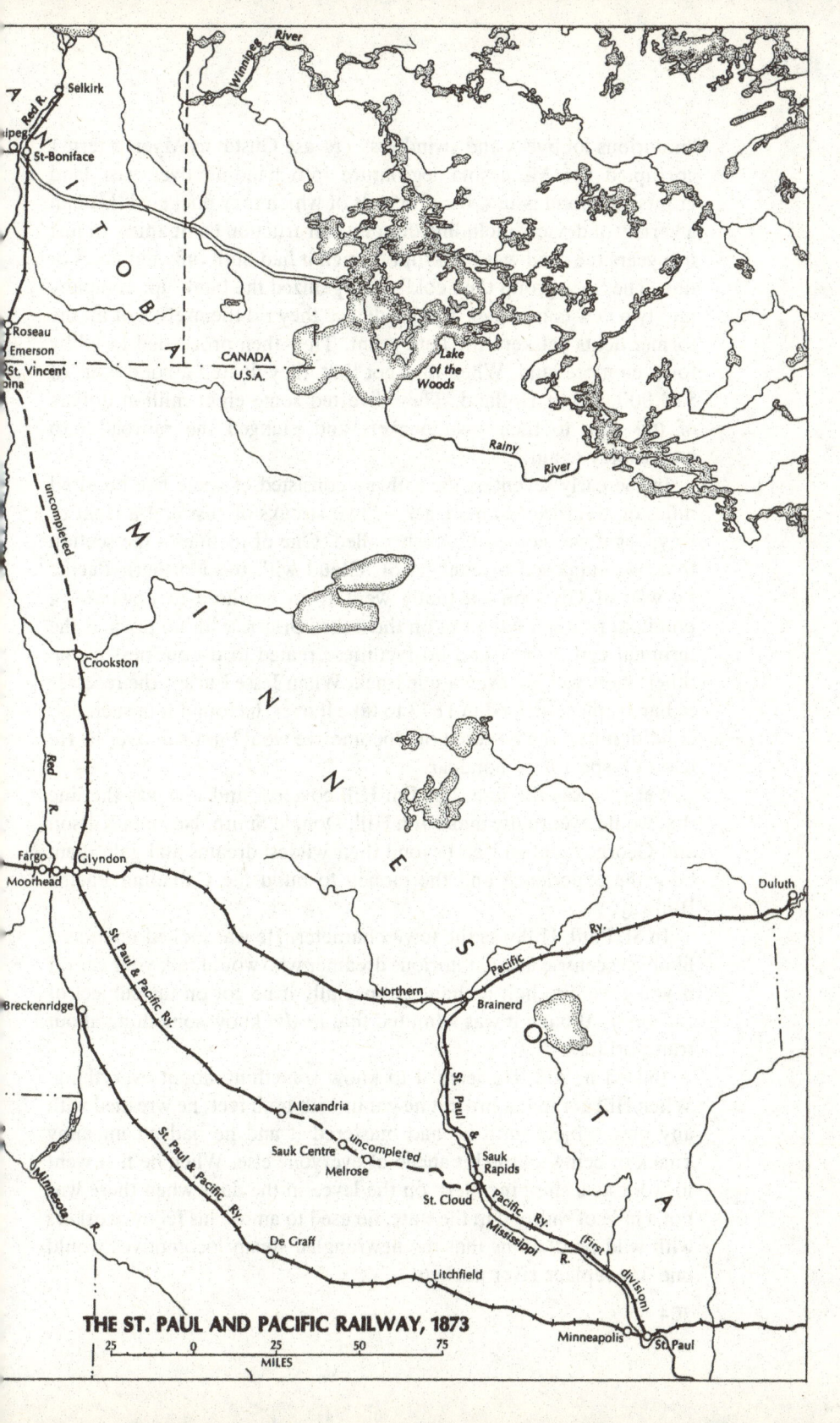

THE ST. PAUL AND PACIFIC RAILWAY, 1873

25   0   25   50   75
MILES

"notorious lobbyists and swindlers" (to use Gustavus Myers's term) corrupted the Minnesota legislature into handing over vast land grants and bond issues, the proceeds of which they pocketed through a variety of devices including dummy construction companies. In just five years the road was bankrupt though it had built only ten miles of line. The Sage group then coldly reorganized the bankrupt company into two new companies. By this device they rid themselves of all the former debts yet kept the land grant. They then proceeded to lobby for even more land. When they got that, they floated a bond issue of $13,800,000 in Holland. They diverted some eight million dollars of this sum to their own pockets and plunged the railroad into bankruptcy again.

In the early seventies the railway consisted of some five hundred miles of almost unusable track – "two streaks of rust and a right of way," as it was contemptuously called. One of its lines – the section that was supposed to connect St. Cloud with the Northern Pacific by way of Glyndon – actually went from nowhere to nowhere, a phantom railroad lying out on the naked prairie with no town at the terminal end of iron and no facilities created to do business at the other; there was not even a side track. When Jesse Farley, the receiver in bankruptcy, arrived in 1873 to take it over, he found it in such bad condition that the battered old locomotive would not run over it. He had to inspect it by handcar.

Yet this was the line that Jim Hill coveted; and this was the line that would eventually make Jim Hill, Donald Smith, Norman Kittson and George Stephen rich beyond their wildest dreams and gain them both the experience and the money to build the Canadian Pacific Railway.

In St. Paul, Hill was the town character. He was looked upon as a likable eccentric and a notorious dreamer who would talk your ear off if you gave him half a chance, especially if he got on the subject of railways – though it was admitted that he *did* know something about transportation.

Indeed he did. He seemed to know something about everything. When Hill got into a project he got in with both feet; he wrestled with any new subject until he had mastered it and he had an uncanny knack of being a little bit ahead of everyone else. When he first went to work as a shipping clerk on the levee in the days when there was not a mile of railroad in the state, he used to amuse his fellow workers with wild predictions that the newfangled steam locomotives would one day replace river packets.

Hill was the kind of man who could look at a village and see a city or gaze upon an empty plain and visualize an iron highway. He took a look at St. Paul when it was only a hamlet and realized he was at one of the great crossroads of western trade. Accordingly he set himself up as a forwarding agent and began to study the movement and storage of goods. When the railway first came along Hill began to sell it wood, but he saw that coal would swiftly replace the lesser fuel and so he studied coal. He made a survey of all the available sources of coal and became the first coal merchant in St. Paul; he also sold the first bagged coal in town. *That* was not enough for Hill. He became an expert on fuel and energy of all kinds. He actually joined geological parties exploring for coal. Years later, when the great coal deposits were discovered in Iowa, it turned out that one-eyed Jim Hill held 2,300 of the best acres under lease. Until his death he was considered one of the leading experts on the continent on the subject of western coal.

But in the early seventies, no one took Jim Hill seriously. Perhaps it was because he talked so much. There he sat in his old chair in front of his coal and wood store talking away, a stocky, powerful man with a massive, leonine head, the hair almost down to the shoulders, a short-cropped beard, a face scorched by the prairie sun and that single black eye – a glittering orb that, like the Ancient Mariner's, burned itself into the listener's consciousness.

Napoleon was his hero. He first read his biography back in Canada at the age of thirteen and nothing else that he read (and he seemed to read everything – Byron, Plutarch, More, Gibbon) made such an impression on him. From that moment, he believed that when a man set his mind to something it was already half done. Later in life, when he had built a mansion in St. Paul and stocked it with costly paintings, he began to think of himself as a Bonaparte, or perhaps a Genghis Khan. But in those early days, long before he fought his own Borodinos with Vanderbilt and Villard, he simply brought his Napoleonic determination to bear on the matter of the decrepit railroad. Hill saw it not as two streaks of rusted iron but as the nucleus of a transcontinental line. It was, everyone agreed, a crazy dream, but then Jim Hill had always been a dreamer – a "romancer," in the phrase of a boyhood companion. He had played hooky at the age of nine to read histories of the days of chivalry. He had sung old Scottish songs of love and derring-do while his Irish father played them on the flute. He had wild ambitions. He was going to be a doctor. He played at wild Indians until an arrow through the eye ended his medical future. But the romantic ambitions remained. He was going to be a sailor before the mast. He was going to run a steamboat line in India. He was going to conquer the world.

He was Canadian by birth and a Celt by heritage – half Scottish, half Irish. He was born in a log house at Rockwood, Ontario, and was much influenced by his teacher, the great Quaker educator, William Wetherald, father of a leading Canadian poetess. Wetherald was the founder of the Rockwood Academy, famous enough to be preserved in the next century as a National Historic Site. He taught young Jim Hill the value of books and of study and for all of his life Hill remained a student. He studied scientific treatises, classical art, geology, finance – everything he could get his hands on. Rockwood could not hold him; at eighteen, his heart fired by the idea of adventure, he set off for the Orient, wearing a new felt Horace Greeley hat, which was blown off at the Grand Trunk station in Toronto. He worked his way through New York State as a farm labourer, pushed on to Philadelphia (where he went straight to the opera and emerged much impressed) and then south to Richmond, seeking the ship, the tall, white ship, that he thought would take him to India.

But there was no ship in Richmond that would employ him. Hill turned to a closer frontier, the American West. When he reached St. Paul in July 1856, it was the jumping-off place to nowhere; the serpentine brigades of Red River carts, caked with the grime of the prairies, attested to that. Hill's imagination spanned the plains in a single leap and he saw the blue Pacific beckoning. He would join a brigade of trappers and go overland to the coast where he could find a ship bound for India. He looked at the steamboats pouring into St. Paul – three hundred in a single season – and again he began to dream. He would build a steamboat line on the Ganges, or the Hooghly, or the Brahmaputra. But he was too late; the final brigade had left for the season. And so Jim Hill stayed in St. Paul for a year, and then for another year – and another. The accident changed the pattern of his life, not to mention the pattern of the city he made his own.

For eight years, while he worked at a variety of jobs in St. Paul, he read and he studied; and when he was not reading he was trying his hand at painting. His first job was as a clerk on the levee and he read his way through that. He read voraciously, at all hours and in every setting. Once, the mother of a sick friend whom Hill was attending found him devouring a book on engineering. She asked him if he intended to be an engineer. Hill replied that he did not know what he might be: "You see I am only a young man yet, and a little knowledge of engineering might prove useful some day." It was the sort of thing Horatio Alger was putting into his books, but then Hill is the perfect Alger hero. When the long five-month winter of isolation settled upon St. Paul and others found amusement in saloons, Hill read his way through that, too. One winter he took a job as a watchman on a steamboat wintering on the levee. He arrived with an armful of books, ranging from Gibbon's *Decline and Fall* to several difficult scientific treatises. When he emerged the following spring he had read and annotated them all.

By the time he decided to try his hand at business, Hill's knowledge was encyclopaedic and his memory prodigious. He could repeat page after page of Byron or Plutarch. Years later, when he was wealthy enough to possess a herd of blooded cattle, he could cite the pedigrees of each one of them for generations back.

One of the things Jim Hill studied was the Toonerville operation out of St. Paul; and one of the things he learned was that whoever owned the railway could come into possession of two and a half million acres of the richest agricultural land in the American midwest. The time would come, Hill reckoned, when the railway could be bought for a song. It was all a matter of waiting.

2

In Winnipeg, Donald A. Smith had a similar idea. The community, which he represented in Parliament, needed a railway, and, perhaps more important, the Hudson's Bay Company, with nine million acres of land to sell, needed one, too. In 1873 the Canadian Pacific was dead by the hand of Sir Hugh Allan; a transcontinental line lay far in the future; but the Red River needed a lifeline to the East. If such a line could be built from Selkirk to the border and if the bankrupt American line out of St. Paul could somehow be revived to meet it, that connection would be effected.

Smith, like Hill, was a man who liked to look ahead: a month sometimes, a year perhaps, even a decade or more. He saw, for instance, the coming extinction of the buffalo and kept some captive

"Donald Smith is ready to take hold"

animals in a corral at Silver Heights against the day when they should vanish, as they did with dramatic and almost supernatural suddenness in 1880. When he emerged from Labrador as a junior factor on his first visit to Montreal, Smith decided to learn to cook, for he saw future advantages in that art. He took a job in a bakery and another later in a restaurant to absorb culinary techniques, which at the time were non-existent in the wilderness. He returned and gave all his employees and colleagues instruction in cooking and serving wholesome meals in order to preserve their health and sometimes their lives in the wilds. More, he picked up a knowledge of primitive medicine and learned to make an antiseptic for wounds by boiling the inner bark of the juniper tree. It was this kind of preparedness that undoubtedly saved Smith's own life when his guides faltered and died on the snow-blind journey back to Mingan, and on many other occasions as well. No matter what the weather, Smith always had the foresight to carry extra warm clothing and additional provisions with him wherever he went. When a blizzard sprang up, Smith was always ready for it; he was generally ready for any eventuality.

Like Hill, he foresaw the death of the steam packet at a time when the river trade seemed to be at its height. Smith also saw the threat to the fur trade as he and his colleagues had known it, even when the fur trade seemed invulnerable. As early as 1860 he predicted that the Company could not go on forever sealing off the North West from the rest of the continent; and he realized that once the Company's charter was modified or cancelled there would have to be a railway from Lake Superior to the Red River.

"You will understand that I, as a Labrador man, cannot be expected to sympathize altogether with the prejudice against settlers and railways entertained by many of the western commissioned officers," he said in 1860. "In all events it is probable that settlement of the country from Fort William westward to the Red River, and even a considerable distance beyond, will eventually take place and with damaging effect to the fur trade generally." It was a remarkable statement for the time, especially when it fell from the lips of a Company officer. And it was significant that, as a fur trader, Smith thought geographically in horizontal terms, and not on a vertical, north-south axis, as the Red River farmers did. The furs moved laterally from west to east but the grain went south.

Thirteen years after that forecast was made, Smith contemplated the twin streaks of rust out of St. Paul and saw in them the nucleus of a line to the Canadian North West. The twin railway companies (one was known as the St. Paul and Pacific, the other as the First Division of the St. Paul and Pacific) were in a terrible legal and financial snarl. One was in receivership, the other was about to go into trusteeship. There were suits and countersuits by unpaid contractors, chagrined stockholders and swindled bondholders. It was not easy to fathom the complicated financial situation, since there were several classes of bonds for the two lines and most of these were held out of the country by Dutch investors.

The railway was thought by the experts to be as dead as the CPR but Smith was looking farther ahead than the experts. A parliamentary colleague told him that his constituency seemed ill-fated in the matter of railways: "The Canadian Pacific is shelved for another generation and no capitalist will ever touch that Yankee railway to the south of you; those Dutchmen would do well to come over and sell those rails for old junk." Smith gave him a bleak smile. "The railway isn't dead," he said quietly. "A traveller isn't dead when he sits down by the wayside to rest." He went on to predict that both of them would be riding on the Canadian Pacific within ten years. Already he was seriously considering the revival of the "Yankee railway to the south."

In the fall of 1873, on his way through St. Paul en route from the Red River to that stormy session in Ottawa, Smith had dropped in on "Commodore" Norman Kittson, the Hudson's Bay representative and the president of the steamboat line which, with the Company's secret connivance, held a monopoly on the river.

The two men were old friends and they had much in common. Both sprang from the harsh background of the fur trade. It was in their blood: Smith's uncle, John Stuart, had been at Simon Fraser's side when that nerveless Scot took his canoes to tidewater down the great river that bears his name. Stuart became master of New Caledonia, the fur-trade empire that stretched from the Rockies to the sea coast and as far south as Oregon; Stuart Lake and the Stuart River enshrine his memory. Kittson's antecedents were equally spectacular; his grandfather was Alexander Henry the elder, the fur trader whose book of travel and adventure among the Indians became a primary source for early historians.

In 1873 and 1874, when Kittson and Smith discussed the St. Paul railroad and its prospects, Kittson had already reached his sixties – a patriarchal figure with a long grey beard and bright searching eyes, which peered out of a face long battered by the elements. Reserved, reticent and largely unlettered, he was a respected leading citizen of St. Paul. He had been a member of the Minnesota Territorial Council in the days when it required a snowshoe trip of five hundred miles to attend a session. In 1858 he was elected mayor of St. Paul. He, too, was born a Canadian but he had left his home in Sorel, Quebec, at the age of sixteen to seek his fortune with John Jacob Astor's fur company.

By 1843, semi-independent, he was king of the border, brazenly bank-rolling Canadian merchants to bootleg furs out of Red River under the very noses of the Hudson's Bay Company, which held the legal monopoly. Within five years, Kittson's very existence near Pembina threatened not only the Company's fur trade but also its control of the valley. It tried every means short of assassination to knock him out of business. Price wars, harassment, legal action – none of these could budge the stubborn upstart. In the end the Company employed the tactic it always adopted: it swallowed Kittson whole. Miraculously, the thorn in their side was transformed into one of the Company's most honoured traders.

It was in this capacity that Donald Smith first came to know and admire Norman Kittson. He never failed on his journeys through St. Paul, between the Red River and Montreal, to look in on his old friend. Now he wanted a favour: could Kittson find out everything possible about the financial and legal position of the St. Paul and Pacific Railroad, especially about the bonds held in Holland and the various prices the Dutch were asking? If the price was right, Smith thought, he might consider raising the money to buy the line, complete it to the border and join it to the Canadian railway that he hoped to build from Winnipeg south. Or perhaps he could convince the Dutch to take over the line and complete it themselves. Smith was not a railwayman; he saw the line of steel merely as a means to link his constituency with eastern Canada. He did not really care who controlled the route.

The project did not interest Kittson personally. He was well-to-do; he was getting on in years; it was all too rich for his blood. But he mentioned it to his other silent partner, Jim Hill, and it was as if a light had flashed on above that lion's head. Of course! For all these months Hill had been grappling with the puzzle of the bankrupt railway, wondering where the money would come from when the time was ripe to buy it. Now he had the answer: Smith was one of the chief officers of the Bank of Montreal as well as of the Hudson's Bay Company. He was wealthy in his own right. Smith was his man.

From that moment on, Hill became a monomaniac on the subject of the St. Paul and Pacific, especially to his friend Henry Upham, a clerk in the bond department of the First National Bank. Upham was Hill's next-door neighbour and confidant; he knew a great deal about finance and specifically he knew a great deal about the various bond issues of the St. Paul road. It was a profitable friendship.

When Donald Smith passed through St. Paul again, early in 1874 (he was on his way to campaign in his constituency), both Hill and Kittson were ready with the information he needed: most of the bonds were now held by Dutch investors who had formed themselves into a committee of bondholders. There were various classes of bonds totalling almost eighteen million dollars, face value; some were being quoted on the market at five cents on the dollar. The bonds were secured by the land grant on the unfinished portion of the line and this land grant was worth, in total, between two and three million dollars. In addition there were some five hundred miles of more or less completed railroad. Hill figured it would take two or three millions to complete it. He had learned that the Dutch had no intention of taking on that task. Smith, as a last resort, indicated he would be prepared to form a company to do the job if the bonds could be bought at reasonable prices.

The strategy was clear: buy the bonds as cheaply as possible, form a new company, force a foreclosure, buy the bankrupt railroad, complete it to the border, cash in on the resultant land subsidy and reap the profits. But there were many obstacles. It was no use buying the railroad without being certain of getting the free land that was supposed to come with it. The Minnesota legislature, however, had passed a law (no doubt with the bitter memory of Russell Sage's plundering) making the land grant non-transferable to any new company after foreclosure. A good deal of lobbying – and perhaps more than lobbying – would be needed to get that law revoked. There was also a variety of lawsuits pending against the railway lines. Then there were the stockholders, in addition to the bondholders, to be considered. Most of the stock was held by a speculator named Edwin Litchfield, a notoriously difficult man to deal with. Litchfield was trying to get control of the railway for himself through court action. The depression was at its height, money was hard to come by, plagues of grasshoppers were ravaging the land. For the moment nothing could be done.

"There was a time," Hill later recalled, "that everybody waited. There seemed no way to get in."

They bided their time for two full years – Smith and Hill, who was now deeply involved, and Kittson, who was reluctantly being pushed to the point of committal by his enthusiastic partner.

During that time, Hill studied the faltering railroad in all its economic ramifications – studied its finances, studied its operation, studied the quantities and values of the various bonds and where they were held; figured out the number of acres of land owned by the twin companies, the number of miles completed, half completed and still to be completed; worked out the value of the future land grants, the value of the terminals in St. Paul and in Minneapolis across the river, the value of the franchises that were granted before the state was admitted to the union; added up the number of locomotives, freight and passenger cars; kept up with all the law cases; made friends with the legislators and lobbied for changes in the law. Within two years, it was said, Jim Hill knew more about the railway than the men involved in running it. Two things he certainly knew that few others knew: it was worth far more than it appeared to be; and it could be made to show a profit.

He made no secret of his dream. Everybody in town knew that Jim Hill wanted the railroad and hoped to get the money from Donald A. Smith. His banker friend Henry Upham said that over a period of four years Hill must have talked to him on the subject several hundred times: "It was a favourite recreation with him. . . ."

Upham admitted that Hill "used to talk so much about this that people were a little tired of it." In the old Minnesota Club, Hill would corner fellow members and, his finger waggling in a characteristic gesture, harangue them for hours on the subject of the railway. "It was quite noticeable and it was talked of some time afterward by the boys," Upham recalled. He particularly remembered one evening early in May, 1874, coming across Hill in the club, gesticulating wildly, with Kittson who, having had two hours of the same thing late the night before, was almost numb with fatigue. The exhausted commodore sat totally immobile in the front of Hill, letting his young colleague rave on and on, his own face an absolute mask. As Upham came by he caught Kittson's eye, which closed slowly and then opened again, while his face remained totally expressionless.

Hill lived and slept the railway. Another friend, Stanford Newel, remembered that no single day passed after February, 1874, that Hill did not talk about it. Newel, who admitted that he found the whole subject tedious, said that "it became from day to day an all-absorbing subject with him. I used to tell him that he was getting it on the brain. He thought of nothing else. . . ." Indeed, he neglected his work because of it, as his partner Edward N. Saunders was to testify: "It seemed to occupy his mind to the exclusion of the coal business." Saunders felt injured; when Hill did turn up on the job all he would talk about was acquiring the railway.

One of the men he talked to, long and intimately, was Jesse P. Farley, an old railroad man from Dubuque, Iowa, who had been appointed receiver of the bankrupt St. Paul railroad. The twin to the bankrupt company was under trusteeship and the trustees made Farley general manager of it, so that he was actually in charge of the entire St. Paul and Pacific line and its branches. As such he was supposed to keep the railroad profitable, try to get it out of trouble and build more track. He was singularly unsuccessful in doing this, spending in three years only about one hundred thousand dollars on construction and repair. It is clear from subsequent sworn testimony that he and his assistant were on intimate terms with both Hill and Kittson, whom they saw almost daily, and that they were pleased, on occasion, to do Hill's bidding. The question, which was the subject of a prolonged series of legal battles, was whether or not the two were simply pumping Farley for information or whether Farley was in collusion with them to keep the railway in a rundown condition so that it could be bought cheaply. That is a mystery that has never been conclusively unravelled.

But then, there are several mysteries connected with the complicated finances and eventual disposition of the St. Paul and Pacific. Another has to do with the role played by John S. Kennedy, a New York banker, and his partner, Capt. John S. Barnes. Kennedy and his company were the agents of the Dutch committee that held almost all the bonds of the bankrupt railroad. Kennedy recommended Farley as trustee. Farley was a generally ignorant and almost illiterate man and "his cupidity was well known," according to Gustavus Myers the muckraking business historian (who was not entirely unbiased). Farley, previous to his appointment, had worked for Kennedy on a small Iowa railroad and generally did what the banker told him. What was Kennedy's real role? He was officially the man charged with looking after the bondholders' interests but he himself was to become a multimillionaire as a result of his association with Jim Hill and associates – the men who finally bought the Dutch bonds.

The bondholders in Holland appointed one of their number, Johan

Carp, to visit St. Paul and look over the railway, which had cost them so many headaches and so much financial loss. Carp later testified under oath that in 1876, and again in 1877, he discussed the future of the railway with Farley and that Farley was pessimistic: "He related to me the various difficulties we were to meet from competing railroads and opposite parties." Farley urged Carp to get the bondholders to put up more money to finish the road, but it was quite clear that this was not financially possible. "I was induced to believe that it would last many years before all these troubles should come to an end," Carp recalled. Persuaded of this, he decided it was time to sell the bonds; when Farley asked him if the committee was willing to sell, Carp replied that he thought so, if a reasonable bid could be obtained. Meanwhile Farley had introduced Carp to Hill and Kittson.

The time for waiting was over. While Farley was telling Carp that the railway would be tied up for years, Hill realized that solutions to many of the problems were at hand. Chief of these was the new legislation his political friends were pushing through the Minnesota legislature. Until that time, bankrupt railroad companies stood to lose their land grant. Under the new law companies could be sold under foreclosure and reorganized with the grant intact. Hill had always known that the real value of the railway lay in its capacity to claim free land.

The new legislation was passed on March 6, 1876. With this huge obstacle removed Hill left, on March 17, for Ottawa. At Smith's invitation the two men breakfasted in the cottage belonging to the Bank of Montreal where Smith made his headquarters while in the capital. Hill told Smith that it was now or never, and explained why: matters were moving swiftly with the railway. Edwin Litchfield, the chief stockholder, was trying to reach a compromise with the Dutch bondholders which would leave him in effective control of the property and prevent foreclosure. Hill's whole scheme rested on the certainty of foreclosure. Whoever owned the bonds could foreclose if mortgage payments were in default. Then the railroad would go on the block and the new bondholders could buy it for a song. But how much did the Dutch want for their bonds? If the price was right, Smith told Hill over breakfast, it was probable that the money could be raised in England. He mentioned Sir John Rose, long the government's unofficial representative in London and a partner in the financial house of Morton, Rose and Company.

"I wish you and Mr. Kittson would go on now and see at what

314

price, if you can determine or find out, these bonds can be bought," Smith said.

Hill departed for St. Paul in a state of jubilation. On the train out of Chicago he ran into his old friend Stanford Newel. "Donald Smith is ready to take hold," Hill exulted. Newel was impressed. Could it be that Hill, the voluble dreamer, had something after all?

When Johan Carp, the Dutch representative, first met Hill and Kittson in St. Paul in December, 1876, and learned that they might be interested in buying eighteen million dollars worth of bonds at a discount, he refused to take them seriously. An aging steamboat man and a garrulous coal merchant! Why, said Carp, there simply wasn't that kind of money in St. Paul. It took some convincing to explain that the money could be raised through Canadian and British capitalists. When Carp learned who Donald A. Smith was he began to pay attention.

It was now Hill's task to figure out the price at which the Dutch were prepared to sell their bonds. The partners had determined to buy them as cheaply as possible. But how cheap was cheap? Hill worked night after night, making detailed estimates of costs and assets. He figured the value of the railway property alone at $12,216,718. Then he went to work on the land grant and he figured that, right down to the last dollar, at $6,585,205. He figured net earnings at seven hundred thousand dollars a year and he listed every fraction of debt and every detail of assets. Meanwhile Farley was warning Carp of the complications that lay ahead and urging him to sell the line.

In January, 1877, Hill was ready to deal, or at least he pretended he was. Actually his plan was to write a letter to the Dutch committee that would sound like an offer so that he might get some idea of the actual price they would sell for. He had two other purposes. He wanted to keep Carp interested and in a good humour, and he wanted to word the letter in such a way as to convince the Dutch bondholders that the railway was practically worthless. Faced with an apparently *bona fide* offer, Hill rightly believed, the bondholders would grasp at any straw to sell the white elephant. He and Kittson "puzzled over the thing a good deal." They spent an entire evening working out the delicate wording and then a full morning with their lawyer rephrasing it. Since they had no cash they did not dare at that moment to risk outright acceptance. The letter contemplated buying the railroad property for three and a half million dollars in cash and letting the land grant go to the Dutch. But the cash was not to be paid over until the property was unencumbered, and that happy day seemed a long time distant. "We did not consider we were running much risk in making that offer," Hill was to recall.

The Dutch rejected the offer, as Hill had forecast they would; but their reply contained enough information to give him a clue to the kind of deal they would accept. The time had finally come to stop dreaming dreams and playing games. The time had come to put some money on the line. The time had come to broach the subject to George Stephen, the President of the Bank of Montreal, one of the keenest financial minds in Canada and a first cousin of Donald A. Smith.

3

Enter Ever since 1874, Donald Smith had been boring his cousin with talk
George about the St. Paul railway, in the same way that Hill had been boring
Stephen his friends. George Stephen saw Smith several times a year in Mont-
treal and listened politely to his enthusiastic accounts of the future of
the North West. Stephen, like most Montreal businessmen, had a confused and inaccurate picture of the country west of the lakes: "He
thought of Minnesota . . . that it was at the North Pole somewhere,"
Smith later recalled.

Stephen cheerfully concurred in this assessment: "This Minnesota
railway matter was constantly coming up. He [Smith] was very hot
upon the matter and I was lukewarm." Stephen thought the railway
scheme "an impossible thing for us to accomplish." Nevertheless he
agreed to meet Hill and Smith early in 1877 to discuss the matter.
Hill, armed with facts and figures, papers and documents, talking his
usual blue streak, gesturing with that insistent finger, never letting
up for an instant in his infectious enthusiasm, changed Stephen's
attitude from one of "languid attention" to whole-hearted interest;
and Stephen's interests were never idle ones.

Stephen is a shadowy figure in Canadian history. The immense
granite peak that overshadows Field, B.C., and bears his name is
better known than he. His official CPR portrait, painted when the
ordeal of railway building was at an end and his hair had gone white,
is reasonably familiar: it shows a slender, graceful man, impeccably
attired, with a long, grave Scottish face and a neatly trimmed beard.

316

That is about all most school children know of George Stephen. In Canada's Centennial year, a group of distinguished historians was invited to name the twenty-five greatest Canadians of the century, apart from politicians. Sandford Fleming, Donald Smith and William Van Horne all made the list but George Stephen was not even considered. Yet, apart from the politicians, he, more than any single man, was responsible for the shape and direction of the new Canada that sprang up west of Toronto after 1881.

Stephen would have been delighted with his own historical anonymity for he was a man who shunned the limelight. Four separate biographies of Donald Smith were published within a few years of his death. Stephen was dead for forty-four years before he was so enshrined and then the work was necessarily incomplete. The biographies that appeared of Van Horne, Smith, Hill and the others provoked in him an amused contempt. He saw to it that his own personal papers were destroyed. He had no use for scribblers. He thought the newspapers printed a lot of damned nonsense. In his later years he banned the newly invented telephone from his home; it would be used, he said, for no better purpose than to spread trivialities and gossip.

Outwardly reserved, publicly reticent and privately unassuming, he was inwardly subjected to the tugs and pressures of a mercurial psyche, reckless in its enthusiasms, magnificent in its audacities, faithful in its loyalties, consuming in its antipathies and single-minded to the point of intolerance. He was used to the blunt directives of the business world and was maddened by the circumlocutions of the political. Unlike Macdonald, to whom he poured out his inner soul in an astonishing series of personal letters (the only real record we have of that hidden turbulence), he indulged himself in the luxury of maintaining his animosities. As far as Stephen was concerned, you were either for him or against him. There was rarely a middle ground.

This apparently conservative business figure with the courtly manner could operate with a gambler's daring when the occasion demanded it. His sudden espousal of Hill's scheme to capture the St. Paul railroad is the first major example of it; but there were hints in his background. The story goes that when he was nineteen and looking for a job in Glasgow (he had been a draper's apprentice in Aberdeen) he happened past the Mansion House and was attracted by a large crowd outside; some dignitary was being accorded a civic welcome. On a sudden mischievous impulse, the brash young man moved into the ranks of the reception committee and gravely shook hands with the pear-shaped guest. It was, he discovered later, none other than Louis Philippe, the recently abdicated King of France.

The same audacity provided him with a business coup early in his career in the drapery business. As a junior partner and buyer for a Montreal firm he came under the influence, during his trips to England, of James Morrison, the most romantic business figure in the country – a man whose swift and daring rise to fortune had inspired the phrase "Morrison's Millions." Morrison had got his start as a result of an impetuous incident: as a draper's apprentice he had been so struck by the beauty of a young woman in his master's home that, on a sudden impulse, he flung his arms around her and kissed her. He thought her a maidservant; she turned out to be the master's daughter. He married her and assured himself of a career in the business. The story has all the aspects of a cheap Victorian novel but it convinced Morrison of the value of making instant decisions. By moving swiftly and operating on the principle of "small profits, quick returns," Morrison became a millionaire.

With England on the verge of war in the Crimea, Morrison urged Stephen to buy up all the cottons and woollens he could lay his hands on and ship them across the Atlantic to Canada before wartime scarcity shot the price up. Since Stephen had no way of consulting his superiors back in Montreal, there being no Atlantic cable, he took the plunge himself. The gamble must have dismayed his senior partner, who from time to time entered into young Stephen's financial adventures with the comment: "Well, it is clear George is going to ruin the firm, so it might as well come now as at a later time." But, of course, he did not ruin the firm. The corner he secured on cotton and woollen goods allowed him to bring off a financial coup. He eventually took over the firm, later formed one of his own, and soon found himself a member of the Montreal business establishment.

In Smith and Hill, Stephen found men like himself: shrewd in business, willing to take long risks, and, perhaps above all, wedded to the idea that a man was placed on earth to work, day and night if need be. To them, idleness was anathema and the concept of leisure almost unknown. Hill had never known an idle moment. Of Smith, it was said (by an old Hudson's Bay factor) that he "was a wonder to work. He did not seem to take any sleep. We used to say, indeed, that he stopped up all night. No matter how late at night you looked, you would see his lamp burning in his house. . . ." Work, indeed, was

318

Smith's real religion. There is a revealing story about Smith and his secretary, a God-fearing man who refused to work on Sunday in spite of a pile of correspondence waiting for the Monday post. Smith allowed him the Lord's Day off and then, at exactly one minute after midnight, put him to work until dawn answering the mail.

As for Stephen, late in his career when he was presented with the freedom of Aberdeen, he ventured to reveal what he considered to be the secret of his rapid rise in the business world:

"Any success I may have had in life is due in great measure to the somewhat Spartan training I received during my Aberdeen apprenticeship, in which I entered as a boy of 15. To that training, coupled with the fact that I seemed to have been born utterly without the faculty of doing more than one thing at a time is due that I am here before you today. I had but few wants and no distractions to draw me away from the work I had in hand. It was impressed upon me from my earliest years by one of the best mothers that ever lived that I must aim at being a thorough master of the work by which I had to get my living; and to be that I must concentrate my whole energies on my work, whatever that might be, to the exclusion of every other thing. I soon discovered that if I ever accomplished anything in life it would be by pursuing my object with a persistent determination to attain it. I had neither the training nor the talents to accomplish anything without hard work, and fortunately I knew it."

It was this hard ethic, so forcefully expressed by Stephen, that explains the dominance of the Scot in pioneer Canada. The Irish could loll in the taverns, sing, brawl, engage at ward level in the game of politics and otherwise disport themselves with the religious bickering that so engrossed their time and energies. For the Scots it was work, save and study; study, save and work. The Irish outnumbered them, as they did the English, but the Scots ran the country. Though they formed only one-fifteenth of the population they controlled the fur trade, the great banking and financial houses, the major educational institutions and, to a considerable degree, the government. The CPR was built to a large extent by Irish navvies and Irish contractors; but it was the Scots who held the top jobs. Almost every member of the original CPR Syndicate was a self-made Scot. In the drama of the railway it is the Scottish names that stand out: Macdonald and Mackenzie, Allan and Macpherson, Fleming and

Grant, Stephen, Smith, Kennedy, McIntyre, Angus and Hill (who was half Scottish) – living embodiments of the popular copybook maxims of the time. *Waste not, want not. . . Satan finds more mischief still for idle hands to do. . . . God helps those that help themselves. . . A penny saved is a penny earned. . . Remember that time is money. . . Early to bed, early to rise. . . Keep your nose to the grindstone. . . See a pin and pick it up. . . . * Stephen, it is said, got a job through following the last of these maxims. Unsuccessful in Glasgow, he had moved to London and sought work in a draper's establishment. The store was in chaos, for it was stock-taking day and no one had time to speak to him. He turned away disappointed and was halfway through the door when he stopped to pick up a pin, which he carefully stuck behind his coat lapel. The foreman, so the story goes, spotted the action, called him over and gave him a job on the spot. Alger could not have improved upon the incident.

Stephen's idea of a spare-time activity was to make a study of banking. The hobby, if one could call it that, led him eventually to the top of the financial pyramid. His only real form of relaxation was salmon fishing, a passion which he indulged at his summer retreat of Causapscal on the Matapedia River in the Gaspé. His love of the sport almost certainly went back to his days at the parish school in his native Banffshire, a name Stephen was to make famous as Canada's best-known Rocky Mountain resort. Here, as a young student, he came under the influence of a brilliant teacher and mathematician, John Macpherson. Top students were rewarded by Macpherson with an invitation to go salmon fishing. Stephen was certainly a top student in Macpherson's specialty; the schoolmaster was to recall that in thirty years of teaching Stephen was one of the three best mathematicians he had known. The salmon-fishing expeditions must have been frequent.

A mathematician must think logically and tidily; above all, he must reason creatively. Stephen had that kind of a mind, able to grapple with intricate problems, to rearrange the components into a rational pattern and then make deductions from the result. He has been called with truth "the greatest genius in the whole history of Canadian finance." His entire career is a testimony to it.

Stephen met his cousin Donald A. Smith for the first time in 1866 and it was a curiously chilly and awkward encounter. At this point the contrast between the two men was marked. Stephen had been in Montreal sixteen years and had climbed swiftly up the social and

320

mercantile ladder: a prominent man in the woollen business, a member of the Montreal Board of Trade, who mixed easily on the boards of charitable organizations with the Redpaths, the Torrances and the Allans. Smith, who was eleven years older than his cousin, had been walled off from the world in the dark and lonely corners of Labrador for more than a generation. The sophisticated Stephen was faultlessly groomed, as a good draper should be; indeed, for a time he employed a valet. Smith was shaggy and weatherworn, his sandy hair curling around his collar, his eyebrows unkempt, his beard ragged.

Smith was visiting Lachine at the time, staying at the home of his in-laws, the Hardistys. He knew very little about Stephen save that he was in the woollen trade and was a first cousin, but he decided to go into Montreal to look him up during the course of a shopping expedition. He took along his wife and family and, en route, they purchased a great, gaudy carpetbag to take back with them to Labrador; it was the sort of thing the Indians enjoyed seeing. Later, when Smith was asked if Stephen had been glad to see him, his wife burst out: "He wasn't glad at all. Why should Mr. Stephen be glad to see country cousins like us? I wish he had waited until he met Mr. Stephen before buying that red carpet bag. But he wouldn't let me carry it, and the rest of us waited outside."

It is an oddly memorable picture, this initial meeting between two men who came to be numbered among the most powerful in the country: the nervous family group on the doorstep, waiting outside like poor relations and the rustic Smith, clutching his outlandishly brilliant bag in the presence of the elegant Stephen – the country mouse and the city mouse, circling each other warily.

But Smith was no bumpkin as Stephen was speedily to realize. He was a man of parts, who had earned the praise of a future Smithsonian director with his scientific experiments in farming at Esquimaux Bay where, in subarctic conditions, he had managed to raise sheep and cattle and cultivate seven acres of land. His active correspondence with colleagues all over the world kept him abreast if not ahead of international affairs. More, he was an astonishing businessman. For many years his fellow officers in the fur trade had entrusted him with their salaries and this gave him control of large sums of money. He guaranteed the fur traders three per cent a year and invested their money in securities. He was, in short, a kind of one-man Labrador bank and this became the basis of his fortune. One of the stocks he bought was that of the Bank of Montreal;

another, the Hudson's Bay Company. He ended up as one of the bank's largest shareholders and in total control of the Hudson's Bay Company. But, true to the copybook maxims, he was not above counting and sorting all the nails in the packing cases that were shipped to him.

When Smith met Stephen and Hill in Montreal in the spring of 1877, he was already a director of the bank. Stephen was its president. The two had become associated since that frosty meeting ten years before. Smith was moved permanently to Montreal in 1868 and he and his cousin soon found themselves co-directors and leading shareholders in several industries, including one that manufactured railway rolling stock. Bit by bit Stephen found himself getting involved with railways, almost by osmosis. As early as 1871 he and Smith had both been allied in a small way in an attempt to get a charter for a railway from the Red River to the border and another from the lakehead to Fort Garry. Macdonald's plans for the CPR frustrated this project but it was almost impossible for any business-man of stature not to be connected with railways. Stephen moved into a locomotive works in Kingston, arranged for the sale of bonds on the Toronto, Grey and Bruce line, and was appointed to the provisional board of a Quebec railway. Now, in 1877, he found himself leaning across the table while a one-eyed ex-Canadian jabbed his finger at him and talked about launching a daring financial adventure.

Stephen's precise mathematician's mind easily grasped Hill's Niagara of statistics and sorted them into a pattern. His gambler's instincts tugged at him insistently. If the coup could be pulled off – it was an immense "if" – it would be a master-stroke comparable to the exploits of a Gould, a Fisk or a Morgan. If it failed, it would literally beggar them all.

What did Stephen have to gain at this point in his career? He was president of the most important financial institution in Canada, director of innumerable companies, respected by his peers, socially impeccable. The preposterous scheme of buying into an obscure and rundown railroad somewhere off beyond the mists of the horizon could, unless it worked, bring him nothing but discredit. Perhaps if he could have seen the tortured succession of events that this would finally lead to, the terrible moments when he saw his world, everything that he had built and toiled for, crumbling around him, the sleepless nights when he was close to a nervous and physical breakdown, perhaps even to suicide – George Stephen might have hesitated and backed away. A decade later, after it was all over and the years hung heavy upon him, he gave more than a little indication of this when, on the eve of his birthday, he wrote to John A. Macdonald:

"Tomorrow I begin my sixty-first year, and looking back ten years I am far from being the free man I then was. . . . When I think of the misery I have suffered in these ten years I cannot help thinking what a fool I was not to end my work and enjoy the leisure which I had earned by forty years hard work. I began to earn my own living at the age of ten. 'But what maun be maun be.' It was not so ordained. . . ."

He could not resist the adventure. He sat down and began to figure, with Hill and Smith, at what price the bonds should be purchased. They worked it out together at a little more than four million dollars. If the Dutch bondholders indicated that price was acceptable, Stephen said, he thought he could raise the money in London that fall. He still had to see the railway for himself – he was nothing if not thorough – but from that day on George Stephen was, for all practical purposes, totally captivated, body and soul, to the exclusion of everything else.

4

The new associates – they were not yet even partners and had signed no formal agreement – had a great deal of delicate negotiating ahead of them. Before Stephen could leave for Europe it would be necessary to make a firm and final deal with the bondholders. Then, in order to forestall a legal battle, an attempt must also be made to corner the stock. After that Stephen would have to raise enough money to buy both the bonds and the stock.

Hill left Montreal for New York to see Litchfield, the man who owned almost all of the stock. He drew a blank. "The old rat," as Stephen called him, would not even name a price. Then, on May 26, Hill fired off a carefully worded letter to the Dutch committee, proposing various discounts on the different classes of bonds ranging from eleven cents to eighty cents on the dollar, but adding up to the price the associates had agreed upon in Montreal. Hill, the master

A railway at bargain rates

letter-writer, had worked at this one all night. It was so ambiguously worded that, although it looked like an offer, it was actually only an option. Lengthy negotiations followed. The Dutch tried to bargain. In July, Hill began to get tough. The value of the bonds was actually decreasing, he suggested: the grasshopper plague had caused land values to plunge and the Northern Pacific was threatening to build a competitive line, which would reduce the value of the property still further.

Just before he left for Europe, on September 1, 1877, Stephen found an opportunity to see the property for himself. He was in Chicago on business with R. B. Angus, the bank's general manager – another bearded, self-made Scot – and the two decided to spend the weekend in St. Paul. Smith immediately came down from Winnipeg and on Sunday the four associates together with Angus and Farley, the receiver and manager, took the pay car out along the completed portion of one of the lines.

Stephen was dismayed at what he saw when the train chugged past the last hamlet of Litchfield and out onto the sere prairie. This was the worst year of the great depression of the seventies. The economic panic had been followed by drought years, which drove settlers from the land, and – worse – by a grasshopper plague of truly terrible proportions. The hoppers came by the millions, covering the roads and fences so thickly that they obscured them. They ate everything that grew. James Trow, the M.P. who visited the Red River country at the time of the plague, left a graphic description:

"In looking toward the sun the sight resembled a heavy snowstorm of large flakes, passing through the air with great rapidity. They were upon the ground piled one upon the other so that we crushed thousands with every revolution of the carriage wheels. For the novelty of the thing, we would occasionally alight, walk ahead of the horses, when millions would rise out of our path."

It was through such ravaged country that Stephen was now passing, shaking his head ominously: it looked for all the world like the top of a rusty stove. The others watched in growing alarm. Would he back out now? Stephen began to ask some pointed questions: where would the business come from in this tenantless desert? When, if ever, would there be settlers here on the parched and plundered grasslands? Then suddenly the little station of De Graff was reached, named, ironically, for a contractor who was suing the company for unpaid bills. Here there was "a rude but good sized structure" with crowds around it. There were several trails leading into the community and these were speckled with carts loaded with people.

"What is all this?" Stephen wanted to know.

Somebody, probably Hill, made a reply which Smith was later to remember:

"Why, this is but an instance of what is to occur along the whole line of the railroad. This is a colony opened by Bishop Ireland one single year ago. Already the settlers brought in by the Bishop are counted by the hundreds, and hundreds of others are coming to join them from different parts of America and Europe. This is Sunday morning and the settlers are going to Mass."

The scene made an enormous impression on Stephen: the vision of a railway tied to colonization – bringing in the very settlers who would then provide it with its future business – was limned in his mind. His old mentor, James Morrison, had always advised him: "Hold to your first impression of a bargain." Stephen's doubts evaporated and, in Smith's words, "from that moment he was won over to the new enterprise." As for Bishop Ireland, he benefited hugely from the incident. A grateful Jim Hill saw to it that his church got all the land it needed for next to nothing.

Hill had by this time made a detailed inventory of the railroad's assets and liabilities, listing every fraction of debt and describing the securities in detail. His supple mind had grasped a point that eluded everyone else: though the net earnings of the First Division Company seemed to have dropped, they had in reality almost doubled because almost two hundred thousand dollars had been charged to operating expenses instead of to construction and equipment. This meant that the railroad was doing much better than the books seemed to indicate.

Hill knew something more: although he figured that the total cost of the bonds plus the cost of completing the remainder of the line would require some five and a half million dollars, he was able, by close reckoning, to estimate the total value of the railway, with its equipment, track, townsites and land grants, at almost twenty millions. In short, Hill realized that, if the bondholders accepted the offer, he and his associates would get the railway for about a quarter of its real value.

In mid-September, Kennedy's partner, Captain Barnes, representing the Dutch committee, met Stephen in Montreal. The Dutch were ready to deal and, though there was some internal shuffling, the over-all asking price remained the same. If Stephen could raise the money, the partners could buy themselves almost eighteen million dollars worth of bonds for slightly more than four million. It was a fantastic bargain.

The four partners agreed to share the risks and the profits equally, each taking a one-fifth share in the enterprise. "We are all in the same boat to sink or swim together," was the way Stephen put it. The remaining one-fifth went to Stephen to use at his discretion in raising a loan. Indeed, Stephen was given a wide latitude in negotiating terms. At the end of September he set off for England, full of optimism.

But in London, the bankers were gun shy. The panic of 1873 had made American railway securities a bad risk. And among all the bad risks, the St. Paul and Pacific was held to be the worst. Canada's unofficial ambassador in London, Sir John Rose, might pave the way, through his firm of Morton, Rose and Company, but Stephen was not able to raise a shilling. As he described it: "After considerable negotiation I utterly failed. Nobody believed – or at least I failed to induce anybody to believe – that the property was good for anything."

In Montreal, on Stephen's return, four bitterly disappointed men met on Christmas Day, in no mood for Yuletide merriment. The grand scheme on which Hill and Smith had been pinning their hopes for four years lay shattered. Stephen, however, had no intention of giving up. The tumblers of his precise mind were already clicking over, forming new patterns. An unconventional plan was taking shape which, if accepted, would be far better than the original. Stephen decided to take the negotiations into his own hands and deal directly with the Dutch committee's New York agent.

Early in January, Stephen met John S. Kennedy for the first time. Kennedy was yet another self-made Scot and the two swiftly became friends and, not long afterward, business associates. Stephen's plan was as bold as it was simple. He offered to buy the bonds on credit, depositing a mere one hundred thousand dollars on account and paying the balance *after* foreclosure. The payment could be made either in cash or in the new bonds of the reorganized company. The Dutch were encouraged to accept the paper rather than the money by the offer of a bonus of $250 in preferred stock for every thousand-dollar bond they took. The partners, in turn, agreed to finish the railway and put it into working order.

They were, in short, proposing to get control of eighteen million dollars worth of bonds for a cash outlay of only one hundred thousand dollars. The Dutch bondholders were psychologically in the position of horse traders who, having had various offers dangled before them and then withdrawn, had worked themselves into a frame of mind to deal at any price. Under Kennedy's prodding they accepted. The purchase was concluded on February 24, 1878, and the partners took control of the railway on March 13.

One of the mysteries surrounding this remarkable transaction is the disposition of the extra one-fifth share that Stephen was given to negotiate with. What happened to it? Did Stephen keep it for himself? If not, to whom did he give it? That it was not divided among the four partners seems clear from their subsequent court testimony, in which they appeared remarkably casual, unconcerned and even evasive about a slice of stock that came to be worth many millions.

"We showed our satisfaction and contentment in the whole matter by each of us releasing Mr. Stephen. There, with us, was the end of it," Smith said airily. "We did not ask Mr. Stephen to account for it." The agreement, as Smith recalled it under oath, was that Stephen would use the extra one-fifth "as might be necessary in getting the aid of friends or in getting the money." But what friends? Smith did not say; Stephen was not asked.

One man Stephen did *not* give the one-fifth interest to was Jesse P. Farley, the receiver in bankruptcy of one of the twin St. Paul companies and the general manager of both. Farley later sued Kittson, Hill and the newly organized company, charging that in 1876, before the meeting with Stephen, both Kittson and Hill had promised him a one-fifth share in the enterprise in exchange for his help, co-operation and special knowledge. It was clear that that help consisted in deceiving the courts, which had put him in charge of the property on Kennedy's advice. What Farley was saying, in effect, was that he had devised a plan and arrived at a secret agreement with Hill and Kittson to keep the line in such condition that it could be bought cheaply. The circuit court judge who heard the case in 1882 tended to believe Farley. "The plaintiff," he said, "conceived a scheme to wreck the vast interests which it was his duty to protect"; but he threw the case out because "courts will not and ought not to be made the agencies whereby frauds are to be in any respect recognized or aided." Farley appealed and a trial was ordered. It took place in 1887, when Kittson was dead. This time the judge did not believe Farley. He said, with some sarcasm, that in his opinion Farley did not fail in his official duty "and although such conclusion carries an imputation upon his recollection or veracity as a witness, it sustains his integrity as an officer."

Farley persisted in the courts for a total of thirteen years. By the time the final judgement was read against him in the Supreme Court in 1893, he, too, was dead and the matter was closed. From all this testimony – two thousand pages of it in one case alone – several puzzling pieces of information emerge which do not quite fit together. It is reasonably clear that Farley *thought* he had a secret deal with Hill and Kittson. It is equally clear that Hill emphatically did not think so. It is also reasonably clear that Hill, Kittson and Farley did a good deal of talking together about the railway and that at a time when Farley knew that Hill wanted to buy it, he, Farley, did his best to disparage the line to the Dutch representative.

There is also the puzzling question of Kennedy's role. Farley was Kennedy's man. At a time when the bondholders were in their final negotiations with Stephen – on Kennedy's advice – Kennedy was also writing to Farley, urging him to get in on a good thing. "We think it will pay you to take an interest with K. & H. and we are glad to hear that they have offered it to you," he wrote on February 25, 1878, in a reply to a letter from Farley soliciting his advice.

All of this can be subject to innocent interpretation but the question continues to rankle: who got the extra one-fifth? After the St. Paul line grew into the Great Northern it was revealed that John S. Kennedy held an enormous quantity of its stock. He, Hill and Stephen all became close friends and when the CPR board was formed Kennedy was a director. When he died he left an estate estimated at between thirty and sixty million dollars, depending on the book value of the immense mass of railway stock he had acquired. Did Kennedy simply buy into the railway that he had urged his Dutch clients to sell so cheaply? Or was it he who was promised George Stephen's extra one-fifth during those delicate negotiations, which allowed the sale of eighteen millions in bonds for almost no cash at all.*

*The Canadian historian O. D. Skelton, in his book *The Railway Builders* (Toronto, 1916), says that Stephen, Hill, Smith and Kennedy each took one share and that Kittson took half a share, the remaining half share going to Angus after he left the service of the bank and became general manager of the railway. He gives no source for this statement, which does not square with the court testimony of the principals in 1888. Nonetheless it is a plausible suggestion: Kittson's energies were not really involved in the enterprise to the same extent as the others; Angus

Perhaps Stephen himself kept the extra one-fifth, though that is hardly in character. If he did, no one could say he had not earned it. As for the Dutch, they seemed perfectly satisfied: most of them preferred to take more bonds in the new company rather than cash, a wise decision as it turned out. It was true that they had sold the railway cheaply; it was also true that the line was worth eighteen million dollars only if and when it could be put into working order. If Hill and his associates had not come along, it is doubtful whether the bondholders would have realized anything on their original investment. As it developed, they were so well pleased that they made a gift to Stephen of a valuable bowl commemorating a great victory in which a Dutch admiral, in 1666, burned the best of the British fleet. Years later, when Stephen was entertaining George V of England, that old sailor's eye caught sight of the trophy. The monarch was not amused at this symbol of naval humiliation.

"Why don't you destroy the damned thing?" His Majesty asked.

5

The Syndicate is born

The four partners had possession of the bonds but they were by no means out of the woods. A whole series of complicated problems now faced them simultaneously. Any one of these could wreck the enterprise and ruin them.

First of all, there was more money to be raised. The line owed $280,000 in debts, which had to be paid immediately. Then there was the one hundred thousand dollar deposit to the bondholders. There was also the half-yearly dividend of $140,000 which could not be passed. The stock, if it could be purchased from Litchfield, would cost around half a million dollars. Finally, the railroad itself must be finished swiftly if the land grant was to be earned.

There was only one conceivable place to get this kind of financing and that was from the Bank of Montreal. Stephen was president and

could probably be lured away from the bank only on the promise of a sizable interest; and Kennedy's subsequent involvement makes it clear that he was a substantial shareholder. It is reasonably certain that Kennedy was brought into the syndicate by Stephen at the time he convinced the Dutch committee to accept the offer.

Smith was a director and they were now proposing to borrow money personally from an institution under their care.

It did not look well; there would certainly be stockholders' questions and newspaper comment, but there was no help for it.

Stephen wrote to Hill on February 10, 1878, that he and Kittson must pledge everything they owned – and he meant *everything* – in order to get a line of credit from the bank. He and Smith had already handed over "every transferable security of every kind we have got" in order to get the initial $280,000 to pay off the debts. Now it was all or nothing.

"The risks were very great," Hill later recalled, "and in case of failure so great as to entirely ruin the entire party – financially; wipe out every dollar we owned in the world and leave us with an enormous debt if the enterprise failed."

Kittson was almost sick with worry. To him, the scheme had always seemed wild; he had gone into it solely because he trusted Jim Hill. Now, if at any stage of the sensitive manoeuvres that were required something went wrong, he faced the poorhouse. He kept his participation a secret, lest his friends should talk him out of it. "An enormous risk at my time of life," he told his friend ex-governor Sibley of Minnesota after it was over. "I did not dare tell you of it." But in his old age, Norman Kittson, the one-time border trader, wealthy beyond his wildest visions, would be able to purchase and maintain one of the largest and finest racing stables on the continent.

Stephen's next move was to go straight to Ottawa and negotiate with Mackenzie for a ten-year lease of the Pembina Branch so that the St. Paul road, when it reached the border, would have a connection to Winnipeg. This, too, was fraught with uncertainty. Smith's name was already being mentioned as a major shareholder in the company and it was impossible for him in Parliament to maintain the fiction that he was disinterested. So unpopular was he with the Conservative opposition that Mackenzie, as we have seen, was flatly denying any meeting at all with the Stephen group.

Almost simultaneously a new problem arose. The Minnesota legislature passed a new law setting a series of deadlines for the construction of the railway. Two sections had to be completed by the end of the year, otherwise the land grants, franchises – everything – would be forfeited. Now it became doubly important to push the foreclosure suits. Hill was fearful that one of the twin companies might actually start making money. If that happened the new trustees would be forced to give up their control over it, since it could pay the defaulted mortgage interest with the increased revenue; and then the St. Paul terminus, among other assets, would be lost and the value of the second company's property would be reduced.

The partners were juggling several problems at once: they must lobby in Ottawa for the Canadian lease; they must raise funds to build the rest of the railway before the rapidly approaching deadline; they must haggle with Litchfield to try to get his stock in order to press foreclosure. Finally, they must fight off the rival Northern Pacific, which was now threatening to move in with its own line to the border and launch a railway war. It seemed an impossible task, especially in view of the precarious state of their finances. If either Litchfield or the rival railway knew how badly off they were, the game would be over. This is where Stephen's control of the bank became so valuable: there would be no leaks from that source.

But there was not a million dollars available for the additional railway construction to the border. The only way to raise money was for the receiver, Farley, to get a court order permitting him to issue receiver's debentures. Thirty-five miles of railway had to be built by August, 1878, from Melrose to Sauk Centre and another thirty-three by December (to Alexandria) in order to hold the land grant. Farley was persuaded by Hill to go to court, but the courts were dubious. There had been a great deal of profiteering in St. Paul railroad bonds. Once before Farley had been charged with raising money in this manner and had failed. There were two court hearings and a commission. The sessions were maddeningly slow. Every day counted but the hearings dragged on and on. The judge refused to issue the order. Hill himself went to see him and, using every persuasive power, managed to change his mind. The judge was impressed by Hill but even as he signed the order, he had his doubts: he said candidly that if the associates failed to carry it out, it would destroy them and ruin him.

From this point on the financing of the railway was left to Stephen while Hill moved in to build the line. It was almost a rehearsal for the future and grander project of the CPR, when again it was Stephen's task to keep the money flowing while Hill's protégé, Van Horne (who later became his deadly enemy), would drive the steel.

Hill had two months in which to lay track from Melrose to Sauk Centre. Though Farley was still technically general manager, it was Hill who took charge of construction. He had to find rails, ties, rolling stock and labourers in a hurry. The task took all his waking hours. At 10.30 p.m. his wife Mary would come to his office where he worked long after dark to take him home, but Hill would keep on working away and she would sit in a chair by the window and doze until he was ready to leave, rarely before 1 a.m. By the time the men and equipment were assembled, Hill realized that he would have to lay at least a mile of track a day to make the deadline. He took charge himself, fighting mosquitoes, sunstroke, rattlesnakes and dysentery, firing bosses on the spot if they could not maintain the mileage. When one crew rebelled at Hill's methods and quit, he wired St. Paul for replacements, taking the precaution of paying the fares in advance and hiring the toughest navvies he could find to guard each car door to prevent the new workers from skipping out before they reached the end of track.

In the midst of this another crisis arose. The rejuvenated Northern Pacific, which for a brief time before its collapse in 1873 had controlled part of the St. Paul road, decided to move in, force it into bankruptcy and buy it cheap. The rival company still held some St. Paul stock, which meant it could harass and delay the foreclosure proceedings. But worse, it was threatening to build a line to the Canadian border parallelling the St. Paul line. That would be disastrous.

In the American midwest there is a particularly stubborn and obnoxious weed to which the early settlers gave the name of Jim Hill Mustard. It fitted. In his battle with the Northern Pacific, Hill showed his mettle. He met the rival company head-on – the first of a series of bold encounters which would, one day, see him best a Vanderbilt. Hill was convinced that the Northern Pacific was bluffing. It was his tactic to convince his rivals that he himself was not. The Northern Pacific was at the time using St. Paul tracks. Hill threatened to cancel the agreement immediately, raise the fees for running rights and boost the rent on the St. Paul terminal. More, he would start at once, he declared, to survey a line all the way to the Yellowstone River and would ask Congress for half of the land grant that had been promised the Northern Pacific as far west as the Rockies. In the face of this bluff – it could be nothing else – the rival railway knuckled under and an agreement was reached in November, the chief articles of which were that the Northern Pacific would withdraw from competition with the St. Paul and Pacific in return for certain running rights and terminal space in the Twin Cities. Hill had won his first corporate dogfight handily.

He met his first construction deadline with just twenty-four hours to spare and secured the vital land grant. He did not slacken his pace, for he had to finish the second stretch before December 1. The enemy was no longer the dysentery and sunstroke of the summer but the bone-chilling cold of the Minnesota prairies. Hill walked the line himself, stopping here and there to counsel one or other of the navvies – he knew them all by their first names – on the way to treat frostbite. On one memorable occasion he leaped from his private car, seized a shovel and began attacking the snow, spelling the workmen off one after another while they went inside for a dipper of hot coffee. He made his deadline well ahead of time and kept on going, for he wanted to get the full railway operating as swiftly as possible. The line would be useless until he completed the gap between Crookston and St. Vincent – across from Pembina at the Canadian border. On November 11, Hill had the satisfaction of seeing his first through locomotive arrive at Emerson, Manitoba.

Stephen meanwhile was having his own problems – a whole irritating series of them. The Senate had thrown out Mackenzie's bill, making a straight lease of the Pembina Branch impossible. Mackenzie had, however, in August given the St. Paul line running rights on the Canadian road. Then the Government changed and, to add to the complications, the contractors still had legal possession of the line and were not about to give it up. Their rates were so exorbitant that they amounted to an embargo on all through rail traffic from St. Paul. In the House, Tupper used the difficulties with the contractors as an excuse to frustrate Mackenzie's arrangement and make a new contract with Stephen. The St. Paul group could use the line only until the completion of the Canadian Pacific Railway. It was, at least, something. To speed up the transaction, Hill had one of his own men buy into the Pembina contract; but it was late spring, 1879, before the Canadian government finally got control of its own road.

Stephen's second problem was the recalcitrant Litchfield. As long as he held the stock he could hamper the foreclosure proceedings and prevent the reorganization of the railroad company. To push matters along, the partners decided upon a squeeze play. They launched a legal suit against Litchfield to attach some of his property and that of his brother in Minnesota to recover money that had been furnished to complete the main line and that he had converted to his own use. "The more he is worried and annoyed the sooner are we likely to bring them to terms," Stephen advised Hill. The financier remained stubborn. "We shall not be at peace or comfortable until we settle with Litchfield," Stephen said. In mid-January Stephen personally went to see "the old rat" in New York and managed to secure all the stock for a half million dollars. It was a considerable piece of negotiation. Stephen warned Hill to say nothing to anybody, not even to Litchfield's lawyers, since "it is the old rascal's idea to bring [them] to New York to *make* an *agree*¹. They must not know or have an idea that we have made one already or all the fat would be in the fire. Old L. wants to cheat both of them and it is not our policy to interfere." Stephen added that he had had "a terribly worrisome 4 or 5 days with the old fellow."

But it was done; there could be no conflicts now between stockholders and bondholders since they were one and the same. The partners got their half million from the Bank of Montreal and moved for foreclosure. It was granted in March. In May, they formed a new company, the St. Paul, Minneapolis and Manitoba Railroad Company. In June, the new firm bought up all the property at the foreclosure sale. It is said that they paid $6,780,000 for it, not in cash but in receiver's debentures and bonds. They floated a sixteen-million-dollar bond issue at once, some of which was used to pay back the Dutch. Immediately after the foreclosure sale they sold the greater part of the land grant for $13,068,887. Already they had realized an incredible profit. It was only a matter of deciding how much stock to create and that took some time and care. Years later, Smith remembered that Hill's ideas were so big in this direction "as to cause me, a man of moderation, considerable perturbation."

Hill wanted to create fifteen million dollars worth of stock.

"Aren't you afraid that the capitalization will startle the public?" Smith ventured. "Isn't there some danger that we will be charged with watering the stock?"

"Well," Hill replied, "we have let the whole lake in already."

When the stock was issued, each of the original partners received 57,646 shares. Within three years, each share was worth $140, which meant that each partner had made a clear capital gain of more than eight millions. At that point – 1882 – the partners issued another two million dollars worth of stock to themselves and then, in 1883, they issued to themselves ten million dollars worth of six per cent bonds for one million dollars – an additional profit of nine millions. Yet at the time the railroad was still sneered at as "Hill's Folly." The attorneys who worked out the corporate structure were offered a fee of twenty-five thousand dollars in cash or half a million in stock. If they had taken the stock and held it for thirty years, they would have had in principal and interest something close to thirty millions.

From the beginning, the railroad was fabulously successful. The grasshoppers magically disappeared. The soil began to yield bumper crops. Hill had to scramble to find extra freight cars to handle the business. In 1880, the net earnings of the railroad exceeded the interest on the bonded debt by sixty per cent – an increase of one million dollars in a single year. The "Manitoba" road, as it came to be called, formed the nucleus of Jim Hill's Great Northern, the only transcontinental line in the United States that never went bankrupt or defaulted on a dividend. Within two years its four promoters went from the brink of disaster to a position of almost unlimited wealth.

They had also become controversial figures in Canada. The deal with the Bank of Montreal was looked at askance by press, public and shareholders. There was a flurry at the stockholders' meeting in June of 1879, when pointed questions were asked about the propriety of directors appropriating bank funds for a private venture. The criticisms increased when R. B. Angus resigned as the bank's general manager in August to take a job as general manager of the new railway.

Stephen disdained to stoop to any explanation at all. Meanwhile, he and his colleagues were being attacked on another front. The new company, which operated the only trains from St. Paul to the Red River, had also taken over the Kittson Line and thus had a monopoly of all traffic to Winnipeg. That aroused the full ire of the Conservative press, to whom the name of Donald Smith was still a profanity. Railway policy, cried the Montreal *Gazette*, "has already been too long dictated simply by regard for the interests of Mr. Donald A. Smith and his associates." The pact between the Government and the St. Paul group was suicidal, the paper said; it called for the immediate construction of the Canadian Pacific to remove their pernicious influence. The Winnipeg *Times* was even more caustic. "The wily Jim Hill," it charged, "had to 'grease' other interests, legislative, judicial and private to the tune, it is said, of a million." The paper went on to ask where the money had come from "to buy up the bonds and meet the scarcely less cost of *controlling* the interests in St. Paul that were necessary? Let the two confiding stockholders of the Bank of Montreal ask the question." On the other hand, the Manitoba *Free Press* a year later was hailing the coup as "a great triumph of Canadian sagacity."

This was the climate in which the CPR Syndicate was eventually formed. For all the controversy served to illuminate one fact: there was now available a remarkable group of successful men who had experience in both railway building and high finance. In the summer of 1880, the Macdonald government was looking for just such a group. It was John Henry Pope, the homely and straightforward Minister of Agriculture, who had first drawn his prime minister's attention to the St. Paul associates.

"Catch them," he said, "before they invest their profits."

Chapter Nine

1

"Capitalists of undoubted means" There is something akin to a sprightly look in the earlier photographs and portraits of George Stephen: the head is tilted upwards, the wide, clear eyes sparkle a little and there is almost to be seen in those unlined features – one hesitates to use the word – a quality approaching innocence. The later famous painting by Sir George Reid, which hangs in the CPR board room, portrays a different man. The head is sunk forward on shoulders that have become slightly bowed; the greying moustache droops down, giving the bearded face a morose, hound-like appearance; the eyes, once so wide, are shrewd, knowing and not a little sad. It is perhaps unwise to make too much of Victorian portraits; and yet all the evidence suggests that Reid did not exaggerate the change in his subject.

When the first annual report of the "Manitoba line" electrified the public in 1880, Stephen must have believed that his life's struggle lay behind him. In reality, it had only begun; the troubles he faced would be far more consuming and far more nerve-racking than anything he had yet experienced. For when Stephen said "yes" to Jim Hill in 1877 he unwittingly catapulted himself into the great project of the Canadian Pacific Railway.

From the moment that Stephen's success became public property, he was transformed, whether he knew it or not, into a leading candidate to build the great railway. Long before Macdonald took power, Mackenzie had been seeking just such a man – a successful Canadian financier, in league with other Canadians of means, with practical experience in financing and constructing a profitable North American railway. After Mackenzie's fall, Macdonald took up the vain search. Just when it seemed impossible to find such a man, an entire group of them – Stephen, Hill, Smith, Kittson and Angus – suddenly popped out of nowhere, loaded with credentials.

Macdonald's fruitless quest had already occupied more than a year. It was clear from Tupper's speech in the House in May of 1879 (the doctor was hoarse and ill at the time) that the Government intended to prosecute its railway policy with as much energy as it could muster. Tupper on that occasion talked about the future of Manitoba, the necessity of introducing more English immigrants into the North West and the Government's intention to seek an Imperial guarantee to help build the railway. That fall, Macdonald, Tupper and Tilley set out for England on just such a mission. The delegation was the most influential to cross the water since Confederation and the country was convinced that it would succeed. One rumour from Ottawa had the Brassey firm of Great Britain, which had built the Grand Trunk, combining with five other contractors to construct the railway without a guarantee. Another said that the Bank of England would supply all the funds necessary to complete the entire line. The Chicago *Tribune*, hailing a rumoured British loan of one hundred million dollars, urged that the government seek more like it, since Canada would eventually become part of the United States anyway and the money would, therefore, ultimately benefit the republic.

It was all premature and overoptimistic. There was no Imperial loan and no guarantee; nor were any contractors willing to gamble on such a lunatic undertaking. One English financier laughed aloud when he first heard of Macdonald's plan to raise a loan to build a railway across the half-frozen continent. Years later he related to Donald Smith his impressions at the time: " 'Good Heavens,' I thought, 'somebody will have to hold these Canadians back, or they will go plunging themselves into hopeless bankruptcy before they come of age.' I felt I would as soon invest in a Yankee 'wild-cat' mine."

Ironically, one of the elements of Macdonald's National Policy was working against another. The protective tariff was unpopular in England. Macdonald did not receive a turn-down from the Imperial authorities; he was simply asked to wait until the political climate improved. Help at the moment was out of the question.

But by 1880 the Government could no longer wait. Little George Walkem, back again in power in British Columbia, was bluntly threatening secession; he had, in fact, been elected on a "Fight Ottawa" platform. It was clear that the Canadian government would have to go it alone and swiftly if it was to keep the nation whole. The contract for the Yale-Kamloops section had to be let hurriedly as a sop to the British Columbians, and by the spring of 1880, to everyone's relief, Andrew Onderdonk was on the spot preparing to blast his way through the canyons of the Fraser. In April, Blake made one of his interminable speeches – this one lasted more than the usual five hours – in which he demanded that Onderdonk be stopped and that all construction cease west of the Rockies. The Government, he declared, was risking the ruin of the country for the sake of twelve thousand people. In his resolution Blake urged a policy of prudence:

the prairie section, it said, should be built ony as fast as settlement demanded. The resolution was, of course, defeated, but every member of the Opposition voted for it, including the rising young star of the Liberal Party, Wilfrid Laurier.

Blake's remarks, however, had considerable effect. The Government, while placating British Columbia with the Onderdonk contracts, determined to move slowly on the prairies. Its plan was to build "a cheap railway . . . incurring no expenditure beyond that absolutely necessary to effect the rapid colonization of the country." Only two hundred miles would be placed under contract, and the construction would be as flimsy and as cheap as possible. The line would not even be properly ballasted and only enough rolling stock to handle minimum traffic would be ordered. The steel would creep across the plains, year by year, a few miles ahead of advancing settlement. After the House rose, Macdonald told his dubious council that such a local railway was necessary to attract immigrants. He proposed a bonus of land to bring settlers and he spoke of going to England that summer to raise money for the project.

This was anti-climax after all the brave talk of a two-thousand-mile transcontinental line built to Union Pacific standards and it did not sit well with Charles Tupper. The Fighting Doctor was not one to admit defeat and this looked very much like surrender. To Tupper must go much of the credit for pushing through the project in its original form in the face of the hesitancy of his more timid colleagues.

"Sir John," he said, "I think the time has come when we must take an advance step. I want to submit a proposition for building a through line from Nipissing in Ontario to the Pacific Coast."

Macdonald remained sceptical. He told Tupper that he was afraid that it was "a very large order." Nonetheless he added, "I shall be pleased to consider anything you have to submit."

If the conversation (as reported by Tupper in his memoirs) sounds stilted, it may have been because the two were not speaking to each other except on matters of public necessity. The rift sprang out of Tupper's elastic political morality. (His private morality was similarly flexible, his propensity for handsome women earning him the nickname of "the Ram of Cumberland.") The sons of the two men, Charles Hibbert Tupper and Hugh Macdonald, had opened a law practice in Winnipeg. Tupper wanted the Government to throw business their way; Macdonald felt that to be improper. It is said that the two did not communicate in private for two years.

Tupper was more sanguine than his leader on the matter of the railway because he had learned of the incredible success of George Stephen and his colleagues and in his memo of June 15 to the Privy Council he made reference to it. He believed that the entire line from Nipissing to Pacific tidewater, including the sections already commenced by the government, could be completed for a cash expenditure of $45,500,000 and a land subsidy of twenty-five million acres and that, since there would be land left over, the government could recoup all the cash through sales to settlers. He recommended that "authority be given to negotiate with capitalists of undoubted means and who shall be required to give the most ample guarantee for the construction and operation of the line on such terms as will secure at the same time the rapid settlement of the public lands and the construction of the work." The memo bore the endorsement of Fleming's successor, Collingwood Schreiber, the former chief engineer of the government's Intercolonial Railway.

There was no doubt about who the "capitalists of undoubted means" were. Tupper had his eyes clearly focused on the St. Paul Syndicate. But even as the Cabinet met to consider the terms it was prepared to offer – a twenty-million-dollar subsidy and thirty million acres of prairie land – it was obvious that the atmosphere was changing and that other capitalists, some substantial and some shadowy, were sending feelers to Ottawa. The depression was at an end; the harvest of the previous autumn had been a bumper one; the climate for railway building suddenly looked better. There was word that the principals behind Andrew Onderdonk were interested; so was the Brassey firm. And up from New York came a British peer, Lord Dunmore, "a spendthrift and most probably a dupe of some knaves or other," according to Alexander Campbell. Dunmore was a front man for Puleston, Brown and Company, a British financial house, whose senior partner, Colonel John H. Puleston, had once been the head of Jay Cooke's office in London. The new governor general, Lord Lorne, was as suspicious of Dunmore as Campbell: "Mr. Brassey has a very good head, and plenty of money," he wrote to Macdonald. "Ld. Dunmore has a very good heart, no head and no money. . . . He is very capable of getting up good musical concerts but pray examine his financial concerts . . . his very name will probably be enough to give the C.P. a bad one. Mr. Brassey now on the other hand wd. be a tower of strength." Two days later His Excellency had second thoughts about Brassey: "Much as I would like to have Brassey take over the business of the aid of a company bound to settlements and to complete all the line, I cannot help feeling somewhat nervous as to the possibilities involved in any unqualified tying of the country to a company which might be far stronger than the Hudson's Bay and as strong as the old East India Company. If the money were got in New York, as I believe it might be, the Yankees cd get such important interests to guard that it cd well be justification of the U.S. to take charge of the whole of our Railway & 'fertile belt' in case of difficulty." The young governor general, who could not resist an opportunity to play with words, added that "my imagination becomes as you see 'fertile' in contemplating our possible slavery to any gigantic vested interest."

There was another offer before the government that June. It came in the name of Duncan McIntyre, who was engaged in building the Canada Central Railway from Ottawa to Lake Nipissing. Though McIntyre's name was appended to the preliminary correspondence, it was no secret that his principals were George Stephen and the other members of the St. Paul group. The arrangement between Stephen and McIntyre was a marriage of convenience. As the virtual owner of the Canada Central, McIntyre would be a valuable ally if Stephen's group secured the contract, for McIntyre's line stopped where the CPR was to begin. The alliance could mean that the through route from Ottawa to the Pacific Ocean would be controlled by a single company. McIntyre, a heavy-browed Lowlander with a great soup-strainer moustache, was another self-made Scot who had begun life in Canada in 1829 as a clerk in a mercantile firm. Although he became a spokesman for the new syndicate in its formative period, he was always something of an outsider within the group; and when the ultimate crisis came he would be found wanting. He did not have Stephen's stamina, nor Smith's, and the day would come when Stephen could not stand to be in the same room with him.

The Stephen-McIntyre offer was a tempting one, especially as it was the only one that came from Canada, but it asked more than the Cabinet was prepared to grant: a subsidy of twenty-six and a half millions and a land grant of thirty-five million acres. The Syndicate would not budge or bargain. The subject, McIntyre told Macdonald, was closed "for the present"; but the door was obviously being left ajar. On June 29, at a picnic at Bath, Ontario, Macdonald was emboldened to announce that there were a number of capitalists in Ottawa bidding for the construction of the railway and that negotiations had reached the point where a deputation of ministers to England was indicated.

Macdonald and Tupper sailed for England on July 10. The Prime Minister intended to see both Puleston, Brown and Company and Sir Henry Tyler, president of the Grand Trunk. Campbell was left to negotiate with Onderdonk and his backers. As for McIntyre, he was sailing on the same ship – not entirely by coincidence – and, as the mail steamer touched at Rimouski, a letter arrived for Macdonald from George Stephen, from his fishing camp at neighbouring Causapscal. It was an odd missive, diffident yet wistful, and it opened the door a little wider.

"I am aware," Stephen wrote, "it is often impossible for a Government to adopt the best course; and it is the knowledge of that fact that makes me rather hesitate to commit myself to the enormous responsibilities involved in this undertaking. You will have no difficulty, I feel sure, in finding men on the other side, more or less substantial and with greater courage – mainly because they know less of the difficulties to be encountered but also because they will adopt measures for their own protection which I could not avail myself of."

It was a clever letter, though Stephen may not have consciously intended it as such since he himself was of two minds regarding the project. Nevertheless, he managed very subtly to damn all other aspirants to the contract while obliquely selling his own group. He pointed out the difficulties of a large bonded indebtedness in which "the real responsibility is transferred from the Company to the people who may be induced to buy the bonds . . . while the Company or projectors pocket a big profit at the start. . . ." He suggested any English financial organization would indulge in this kind of manipulation at great risk to Canada: "It would indeed be a disastrous affair to all concerned, if the English public were induced to invest in a bond issue which the road could not carry. . . ."

His own plan, Stephen remarked, would have been to limit the borrowing to the smallest point "and if we issued a bond at all to take care it did not much exceed $5,000 a mile." He would expect his profit to come from the growth of the country after the railroad was built.

"I could not be a party to a scheme involving a large issue of bonds on a road which no one can be sure will earn enough to pay working expenses," Stephen declared. He had no intention of going to England; he would be outbid there. No English or American organization could do the job as well or as cheaply, yet they would

343

want to pocket the profits in advance while Stephen was willing to take the risk and wait.

Then, once more, the soft sell: Stephen was satisfied that he and his group could construct the road without much trouble and if anybody could operate it successfully, they could. The line from Thunder Bay to Red River would be profitable and they would use the experience gained in Minnesota in the management and settling of the lands. The Canada Central to Ottawa and certain Quebec roads would, of course, have to be incorporated because the terminus must be at Montreal or Quebec City, not Lake Nipissing, far off in the wilds of northern Ontario.

It was a letter dictated from a position of strength and confidence, written when Stephen was salmon fishing with Angus; indeed, the two had discussed nothing else all week, the fishing having been poor. In it, Stephen played Macdonald like an angler. He had thrust the bait towards him: the Minnesota experience, the desire to take risks, the special knowledge of Canadian conditions, the unquestioned ability of his group to do the job. Then, in a final paragraph, he pulled back slightly but left the bait dangling: "Although I am off the notion of the thing now, should anything occur on the other side to induce you to think that taking all things into consideration, our proposal is better upon the whole for the country than any offer you get in England, I might, on hearing from you, renew it and possibly in doing so reduce the land grant to some extent. . . ."

The Opposition, he reminded Macdonald – if one believed the *Globe* – would prefer limiting the land grant and increasing the cash subsidy.

It was a hard letter for Macdonald to resist, since Stephen's was the only Canadian group bidding and it was clear that he was prepared to do the job for about twenty-five millions in cash and an equal number of acres of good prairie land. Moreover, the other aspirants were dropping away. In August, the Onderdonk group passed: they were interested, but the Fraser canyon was occupying their efforts and they did not feel they had enough time to consider the matter. In London Macdonald and Tupper approached Sir Henry Tyler, the debonair and witty president of the Grand Trunk. The company was a political force in Canada and such a strong supporter of the Government that Grand Trunk employees, at election time, were given strict orders on how to vote. It was important that Tyler be given a chance, at the very least, to refuse the contract.

He did just that. Tupper reported his reaction, given in the tea room of the House of Commons, where Tyler was a sitting member: "If you'll cut off the portion of the railway from Thunder Bay to Nipissing I'll take up the project; but unless you do that, my shareholders will simply throw the prospectus into the wastepaper basket." There it was again: the terrible geography of North America conspiring against the efforts of the struggling nation to consolidate. Tupper replied that Canada could not consent to be for six months without any communication with Manitoba, the North West and British Columbia except by a long detour through a foreign land. That was that; Tyler would become an implacable enemy of the CPR and would almost succeed in smashing the line financially. The Grand Trunk's philosophy did not encompass a transcontinental nation; in the eyes of its absentee owners Canada was not much more than a way point on the route that led from the Atlantic to Chicago. Sir Henry's blunt refusal, though he could not suspect it at the time, would reduce the Grand Trunk to a secondary railroad; the CPR would shortly outrank it and, in the end, outlive it. By the time the older company caught the spirit of the new Canada and decided to push its own line of steel to the Pacific it would be too late. That belated and disastrous undertaking spelled the end of the company which might have been the greatest in the nation.

The offer from Puleston, Brown and Company, which Macdonald pushed, or pretended to push – it was financially more attractive than Stephen's – also dissolved. Puleston, the Civil War colonel who was to become a British knight and Member of Parliament, was a solider citizen than his front man, Lord Dunmore, but he could not, in the end, get the European backing he promised. It is possible the Prime Minister was relieved. A transcontinental railway built by a British promoter with American roots using French and German money was scarcely a great national undertaking. Stephen's letter was in his pocket and McIntyre, as he well knew, was in England. He began a series of discussions with McIntyre in London. Sir John Rose, who represented one of the smaller British financial houses and had some connection with the wavering European group, was present. George Stephen, in Canada, was at the end of the cable line. By September 4, the provisional agreement was made. Twenty-five million dollars and twenty-five million acres it was to be. McIntyre returned to Canada at the end of the month and so did the Prime Minister, to whom Stephen immediately wrote. He had seen "the important document," he said,

345

and he hoped there would be no difficulty in coming to terms on all points.

He and his colleagues had taken on a job that no one else in the United States, Britain, Europe or Canada had been persuaded to tackle. It was a huge responsibility and already in Montreal financial circles there were murmurings that this time the reckless Stephen had bitten off more than he could chew.

". . . my *friends* and my *enemies* agree," he wrote, "in affecting to think [that it] will be the ruin of us all."

And it almost was.

2

Success! All during late summer and early fall the newspapers of Canada were alive with rumour and speculation. During August, the *Globe*, with glee, continued to report the failure of Macdonald's mission, announcing the collapse of the Puleston, Brown offer and that of several other totally non-existent negotiations ranging from the Rothschilds to Sir Hugh Allan, a tactic which the rival *Mail* charged "was unprecedented in the newspaper annals of any country." On September 7, the Manitoba *Free Press* reported that on the basis of "the most positive information from London," the mission to Britain was a failure. By mid-September word of actual negotiations began to leak out. The Montreal *Daily Witness*, reporting the rumours, described the prospective deal as "utterly ruinous." Even the *Mail*, having disposed of the *Globe*, was remarkably hesitant: there was "no great reason for rejoicing . . . but it is quite likely that a reasonable bargain has been made." In the *Bystander*, Goldwin Smith was his usual acerb self: "Our deliverance from Government contracts and their pestilent influence is almost as great a cause for rejoicing as our deliverance from the mad undertaking itself."

The English press, covering Macdonald's visit, was generally hostile and its editorial remarks were cabled back to the Canadian newspapers. Much was made of the fact that the Canadians, having built small portions of the transcontinental line, had exhausted their means and were, at a late moment, appealing to the mother country for help. The all-Canadian route through the bleak Lake Superior country was universally condemned as useless. "The climate, too, is painted in black colours," the *Mail* reported.

Of all the adverse British comments, that of *The Times* was the most moderate. Referring to the Lake Superior section as "the pauper the rest of the family will have to support," the newspaper asked "whether the Dominion would not have been wise to retain for itself this special burden and not endeavour to throw it on European capitalists. If they accept it, they do so solely because they believe the dose to have been sweetened to an extent which will be very costly to the Canadian taxpayer."

The London *Examiner* launched an all-out attack on Macdonald and his colleagues: "The Dominion Ministers have grossly mismanaged their mission. They have repelled confidence where they should have nourished faith, and have sown distrust where they should have cultivated hope. They have been mysterious and fussy at the same time. They have flourished about their object and have inspired communications that have proved to be misleading. The upshot is, with the best intentions, they have cast no credit on the Canadian Pacific Railway."

The American press was equally scathing. The New York *Herald* referred to the mission as "abortive" and predicted that Macdonald would fail "in spite of all his financial juggling and the apocryphal rumours he has set afloat to influence public opinion." The hard truth was that the railway would be "constructed through a wilderness, with long stretches of absolute barrenness and in a climate of such severity that the road would be closed for four months of the year.... For fifty years to come it would be a sheer waste of capital to build the Canadian Pacific Railway, and the investing classes understand this so well that Sir John Macdonald's hypothetical syndicate could have no success in selling its shares."

The New York *Commercial Bulletin* reported that Macdonald had got himself "out of one very embarrassing scrape, but in a way which threatens to put him and the Dominion in a worse position than ever. Such an exhaustive accumulation of debt is something more than four million of population can be expected to stand."

Yet in spite of all this hostility there was enormous excitement when it was learned that Macdonald would be arriving at Hochelaga station, Montreal, on the afternoon of September 27. Early that morning a rumour sped around the city that the Prime Minister had passed through secretly the previous night, having failed in his mission and "anxious to reach without delay the obscurity the capital affords." Then it was learned that Macdonald had spent the previous evening in Quebec City. Would he stop in Montreal? The excitement grew. Early in the afternoon both telegraph companies posted notices that the ministerial train would arrive in Montreal at 4.40 p.m. With that the sense of expectation became acute. The *Daily Witness* reported that "rarely have political and financial circles been so agitated over any public event" and the *Mail*'s correspondent wrote that never in a long experience had he "witnessed such intense anxiety to see a public man and hear what he has to say upon a great question of public interest."

By late afternoon people of all classes were streaming towards the station. Almost every prominent Montrealer was present, no matter what his politics. A reception committee of some fifty leading Tories was waiting on the platform; packed behind it, pushing, craning and buzzing with anticipation, was an immense throng. Suddenly from a distance came the sharp reports of fog signals being fired as a salute along the right of way and then the train itself appeared, dead on time.

Macdonald's special car was shunted to a siding and a few moments later the Prime Minister appeared, his face wreathed in smiles. Almost everybody who knew him remarked on how healthy he appeared – "ten years younger" was the common remark. The English trip had done him good. More important, success was written on his features.

Macdonald, full of "animal spirits" in the *Mail*'s phrase, was, in his usual fashion, greeting friends and enemies alike with gibes and sallies. He caught sight of Amor de Cosmos in the throng – perhaps his most vitriolic opponent from British Columbia – and he remarked that the first news he had read in the papers when he touched at Rimouski was that British Columbia had obtained another representative in the form of a great sea serpent. Macdonald remarked jovially that he thought it would now be hard to match the Pacific province.

The Club Cartier, an organization of young Conservatives, had the inevitable address of welcome to present and the crowd waited as patiently as it could until this formality was over. Then every neck strained forward as the Prime Minister prepared to speak. It was a brief, somewhat vague statement but it was what everyone wanted to hear. The Government, Macdonald indicated, had secured financing for the great railway. He could not spell out the details, for these must first be presented to the Governor General.

As was often the case he appeared to say more than he really did

348

and much of what he did say was deceptive. From his short speech in Montreal and the interviews with friendly reporters that accompanied it, no one could have divined that the railway was to be built by a predominantly Canadian group. Macdonald made a good deal of the German element in the Syndicate, which was, in point of fact, very small. But it was considered politically important to get token money from Germany, which would, as Macdonald told the crowd at the station, divert the tide of immigration to Canada. He mentioned no financial houses or individual capitalists but in an interview with the friendly *Mail* talked about "a Syndicate composed of eminent capitalists from Frankfurt, Paris, London, New York and Canada thus forming a combination of interests in order to further emigration from all those countries." Since McIntyre had returned home on the same boat, his connection with the new syndicate was generally accepted. The United States element was played down to a point where the Conservative Winnipeg *Times* even denied its existence. But the Prime Minister was able to reassure the cheering crowd on several points: the new syndicate would finish the line in ten years, it would not build the easy portions first or save the hard ones for the last, and, finally, the road would not cost as much as Sir Hugh Allan had offered to build it for in 1872. Moreover, it would not cost the older provinces of Canada one cent: the sale of western land would pay for it all.

Before he finished Macdonald could not resist a political gibe at his opponents. (The *Globe*'s James Harper, the only shorthand reporter present, squeezed between a mass of jocular Tories, was taking it all down verbatim.) The time would come, Macdonald said, when Canada's teeming millions would remember that it was the Conservative Party that had given the country its great railway.

"I shall not be present," said the Prime Minister. "I am an old man, but I shall perchance look down from the realms above upon a multitude of younger men – a prosperous, populous and thriving generation – a nation of Canadians who will see the completion of the road."

This sobering reminder of the Prime Minister's mortality produced a curious lull in the jollity. It was not easy to contemplate a Canada without Macdonald. Loved or hated, despised or revered, he had become a kind of permanent fixture with his silver-knobbed cane, his fur-collared coat and his familiar Red River sash.

Almost as soon as the ministerial train puffed out of the station towards the capital the great debate over the Syndicate, as it was now called, began. By October, the composition of the new group had leaked out even though the actual contract was not signed and the specific details had still to be worked out. The members were George Stephen and Duncan McIntyre of Montreal; John S. Kennedy of New York; James J. Hill and Richard B. Angus of St. Paul; Sir John Rose's old firm of Morton, Rose and Company, London; and the German-French financial syndicate of Kohn, Reinach and Company. Norman Kittson, who had an interest, was not named at the time: too many men with St. Paul addresses would have caused a storm in the Opposition press. There was, as well, another name far more conspicuous by its absence – that of Donald A. Smith. Smith, of course, was to be a major shareholder in the CPR; but since his name was an obscenity to Macdonald and the entire Conservative Party there was no way in which he could be publicly connected with the Syndicate.

It had been a bad year all round for Smith, politically; indeed, it marked his withdrawal from the political scene. Following his successful re-election to the constituency of Selkirk in 1878, a petition was filed in court charging that his seat had been secured through bribery and corruption. Behind this move was seen the fine hand of the Prime Minister himself, for Macdonald was still smarting from the parliamentary skirmish of the previous spring. The matter did not come to trial until after the House recessed in 1879 at which time Smith was confirmed in his seat. But a local journalist discovered that the judge who gave the decision had borrowed four thousand dollars from Smith and that a mortgage was registered on the jurist's property in Smith's name as security for the loan. The case was appealed to the Supreme Court, which thought a clear case of corruption had been made – not against Smith personally, but enough to void the election. Smith ran in a by-election in September, 1880, spending, as he later admitted, thirty thousand dollars. His connection with the St. Paul and Manitoba railway told against him and he was defeated.

"Donald A., the —— voters have taken your money and voted against you," the secretary of his campaign committee is said to have complained.

"You have properly expressed the situation," Smith replied quietly.

The result was scarcely known, to the immense jubilation of the Tory press ("SELKIRK REDEEMED" trumpeted the *Mail*), when Smith suffered a second blow to his ego: the knowledge, imparted to him by

Stephen, that he could not be publicly associated with the greatest of all national enterprises. The Syndicate would take his money but it did not want to be saddled with his name. Nonetheless, his presence as a silent partner was assumed by both press and public and a great to-do resulted.

The usually imperturbable Smith briefly dropped his mask and gave Stephen a rare, private glimpse of his very human ambitions. "You will have heard of the trouble that Smith has given me . . . because I did not put his name into the contract," Stephen wrote to Macdonald. "I had to tell him that I omitted it to avoid discussion in the House but rather than he should be unhappy I would let him out of the business. He is excited almost to a craze and so troublesome that I do not care if he does withdraw though his money and co-operation would be useful, so would his knowledge and influence in the North West."

Smith did not want to withdraw his money but he did want recognition, and so the fuss continued. A week later Stephen told Sir John Rose that he had had "a terrible bother with D. Smith because his name is not printed in the papers to submit to the House." Actually both Stephen and Angus thought they were doing Smith a good turn by keeping it out; public mention could only bring down further calumny upon that shaggy head, but "he has been like a baby over this thing," Stephen reported. Late in January, Smith was still at it – "so sensitive as to his position in the company and . . . so sore at me and Angus for omitting his name in the Contract."

Stephen was equally exasperated with the French-German element in the Syndicate which Macdonald had insisted upon for entirely political reasons. "It gives us prestige in the province of Quebec and frees the Company – (in public opinion) – from the tyranny of the English stock exchange," the Prime Minister had explained. Kohn, Reinach and Company was a French-German group which included the French Société Générale. The Europeans were in the Syndicate for two reasons only: first, they expected to make a quick profit, and, second, they hoped to get further business from the Canadian government, as did the English house of Morton, Rose and Company. Without the inducement of further business it is doubtful if either firm would have entered the venture. Even at that, the French at the last moment threatened to back out unless they could get assurance either of a speedy profit or of Stephen's pledge to buy up their shares if the operation proved unprofitable. "If we had our Charter I would be inclined to make short work of the Frenchmen," the impatient Stephen wrote to Macdonald. "Meanwhile I suppose we must not break with them until we're through Parliament."

In the end, Stephen told the nervous French that he would build the railroad himself, with or without their help, and "this confidence . . . did them good." Macdonald sent a hurried letter to Rose in England, pointing out the political importance of the French-German involvement and Rose wrote at once to Stephen: "I quite see that they will be troublesome and minute, but I don't think to an extent that patience and good temper won't enable you to deal with." After the contract was signed, Stephen himself went to Paris to stiffen the Frenchmen's resolve.

It was Stephen's first venture into the periphery of politics and the inability to deal directly, swiftly and conclusively with matters he considered to be purely business had already begun to torment him. The wretched contract seemed to be taking weeks to complete and after it was signed Parliament would have to consider it before any company could be formed and the actual work of building the railway could be begun. He began to fire off letters to Macdonald urging speed: not a day must be lost in the preparation of the contract and in the Act of Incorporation. "Unless we have *cars* running over a long piece of the road west of Winnipeg by this time next year, both the Government and the Contractor will be put to discredit with the public." There must be parliamentary sanction "at the earliest possible day"; the European signatories must rush to Ottawa and thence to Montreal to iron out all the differences as swiftly as possible. Stephen was almost breathless with impatience.

Nothing, of course, moved as swiftly as he hoped. He had expected to embark for London at the end of October to meet Tupper. He had to postpone his sailing date.

Among other things, the status of the Pembina Branch had to be ironed out. John Henry Pope talked to him about giving the government a share of its net earnings for fifteen years; Stephen wanted none of that. He wanted the line, complete, for the CPR and he wanted a monopoly. If the CPR's main line was tapped at Winnipeg by other, rival lines running to the boundary, "no sane man would give one dollar for the whole line east of Winnipeg." This was the original bargain that the Syndicate had made with the Government. Like everyone else, Stephen was reluctant to build a foot of railroad north of Lake Superior. When Macdonald insisted, he agreed – but

352

on one condition: he must have a monopoly of all rails running from the Red River to the United States border. On this he was adamant and in mid-October he made it clear that he was prepared to cancel the entire contract if there was any change in this arrangement. The Pembina Branch would have to subsidize the lonely line that ran through the Precambrian desertland. Macdonald was reluctant: he saw the political disadvantages of granting a western rail monopoly to an eastern company. And yet he was caught between two unyielding points of view. He must have an all-Canadian railway; to get it he would have to concede to the importunate Stephen who again and again in his letters was hammering home the point. Stephen feared "strangulation in the hands of our Chicago rivals hanging over our heads." The danger "is *real* and *imminent*." If any other railway except the CPR made connection with Winnipeg the money spent east of that city "might as well have been thrown into the Lake."

Stephen had never talked so toughly before and only Macdonald knew, perhaps, how hard a bargain he was driving. For this was the basis of the "Monopoly Clause" in the CPR contract, which would turn the West against the railway and against the East and lay the basis for almost a decade of bitterness before it was voluntarily revoked. The impotence of the Manitobans in the matter of building their own railway lines became, in that province, a *cause célèbre* which was to lead to a long-term disaffection towards Ottawa and towards the railway itself. Macdonald could see that clause returning to haunt him – returning to haunt the nation. But there was nothing he could do.

3

The contract was finally signed on October 21 and the battle lines were drawn for the greatest parliamentary struggle since the Pacific Scandal. The comments in the Opposition press, before and after the contract was tabled in the House in December, give some evidence of the virulence of the attack. The Ottawa *Free Press* referred to the whole thing as "a stupendous outrage." The paper declared that "nothing that ever entered the human mind can equal it . . . the terms are more like what would be imposed by a military conqueror after the country had been prostrated by an unsuccessful war." The Montreal *Daily Witness* cried that "one stands aghast before this Pacific

The Contract

Railway contract, so monstrous are its provisions and so monstrous its omissions. We take days to gather breath to discuss it and then we quail before the uselessness of the task." The Manitoba *Free Press* called it "a ruinous contract" and the *Globe*, as may be imagined, was apoplectic.

The trouble with the *Globe*'s apoplexy was its very inevitability. The *Bystander*, no friend of the railway, was finally driven to attack the *Globe* for its intemperance: "It would surely be difficult for a political party to be worse served than the Canadian Opposition has been served on the present occasion by its reputed organ . . . [which] represented them as mad with factious malevolence, passionately desiring the failure of the operation, agonized by any favourable intelligence, hailing any adverse report, no matter how frivolous, as a crumb of comfort." It was true. The *Globe* had assumed a variety of positions during the previous three months, alternately laughing at Macdonald for bungling the financing of the railway and attacking him when he was successful. "The gain of the Opposition," said the *Bystander*, "has thus been ruined, and the leaders will go to Ottawa without a shred of moral authority left."

The contract was the most important Canadian document since the British North America Act and one of the most important of all time, for it was the instrument by which the nation broke out of the prison of the St. Lawrence lowlands. It represented a continuation of the traditional partnership between the private and the public sectors, which always had been and would continue to be a fact of Canadian life whenever transportation and communication were involved. The geography of the nation dictated that the government be in the transportation business – either fully, as in the case of the canals and the Intercolonial, or in a kind of working partnership with private industry, as in the case of the Grand Trunk and the Canadian Pacific Railway. In these matters the Canadian government was to be involved far more deeply than its counterpart south of the border and this mutual participation was to broaden and deepen as the nation developed. The express and telegraph systems, the future transcontinental railways, the airlines and the pipelines, the broadcasting networks and communications satellites – all the devices by which the nation is stitched together are examples of this loose association between the political and business worlds. Like the original CPR they are not the products of any real social or political philosophy but simply pragmatic solutions to Canadian problems.

Apart from the all-important subsidies of twenty-five million dollars and twenty-five million acres of land, the chief provisions of the CPR contract were these:

The government would turn over to the Company all the lines built with public money – the Onderdonk section in British Columbia, the Pembina Branch and the Thunder Bay–Red River line – upon completion.

The government would waive duty on the import of all railway materials, from steel rails to telegraph cable.

The free land would be taken in alternate sections of 640 acres each from a strip forty-eight miles wide running along the route between Winnipeg and Jasper House. The Company could reject land "not fairly fit for settlement." It could issue up to twenty-five million dollars worth of land-grant bonds, secured against this acreage. It must deposit one-fifth of the bonds with the government as security, but it could if it wished sell the rest of the bonds, as the land was earned by construction, in the proportion of one dollar per acre.

The land would be free from taxation for a twenty-year period or until sold. Stations, grounds, workshops, buildings, yards, etc., would be free from taxation forever and the land for these would also be provided free.

For twenty years no other line could be constructed south of the CPR to run within fifteen miles of the United States border.

The Company, in return, promised to complete the road within ten years and forever after to operate it "efficiently." That adverb was significant since it relieved the CPR of future responsibilities for unprofitable aspects of its operations – passenger service, for example.

The contract was drawn up by J. J. C. Abbott, Sir Hugh Allan's one-time solicitor and now solicitor to the new syndicate and eventually to the new company. It was a document free of loopholes, "one which has since borne the test of judicial scrutiny," in the words of a later CPR president.

The Ottawa *Free Press* figured out that, in one way or another, the Syndicate was being handed a gift amounting to a cash equivalent of $261,500,000. Stephen's private estimate was considerably lower but he neglected to count such items as freedom from taxation, duty-free imports and free land for company property. He figured the value of the 710 miles of completed government line at thirty-two millions and the cost of the work to be completed by the Company at forty-five millions. The Syndicate had thirty millions in hand, including the cash subsidy, and could raise fifteen millions from its own resources. But this was a wildly optimistic piece of reckoning, as future events were to prove.

The press attacked on several fronts. Even such loyal western papers as the Winnipeg *Times* found it hard to stomach the monopoly clause, especially in the light of the experience with the Kittson Line's exorbitant rates. The eastern Opposition press hit hard at the monopoly clause and also the proposition regarding duty-free construction materials; after all, Macdonald's victory had been secured by the promise of increased protection. The great debate on the contract was not without its ironies: one was the spectacle of traditionally free-trade newspapers and politicians bitterly attacking the entry of construction materials free of tariff.

Nor did the press believe the Syndicate would actually commence building the Lake Superior section at once, as the contract stipulated. "Who is going to hold them to the bargain?" asked the *Witness*, pointing out that it would be cheaper to sacrifice the security held by the government, which was, after all, only one million dollars. (As it turned out, the prairie section was begun well ahead of the Lake Superior stretch.)

But more than anything else, the press harped upon the American influence in "the St. Paul Syndicate," as its opponents called it. The *Globe* cried that "all the outlets from the Canadian North West . . . will be handed over to the grasp of the St. Paul and Manitoba Railway." The Ottawa *Free Press* reported that not only the St. Paul interests "but also the railway kings of Chicago and New York" were behind the scenes. The headquarters of the Syndicate, the paper insisted, would be only nominally in Montreal; the real nerve centre would be in St. Paul. Much was made of a dispatch in the St. Paul *Globe*, which declared that "the position of the company's roads is such that it cannot acquire interests or form alliances adverse to St. Paul." Attacks were launched on the American influence in the shape of Jim Hill and Norman Kittson. Even Angus, a Montreal Scot, was labelled an American, since his address was given as St. Paul.

The anomalous presence of Donald A. Smith – a Liberal in what everyone assumed was a Conservative hive – created confusion and embarrassment. The fiction of keeping his name off the list of Syndicate members fooled no one; it was quite obvious that he was deeply involved. To the Conservative newspapers Smith had been a villain of the deepest dye; how could they praise any enterprise with which he was connected? The Liberal newspapers, on the other hand, had been praising Smith; how could they now attack what some were calling "the Donald A. Smith Syndicate"? The Montreal *Gazette* found itself in an invidious position. On November 3, it attacked Smith and his connection with the Pembina Branch. On November 16, it congratulated the Government on its choice of men to build the CPR and praised them for their experience in building the same Manitoba line which it had just attacked. As the Manitoba *Free Press* commented, "that is eating humble pie with a vengeance!" Some papers – the *Gazette* was one – simply continued to pretend that Smith was not involved, but this did not wash.

"The *personnel* of the Syndicate is not acceptable to our people," a Winnipeg supporter confided to Macdonald. "Mr. J. J. Hill is one of the old Kittson Co. whose crushing rates were felt so severely here for many years and it is supposed that he represents in the Syndicate Mr. D. A. Smith who is also regarded with suspicion and dislike."

Stephen did his best to defend his colleagues: "Kittson is one of the best old gentlemen you ever knew, honourable to a degree; he takes no *personal* interest in these matters being content to do just as the rest of us tell him. Hill is a very able fellow, without whom we could not easily do the work. He has scrambled from a very humble beginning to a very high position, and of course, those he has passed on the road do not like him. The real control and govt. of the enterprise will be in the hands of Angus, Kennedy, McIntyre and myself . . . so you see there is no danger of the control getting into the hands of our St. Paul friends." That was not strictly true. It was inconceivable that Jim Hill could be connected with such an enterprise without taking an active role.

In spite of Stephen's reassurances, the editorials hit home to Macdonald. Two years before he had publicly called Smith the greatest liar in the world. Now he had handed the former fur trader's closest friends – and Smith, too, by all accounts – an enormous slice of Canada. Two years before he had gone to the country with a policy of protecting local manufacturers. Now he had given the Syndicate a unique opportunity to buy on the open market; in Montreal, a delegation of iron manufacturers, appalled at this threat to home industry, were already preparing an onslaught on the capital. Almost ten years ago he had boasted that he had resisted with every atom of his being the attempts by Americans to buy into the Allan railway syndicate. Now he appeared to be welcoming even more Americans with open arms. As Peter Mitchell told a group of friends, the whole affair was very badly mixed: the Tories liked the terms but hated the men, whereas the Liberals hated the terms and liked the men.

It did not go unremarked that much of the Government press was suspiciously silent on the subject of the contract and that those comments which were made tended to be grudging. The Ottawa *Citizen* said it would be glad to see some of the details amended or at least more clearly defined. "It is not perfect," the *Mail* admitted, "but . . . is it not by far the best scheme yet proposed?" The Montreal *Herald*, a Liberal paper, was in a difficult position because, it was said, Smith and Stephen owned stock in it. Certainly it switched its point of view and went on the attack, upon which its editor tendered his resignation.

These misgivings, implicit in the attitude of the ministerial press, only reflected the doubts and, in some cases, the shock of Macdonald's own followers. Some said the contract would be the ruin of the country; the obligations were so great the credit of Canada would be destroyed, making it impossible to borrow for other purposes. That was the theme on which many back-benchers harped: where was the money to come from? Others saw in the contract the ruin of the party; the undertaking was so clearly onerous that the country would be alarmed and turn against the Tories. There were other murmurings. It was an American syndicate whose members were either Yankees or annexationists. It was a Montreal syndicate without a single name from Toronto or Ontario; the Ontario members who had tried so hard to seize the transportation initiative from Montreal were incensed about that. The Manitoba members were angry about the monopoly clause. The Victoria members were disturbed because there was no mention of the island railway. As the session opened the Ottawa *Free Press*, reporting this dissension, declared that "sufficient has transpired to show that Sir John Macdonald cannot carry the Pacific Railway Bill. . . ."

Already some papers, remembering the days of '73 and seeing another political crisis in the making, were coining slogans like "the Pacific Swindle" and "the Pacific Disgrace." And the rumours were beginning to fly: Charles Tupper had joined the Syndicate (scandal!); the Governor General had urged that there be a dissolution of Parliament so that the matter could be decided by the people (crisis!);

John A. Macdonald had privately announced his intention of retiring (sensation!).

Macdonald had no intention of retiring, any more than Tupper had of joining the Syndicate or the Governor General of dissolving Parliament; the press treated the flimsiest gossip as news. It was an indication that the great Canadian debate, which had been going on since 1871, was about to reach its immediate climax. Was the country prepared to stand behind this first great national undertaking? How much did the nation care whether it was united by these costly bands of steel? Was the price too high? Was the bargain a fair one? Could the country afford it anyway? Was it just another piece of railway jobbery (as the Grits suspected) or a great nation-building device (as the Tories proclaimed)? Could the opponents of the great railway prolong the debate long enough to rally public opinion, as they had in 1873, and force the Government to climb down? Would Macdonald's own supporters stand behind him or would they again fall away like dying leaves? The battle lines were drawn. As the opening session approached, Macdonald, though ill once more, was reasonably confident of victory. But, unlike the impetuous and optimistic Stephen, he knew the fight would be long and consuming.

4

Ottawa, Thursday, December 9, 1880. The weather is bitterly cold: The *two below zero at 8 a.m. with the skies heavy, dreary and grey. Port-* Great Debate *land and Phaeton sleighs are skimming along the hard-packed roads,* begins *their occupants swathed in heavy robes of bear, wolf and buffalo. The streets are crowded despite the cold. The town is alive with visitors, muffled in furs, steam pouring from frosted nostrils. Newspapermen and Senators are flooding into town. Back-benchers are hand-shaking their way through the hotels. The Russell House is preparing to accommodate one hundred and fifty dinner guests at a single sitting, all crowded together at long tables under great chandeliers and all discussing the topic of the day: the contract with the Syndicate.*

Ottawa has grown since Lord Dufferin first saw it in 1872. Then it was "a very desolate place, consisting of a jumble of brand new houses and shops . . . and a wilderness of wooden shanties spread along either side of long, broad strips of mud." Now the Russell

House is adding a new wing to keep up with its enterprising opponents, the Windsor and the Union House. The former has installed fire grates in many of the rooms and the entire structure is lighted by gas; only the early calling of the session has prevented the building from being equipped with steam pipes. The Union House is now five storeys high and it has an elevator which works by hydraulic power, as well as hot and cold running water throughout. Patent "enunciators" connect every room with the main office, making the Union House so grand that it will henceforth be known as the Grand Union. "It is safe to say," declares the Free Press, *"that Ottawa can now give as good hotel accommodation as any place on the continent."*

For lesser M.P.s *there are rooms advertised with open grates on Albert Street opposite the Opera House, where Nicholas Flood Davin is about to lecture in aid of the St. Patrick's Orphan Asylum under the distinguished patronage of John A. Macdonald. Davin is one of tens of thousands whose lives and careers will be totally changed by the construction of the railway. Far out on the darkling plains lies a pile of bleached buffalo bones, the site of a future city named Regina whose voice he is to become.*

It is the Christmas season. Yuletide fancies are on sale: papier mâché brackets, glove boxes, card plates and solitaire boards. On Sparks Street, Stitt and Company announce "novelties for the opening" – kid gloves in pale, opera shades and lace jersey collars. "The Speech from the Throne is speechless about our beautiful Countess Coal Stoves," trumpets one enterprising emporium.

The newspapers, as usual, are crammed with odd and revealing trivia: Princess Louise, whose boredom with the capital is a matter of public speculation, has whiled away the hours writing something called "The Doctor's Galop." Police are arresting all drivers who have no bells on their sleighs. "Reprehensible" people are throwing refuse into the streets and getting an editorial slapping for it. A local youth has just accomplished the astonishing feat of drinking thirteen glasses of whiskey in as many minutes.

But the big story is the opening of Parliament and the coming debate, which all now realize is the most important in the history of the young Dominion.

Macdonald had called the session two months in advance in order to dispose of the contract before the construction season began. That may have been why the opening seemed a little short of the usual pomp. Not so many ladies attended in full dress and only Sir Alexander Campbell, the leader of the Senate, appeared in a Windsor uniform. A special gallery, set aside for ladies in "half-evening dress," was crowded. Lady Macdonald was not among them nor, to everyone's chagrin, was the Princess Louise, daughter of the Queen and wife to the new governor general. Lord Lorne, a short, handsome man of thirty-five with a cowlick and a wisp of a moustache, arrived slightly early to the usual salute of guns, but Macdonald was not there to greet him; on doctor's orders he remained in the Commons, husbanding his strength for the ordeal to come.

In the Speech from the Throne, His Excellency explained the "extra session," as some were calling it: "No action can be taken by the contractors to prosecute the work, and no permanent arrangement for the organization of a systematic emigration from Europe to the North West Territories, can be satisfactorily made until the policy in Parliament with respect to the Railway has been decided."

As he spoke, a lady in the gallery leaned forward and a red bow dropped from her hair. A young man, described as a "beau," rushed forward and pressed it close to his heart.

The pageantry was ended; it was time for the politics to begin. Macdonald was ill and so was Mackenzie, the latter an unhappy ghost in the bulky shadow of Edward Blake, who had, in effect, overthrown him as Liberal leader. Blake was full of fight; he was outraged by the contract, which he considered a national scandal, and he meant to oust the Government on the strength of it, as he had seven years before. Across from him sat the bulldog figure of Tupper, eager for the contest.

Blake's strategy was to be delay. He was totally convinced that he held in his hands a political issue as explosive as the Pacific Scandal. What he lacked in parliamentary power he felt he could make up in rising public wrath over such a massive giveaway to private capitalists. The ghost of the Scandal, which had frozen attitudes for all of that decade, still hovered over the House. The Opposition press would hit as hard as it could, opening the old sores of 1873, whipping up anti-American sentiment and linking it to the present syndicate, hinting at bribery, corruption and shameless political handouts. The Opposition tactic was to talk forever, to speak at every stage of the debate, to propose amendments at all points, to divide the House at every opportunity and to portray themselves as the saviours of the country. They would paper the nation with tracts, engulf it with oratory, arouse it with mass meetings and expose Macdonald's attempt to ride rough-shod over Parliament with his steam-roller majority. Blake believed that history would repeat itself, that he could force an election and carry the issue of the contract to the country. If that happened he had no doubt that he would win.

He had some powerful speakers on his team. The aristocratic Cartwright (back in Parliament after a by-election), vigorous and trenchant, was an orator of the first rank, fairly itching to tear into his old foe, Charles Tupper. A physical giant with muscles of iron and nerves of steel, his invective was unequalled. In political warfare, said Sir John Willison, "he knew only the law of the jungle" and in the debate that followed he was to prove it. Timothy Warren Anglin, the Speaker of the House during Mackenzie's regime, had made himself the tribune of the Irish-Catholics in New Brunswick through his newspaper the *Morning Freeman*. He had small, pinched eyes, a worried face, sensuous lips and tiny spectacles but he was the most eloquent Irishman in the Commons; he would pass on that histrionic ability to his four-year-old daughter, Margaret, whom Sarah Bernhardt was to call "one of the few dramatic geniuses of the day." And then there was the 49-year-old former Minister of the Interior, David Mills, "the philosopher of Bothwell" as Macdonald called him, half in jest, half in admiration, for he was the best-read man in Parliament and so expert on constitutional law that even the Prime Minister deferred to him.

They were a sober-looking group, these parliamentarians of 1880, in their dark suits and waistcoats. They wore broad ties, bows or four-in-hands, with vast knots – so large they often entirely hid the shirt beneath. The predominant colour was black or grey, though here and there a checked trouser or spotted vest broke the pattern. Their coats were long, often with velvet collars, and in the fashion of the era they carried cane and gloves when stepping out.

They sought individuality not in colour but in whisker styles. In the Commons of 1880, every conceivable fashion was to be found and it seemed to bear little relation to age. Macdonald, who was sixty-five, and Laurier, who was thirty-nine, were totally clean shaven with manes of curly hair that almost touched their collars. The young and dapper James Domville wore a thin, jet-black anchor beard and matching moustache, while the elderly Langevin sported, beneath his underlip, an infinitesimal *mouche*. Pope and Blake each wore chin curtains, the latter's so tenuous that it could hardly be seen in photographs. Tilley wore long sideburns to the jaw line. Tupper sported handsome greying mutton chops. Mackenzie had a thin goatee. Anglin wore weeping sideburns that looked like squirrels' tails. Cartwright and Edgar Dewdney both sported astonishing Dundrearies, named for the titled and popular character in Tom Taylor's *Our American Cousin*, the play Lincoln was watching at the time of his assassination.

The beard styles were endless, ranging from Phillippe Baby Casgrain's dashing Imperial to the immense pioneer beard of Alfred Boultbee of York East. There were spade beards, forked beards, Vandykes, goatees, ducktails, Hulihees and chin puffs. The moustache, however, was growing in popularity. David Mills had a handsome black waxed moustache, Josiah Burr Plumb of Niagara a shaggy, greying soup-strainer, Auguste Landry of Montmagny a wispy walrus. The whisker styles were as varied as the men who wore them and so were the devices that were advertised to keep them flourishing – the pomades and beeswaxes, the iron curling tongs, the patent moustache trainers, the special brushes of varying sizes and that magic lotion known as "Ayre's Formula," which was guaranteed to grow whiskers in just five weeks.

The great majority of this parliament of individualists belonged to Macdonald. Could he keep them all in line? The job of maintaining party discipline would not be easy; and, Macdonald knew, the debate would be exhausting. Stephen, who was already convinced that what was good for the CPR was good for the country, naïvely supposed that the business would be disposed of by Christmas, "otherwise a season may be lost." Macdonald knew better. "Surely," Stephen wrote, "the Opposition will not be foolish enough to take a line to damage us in the country, too." But the Liberals' whole strategy was to save the country from Stephen.

The debate, which began in early December and ran until the end of January, was the longest ever held until that time and one of the longest in all the history of the Canadian parliament. During that period, more than one million words were uttered in the House of Commons on the subject of the Canadian Pacific Railway contract – more words by far than there are in both the Old and the New Testaments. Though the proceedings were not immune from the kind of bitter, personal invective that marked the polemics of the period, there was a very real sense of the importance of the occasion. Tupper, when he put the resolution to the House, called it "the most important question that has ever engaged the attention of this Parliament" and speaker after speaker on both sides echoed these words when it came his time to stand up and be counted. They realized, all of them, that once the contract was committed, the small, cramped Canada they knew could never again be the same. Some felt the nation would be beggared and ruined, others that it would blossom forth as a new entity. All understood that a turning point had been reached.

Goldwin Smith, who was opposed to any project which attempted to split the continent in two, understood one aspect of the coming debate. "Seldom has any country been summoned to deliberate upon an enterprise so vast in comparison with its resources, or so vitally connected with its fundamental policy," he wrote in the *Bystander*. "What is truly momentous, and makes this a turning point in our destiny, is the choice which our people are now called upon to make between the continental and the anti-continental system, between the policy of antagonism to our neighbours on the south and that of partnership."

Goldwin Smith was talking in extremes when he used words like "antagonism" but he managed to catch the sense of the issue. To Macdonald, "partnership" meant something perilously close to engulfment; to the Liberals, it was not a danger but an economic asset. The echoes of that argument have yet to be stilled.

Meanwhile, the misgivings among Macdonald's followers had to be met head-on. This became Tupper's task. The party caucused in the railway committee room on Saturday, December 11, in a session that lasted all day. It was the first time the members had been able to examine the actual bill for, until that moment, everything published about the contract had been newspaper rumour. According to George Ross, "the caucus was so shocked and overwhelmed at the enormous concessions made by the Government that not a single member of the party expressed approval." Tupper let them talk, and they talked all day. Then, in a forceful speech, in which he dealt with all their misgivings point by point, he brought them round. His most telling argument was not nationalistic but political: the construction of the railway would give the party such *éclat* throughout the nation that they would be rendered invincible in the next election. "They would all live to see the Canadian Pacific Railway contract become the strongest plank in the Conservative platform." After this coldly pragmatic assessment, they gave him a unanimous vote of confidence.

In Parliament there were two days of minor in-fighting around the Speech from the Throne before Tupper put the resolutions regarding the subsidy and the land grant before the House. On the very first day, Blake came close to asking for a plebiscite on the contract, and though he did not use that word, the Opposition press immediately took up the cry. This Macdonald rejected: "It is contrary to the British constitution to submit any complicated measure for the discussion of the whole people." It was up to the representatives of the people to argue it out, clause by clause; that was what they had been elected for. Mackenzie tried to get the details of all the other offers tabled but Macdonald rejected that, too; it would scarcely be fair, in a business sense, to state that "these persons failed in being strong enough to undertake the work." All Macdonald would say was that the present offer was the most favourable one the Government had received. In this, he was correct; in point of fact, it was the only one.

Blake tried another gambit. When Tupper moved that the House go into Committee of the Whole to consider the contract on Tuesday, December 14, he tried to get the matter postponed until January 5. The Government majority, of course, beat him down, but it gave him a debating point to take to the public during the Christmas recess: the Government was trying to rush the charter through without giving the country a chance to consider it.

Tupper rose that Tuesday, heavy-jowled and solemn-eyed, and launched into an exhausting speech, one of the best of his career. Like a good general, he anticipated enemy attacks by embarking on a detailed history of the entire transaction, pinning down the Liberals by enumerating their own acts and declarations, showing that the policies of both governments had been, in practice, nearly identical and quoting exhaustive figures to prove that under the present contract, the people of Canada were getting a railway for thirty million dollars less than Mackenzie's Railway Act of 1874 had promised (he conveniently forgot the free gift of seven hundred miles of finished government-built line). He dealt with the Syndicate and pointed to the successful launching of the St. Paul railway. He dealt with the duty-free clause and pointed out that the United States government had made similar concessions to its railway builders. He dealt with the tax-free land and called attention to the fact that as soon as it was sold – and the Syndicate was anxious to sell it – the new owners must pay taxes like anybody else. On and on he went, hour after hour, pausing for the dinner period and then taking up the cause again until he had spoken for almost six hours. He wound up passionately:

"If I have no other bequest to make to my children after me, the proudest legacy I would desire to leave was the record that I was able to take an active part in the promotion of this great measure by which, I believe, Canada will receive an impetus that will make it a great and powerful country at no distant date."

The following day was Blake's. His speech was almost as long as Tupper's – indeed, in that great debate any speech of less than two hours' duration would be called short. It seemed much longer. It was a great effort, wrote Goldwin Smith, but "somewhat marred by a tendency which besets lawyers, and Chancery lawyers especially: he laboured all the points of the case, great and small, as he would be bound to do in pleading before an Equity Judge." Though the galleries had been full and the House, too, at the outset, there was a dwindling as Blake droned on and on. Macdonald was not present; his illness kept him out of the House for most of the week. Mackenzie, whose own ailments would soon force him to his bed, seemed half asleep. It was an elaborate speech, designed to show that the contract would "prove disastrous to the future of this country" – but it was a little *too* elaborate. Blake's speeches, as George Ross noted, were always too long. So were Tupper's, but Tupper's had some air in them. Tupper fired off a fact and let his listeners chew on it while he indulged in lively oratory. Blake's speeches "contained more matter than even the House of Commons could assimilate, and to that extent his labours were lost."

Blake got in some telling sallies, especially when he pointed out that one of the men Tupper was praising – Donald A. Smith – had been called a coward by that same Tupper and a liar by Macdonald.

"His name is not there," called out one of the Government members.

"I know you do not see it, but it is there for all that, you know it well," Blake retorted. But generally, most of what he said was indigestible.

In his speech Blake had hinted darkly at corruption. When Cartwright rose, he brought the hint out into the open in the most shameless fashion, twisting Tupper's closing remarks in such a way as to cause a verbal Donnybrook. Of Tupper he said: "If I understand him aright, the fact of his being a permanent party in conducting this

366

negotiation would enable him to leave a substantial legacy to his children."

Tupper, red-faced, jowls quivering, leaped to his feet; he had, he cried, insinuated nothing of the kind. Cartwright proceeded to read from Hansard, which did not carry the adjective "substantial." He smoothly retracted his remark: if it was only a legacy of fame and not a substantial legacy, he was sorry for his mistake and also for the children. The Opposition burst into laughter, whereupon Cartwright could not resist adding that it was sometimes as hard to find out what Ministers meant as it was to ascertain what became of the memorable thirty-two thousand dollars in connection with the former contract. Langevin led the hissing from the Government benches. As soon as Cartwright could be heard over the uproar, he remarked that he did not wonder that Tupper did not like to be reminded of a contract that eight years before had hurled his party from power.

Cartwright's speech was a mass of insinuations. He was a vengeful man, full of bitterness against Macdonald, as his memoirs show, unforgiving because he had once been passed over for Cabinet material in favour of Hincks, and permanently obsessed by the Pacific Scandal. In his speech he insinuated that Tupper had taken a bribe and hinted that as a result of arrangements with the present syndicate, Sir Hugh Allan would be reimbursed. He returned again and again to 1873. "We are not dealing with men whose characters and antecedents in managing Pacific Contracts are unknown to us," he thundered. Tupper, he charged, was "an accomplice after the fact, and very nearly as guilty, in intention, as the man who was himself the criminal."

When Cartwright was finished, Tupper rose to reply and the Members rushed to their seats. The Cumberland War Horse was beside himself. He peppered his retorts with such phrases as "lying," "slander," "most dishonourable" and "base and unmanly insinuations." Before he was finished, Tupper turned to the press gallery and upbraided the editor of the *Globe,* Gordon Brown, the late founder's brother, who was, he cried, "drawing venom from the depths of his own black heart." An argument about who was the more un-parliamentary speaker was broken up only by the adjournment of the House.

Cartwright's speech did not advance his party's cause. The Montreal *Daily Witness,* a Grit paper, found it "objectionable in tone as well as in subject matter." The Commons settled down after that and

367

the speeches were more moderate. One of the mildest and shortest was that of Wilfrid Laurier, who pointed out that "this is not a time for recrimination, it is a time . . . when every man should apply himself to discharging his duties to the best of his lights and conscience." Laurier urged a go-slow policy. He suggested building the line through Sault Ste Marie and the United States, rather than through the Superior country, and declared that "to surrender unconditionally to the Syndicate" would be "a great calamity to the Dominion at large."

By December 21, the Opposition was itching for a Christmas recess. It needed as much time as possible to take the case to the people through public meetings and to appeal, in Laurier's phrase, to the best lights and conscience of Macdonald's supporters through massive petitions from constituents opposed to the deal with the Syndicate. But Macdonald did not intend to give them any more time than necessary. In spite of strong agitation, he intended to keep the recess as short as possible.

On December 23, the unquenchable Cartwright was proposing a new bill before the House. The bill itself was an insinuation against the Syndicate and the Government. Its main clause provided that if any corporation that was granted a charter to construct the Canadian Pacific Railway was found to have contributed funds to any M.P. for campaign expenses, then that corporation would forfeit the charter. It was a pale attempt to revive the spectre of Sir Hugh Allan and the Conservative majority doomed it to failure.

With that, the House adjourned. As Timothy Anglin put it, whatever became of the Pacific goose they were now cooking, the Members would like to eat their Christmas goose at home (Canada was still British enough apparently to ignore the Yankee turkey).

For most of them it would be a busy Christmas season. Macdonald had called them back for January 5, the first Wednesday after the New Year. That left Blake with less than two weeks in which to rouse the nation.

5

The "avenging As the session closed, the Conservatives caucused again. Macdon-
fury" ald's following, rallied a fortnight before by Tupper's eloquence, had

368

grown alarmingly shaky. A new attempt was made to persuade Macdonald to modify the contract terms. The Manitobans were in open revolt over the monopoly clause in the contract. John Norquay, the Premier, had already written Macdonald of "grave apprehensions" in the province, even among the best friends of the Government. Resolutions were read in caucus from the Manitoba Tories and the Manitoba legislature urging that the clause be changed. Macdonald knew how impossible that was. Several other prominent members rose to press for the abandonment of the promised tax exemption on railway materials. Others pooh-poohed the idea of building the railway through the rock of Superior. Forty years later, an old CPR hand, William Pearce, recalled that "fully fifty percent of the . . . followers of Sir John never imagined that the road would be built between Sudbury Junction and Fort William nor that it would ever be built through the mountains." The Quebec contingent offered to vote for the contract, but only if the Dominion government promised to purchase the province-owned white elephant – Q.M.O. & O. Railway along the north shore of the St. Lawrence, presumably at an inflated figure.

The Opposition newspapers had their pipelines into the caucus room. The *Free Press* in Ottawa reported that "the breach in the ranks of the ministerialists had widened considerably. . . . There was a hope the Government would pause and find some way out of the dilemma; now this hope has been taken away there is nothing left for those who cannot conscientiously support the Government but to vote against them." This was a broad hint to the dissidents to follow the example of 1873. The *Daily Witness* reported "a general weakening of Government supporters all along the line before they left for home. They felt they were taking their political lives in their hands but had not the nerve of desperation to enable them to face their constituents with a show of confidence."

Nonetheless, the party leadership stood firm, and Tupper, in a three-hour speech to the dissenters, held them, for the moment, in line.

Meanwhile, the Opposition was in full cry across the country. Blake's five-hour speech in the House was printed as a pamphlet and the Liberals were smothering the nation with it. The Conservatives replied with a similar blizzard of tracts reprinting Tupper's speech. Christmas or not, every Liberal member was under orders to call a series of public meetings, to attack the Syndicate and the contract and to force through a series of resolutions to be forwarded to Ottawa. Coincident with this, petitions were to be circulated on the same theme so that hundreds of thousands of signatures would fall like a storm upon the capital by the time Parliament sat again.

The meetings, which were continued up to and past the reconvening of the House, were lengthy, raucous and often wicked. In London, John Charlton, a big-chested, full-bearded lumber merchant, warned his constituents to watch their representatives in Parliament closely, for it would pay the Syndicate well to spend a million dollars to secure the passage of the measure in the House. In Kingston, Cartwright, laden down with a formidable burden of maps, books and pamphlets, referred to the present arrangement as another Pacific Scandal and suggested that the Syndicate had no intention of building anything save a cheap and profitable prairie section. Up sprang a Tory plant and, before the Liberal chairman could forestall him, moved a resolution supporting the Government, which he proceeded to have carried by a vote of cheers. The chairman, who also happened to be the mayor, refused to accept the tactic and the meeting eventually broke up in confusion.

This had been the Conservative strategy, agreed to at the party caucus: they would initiate no meetings of their own but they would have a man of stature at every Grit gathering to challenge the speaker. The venerable and white-bearded Alfred Boultbee was detailed to appear at the first big meeting in Montreal's St. Lawrence Hall, where Blake and Sir William Howland were both scheduled to speak. Boultbee forced his way in with difficulty and, all the time that the chairman, a grey-haired Liberal senator, was attacking the Syndicate, slowly squeezed his way through the Grit phalanx to the front. As soon as the chairman finished, Boultbee demanded to be heard. The chairman told him that he would have to wait for Blake to speak. Blake spoke for more than three hours while Boultbee, taunted continually by his opponents, held his ground. Immediately Blake finished, Boultbee again demanded to speak. The chairman said that the resolution attacking the Government would first have to be put. Following this, the intrepid Boultbee tried again, only to be informed that there were still more resolutions. Finally, around midnight, Boultbee was grudgingly given the floor but was hissed at and howled down until the meeting broke up in confusion.

The meetings were lengthy, well attended and often full of surprises. In East York, one meeting was convened at two in the afternoon and continued until nine. The Liberal chairman tried to break it up for supper but the farmers insisted on hearing both sides of the question and agreed to forgo their evening meal and continue the discussion. The Liberal orators retired anyway, whereupon the farmers voted another man into the chair, a move that brought the Grits scurrying back, their suppers untasted.

The speaker most in demand was Edward Blake. The Ottawa *Free Press* compared his tour to Gladstone's, previous to his British election victory, and saw him as "a Canadian statesman coming forward on behalf of the people at a great national crisis." Tupper offered to attend Blake's meetings if Blake would grant him half the time for speaking, an offer which the wordy Liberal leader rejected since, he said, he would require an entire evening for his own statement of the case. Blake's meetings opened at 8 p.m. and were rarely finished until long after midnight.

Tupper determined on a change of tactics. He detailed a man to attend every Blake meeting to announce that he, Tupper, would reply to Blake, point by point, the following night and the dramatic spectacle occurred of "the Honourable Member for Duluth," as James Colebrook Patterson, the Member for Essex, called Blake, "flying from city to city, pursued by the Honourable Minister of Railways as though he were an avenging fury."

It made for exciting holiday fare in an era devoid of electronic entertainment and both Blake's and Tupper's meetings were jammed. The climax came at Blake's second Montreal meeting held in the Queen's Hall in early January. By the time Blake and Laurier appeared, hundreds had been turned away. After the Grit leader's speech, the usual resolution was offered demanding that the matter of the contract be decided at the polls. The chairman was about to put the question when two Tories sprang up and proposed an amendment, which stated that – as Tupper was scheduled to follow Blake in the same hall that week – the whole question ought to be held over until both sides had been heard. The chairman tried to put the resolution, the crowd called for the amendment and an "indescribable uproar" followed, with the chairman ruling the resolution carried. Tupper's meeting followed to scenes of similar anarchy. Tupper felt, however, that he had carried the day. Abbott, the lawyer, who was present, told him that he had never before realized the influence of the human tongue. The meeting, Abbott estimated, had opened one-third friendly, one-third neutral and one-third hostile to the Minister. When Tupper finished, he said, one-third was friendlier than ever, one-third was converted and one-third had been silenced.

This series of meetings in Blake's wake convinced Tupper that the Government could stand fast and exert party discipline on its followers. It was slowly becoming apparent that the great wave of public opprobrium, which Blake had so confidently expected, was largely non-existent. Though there were misgivings about certain clauses in the contract, the people manifestly wanted the railway question settled. The feeling had been evident in Montreal earlier that fall when Macdonald arrived with what was almost universally accepted as good news. Canadians had been hearing about the railway now for almost a decade. In 1871 it had been a new and frightening idea. Ten years later they had come to accept it as a probability.

Nor were they put off by the cries of scandal. The shrill press had made them cynical of such red herrings. If there was scandal, the people wanted proof and there was no proof. The Syndicate might be controversial but anyone could see that it was possessed of the kind of boldness that, after a decade of vacillation, could only be refreshing. In vain the *Globe* called for the people to rise up and smother Ottawa with their signatures; the *Globe* had cried wolf too often. A total of 266 petitions arrived at Ottawa, of which 256 came from Ontario. They contained 29,913 signatures, scarcely the avalanche that Blake and his followers had envisioned. Moreover, a suspicious number seemed to be in the same handwriting and one signature, at least, in Sir Richard Cartwright's riding, belonged to a corpse. "Generally speaking," the *Bystander* reported, "the attempts of the Opposition leaders to fire the heart of the people were not very successful. . . . The petitions for which the *Globe*, assuming the leadership of the party, called were almost a fiasco."

But Blake and Cartwright had no intention of giving up. They had almost a month left to fight and one more major card to play.

6

Macdonald   Early in January, as the session began, there was a kind of insistent
versus   buzzing in Liberal circles in Ottawa and Toronto that something big
Blake again   was being planned: the Syndicate, the contract and the Government
were about to be challenged in a dramatic and decisive fashion. In

372

the House, the big guns of the party continued to fire volleys at "these infamous propositions" (Hector Cameron) "fraught with mischief" (David Mills). On Friday, January 7, Macdonald, over Opposition protests, ruled that the contract debate would have precedence over everything save routine proceedings: "I believe that the settlement of the North West will be greatly retarded by delay . . . it ought to be discussed to the exclusion of all other matters until it is finally settled, and the policy of the Government either adopted or rejected by Parliament."

That day the House sat until after midnight but such was the duration of the speeches that only five members were accommodated. They were not very illuminating. Half a continent, said John Charlton, was about to be "handed over to a soulless monopoly and ground down by their exactions." The Government, said C. I. Rinfret from Lotbinière, was about to "bury millions of money in the mountains of British Columbia, in the deserts that border Lake Superior." The members on both sides were starting to repeat themselves.

The Opposition could take heart for by the end of the week the news of the coming surprise was known, at least in part, to the rank and file. George Ross – "that little devil Ross" as Macdonald called him – let out a hint of it on Monday. "How do we know that this is the best bargain?" he asked. "How do we know that we may not have, within a few days, even though no tenders were asked for, better propositions?" By refusing to call for tenders, Ross declared, the Government had violated the general rule of the public works department. At this, several Conservatives, recalling the disastrous system installed by Mackenzie, cried "Hear! Hear!"

Ross retorted, darkly: "Well, they may 'Hear, Hear' in a few days something that will not gratify them very much."

Though the House sat until three-thirty in the morning, there were only four speeches that day. Ross's alone took four and three-quarter hours – "a feat I never attempted again." Years later he admitted in his memoirs that he had spoken at "unpardonable length."

Macdonald had a reasonably clear idea of what his adversaries were planning but he was more concerned with the troubles he faced from his own supporters.

Two days before he had received a letter from John Haggart, Member for South Lanark, regretting that he could not vote for the Government on the Pacific Railway resolutions. "I have tried to view them in as favourable a light as my friends but cannot. As it will be the first vote I ever gave against the party, it causes me considerable uneasiness." (It was a temporary defection and Macdonald, who believed that no politician could afford to hold lifelong grudges, put Haggart into his Cabinet later in the decade.)

From Halifax came word that some of his leading supporters there, prominent businessmen, were expressing grave doubts about the Government's policy as a result of the debate in the House. They felt the party would be crushed under the financial load it was imposing on the country.

The Premier of Quebec, Joseph Adolphe Chapleau, had been in town for a week trying to sell the votes of his federal followers in exchange for a fancy price for the Quebec-owned railway. Macdonald, who could not commit the new company in advance, had to put him off with evasions. As a result Chapleau's paper, *La Minerve*, turned against him on the issue.

The Manitoba members had an interview with both Macdonald and Tupper intimating that they could not support the bill unless it were modified; Macdonald did not yield. He was sixty-seven years old and he was ill with a complaint the doctors eventually diagnosed as "catarrh of the stomach" ("catarrh" was a fashionable medical term in the seventies); the Opposition papers were slyly insinuating that he was drunk again; some of his friends feared that he had cancer. But ill or not, on this issue Macdonald intended to stand firm as a rock. There would be no modification of the contract and no compromise. When the vote came he meant to regard it as a vote of confidence. Let his supporters betray him at their peril! If the bill failed to pass, he intended to resign.

On the night of January 11, when the resolution was finally taken out of committee, the Government whips were busy and at 1.30 a.m. Macdonald's supporters trooped in, filling all the ministerial benches. The Opposition, so the *Mail* reported, was startled by this "sudden display of spontaneous force."

The following day the ailing Mackenzie, absent from his seat for all of that session, made his first speech as the bill was read for the first time. He referred to "public reports that eminent men on both sides of politics are, at this moment, preparing offers to the Government of a much more favourable character than those that are now before it." Mackenzie did not need to get his information from public reports. He knew better than most what was afoot. This was the Opposition's final tactic – to mount a rival syndicate, which would

374

offer the Government a much better proposition divested of all the objectionable clauses in the original contract and at a cheaper price. If the Government refused this offer, the Opposition believed, it would be shown to be in league with the "monstrous monopoly," as Cartwright called it. On the face of it the gambit was irresistible.

Even as Mackenzie spoke, the new syndicate was meeting at the Queen's Hotel in Toronto to draw up a tender to be sent post-haste to Ottawa. The chairman and president was Sir William Howland, a one-time miller and wholesale merchant who had been Lieutenant-Governor of Ontario in 1873, and who had, since that time, been dancing on the periphery of Liberal politics. When he told the press he was not connected with any government, he was technically correct; no government had claimed him since 1867 when the Reform convention in Toronto rejected him. When he added that he was free from party prejudice, he was asking the country to strain its credulity; after all, he had appeared on the same platform with Blake a few weeks before. Howland was a distinguished-looking man, with black, candid eyes and a massive chin fringe, a little Lincolnesque of feature but without the hard resolution to be seen in the Lincoln portraits. He had been on the directorate of Allan Macdonell's abortive transcontinental railway company in the 1850's. His son was a director of Senator David Macpherson's short-lived Interoceanic in 1872. Now he was trying again, in the belief that he was rescuing the country from the jaws of a ruinous monopoly. As chairman of the proposed venture, he was close to being a puppet. "The Telegram, coupling my name with the new Syndicate, was the first intimation I had that anything of the kind was in contemplation," he naïvely told a reporter on January 11.

The Grit newspapers revealed the general terms of the new syndicate's bid: they would ask only twenty-two million acres of land and twenty-two million dollars in cash. There would be no monopoly clause. They would ask no exemptions from the tariff on railway materials. They would ask no exemptions from taxation on either land or railway property. On the matter of the construction of the line, they were equally obliging. They would be willing to postpone the building of both the Lake Superior and the mountain sections and would cheerfully release the government from the liability of building the difficult Fraser River section from Emory's Bar to Port Moody on salt water. They would also be willing to construct a line to Sault Ste Marie to connect with the U.S. railhead in return for a bonus of twelve thousand dollars a mile. "The meeting was strictly a business one," reported the Ottawa *Free Press,* "and there can be no question of the seriousness of the offer made."

Such was the Opposition's ploy – to paint the new syndicate as totally non-partisan and totally businesslike; to convince the country that all objectionable clauses in the contract were unnecessary. First, however, the tender had to reach the government; more delays would be needed.

Macdonald had determined to push the bill through its first reading and accordingly, on January 13, moved that the House waive the motions on the order paper and continue the discussion on the contract. The Liberals, of course, opposed him and the debate on this bit of procedure dragged on until 1.25 the following morning. The Opposition used every technique of filibuster, including lengthy readings from journals of the Ontario assembly of several years previous and, predictably, the terms of the contract with Sir Hugh Allan. In Ottawa, the *Free Press* had already begun the republication of all the infamous Pacific Scandal correspondence and was doing its best to depict Macdonald as a dictator overriding the rules of Parliament in a dangerous and tyrannical fashion "in terror that the new proposal will be in his hands before the resolutions are adopted."

The following day Tupper revealed, on a question from Blake, that the new tender had reached him about an hour before the House sat. He had not had time to consider it. The atmosphere grew more acrimonious. Philippe Baby Casgrain, a scholarly looking Government supporter, began to speak in French. Cartwright pretended to sleep while his colleagues, to Casgrain's discomfiture, engaged in badinage. There followed a vicious encounter between Tupper and Sir Albert J. Smith of New Brunswick, a former minister under Mackenzie. The two portly figures, each with huge grizzled sideburns, heavy jowls and grim eyes, hurled expletives at each other across the floor of the House. Smith had once been an independent. Tupper called him an office seeker, willing to sell out for a cabinet post. Smith called Tupper a slanderer: "There is no man in Canada who has done so much to degrade public life." Tupper charged that a petition had been filed against Smith for "scandalous and wholesale bribery." Smith retorted that no man in Canada was as corrupt as Tupper – "he is notorious for his bribery and corruption."

Macdonald was too weak that day to attend but he knew what he must do. The talk about the new syndicate was having its effect.

It had raised the morale of the Opposition and it had caused new murmurings among his own followers in both House and Senate. Until now he had taken only a minor part in the debate, leaving the in-fighting to Tupper. He saw that he must kill the new syndicate – slay it so thoroughly that no man would ever dare to mention it again. He must lay bare its palpable weaknesses, expose the dangers that it posed to the country and then assassinate it with ridicule.

He rose on Monday, January 17, as soon as Tupper laid the new tender before the House. Blake, he knew, would follow the next day, with one of those earnest, perfectly constructed and brilliantly contrived orations for which he was so well known and for which he was preparing himself with his usual meticulous labour. There was a strange feeling of repertory about it all: the same chamber and the same adversaries of 1873, the same charges of scandal, corruption and dictatorship, the same feeling of age and infirmity (though not from drink this time) and the same subject – the railway. In a sense he was back where he had started, fighting on his feet for the contract as he had fought eight years before. But it was not quite the same; this time Macdonald had no apologies to make.

He had to be helped to his feet, but his words carried all the force of a pile driver: the road *would* be constructed. Period. "Notwithstanding all the wiles of the Opposition and the flimsy arrangement which it has concocted, the road is going to be built and proceeded with vigorously, continuously, systematically and successfully" – the adverbs fell like hammer blows – "until completion and the fate of Canada will then, as a Dominion, be sealed. Then will the fate of Canada as one great body be fixed beyond the possibility of honourable gentlemen to unsettle."

Now the time had come for him to scupper that "flimsy arrangement": "We have had tragedy, comedy and farce from the other side. Sir, it commenced with tragedy. The contract was declared oppressive . . . we were giving away whole lands of the North West. . . . The comedy was that when every one of the speeches of these honourable gentlemen were read to them, it was proved that last year, or the year before, and in previous years, they had thought one way, and that now they spoke in another way. . . ."

And finally the farce: "We had the farce laid on the table today. The tragedy and comedy were pretty successful; but the farce, I am afraid, with an impartial audience, in theatrical phrase, will be damned."

He proceeded to damn it.

"I may say it is too thin. It won't catch the blindest. It won't catch the most unsuspicious. No one of common sense, no man who can say two and two make four, will be caught for one moment. . . . It was concocted here. It was concocted in Ottawa. It was concocted as a political engine. . . ."

Seven of the signatories to the document, Macdonald pointed out, were disappointed or defeated Liberal candidates in former elections. "No man, be he ever so simple, who is fit to be elected, can read else on these papers than that it is a political trick. . . ."

He had to pause for a moment. "I am speaking at some disadvantage," he said, "because I am not well. But I will make myself heard."

He gathered his strength and continued, moving closer to the nub of his argument. The tender for the new syndicate was prepared "for the express object of enabling the most timid man – including Sir William P. Howland, who would not risk five thousand dollars unless he were certain of getting it again – it is drawn for the purpose of enabling the most timid man to sign this document, knowing that he was safe. It was – heads I win; tails you lose."

The joker in the pack was the optional clause in the proposed contract which suggested that the new syndicate had no real intention of building anything but the easiest section of the railroad. The first clause, Macdonald showed, did away with the Superior section, the second provided for a rail line to Sault Ste Marie and the United States, the third provided for the government to abandon the British Columbia section and the fourth gave up building anything west of Jasper House. The scheme, then, was nothing more than "an impudent offer to build the prairie section and to do it by means of political friends." Connecting with the Yankee railways at the Sault would be "to the utter ruin of the great policy under which the Dominion of Canada has been created, the utter ruin of our hopes of being a great nation. . . ."

"They would be relieved from running any portion of the road that would not pay. Canada might whistle for these connections. . . . but the people would gradually see that the colonies would gradually be severed from each other; and we should become a bundle of sticks, as we were before, without a binding cord, and then we should fall, helpless, powerless and aimless, into the hands of the neighbouring republic."

378

He fought next for the monopoly clause; and here all his passionate distrust of the American colossus came to the fore. The Rhine, he said, had a miserable, wretched end, "being lost in the sands of the approaches to the sea; and such would be the fate of the Canadian Pacific Railway if we allowed it to be bled by subsidiary lines, feeding foreign wealth and increasing foreign revenue by carrying off our trade until, before we arrived at the terminal points of Ontario and of Montreal, it would be so depleted that it would almost die of inanition."

What chances, Macdonald asked, would an infant country of four million have against the whole of the United States capitalists? The Americans, he reminded the House, had offered to carry freight for nothing and to pay shippers for sending freight their way.

"It would not all come by Sault Ste Marie. It would come to Duluth. It would come to Chicago. It would come through a hundred different channels. It would percolate through the United States, to New York and Boston, and to other ports and, Sir, after our railway was proved to be useless, they might perhaps come into the market and buy up our lines as they have bought up other lines."

He had some facts and figures dealing with United States railway wars: "The road would become shrunken, shrunken, shrunken, until it fell an easy prey to this ring. We cannot afford to run such a risk."

He was almost finished, but he wanted to nail down in the clearest possible language his vision of the railway and his vision of the nation. He wanted, he said, an arrangement "which will satisfy all the loyal, legitimate aspirations, which will give us a great and united, a rich and improving, developing Canada, instead of making us tributary to American bondage, to American tolls, to American freights, to all the little tricks and big tricks that American railways are addicted to for the purpose of destroying our road."

He had spoken for two hours and a half and he had made his point. The *Canadian Illustrated News*, which was less partisan than the daily press, reported that his criticism of the new syndicate "was so searching that he practically killed it, even in the eyes of the Opposition members themselves."

The morrow would be Blake's, but first there was a respite. Parliament adjourned at six so that the Members would attend the Governor General's reception held that evening in the Senate chamber. Sick or not, Macdonald had to be in attendance in Windsor uniform. Friends and foes mingled and murmured pleasantries, the Members dressed in claw-hammer coats and sporting white kid gloves, the ladies in expensive costumes – scarlet satin and feathers for Lady Macdonald, black silk trimmed with lace for Lady Tilley, black velvet with a white lace overdress for Lady Tupper. The air was fragrant with the perfume of half a hundred bouquets and with the music of a spirited military band, which obliged with waltzes, galops, marches and quadrilles. "Mr. Phil Woods, drummer, used his side drum attachment with excellent effect, particularly in the Mazy Waltz. The invention is quite an improvement on the old-fashioned triangle."

The following day the Commons got down to business again. Blake had been waiting for this moment. He had not been at ease during the debate. The Government speakers, knowing his uncommon sensitivity, had baited him continually. When thus attacked, he found himself unable to stare his opponents down but instead would pick up a book and pretend to read. Macdonald had challenged him the previous day, asking him to get on his feet and say that he could approve, on the basis of his past declarations, some of the essential features of the new tender. He could not rise to that challenge but now, on this afternoon of January 18, he was prepared to deliver another five-hour speech, crammed with facts and figures to prove why the contract was a disaster and why, indeed, the whole concept of the Canadian Pacific Railway was, as in his view it had always been, insane.

The arguments, by this time, were familiar; they had not changed greatly since 1871; nevertheless, they were often telling. Blake, for instance, made a hash of Macdonald's figures, which had been changing from year to year, showing the sums which the Government expected to receive from the sales of raw prairie land. Indeed, on almost every point Blake was convincing. The idea of the railway *was* insane, if you thought in terms of an undivided continent; it *was* perfect madness to try to punch it through that sea of mountains and across those rocky Precambrian wastes. Immigration would not come as swiftly as the Government implied, and events were to prove Blake right on that point. The land sales would not pay for the railway. It would be easier and cheaper for everybody to go west by way of the United States, at least in the foreseeable future. Logic, then, was on Blake's side.

The key to Macdonald's argument was emotion: the only way Canada could hold onto British Columbia – and, thus, the land in

380

between – was to build the railway; that was the point he continued to hammer home. British Columbia would not wait, or at least that was what the British Columbians were saying; Walkem himself was in Ottawa in December making secessionist noises. Meanwhile, the reorganized Northern Pacific was creeping west again; with no parallel line on the other side of the border, this great artery would drain off all the commerce of British North America.

Blake's speech was a model of earnest, logical argument. On a previous memorable occasion he had used earnestness accompanied by pitiless fact to bring Macdonald down. In this contest between logic and passion, would logic win again? Blake, the nineteenth-century liberal, was properly suspicious of the "big interests," critical of business speculation, and committed, philosophically at least, to the one-world concept of free trade and all that it connoted. But the climate of the times was not conducive to this kind of idealism, especially in Canada where free trade could mean economic strangulation. Macdonald, the pragmatic politician and hard-nosed Conservative, was in tune with his era – an era which saw the commercial interests working hand in glove with the politicians to develop, exploit or consolidate the nation (one could use all those verbs) for personal profit, political power and (sometimes incidentally) the national interest. Given the political morality of the day and the prevailing public attitude, this traditional Conservative partnership with business was probably the only way in which the nation could be constructed in a hurry. To Blake, with his literal, legal mind, Macdonald was all bombast and humbug. He himself never stooped, in the House or out of it, to the kind of witty sallies, gossipy small talk or passionate declarations that were among the Prime Minister's trademarks. Macdonald, though a cynic, was also an optimist and a gambler. Blake, though an idealist, was a pessimist by temperament as well as by conviction. He could see the pitfalls in Macdonald's program – and they were real enough. He himself understood the value of a dollar: he had vowed to make one hundred thousand dollars so that he would have personal security (and moral security as well) before entering the political lists. The wild extravagance of the railway appalled him. But Macdonald had thrown aside all personal security and bankrupted himself in order to enter and remain in politics.

Blake, the man of ideals, had a strong political philosophy and little imagination. Macdonald, the practical politician, whose only real philosophy was expediency, was endowed with a lively imagination.

That, really, was where Blake foundered in the matter of the railway. He could not see the new Canada as Macdonald could see it; nor would he ever see it. Long after Blake had departed Canada for Ireland, expressing the gloomiest of forebodings about the future, the political analysts continued to discuss the mystery of why he had never quite fulfilled his early promise. But there was really no mystery. Canada in the seventies was an imaginative dream more than a nation. Blake lacked both the imagination and the daring (he thought of it as recklessness) to lead in the development of that dream. If Macdonald's political gamble had failed, if, after all the passionate talk in the House, the railway had foundered, then Blake might have been hailed as a Cassandra and have gone on to become the leader of his country – the very epitome of a sober, sensible, frugal Canadian prime minister. But that was not to be.

7

The dawn of the new Canada The long, exhausting drama was drawing to its close but it was not quite over. In Europe, where he had successfully talked the impatient French into waiting for their profits, Stephen was "literally disgusted" with the conduct of the Opposition. "I did not think it possible for political malignity to go so far as it has done in this discussion . . . a fair and unbiased consideration of the whole situation must result in the conviction that the interests of the country and the Company are identical."

The "political malignity," however, continued. The *Globe* asked: "Can the rumour that Sir Hugh Allan is really a silent partner in the Syndicate be true?" It added that Stephen and his colleagues would not scruple to spend lavishly in order to carry the contract and inquired, rhetorically, whether or not Canadian Tory politicians could stand the test. The Ottawa *Free Press* later reported that a member of the Syndicate (unnamed) had given seventy-five thousand dollars worth of stock to a Government member (unidentified). In the House on January 25, Joseph Rymal, the Grit from South Wentworth with the pinched face and billy-goat's beard, delivered himself of a particularly vicious speech in which he called the Government members traitors and branded one of them, George Turner Orton of Wellington Centre, as a "pocket edition of Judas Iscariot." In the rising uproar, Rymal charged that there had been "two or three million dollars distributed by this Syndicate in order to consummate this swindle." When the Government benches chorused their protest, Rymal cried that their skins were thin and that they themselves were "sharers in the ill-gotten gains."

That night, the word spread about Ottawa that Parliament was to see the end of the longest debate in history. The galleries began to fill up with the wives of Senators and M.P.s as well as members of the general public. Macdonald meant to force a vote through even if he had to keep the House in session all night. The debate droned on while the Members, many of them grey with fatigue yet bolstered by the excitement of the evening, moved out into the corridors and smoking rooms in small buzzing clusters. From one smoking room came the faint strains of several Quebec members singing *La Marseillaise* while an Irish jingle rippled from the parliamentary restaurant. Several card games were in progress throughout the building.

As the night wore on the Members began to drift back to their seats but they were in no mood for speeches. They had been drenched with speeches since December. David Mills, clear-eyed, moustache bristling, was on his feet. He spoke for two hours and for all of that time the chamber resounded with catcalls, desk-hammering, whistling, squeaking, coughing and groaning. Mills continued unperturbed but, when he sat down, no other speaker would face the crowd.

It was time for a division on the first amendment to the resolution, offered by the Opposition leader. The amendment was typical of Blake, being the longest ever offered in Parliament to that moment. It covered three and a half pages of Hansard's small type and raised fifty-three distinct objections to the proposed legislation.

This was the moment of truth. Macdonald had told his wavering supporters in the bluntest terms that if the bill was lost the Government would resign immediately and they would be forced to go to the country with all the opprobrium of a parliamentary defeat hanging over them. The threat was enough: the first amendment was defeated by a vote of 140 to 54. The House adjourned that morning just before six.

It was not yet over. The Opposition had twenty-three more amendments and it proposed to move them all. The galleries were thin the following day; all the old habitués were asleep. The House reconvened at three and sat until eleven that night. Five more amendments were defeated.

The long nights and the gruelling verbal skirmishes were taking their toll. Macdonald, Mackenzie and Pope were all seriously ill. So was the indomitable Tupper, suffering from a complaint later diagnosed as "catarrh of the liver." Amor de Cosmos was ill. Keeler of Northumberland East was ill. Bannerman of South Renfrew was ill. Others, the press reported, were breaking down under the strain. And still Macdonald drove them on. Illness of some sort seemed to be a permanent condition of the political leaders of the day; Macdonald's letters and those of his cabinet colleagues are full of earnest inquiries about each other's health, reports of doctors' advice and descriptions of their own symptoms. Rheumatism, chest pains, bronchitis and catarrh—the all-purpose disease—were high on the list of complaints; and no wonder: the parliamentarians came in from the frigid atmosphere of the Ottawa winter to sit for long hours in the closeness of the House, swathed in sweaty flannel underwear and thick, layered suits of heavy wool. Germs and sanitation were not really understood — surgeons did not even sterilize scalpels let alone themselves — bathing was infrequent and medical knowledge rudimentary. On Government leaders, such as Macdonald, the work load was crushing. Although the business of government was relatively uncomplicated compared to that of a later century, there were few executive short cuts. One could not pick up a telephone to transact a piece of business with dispatch. A rudimentary typewriter had been invented but it was rarely used; Macdonald considered it almost an insult to employ it in a letter of any substance. Though he did have a single secretary, he wrote almost all of his vast personal correspondence himself — thousands and thousands of letters in a lazy, angular hand. The wonder was not that he was ill; the wonder was that he was alive. The secret lay in his ability to relax totally after a harrowing parliamentary session — to push the fevered events of the day out of his mind, for an hour, a day, or, as in the case of the Pacific Scandal, forever. One of his methods was to devour cheap yellowbacks, novels of blood-curdling horror that were the popular mass reading of the day.

Now, ill and exhausted, he was nevertheless determined that, though there be a thousand amendments, the first reading of the bill should be voted on before the next day's sitting ended.

He kept his word. The House sat from three until six, recessed briefly for dinner, and then remained in session for twelve hours without a break while amendment after amendment was offered and voted down. It had become a game, nothing more, and because it had become a game, a kind of gay lunacy settled over the House of Commons. The bitterness drained away and, as each amendment was offered, it was greeted with cheers by both sides. The speeches were mercifully short but even these were interrupted by whistles, chirps and desk-pounding. Paper pellets were flung about and caps placed over the heads of slumbering members. As evening gave way to night and night to morning, a choir was organized and the members began plaintively to sing "Home, Sweet Home." Josiah Burr Plumb, known as the poet laureate of the Tory party, led one group in singing "When John A. Comes Marching Home." Dr. Pierre Fortin, from the Gaspé, led the French members in the traditional voyageur song, *"En Roulant, Ma Boule, Roulant."* The dapper James Domville, from King's, New Brunswick, arrived at 6 a.m. after an all-night dinner party and commenced what the *Globe* referred to delicately as "most unseemly interruptions."

There were other diversions. While one French Canadian was speaking, a dummy telegram was thrust into his hand; he asked the indulgence of the House to pause and read the contents, which were unprintable. Auguste-Charles-Philippe-Robert Landry, a young gentleman farmer from Montmagny, devised an original jape. Landry, who was well known as the most mischievous member in the House, went to a hairdresser about midnight and had his hair and moustache powdered iron grey; then he donned an old pair of green goggles, turned up his coat collar and took his seat at the back of the ministerial benches. The deputy sergeant-at-arms, not recognizing him, tried to throw him out; Landry refused to go. When the votes were being recorded on the latest amendment, the strange figure, gesturing ludicrously, stood up to be counted amid cheers and laughter. The clerk, whose duty it was to name each member as he voted, did not recognize Landry, looked again, puzzled, hesitated and blushed, then looked again and again until at length he pierced the disguise.

Finally, the last amendment was voted down and the main divisions on the two resolutions – the first on the land and the second on the cash subsidy – were carried. In Tupper's absence, Macdonald introduced the bill founded on these resolutions respecting the Canadian Pacific Railway. Not until it was read for the first time did he allow the weary, punch-drunk House to adjourn. By then it was eight in the morning.

The Ottawa social season, held back for some weeks by the dike of the great debate, had already burst out like a flood. "Balls, dinners, routs of all kinds, extravagant dressing and fashionable follies, in which half a dozen ministers are the moving figures, and foolish civil service clerks the puppets, are the order of the night at Ottawa," the Saint John *Globe*'s correspondent reported primly. "The social world is full of unhealthy excitement."

Sir Leonard and Lady Tilley's grand ball in the Geological Museum was "the social event of the season," according to the Ottawa *Free Press*, which devoted four solid columns to a description in which every minuscule detail of décor, dress and deportment was lovingly detailed. The reception room was "simply oriental in its splendour and luxuriousness . . . the refreshment portion of the hall was conducted on entirely total abstinence principles, therefore some 'gentlemen' did not have a chance to 'forget themselves' . . . at either end of the table were oyster tureens of solid ice – great blocks of the frigid crystal with a square hole cut in the top in which were the bivalves in their natural condition."

The paper devoted a full paragraph of description to each of the dresses of 123 ladies, ranging from that of Mrs. Collingwood Schreiber, wife of the new engineer-in-chief ("Black gros grain silk and garnet satin dress; ornaments, pearls") to that of Mrs. St-Onge Chapleau, wife of the contractors' paid informant in the public works department ("Dress en train of gros grain and brocaded white silks combined, trimmed with maroon silk and fringes of flowers and wild grass; ornaments, diamonds and gold").

Such affairs called for a considerable wardrobe, especially for the wives of cabinet ministers, who were invited everywhere. In the course of five days, for example, Lady Tilley attended three major social functions and wore a different formal gown to each one: black silk trimmed with lace for the Governor General's reception, ivory-coloured grosgrain silk with black lace train, garlands of roses and feathered headdress to her own, and a cream-coloured silk *à la princesse* with plush velvet bodice "richly trimmed with lace" to Senator David Macpherson's reception. In each instance, the finance minister's wife also wore a different set of jewellery – diamonds one night, pearls the next, gold ornaments the third.

It must have astonished and perplexed many a visitor from London or Washington to encounter such a glittering assembly within the make-believe palaces of what was, in many respects, still a brawling, backwoods village. From Senator Macpherson's reception in the

Senate chamber, the strains of the overture to *The Bohemian Girl* drifted out across the snowswept Ottawa River where millions of board feet of lumber – the red and white pine of Canada – lay ready for shipment. Every midwinter the city was a battle ground for Irish lumberjacks who drank, fought with bare knuckles, roamed the streets in gangs, smashed entire saloons, toppled buggies and sometimes even blew up houses. Only, perhaps, in Canada could such a town become the federal capital – selected for no other reason than that it neatly straddled the boundary between the two founding cultures.

To one American lady visitor, reporting back to her home town paper, the Cleveland *Herald*, Ottawa, at the time of the great debate, was "a city of frightful contrasts." As for the social pretensions of the citizenry, they were a little much:

"The cordiality of the welcome (if you have *letters*) is most delightful though the satisfied air of self superiority is funny to behold. Society is, in Ottawa, a trifle *shaky*. There are so many grades, and inter-grades, as to bewilder the uninitiated. The Governor-General is placed on the same footing as the President of the United States, with a feeling in the Canadian breast that the President is complimented thereby."

Watching the events in the House she was as puzzled by them as she was by the contrasts within the capital. "Canadian politics are kaleidoscopic. You turn one way, and the French Canadian Conservative with his English ally meet the English Grit in deadly political combat. Again, you turn, and they separate to fight by nationality for their religion, again to divide as Ultramontane and Liberal, until the whole thing becomes a tangle of confused opinions."

And, if the booted lumberjacks were hooligans who gave no quarter when they met in sodden combat, the parliamentarians, engaged in their own verbal Donnybrooks over the future of the nation, were little better: "To the fair-playing average American, it is shocking to hear the way the rampant party in Parliament heaps insult and blatant invective on the minority party. There seems to be not the slightest sense of honor towards the mighty fallen. I doubt if in all the annals of the American Congress such indignities were ever offered to the party out of power even by a Democrat."

Yet the Donnybrooks would have to continue, for the game was not yet played out. There were two more readings to go through before the bill could become law. The first of these was a clause by clause consideration of the full text and this was bound to take time. Even the Governor General's fancy-dress ice carnival on January 31 could not lure Macdonald from his duties in the House. At 12.30 that night, while Lord Lorne and his costumed guests were skating under the glare of two locomotive headlights beneath flag-draped arches, festoons of evergreens and Chinese lanterns – "an overhanging panorama of grotesque and fanciful figures" – the bill passed its second reading.

The following day, February 1, just before midnight, the bill was given its final reading. The formality of Senate assent was still needed but it was now as good as law and the Canadian Pacific Railway Company was a reality.

Finally, it was over. It had been ten years, almost to the month, since the subject of a railway to the Pacific had first been broached to the House of Commons. For all concerned it had been a desperate, frustrating and often humiliating decade; yet it had also been exhilarating. Macdonald was ill with fatigue, stomach trouble and nervous tension – so ill, in fact, that it would take him six months to recover; but he was triumphant. The railway, which had hurled him into the abyss of despond, had now hoisted him to the pinnacle of victory. It had consumed many of the men who were closely allied with it. Mackenzie was a political has-been. Blake was in retreat. Sir Hugh Allan had never lived down the events of the Pacific Scandal. Fleming had been driven back to England. Moberly had quit his profession. Marcus Smith hung grimly on but in a minor post. Joseph Whitehead was out of business. In every instance, the railway had changed and twisted their future, as it had Macdonald's, as it had the nation's.

Far out beyond the Red River, the prairie land lay desolate under its blanket of shifting snow, still bereft of settlers. In just twelve months, as Macdonald knew, all that must change. Before the present parliament was dissolved, cities yet unnamed would have their birth out on those windswept plains, passes yet uncharted would ring to the sound of axe and sledge. Within one year an army of twelve thousand men would be marshalled to invade the North West. Other armies would follow: ten thousand along the Fraser, twelve thousand attacking the mountain crevices, fifteen thousand blackening the face of the Shield. Nothing would ever be the same again. The tight little Canada of Confederation was already obsolete; the new Canada of the railway was about to be born. There was not a single man, woman or child in the nation who would not in some way be affected, often drastically, by the tortured decision made in Ottawa that night.

The future would not be easy and all the cries of dismay that had echoed down the corridors of the seventies would return to haunt the eighties. The granite shield of Canada had to be cracked open to let the railway through. The mountain barrier must be breasted and broken. There would be grief aplenty in the years to come — frustration, pain, hard decisions and, as always, bitter opposition.

But the great adventure was launched. Tomorrow would take care of itself, as it always did. At last the dream was about to become a reality. The triumph lay just a few short years ahead.

Chronology

1871

Feb. 20	William Francis Butler arrives back at Fort Garry following his exploration of "The Great Lone Land."
Mar. 13	Minister of Public Works recommends the organization of the Canadian Pacific Survey.
Mar. 17	Resolution incorporating British Columbia in Confederation put before House of Commons.
Mar. 18	George W. McMullen arrives in Ottawa from Chicago with canals delegation.
Mar. 24	William Kersteman and Alfred Waddington petition Parliament to incorporate their Canadian Pacific Railway Company.
April	Sandford Fleming appointed Engineer-in-Chief.
May	Jim Hill's steamboat *Selkirk* arrives at Fort Garry.
May 16	Resolution regarding British Columbia confirmed by Her Majesty in Council.
June 10	Twenty-one survey parties dispatched to explore and locate line in British Columbia and Lake Superior–Red River areas.
June 17	W. B. Ogden, U.S. railroadman, urges banker Jay Cooke to move to control the Canadian Pacific Railway project.
June 23	Marcus Smith quarrels with Indians on Homathco river.
July 14	McMullen, Waddington, Kersteman and associates meet Sir Francis Hincks and Sir John A. Macdonald in Ottawa.
July 20	British Columbia formally admitted to Confederation. Walter Moberly's survey parties set out for Columbia River.
Oct. 2	E. C. Gillette's survey party reaches foot of Howse Pass.
Oct. 5	Sir Hugh Allan and McMullen meet Cabinet. Decision postponed.
Oct. 29	Member of W. O. Tiedeman's survey party lost and almost dies in Chilcoten country.

Nov. 15	Roderick McLennan's survey party returns to Kamloops from Tête Jaune Cache after losing all its pack animals.
Dec. 4	Moberly sets out across Selkirks.
Dec. 23	McMullen, Smith and associates sign contract with Allan.

1872

Jan. 4	Moberly falls through ice of Shuswap Lake and barely escapes drowning.
Jan. 24	Allan asks McMullen for $200,000 to lure Charles Brydges into Canada Pacific Company.
Feb. 24	Allan reports to American principals that he has made an offer to Senator David L. Macpherson.
Feb. 26	Waddington dies of smallpox.
Feb. 29	Senator David L. Macpherson turns Allan down.
Mar. 13	Robert Rylatt puts down a mutiny on the Upper Columbia.
Mar. 28	Allan authorized by Americans to spend $50,000 on "influence."
April	Fleming settles on Yellow Head Pass as the best route through the Rockies.
May 15	Moberly, back at Howse Pass, tells his party to abandon further surveys there.
June 12	Allan reports to McMullen that he has George Etienne Cartier on his side.
	Fleming and Grant meet in Halifax to plan their journey "Ocean to Ocean."
July 1	Allan reports to General Cass on his use of the Americans' funds to bring Cartier around.
July 17	Fleming meets John Macoun, the botanist, aboard lake steamer.
July 26	Macdonald authorizes Cartier to tell Allan that Government influence will be used to get him the presidency of the CPR.
July 30	Allan and Cartier reach an understanding. Cartier asks Allan for campaign contributions.
	Fleming, Grant and Macoun reach Oak Point and get their first view of the prairie.
Aug. 2	Fleming's party leaves Fort Garry.
Aug. 9	Allan helps Cartier open his election campaign.

Aug. 26	Macdonald wires: "I must have another ten thousand."
Sept. 1	Macdonald government returned in federal election.
Sept. 14	Fleming meets with Moberly in Yellow Head Pass.
Sept. 16	McMullen learns that Allan has spent $343,000.
Sept. 28	The "Grand Ball" at the Boat Encampment on the Columbia River.
Oct. 11	Grant and Fleming end their journey in Victoria.
Oct. 19	Robert Rylatt, en route to the Athabasca Pass, learns his wife has died the previous fall.
Oct. 24	Allan breaks news to McMullen that Americans can have no part in Canadian Pacific Railway.
Dec. 12	Moberly explores and rejects Athabasca Pass.
Dec. 31	McMullen meets Macdonald in Ottawa and tells him of Allan's double dealings.

1873

Jan. 23	McMullen and associates return to Ottawa for second meeting with Macdonald.
Feb. 25	Hincks reports to Macdonald from Montreal that Allan has paid off McMullen and purchased his indiscreet correspondence.
Mar. 6	Parliament opens.
April 2	Lucius Seth Huntington's motion touches off the Pacific Scandal.
April 8	Macdonald announces select committee to investigate Huntington charges.
April 18	Oaths Bill introduced in House.
April 29	Oaths Bill passes Senate.
May 3	Oaths Bill gets royal assent.
May 5	Select committee meets; adjourns until July.
May 13	Robert Rylatt and Henry Baird set off for Kamloops.
May 23	Parliament ajourned until August 13.
June 14	Rylatt and Baird reach Kamloops.
June 27	Oaths Bill disallowed.
July 3	Select committee meets again; refuses to take evidence.
July 4	*Globe* (Toronto) and *Herald* (Montreal) publish Allan correspondence.
July 17	Opposition papers publish McMullen revelations.
July 19	Esquimalt named as terminus for CPR.
July 23	Lord Dufferin, in Charlottetown, gets news of McMullen revelations.

August	Jesse Farley appointed receiver of St. Paul and Pacific Railroad.
Aug. 13	Parliament meets and is prorogued.
Aug. 14	Royal Commission appointed to take evidence based on Huntington charges.
Sept. 17	Jay Cooke's banking firm fails, touching off financial panic.
Oct. 1	Royal Commission ends hearings.
Oct. 23	Parliament opens "short session."
Nov. 3	Macdonald's speech.
Nov. 5	Macdonald government resigns.
December	Donald Smith passes through St. Paul and asks Norman Kittson to investigate bankrupt St. Paul and Pacific Railroad.

1874

January	Party under E. W. Jarvis prepares to explore Smoky River Pass in Rockies.
Jan. 22	Liberal Party under Alexander Mackenzie re-elected.
Jan. 26	Fire in engineering department, Ottawa, destroys valuable survey records.
Feb. 3	Edward Blake resigns from Mackenzie cabinet.
Feb. 7	Victorians (B.C.) attack "Bird Cages" and create Terms of Union Preservation League.
Feb. 15	Jarvis party reaches Smoky River Pass.
Mar. 9	J. D. Edgar arrives in British Columbia to renegotiate terms of union on Ottawa's behalf.
Mar. 15	Jarvis party lost and starving.
April 3	Jarvis party manages to reach Edmonton.
May 11	Premier George Walkem questions Edgar's credentials.
May 18	Edgar leaves British Columbia in a huff.
May 21	Jarvis and party arrive at Fort Garry.
June 12	Lord Carnarvon offers to arbitrate dispute between British Columbia and Ottawa.
June 29	Some two hundred angry passengers on Dawson Route are stranded at North West Angle without transportation.
Aug. 30	First contract on transcontinental railway—for the Pembina Branch—signed.
Oct. 3	Blake's Aurora speech.

Nov. 17	Lord Carnarvon lays down terms of settlement between Ottawa and British Columbia.
Dec. 19	Adam Oliver goes to Ottawa to get telegraph contract between Fort William and Red River.

1875
Feb. 19	Adam Oliver and friends awarded telegraph contract.
April 2	Senate rejects bill to build Esquimalt and Nanaimo railway.
May 14	Blake re-enters Mackenzie cabinet.
	Manitoba, stern-wheeler of newly created Merchants' Line, arrives in Winnipeg.
June 1	First sod of main line of Canadian Pacific Railway turned at Fort William.
July 14	Marcus Smith, sick with fatigue, builds an Indian fly-bridge across the Homathco River.
August	Construction commenced on Neebing Hotel at Fort William.
Sept. 20	Order in council offers British Columbia $750,000 cash in lieu of Esquimalt and Nanaimo railroad.
	Merchants' Line sells out to Kittson Line.

1876
Jan. 10	British Columbia rejects Ottawa overtures, threatens secession.
Mar. 17	Jim Hill leaves St. Paul for meeting with Donald A. Smith in Ottawa regarding purchase of bankrupt St. Paul railway.
May	Fleming given leave of absence; goes to England.
Aug. 16	Lord Dufferin arrives at Esquimalt for viceregal visit.
Sept. 20	Bids opened for Section Fifteen contract, CPR.
Nov. 18	Dufferin, Mackenzie and Blake almost come to blows over British Columbia issue.
December	Fleming called back from leave.

1877
Jan. 9	Joseph Whitehead awarded contract for Section Fifteen.
Jan. 29	First proposal by Jim Hill to Dutch bondholders.
May	Hill and Smith meet George Stephen in Montreal.
May 22	Marcus Smith orders Henry Cambie to launch a secret expedition to examine the Pine River Pass.

May 26	Hill and Kittson make a second offer to the Dutch which is construed as an offer to purchase.
Sept. 1	George Stephen visits the St. Paul and Pacific Railroad for the first time.
Oct. 9	*The Countess of Dufferin,* first locomotive on the prairies, arrives in Winnipeg.
Dec. 25	Stephen, back from Europe, reports his failure to raise funds to buy bankrupt St. Paul line.

1878

Jan. 2	Stephen's first meeting with John S. Kennedy in New York.
Jan. 5	New offer to Dutch bondholders drawn up.
Jan. 21	Agreement reached between Stephen-Hill group and Dutch.
Mar. 13	Final agreement of sale between Dutch bondholders and Stephen-Hill group.
Mar. 18	Mackenzie introduces bill into Parliament to lease Pembina Branch of CPR to unspecified parties.
Mar. 27	"Montreal Agreement" among partners in St. Paul syndicate: Stephen, Hill, Smith and Kittson.
Mar. 29	Marcus Smith's official report urges acceptance of Pine Pass–Bute Inlet route but asks year's delay for more surveys.
April	Fleming is once again called back from sick-leave in England to deal with Marcus Smith.
May 10	Tupper and Macdonald call Donald A. Smith a "liar" and a "coward" in a stormy scene as Parliament is prorogued.
May 18	George Walkem returned to power in British Columbia on platform of "fight Ottawa" and secession.
July 22	Mackenzie government selects Fraser River–Burrard Inlet route for CPR.
July 31	Hill completes first section of St. Paul line and secures land grant.
Sept. 17	Conservative Party returned to power in federal landslide.
	Last spike of Pembina Branch driven.
Nov. 11	First train of St. Paul and Pacific crosses border at St. Vincent and arrives at Emerson, Manitoba.

396

| December | Macdonald government restores Esquimalt as CPR terminus. |

1879

Jan. 30	Tenders opened on Contract Forty-two of CPR.
Mar. 20	Contract Forty-two signed.
May 10	Tupper in House outlines Government's railway policy, rejects Burrard route and announces 125 miles will be built at once in British Columbia.
June 21	Donald A. Smith's election controverted for corruption.
Oct. 4	Burrard route re-adopted.
Nov. 20	Andrew Onderdonk arrives in Ottawa to negotiate for four British Columbia contracts.

1880

Mar. 1	Government relieves Joseph Whitehead of contract.
Mar. 3	Fleming attacked in Parliament.
Mar. 16	Nitro-glycerine works blows up at Prince Arthur's Landing.
April 22	Onderdonk arrives at Yale, B.C., to commence construction.
April 28	Alexander Mackenzie resigns as Liberal leader. Edward Blake named new leader.
May 22	Fleming resigns and is replaced by Collingwood Schreiber.
June 15	Charles Tupper's memo to Privy Council urges that capitalists be found to build CPR.
June 16	CPR Royal Commission appointed.
June 29	Macdonald, at political picnic, Bath, Ontario, announces capitalists in Britain stand ready to build railway.
July 10	Macdonald, Tupper and Pope sail for England.
July 18	Michael Haney, thrown from a moving train, narrowly escapes death on Section Fifteen.
July 30 (approx.)	Whiskey dealer Dan Harrington shot at Hawk Lake.
Aug. 12	CPR Royal Commission begins hearings.
Sept. 4	Macdonald signs a provisional agreement in London with Stephen–McIntyre–Hill Syndicate.
Sept. 11	Donald A. Smith defeated in Selkirk by-election.
Sept. 27	Macdonald arrives back in Montreal.

Oct. 21	Final contract signed with Stephen Syndicate.
Nov. 2	Father Albert Lacombe arrives at his new mission at Rat Portage.
Dec. 9	Parliament opens; details of contract made public.
Dec. 11	Tupper rallies Conservative caucus.
Dec. 13	Debate on contract opens.
Dec. 23	Christmas recess.

1881

Jan. 5	Parliament reconvenes.
Jan. 12	Pacific Railway bill read for first time.
Jan. 14	New tender from Howland syndicate reaches government.
Jan. 17	Macdonald's speech in Parliament.
Jan. 18	Blake's speech.
Jan. 27	Bill passes first reading.
Jan. 31	Bill passes second reading.
Feb. 1	Bill passes final reading.
Feb. 15	Bill passes Senate.
Feb. 16	Canadian Pacific Railway Company holds first director's meeting.

Notes

page line **From Sea to Sea**

1   21   *Islander*, Dec. 31, 1870.

1   30   *British Colonist*, Jan. 2, 1871.

2   3   *Globe*, Jan. 2, 1871.

2   17   *Ibid.*, Jan. 4, 1871.

3   8   Southesk, p. 70.

Chapter One

6   6   *Parliamentary Debates*, Fourth Session, 1871, Vol. 2, p. 681.

6   34   *Ibid.*, p. 745.

7   15   *Ibid.*, p. 681.

7   21   *Macdonald Papers*, Vol. 252, Morris to Macdonald, April 1, 1871.

8   15   Boyd, p. 307.

8   33   *Parliamentary Debates*, 1871, p. 745.

8   40   *British Columbia and the Canadian Pacific Railway*, Complimentary Dinner to the Hon. Mr. Trutch, Ottawa, Monday, 10th April, 1871.

10   2   Pope, *Correspondence*, p. 124, Macdonald to Charles Brydges, Jan. 28, 1870.

10   7   Quoted in Stanley, *Louis Riel*, p. 40.

10   22   Willson, p. 182.

10   26   Watkin, p. 17.

10   36   Pope, *Correspondence*, pp. 123-124, Brydges to Macdonald, Jan. 25, 1870.

11   3   Irwin, pp. 120 and 128.

11   10   *St. Paul Press*, Feb. 8, 1870, quoted in Gluek, p. 262.

12   6   Johnson, p. 27. The pages of the *Patriot* during this period contain no references to Dalton's vision.

12   15   Smyth.

12   28   Carmichael Smyth, p. 2.

12   30   Johnson, p. 28.

12   39   Carmichael Smyth, p. 3.

13   13   Synge, *Canada in 1848*.

13   21   Synge, *Great Britain*, p. 86.

13   31   Wilson and Richards, p. 238.

page line

13   39   *Ibid.*, pp. 205 and 206.

14   12   *Ibid.*, pp. 228 and 229.

14   14   *Ibid.*, p. 232.

15   1   Macdonell, p. 35.

15   4   *Ibid.*, p. 3.

15   19   Irwin, p. 26.

15   24   Hind, et al, *Eighty Years Progress*: Keefer, *Travel and Transportation*, p. 221.

16   25   *Ibid.*, p. 222.

16   28   *Ibid.*, p. 227.

16   38   Trotter, *Canadian Federation*, pp. 88-90.

17   13   Johnson, p. 30.

17   14   Watkin, p. 62.

18   8   Fleming, *Practical Observations*.

18   37   *Ibid.*, p. 46.

19   25   Quoted in Smith, *Political Destiny*, p. 62.

20   2   Quoted in Wallace, *Growth*, p. 5.

20   5   Quoted in Lower, p. 296.

20   13   Canniff.

20   16   Smith, *Political Destiny*, p. 61.

20   21   Quoted, *ibid*, p. 62.

20   26   *Leader*, April 28, 1870.

21   16   Rose, *Great Country*, p. 286.

23   2   Berry, p. 191.

24   34   *Leader*, Jan. 11, 1870.

24   39   Smith, *Political Destiny*, p. 32.

25   19   Quoted in Young, Vol. 2, p. 83 *n*.

25   34   *Ibid.*, p. 81.

26   4   Pope, *Memoirs*, p. 43, Macdonald to Watkin, March 27, 1865.

26   11   Grant and Hamilton, p. 131.

26   31   Careless, Vol. 1, pp. 228-229.

27   10   Young, Vol. 2, p. 84.

30   32   Pope, *Correspondence*, p. 124, Macdonald to Charles Brydges, Jan. 28, 1870.

32   11   See Spry.

33   30   Palliser, *Further Papers*, p. 5, Palliser to Under-Secretary of State for the Colonies, May 20, 1859.

page line

33 33 Palliser, *Journals*, p. 16.

33 35 Palliser, *Further Papers*, p. 5.

35 12 Gladman, p. 164.

35 14 Hind, *Narrative*, p. 220.

35 17 *Ibid.*, p. 234.

35 21 *Ibid.*

35 34 Hind, *et al*, *Eighty years Progress*, p. 80.

37 13 MacGregor, p. 30.

37 21 Trotter and Hawkes, p. 291.

37 31 D'Artigue, p. 45.

38 30 Southesk, p. 92.

38 41 *Luxton Papers*, Memories of Mrs. David McDougall, p. 3.

39 19 Wolesley, *Blackwood's*, p. 178.

40 10 Butler, p. 7.

40 14 *Ibid.*

40 15 *Ibid.*

41   7 *Ibid.*, p. 197.

41 13 *Ibid.*

41 20 *Ibid.*, pp. 200-201.

41 25 *Ibid.*, pp. 199-200.

42   6 *Ibid.*

42 19 *Ibid.*, p. 351.

43   5 Grant and Hamilton, p. 87.

43   8 *Ibid.*, pp. 97-98.

43 14 *Ibid.*, p. 131.

43 34 *Ibid.*, pp. 47-48 *n*.

44   5 *Ibid.*, p. 143.

46 26 Burpee, p. 147

47   9 Quoted in Stanley, *Birth*, p. 50.

47 26 Grant, *Ocean to Ocean*, p. 74.

47 38 *Fleming Papers*, Folder 131, Grant to Fleming, Sept. 30, 1880.

50   9 Macoun, p. 73.

50 27 *Ibid.*, p. 81.

51   4 Horetzky, *Startling Facts*, p. 4.

51 16 Grant, p. 344.

51 22 *Ibid.*, p. 272.

51 25 *Ibid.*, pp. 272-273.

52 30 Coffin, p. 77.

52 37 Butler, pp. 103-104.

53 21 *Malhoit Manuscript*, pp. 108-109.

56   3 *McQuarrie Papers*, Memoirs of 1882-87, p. 1.

56 24 Willson, p. 197.

56 28 *Nor'wester*, July 6, 1874.

56 37 *Ibid.*

56 39 *Ibid.*

57   4 *Ibid.*, July 20, 1874.

57 11 Trow, pp. 12-13.

57 19 *Ibid.*, p. 17.

57 24 *Ibid.*, p. 36.

57 38 Begg, Vol. 2, p. 261.

58   6 Marchioness of Dufferin, *Journal*, p. 343.

58 10 Fitzgibbon, pp. 110-111.

Chapter Two

61 19 Ormsby, p. 205.

61 34 *Macdonald Papers*, Vol. 123, Waddington to Macdonald, Sept. 10, 1869.

61 36 *Ibid.* (enclosure), Waddington, Alfred, *Elements for a Prospectus of the Canada Pacific Railway*, Aug. 22, 1870.

62 11 *Globe*, March 14, 1873, Letter of William Kersteman.

63 27 Irwin, p. 120.

63 33 *Ibid.*, p. 165, Ogden to Cooke, June 17, 1871.

64 14 *Report of Royal Commissioners, August 14, 1873*, pp. 11-12, Hincks' testimony.

64 17 *Ibid.*, p. 13.

64 19 *Ibid.*, p. 100, Macdonald's testimony.

64 24 *Macdonald Papers*, Vol. 519, Macdonald to George Jackson, July 17, 1871.

64 33 *Report of Royal Commissioners*, p. 11, Hincks' testimony.

64 36 *Ibid.*

65 16 *Globe*, March 14, 1873.

65 23 Quoted *Montreal Daily Star*, Nov. 27, 1926.

67   4 *Report of Royal Commission on Labour and Capital*, Quebec Evidence, Part 1, p. 176.

400

page line

67 16 *Globe*, July 4, 1873.

67 18 Quoted in Stewart, p. 235.

67 26 *Report of Royal Commissioners*, p. 4, Hincks' testimony.

67 35 *Dufferin Papers*, Dufferin to Kimberley, Sept. 26, 1873.

68 4 *Globe*, July 17, 1873, McMullen's statement.

68 10 *Ibid.*

68 11 *Gazette*, July 18, 1872, Hincks' statement.

68 12 *Report of Royal Commissioners*, p. 5, Hincks' testimony.

68 21 *Ibid.*

68 26 *Globe*, July 17, 1873, McMullen's statement.

68 31 Quoted in Willson, p. 183.

68 41 Quoted in Irwin, pp. 171-172, Jay Cooke to H. C. Fahnestock, Jan. 16, 1872.

69 4 *Ibid.*

69 14 Josephson, p. 57.

69 27 Quoted in Oberholtzer, Vol. 2, p. 296, Cooke to Gen. B. Sargent, Feb. 25, 1870.

69 31 *Ibid.*

70 4 *Ibid.*, Vol. 2, p. 351.

70 14 *Globe*, July 4, 1873, Allan to Gen. Cass, July 1, 1872.

70 23 *Ibid.*

70 29 Notman and Taylor, Vol. 1, p. 361.

70 35 *Globe*, July 4, 1873, Allan to McMullen, Dec. 29, 1871.

70 39 *Ibid.*, Allan to McMullen Jan. 1, 1872.

71 4 *Ibid.*, Allan to McMullen, Jan. 24, 1872.

71 8 *Ibid.*

71 35 *Campbell Papers*, Abbott to Campbell, Nov. 13, 1872.

72 8 *Globe*, July 4, 1873, Allan to Charles M. Smith, Feb. 24, 1872.

72 17 *Ibid.*, Allan to Charles M. Smith, Feb. 28, 1872.

73 21 *Ibid.*, Allan to Gen. Cass, July 1, 1872.

73 28 *Ibid.*

74 4 *Ibid.*, Allan to McMullen, June 12, 1872.

74 9 Pope, *Public Servant*, p. 40.

75 8 *Globe*, July 4, 1873, Allan to Gen. Cass, Aug. 7, 1872.

75 10 *Ibid.*, Allan to McMullen, Aug. 6, 1872.

75 26 Boyd, p. 320.

76 12 Tuttle, Vol. 2, p. 417.

76 22 Clarke, p. 103.

76 28 *Ibid.*

76 38 *Report of Royal Commissioners*, p. 119, Macdonald's testimony.

77 3 Smith, *Reminiscences*, p. 429.

77 15 Clarke, p. 105.

77 18 *Ibid.*

77 24 Miller, p. 135.

77 28 *Report of Royal Commissioners*, p. 120, Macdonald's testimony.

77 36 Quoted in Thomson, p. 246.

77 39 *Report of Royal Commissioners*, p. 174, Blumhart's testimony.

78 11 *Campbell Papers*, C. J. Campbell to the Hon. Alexander Campbell, Aug. 28, 1872.

78 19 *Report of Royal Commissioners*, p. 134, Allan's testimony.

78 32 *Ibid.*, p. 134.

78 41 *Ibid.*, p. 160, Abbott's testimony.

79 4 *Ibid.*

79 30 *Ibid.*, pp. 136-7, Allan's testimony.

80 2 *Ibid.*

80 29 *Ibid.*, p. 181, Thomas White's testimony.

81 10 *Macdonald Papers*, Vol. 123, Macpherson to Macdonald, Sept. 17, 1872.

81 18 *Ibid.*, July 27, 1872.

81 23 *Ibid.*

81 24 *Ibid.*, Nov. 29, 1872.

81 29 *Ibid.*, Vol. 521, Macdonald to Macpherson, Sept. 26, 1872.

81 30 *Ibid.*

81 31 *Ibid.*, Sept. 19, 1872.

81 33 *Ibid.*, Sept. 26, 1872.

82 4 *Ibid.*, Vol. 123, Allan to Macdonald, Oct. 7, 1872.

82 8 *Report of Royal Commissioners*, pp. 132-133, Allan's testimony.

page line

105 9 De Kiewiet and Underhill, p. 12, Dufferin to Carnarvon, March 18, 1874.

105 19 Willison, p. 24.

105 24 Quoted in Stewart, p. 177.

105 31 *Gazette*, July 18, 1873.

105 35 See Longley.

105 38 *Ibid.*, p. 234.

106 3 *Macdonald Papers*, Vol. 79, Macdonald to Dufferin, Aug. 7, 1873.

106 11 *Ibid.*, Vol. 125, Campbell to Macdonald, July 18, 1873.

106 20 *Ibid.*, Abbott to Macdonald, July 22, 1873.

106 29 *Ibid.*, Day to Macdonald, July 24, 1873.

106 36 *Ibid.*, Abbott to Macdonald, July 25, 1873.

106 41 *Ibid.*, Campbell to Macdonald, July 31, 1873.

107 5 *Ibid.*, Abbott to Macdonald, July 22, 1873.

107 11 *Ibid.*, Affidavit of Alfred Thomas Cooper, Oct. 2, 1873.

107 19 *Globe*, Aug. 7, 1873.

107 29 *Ibid.*, Aug. 2, 1873, Aug. 8, 1873.

107 32 *Dufferin Papers*, Dufferin to Kimberley, Nov. 6, 1873.

108 3 *Ibid.*

108 17 *Ibid.*, Aug. 5, 1873.

109 16 *Ibid.*, July 23, 1873.

109 19 *Tupper Papers*, Vol. 4, Hincks to Tupper, Feb. 3, 1873.

109 27 *Macdonald Papers*, Vol. 79, Dufferin to Macdonald, July 31, 1873.

109 33 *Dufferin Papers*, Dufferin to Kimberley, Aug. 9, 1873.

109 38 Young, Vol. 2, p. 145.

110 3 Dufferin, *Message*, p. 19.

112 20 *Globe*, Aug. 14, 1873.

112 40 *Ibid.*

113 27 *Dufferin Papers*, Dufferin to Kimberley, Aug. 14, 1873.

113 36 Dufferin, *Message*, p. 93.

113 38 *Ibid.*, p. 94.

114 2 *Ibid.*, p. 99.

114 6 *Canadian Illustrated News*, Aug. 23, 1873.

114 10 *Dufferin Papers*, Dufferin to Kimberley, Aug. 14, 1873.

114 17 *Herald*, Aug. 14, 1873.

114 26 *Dufferin Papers*, Dufferin to Kimberley, Aug. 14, 1873.

115 28 *Globe*, Aug. 19, 1873.

115 35 *Ibid.*

115 38 Dufferin, *Message*, Dufferin to Kimberley, Aug. 18, 1873.

115 40 *Guillet Manuscript.*

116 26 *Dufferin Papers*, Dufferin to Kimberley, Oct. 9, 1873.

116 32 Pope, *Memoirs*, p. 557, Macdonald to Cartier, April 9, 1873.

117 4 *Report of Royal Commissioners*, p. 2, Starnes' testimony.

117 12 *Ibid.*

117 18 *Globe*, Sept. 4, 1873.

117 39 *Report of Royal Commissioners*, p. 9, Hincks' testimony.

118 16 *Ibid.*, p. 20, Beaubien's testimony.

118 23 *Ibid.*, p. 39, Daker's testimony.

118 33 *Ibid.*, p. 125, Langevin's testimony.

118 35 *Ibid.*

118 38 *Ibid.*, p. 123.

119 15 *Ibid.*, pp. 76-77, Hamel's testimony.

119 19 *Ibid.*, pp. 35-37, Murphy's testimony.

119 30 Careless, Vol. 2, p. 307.

119 32 *Report of Royal Commissioners*, Macdonald's testimony runs from p. 99 to p. 121.

120 15 *Ibid.*, p. 119, Macdonald's testimony.

120 29 Quoted in *Globe*, Sept. 20, 1873.

120 35 Quoted in *Globe*, Sept. 29, 1873.

120 39 *Report of Royal Commissioners*, Allan's testimony runs from p. 129 to p. 155.

122 21 *Ibid.*, pp. 156-172, Abbott's testimony.

123 22 Hutchison.

123 26 Pope, *Public Servant*, p. 81.

123 37 *Campbell Papers*, Abbott to Campbell, Nov. 13, 1872.

123 31 Pope, *Public Servant*, p. 43.

124 2 *Report of Royal Commissioners*, p. 165, Abbott's testimony.

124 24 *Dufferin Papers*, Dufferin to Kimberley, Sept. 26, 1873.

124 30 Young, Vol. 2, p. 150.

124 34 *Dufferin Papers*, Dufferin to Kimberley, Oct. 26, 1873.

124 36 *Ibid.*

125 6 *Ibid.*

125 17 *Ibid.*

125 21 *Ibid.*

125 28 *Ibid.*, Oct. 13, 1873.

125 29 *Ibid.*, Oct. 9, 1873.

125 30 *Ibid.*, Nov. 13, 1873.

125 32 *Ibid.*, Oct. 13, 1873.

125 37 *Ibid.*, Oct. 26, 1873.

125 39 *Ibid.*

126 4 *Citizen*, Oct. 23, 1873.

127 24 Ross, George, p. 55.

128 20 *Dufferin Papers*, Dufferin to Kimberley, Sept. 26, 1873.

129 2 *Ibid.*, Oct. 26, 1873.

129 21 *Globe*, Oct. 28, 1873.

129 29 *Dufferin Papers*, Dufferin to Macdonald, Sept. 20, 1873 and Sept. 30, 1873.

129 35 Pope, *Correspondence*, Macdonald to Dufferin, Sept. 29, 1873.

130 3 *Dufferin Papers*, Dufferin to Kimberley, Nov. 6, 1873.

130 21 *Globe*, Oct. 28, 1873.

132 3 *Ibid.*, Oct. 29, 1873.

132 8 *Ibid.*

132 15 *Dufferin Papers*, Dufferin to Kimberley, Nov. 6, 1873.

132 21 *Ibid.*

132 27 *Ibid.*

133 20 *Globe*, Oct. 30, 1873.

133 33 Ross, George, p. 69-70.

133 40 *Globe*, Nov. 4, 1873.

134 19 *Dufferin Papers*, Dufferin to Kimberley, Nov. 6, 1873.

134 24 *Globe*, Nov. 4, 1873.

134 29 Thomson, p. 166 *n*.

137 6 *Mail*, Nov. 6, 1873.

137 14 Pope, *Correspondence*, Countess of Dufferin to Lady Macdonald, Nov. 4, 1873.

137 18 *Ibid.*, Dufferin to Macdonald, Nov. 4, 1873.

138 9 *Canadian Illustrated News*, April 12, 1873.

138 14 Willison, p. 70.

138 27 Ross, George, p. 144.

139 2 Young, Vol. 2, p. 153.

139 13 *Dufferin Papers*, Dufferin to Kimberley, Nov. 6, 1873.

139 40 *Globe*, Nov. 6, 1873.

140 7 Pope, *Memoirs*, p. 194.

140 12 *Edgar Papers*, Edgar to wife, Nov. 5, 1873.

140 22 Ross, George, p. 71.

140 25 *Globe*, Nov. 7, 1873.

140 38 Thomson, p. 167.

141 7 *Globe*, Nov. 7, 1873.

141 12 Preston, *My Generation*, p. 92.

141 21 *Globe*, Nov. 7, 1873.

141 37 Ross, George, p. 73.

142 3 *Edgar Papers*, Edgar to wife, Nov. 5, 1873.

142 9 *Dufferin Papers*, Dufferin to Kimberley, Nov. 13, 1873.

142 24 Pope, *Memoirs*, pp. 195-6.

143 40 Ross, George, p. 80.

144 18 Connery.

145 6 Pope, *Public Servant*, p. 29.

Chapter Four

148 7 *Hargreaves Diary*, July 5, 1872.

148 18 *Rylatt Manuscript*, pp. 176-177.

148 37 Fleming, *CPR Report*, 1877, p. 87.

149 11 *Ibid.*, 1878, pp. 88 and 104.

149 19 *Ibid.*, 1872, App. 6, p. 58.

149 24 *Moberly Diary*, Oct. 8, 1872.

149 31 *CPR Royal Commission*, 1882, Vol. 2, p. 1685, Fleming's testimony.

149 35 Shaw and Hull.

149 39 *Hanington Papers*.

page line

150   4   *CPR Royal Commission*, Vol. 2, p. 1315, Fleming's testimony.

150   14   Fleming, *Letter to Secretary of State*, App. 3, p. 23.

150   16   *CPR Royal Commission*, Vol. 2, p. 1242, Horetzky's testimony.

150   21   *Ibid.*

150   23   *Ibid.*, Vol. 2, p. 1700, Fleming's testimony.

150   35   *Marcus Smith Papers*, PABC, *Diary*, July 20, 1875.

150   39   Fleming, *CPR Report, 1872*, App. 6, p. 58.

151   2   *Ibid.*, p. 68.

151   11   *Marcus Smith Papers*, PABC, Smith to Hunter, May 27, 1874.

151   26   *Ibid.*, Smith to Hunter, Oct. 8, 1874.

151   28   *Ibid.*, Oct. 11, 1874.

151   30   *Ibid.*, Oct. 20, 1874.

152   2   *Marcus Smith Papers*, PAC, Letterbook, Vol. 5, Smith to Fleming, Feb. 25, 1878.

152   9   Gosnell, p. 102.

152   14   Allard.

152   18   *Armstrong Manuscript*, p. 33.

152   33   Quoted in Begg, Vol. 2, pp. 181-182.

152   38   *CPR Bulletin*, Feb. 1, 1936.

153   27   Fleming, *CPR Report, 1872*, App. 6, p. 63, Rowan's testimony.

153   34   *CPR Royal Commission*, Vol. 1, p. 126, Carre's evidence.

154   3   *Ibid.*, Vol. 1, pp. 538-539, Kirkpatrick's evidence.

154   6   Fleming, *CPR Report, 1872*, App. 4, p. 42, by R. McLennan.

154   8   *Ibid.*, p. 48.

154   15   Fleming, *CPR Report, 1877*, App. H, pp. 148-161, Jarvis narrative.

155   4   *Ibid.*, p. 153.

155   9   *Ibid.*, p. 155.

155   11   *Hanington Papers*.

155   21   *Ibid.*

155   23   Fleming, *CPR Report, 1877*, App. H., p. 157, Jarvis narrative.

155   31   *Ibid.*, p. 147.

156   28   Moberly, *Rocks and Rivers*, p. 44.

157   2   Robinson, *Blazing the Trail*, pp. 66-67.

157   28   Robinson, *Walter Moberly*.

157   38   *Moberly Diary*, Jan. 4, 1872.

159   2   Moberly, *Rocks and Rivers*, p. 42.

159   33   Fleming, *CPR Report, 1872*, App. 3, p. 31, by Walter Moberly.

160   1   *Moberly Diary*, Jan. 1, 1872.

160   3   Fleming, *CPR Report, 1872*, App. 3, p. 34.

160   11   Robinson, *Blazing the Trail*, p. 74.

160   16   *Ibid.*, p. 75.

161   5   *CPR Royal Commission*, Vol. 3, p. 57.

161   21   Robinson, *Blazing the Trail*, p. 77.

161   35   *Ibid.*, p. 84.

161   41   Grant, *Ocean to Ocean*, p. 249.

162   10   *Ibid.*, p. 253.

162   16   *CPR Royal Commission*, Vol. 2, p. 1678, Fleming's testimony.

162   22   Moberly, *Address*, p. 10.

162   28   *Ibid.*, p. 13.

162   34   *CPR Royal Commission*, Vol. 2, p. 1826, Moberly's deposition.

163   10   *Moberly Diary*, Sept. 8, 1872.

163   21   Moberly, *Address*, p. 13.

163   29   *CPR Royal Commission*, Vol. 2, p. 1828, Moberly's deposition.

163   35   Moberly, *Address*, p. 14.

163   38   *Ibid.*, p. 15.

163   40   *Ibid.*

164   4   *Ibid.*

164   18   Shaw and Hull.

164   22   Robinson, *Blazing the Trail*, p. 73.

165   12   *Rylatt Manuscript*, p. 1.

165   13   *Ibid.*, p. 3.

165   16   *Ibid.*

166   3   *Ibid.*, p. 8.

167   15   *Ibid.*, p. 36

168   9   *Ibid.*, p. 42.

168   14   *Ibid.*, p. 43.

168   22   *Ibid.*

168   36   *Ibid.*, p. 44

169   10   *Ibid.*, p. 46.

169	14	*Ibid.*, p. 49.
169	20	*Ibid.*
170	2	*Ibid.*, p. 55.
170	4	*Ibid.*, p. 58.
170	17	*Ibid.*, p. 66.
170	23	*Ibid.*, p. 80.
170	28	*Ibid.*, p. 81.
170	38	*Ibid.*, p. 93.
171	10	*Ibid.*, p. 107.
171	27	*Ibid.*, p. 108.
172	3	*Ibid.*
172	8	*Ibid.*, p. 109.
172	19	*Ibid.*, p. 116.
172	29	*Ibid.*, p. 123.
172	40	*Ibid.*, pp. 128-129.
173	6	*Ibid.*, p. 131.
173	15	*Ibid.*, p. 176.
173	20	*Ibid.*, p. 193.
174	7	*Ibid.*, p. 226.
175	1	*Hanington Papers.*
175	3	Markwell.
175	6	*Armstrong Manuscript*, p. 33.
175	8	*Ibid.*, p. 97.
175	11	*Rylatt Manuscript*, p. 20.
175	14	*Fawcett Diary*, June 29, 1872.
175	16	*Hargreaves Diary*, July 3, 1872.
175	19	*McLennan Papers*, Smith to McLennan, Aug. 23, 1872.
175	20	*Marcus Smith Papers*, PAC, Letterbook, Vol. 6, Smith to Helmcken, Jan. 12, 1880; Letterbook, Vol. 4, Smith to J. H. Pope, July 20, 1883.
175	21	*Ibid.*, Letterbook, Vol. 6, Smith to Brydges, Oct. 28, 1879.
175	22	*Ibid.*, Letterbook, Vol. 4, Smith to Schultz, March 21, 1885.
175	23	*Marcus Smith Papers*, PABC, Smith to Joseph Hunter, Feb. 23, 1885.
175	24	Quoted in Fleming, *Letter to Secretary of State*, pp. 24-25, Smith to Fleming, March 24, 1875.
175	25	*Marcus Smith Papers*, PAC, Letterbook, Vol. 5, Smith to Fleming, Dec. 28, 1877.
175	26	*Ibid.*, Smith to Helmcken, May 25, 1877.
175	28	*Ibid.*, Letterbook, Vol. 6, Smith to Helmcken, Jan. 12, 1880.
176	22	Fleming, *CPR Report, 1874*, App. E, p. 109, by Marcus Smith.
176	31	*Marcus Smith Papers*, PABC, *Diary*, July 20, 1873.
176	35	*Ibid.*, June 25, 1872.
177	2	Fleming, *CPR Report, 1874*, App. E, p. 119.
177	10	*Ibid.*, p. 120.
177	35	*Marcus Smith Papers*, PAC, Autobiographical note, Manuscript Group 29, A19, Vol. 12.
177	40	*Hargreaves Diary*, July 3, 1872.
178	8	*Ibid.*, June 23, 1872.
178	21	*Ibid.*, Oct. 30, 1872.
178	25	*Ibid.*, June 23, 1872.
178	30	*Ibid.*, June 26, 1872.
178	33	*Ibid.*, July 3, 1872.
178	40	*Ibid.*, July 5, 1872.
179	4	*Fawcett Diary*, June 29, 1872.
179	15	*Hargreaves Diary*, June 23, 1872.
179	23	*Marcus Smith Papers*, PAC, Letterbook, Vol. 5, Smith to Helmcken, Dec. 8, 1876.
179	32	*Fawcett Diary*, June 16, 1872.
179	35	*Ibid.*, June 22, 1872.
179	36	*Ibid.*, June 29, 1872.
180	2	*Hargreaves Diary*, Sept. 12, 1872.
180	14	*Marcus Smith Papers*, PABC, *Diary*, July 13, 1872.
180	24	*Ibid.*, Aug. 11, 1872.
180	29	*Ibid.*, Smith to Hunter, July 8, 1875.
181	4	Fleming, *CPR Report, 1877*, App. I, pp. 164-165, by Marcus Smith.
181	11	*Ibid.*, p. 166.

Chapter Five

184	1	Preston, *My Generation*, p. 112.
184	5	*Bryce Papers*, James M. Coyne to Bryce, Sept. 9, 1915.
184	22	Ross, George, p. 32.

page line

184 24 *Ibid.*, p. 131.

185 9 Goldwin Smith, *Reminiscences*, p. 436.

185 12 De Kiewet and Underhill, p. 13, Dufferin to Carnarvon, March 18, 1874.

185 35 Willison, p. 19.

186 29 Josephson, p. 169.

187 8 *Globe*, Aug. 28, 1875.

187 11 *Monetary Times*, Dec. 21, 1877.

187 14 *Ibid.*

187 19 *Ibid.*, Nov. 8, 1878.

187 24 *Ibid.*

187 34 *Dufferin Papers*, Dufferin to Sir Michael Hicks-Beach, Sept. 4, 1878.

188 12 *Hansard*, p. 1715, April 23, 1877.

188 14 De Kiewiet and Underhill, p. 259, Dufferin to Carnarvon, Sept. 24, 1876.

188 20 Quoted in Grant and Hamilton, p. 137.

188 34 Fleming, *CPR Report, 1874*, p. 23.

188 36 *Ibid.*, p. 153.

188 40 *Ibid.*

188 41 De Kiewiet and Underhill, p. 267, Dufferin to Carnarvon, Oct. 8, 1876.

189 35 Sarnia, Nov. 25, 1873.

189 39 Ormsby, pp. 249-250.

191 9 *Edgar Papers*, Mackenzie to Edgar, Feb. 17, 1874.

191 18 Rattray, Vol. 3, p. 746.

191 34 De Kiewiet and Underhill, p. 70, Dufferin to Carnarvon, Sept. 11, 1874.

194 28 Fleming, *CPR Report, 1877*, p. 19.

195 22 *Sessional Paper 19a 1875*, p. 19, J. D. Edgar to the Secretary of State, June 17, 1874.

195 26 *Ibid.*, p. 20.

195 28 *Ibid.*, p. 23, Walkem to Edgar, May 11, 1874.

195 28 *Ibid.*, Edgar to Walkem, May 18, 1874.

196 3 De Kiewiet and Underhill, p. 49, Carnarvon to Dufferin, June 27, 1874.

196 5 *Ibid.*, p. 51, Dufferin to Carnarvon, July 9, 1874.

196 8 *Ibid.*

196 14 *Ibid.*, p. 54, July 17, 1874.

196 19 *Ibid.*, p. 75, Sept. 11, 1874.

196 27 *Ibid.*, p. 57, July 20, 1874.

197 4 *Ibid.*, p. 72, Sept. 11, 1874.

197 17 *Edgar Papers*, Mackenzie to Edgar, Feb. 21, 1874.

197 19 *Ibid.*, April 26, 1875.

197 21 *Mackenzie Papers*, Letterbook, Vol. 11, Mackenzie to Holton, Sept. 26, 1876.

197 36 Blake.

198 33 *Hansard*, p. 792, March 19, 1875.

199 6 *Order in Council*, Appendix A.

199 16 De Kiewiet and Underhill, p. 188, Dufferin to Carnarvon, Feb. 9, 1876.

199 22 *Canadian Illustrated News*, Sept. 9, 1876.

199 26 *Order in Council*, p. 9, March 13, 1876.

199 28 *Ibid.*, p. 8.

199 32 *Hansard*, p. 1130, April 7, 1876.

199 34 Quoted in Ormsby, p. 263.

200 11 De Kiewiet and Underhill, p. 232, Dufferin to Carnarvon, May 26, 1876.

200 24 Pope, *Correspondence*, p. 177, Macdonald to Lord Lisgar, Sept. 2, 1872.

200 28 De Kiewiet and Underhill, p. 232, Dufferin to Carnarvon, May 26, 1876.

200 34 Marchioness of Dufferin, *Journal*.

201 24 Smith, *Reminiscences*, p. 458.

202 9 De Kiewiet and Underhill, p. 264, Dufferin to Carnarvon, Oct. 8, 1876.

202 12 See *Mackenzie Papers*, Lieut.-Gov. Richards to Mackenzie, Nov. 23, 1876, for a typical reference.

202 13 De Kiewiet and Underhill, p. 264, Dufferin to Carnarvon, Oct. 8, 1876.

202 20 *Ibid.*

202 25 *Mackenzie Papers*, Richards to Mackenzie, Nov. 23, 1876.

202 38 *Daily Standard*, Victoria, July 15, 1876.

203 5 De Kiewiet and Underhill, p. 270, Dufferin to Carnarvon, Oct. 8, 1876.

203 15 Begg, p. 270.

203 21 Marchioness of Dufferin, *Journal*, p. 252.

203 f.n. Quoted by Anglin, Vol. 2, p. 718, Parliamentary Debates, 1871.

204 4 De Kiewiet and Underhill, p. 238, Dufferin to Carnarvon, June 1, 1876.

204 11 Ibid., p. 274, Dufferin to Carnarvon, Oct. 8, 1876.

204 13 Ibid., p. 264.

204 18 Ibid., p. 263.

204 28 Mackenzie Papers, Littleton to Mackenzie, Aug. 27, 1876.

204 32 De Kiewiet and Underhill, p. 274, Dufferin to Carnarvon, Oct. 8, 1876.

205 14 Ibid., p. 261.

205 20 Ibid.

205 27 Ibid.

206 16 Ibid., pp. 296-297, Dufferin to Carnarvon, Nov. 2, 1876.

207 15 Preston, My Generation, pp. 99-100.

207 17 De Kiewiet and Underhill, p. 331, Dufferin to Carnarvon, Jan. 19, 1877.

207 30 Ibid., p. 288, Dufferin to Mackenzie, Sept. 9, 1876, quoted in Dufferin to Carnarvon, Nov. 20, 1876.

208 1 Ibid., p. 310, Dufferin to Carnarvon, Nov. 23, 1876.

208 5 Ibid.

208 14 Dufferin Papers, Mackenzie to Dufferin, Nov. 19, 1876.

208 35 Meyers, p. 29.

209 5 Quoted in Sulma, Appendix, p. 19.

209 26 Mackenzie Papers, Cartwright to Mackenzie, Oct. 14, 1875.

209 36 Fleming, CPR Report, 1877, pp. 283-300.

209 40 Die Kiewiet and Underhill, p. 387, Dufferin to Carnarvon, Dec. 7, 1877.

210 7 Fleming, CPR Report, 1877, p. 72.

210 13 Ibid., p. 63.

210 19 Ibid., p. 74.

210 27 Ibid., p. 76.

210 34 Fleming, CPR Report, 1878, App. F., p. 63, Admiral de Horsey to Secretary of State, Oct. 9, 1877.

210 40 Ibid., p. 69, Fleming to Mackenzie, Dec. 26, 1877.

211 7 Burpee, p. 8.

211 19 Fleming Papers, Vol. 50, Fleming to Tupper, Feb. 9, 1880.

212 5 Macdonald Papers, Vol. 127, Memorandum (Copy) Marcus Smith to Macdonald, April 22, 1880.

212 9 First Report, Select Standing Committee, re CPR, 1879, p. 120, Rowan's testimony.

212 12 Fleming Papers, Vol. 50, Fleming to Tupper, Feb. 9, 1880.

212 18 Fleming, CPR Report, 1877, App. "I", p. 169, by Marcus Smith.

212 27 Marcus Smith Papers, PAC, Letterbook, Vol. 5, Smith to Mackenzie, April 17, 1877.

212 38 Ibid., Smith to Cambie, May 22, 1877.

213 1 Ibid.

213 8 Ibid., Smith to Hunter, Oct. 1, 1877.

213 18 Mackenzie Papers, Film M.199, Robson to Mackenzie, Sept. 26, 1879.

213 35 Marcus Smith Papers, PAC, Letterbook, Vol. 5, Smith to Hunter, Dec. 7, 1877.

214 11 Ibid., Smith to Helmcken, Dec. 7, 1877.

214 27 Ibid., Smith to Fleming, Dec. 7, 1877.

214 29 Ibid.

214 36 Ibid.

214 40 Ibid.

215 8 Ibid.

215 12 Ibid., Smith to Helmcken, Dec. 7, 1877.

215 19 Ibid., Smith to Fleming, Dec. 7, 1877.

215 37 Ibid., Smith to Helmcken, Dec. 7, 1877.

216 5 Ibid., Smith to Fleming, Dec. 10, 1877.

216 10 Ibid., Smith to Fleming, Dec. 14, 1877.

216 16 Ibid.

216 21 Ibid., Smith to Fleming, Dec. 28, 1877.

216 27 Ibid.

217 5 Ibid., Smith to Helmcken, April 22, 1878.

217 19 Public Accounts Committee, p. 121, Rowan's testimony.

217 22 Ibid., p. 117, Fleming's testimony.

217 31 CPR Royal Commission, Vol. 2, p. 1628, Fleming's testimony.

217 41 Marcus Smith Papers, PAC, Letterbook, Vol. 5, Smith to Helmcken, May 25, 1877.

218 9 Fleming, CPR Report, 1878, pp. 13-14.

218 16 Marcus Smith Papers, PAC, Letterbook,

page	line	
247	31	*Ibid.*, Vol. 3, p. 209.
247	35	*Ibid.*, pp. 194-195.
248	3	*Ibid.*, p. 190.
248	15	*Ibid.*, Vol. 1, p. 189, Charles Mackenzie's testimony.
248	23	*Ibid.*, Vol. 2, p. 1351, Fleming's testimony.
249	6	Willson, p. 200.
249	26	*CPR Royal Commission*, Vol. 3, p. 284.
250	13	Willson, pp. 34-35.
250	20	Bernard.
251	2	Collard, p. 189.
251	10	*Ibid.*, p. 184.
251	18	MacKay, p. 302.
252	14	*Hansard*, 1878, p. 355.
252	18	*Farley vs. Hill et al*, pp. 919-920, Defendants Exhibit No. 20, Stephen to Hill, Feb. 10, 1878.
252	29	*Hansard*, 1878, p. 1072.
253	16	*Ibid.*, Vol. 2, p. 2560, quoted by Smith.
253	23	*Ibid.*, p. 1675.
253	33	*Ibid.*, p. 1680.
253	34	*Ibid.*, p. 1681.
253	39	*Ibid.*, Vol. 2, p. 1682.
254	7	*Ibid.*, pp. 1682-1683.
254	13	*Ibid.*, p. 1683.
254	26	*Ibid.*, p. 1685.
254	34	*Ibid.*, p. 1689.
254	36	*Ibid.*, p. 1690.
255	7	*Ibid.*
255	19	*Ibid.*, pp. 1690-1691.
255	22	*Ibid.*, p. 1691.
255	38	*Ibid.*, p. 2556.
256	3	*Ibid.*, 1878, pp. 2558 to 2564.
257	28	Preston, *Strathcona*, p. 108.
259	40	*Ibid.*, p. 112.
260	4	Ross, George, p. 100.

Chapter Seven

262	19	Pope, *Public Servant*, p. 36.
262	36	*Ibid.*, p. 36.
263	11	Pope, *Memoirs*, Vol. 2, p. 202.

page	line	
263	34	*Dufferin Papers*, Dufferin to Sir Michael Hicks-Beach, Sept. 20, 1878.
263	36	*Ibid.*, Sept. 28, 1878.
263	37	*Edgar Papers*, Mackenzie to Edgar, Sept. 24, 1878.
264	13	Biggar, p. 202.
264	19	*Ibid.*, p. 203.
264	24	Pope, *Correspondence*, p. 243.
264	31	Longley, p. 109.
264	37	Skelton, *Canada*, p. 139.
265	4	Young, Vol. 2, p. 239.
265	10	Goldwin Smith, *Reminiscences*, p. 431.
265	13	*Hansard*, 1876, pp. 488-568; 1877, p. 179; 1878, p. 854.
265	19	*Hansard*, 1877, p. 405.
265	28	Quoted in Porritt, p. 247.
265	30	*Hansard*, 1877, p. 406.
265	37	Porritt, p. 247.
266	13	Pope, *Correspondence*, p. 240.
266	24	*Hansard*, 1879, p. 1909.
266	41	*Ibid.*, p. 1893.
267	16	Macoun, pp. 158-159.
267	19	*Ibid.*, p. 164.
267	21	*Hansard*, 1879, p. 1895.
267	32	*Ibid.*, p. 1890.
267	35	*Ibid.*, p. 1892.
268	6	*Ibid.*, p. 1901.
268	9	Harkin, pp. 98-99.
268	23	*Tupper Papers*, Vol. 5, Memorandum, Department Railways and Canals, March 4, 1880.
269	2	*CPR Royal Commission*, Vol. 2, p. 1020, Vol. 3, pp. 443, 448.
269	18	*Marcus Smith Papers*, PAC, Letterbook, Vol. 5, p. 26, Confidential Memo: Location of the Canadian Pacific Railway, Jan. 20, 1879.
269	19	*Ibid.*, p. 6.
269	20	*Ibid.*, Smith to Tupper, Jan. 23, 1879.
269	30	*Ibid.*, Smith to Macdonald, May 12, 1879.
269	34	*Ibid.*, Letterbook, Vol. 6, Smith to The Editor of the *Mail*, May 22, 1879.
269	38	Cambie.

page	line	
270	6	*Marcus Smith Papers*, PAC, Letterbook, Vol. 6, Smith to Brydges, Nov. 4, 1879.
270	16	*Ibid.*, Smith to Macpherson, Oct. 27, 1879.
270	20	*Marcus Smith Papers*, PAC, Letterbook, Vol. 6, Smith to Hewson, Oct. 30, 1879.
270	22	*Ibid.*, Smith to James Colton, March 5, 1880.
270	25	*Ibid.*, Smith to A. P. Macdonald, Oct. 31, 1879; Smith to Langevin, Dec. 29, 1879; Smith to Brydges, Jan. 5, 1880; Smith to Helmcken, Jan. 12, 1880.
270	*fn*	*Free Press*, Ottawa, April 19, 1881.
271	4	Horetzky, *Startling Facts*, p. 45.
271	13	Fleming, *Letter to Secretary of State*, App. 3, pp. 24-5, Smith to Fleming, March 24, 1875.
271	18	*Canadian Illustrated News*, April 7, 1880.
271	24	*Hansard*, 1880, p. 52.
272	16	*Macdonald Papers*, Vol. 216, Galt to Macdonald, Oct. 18, 1879.
272	20	*Ibid.*, Oct. 30, 1879.
273	1	Macphail, p. 199.
273	14	*CPR Royal Commission*, Vol. 2, p. 1677.
273	17	*Ibid.*, Vol. 3, pp. 83-85.
274	20	*Ibid.*, Vol. 3, p. 70.
274	23	*Ibid.*, p. 226.
274	29	*Ibid.*, p. 711.
274	37	*Ibid.*, p. 78.
275	23	*Select Committee, 1879*, pp. xii and xiii.
275	31	*Hansard*, 1875, p. 1075, April 3.
276	3	*Select Committee, 1879*, pp. 87 and 89, Carre's testimony.
276	7	Quoted by J. B. Plumb, *Hansard*, 1880, p. 465.
276	18	*CPR Royal Commission*, Vol. 2, p. 1711, Horetzky's testimony.
276	23	*Fleming Papers*, Folder 162, Horetzky to Fleming, Sept. 24, 1880.
276	27	Fleming, *Letter to Secretary of State*, App. 3, p. 25.
276	40	*Hansard*, 1881, p. 910, Feb. 9.
277	9	Fleming, *Memo*, 1880, pp. 5-6.
277	20	*Macdonald Papers*, Vol. 127, p. 10, Memorandum, Marcus Smith to F. Braun, Secretary, Department of Railways and Canals.
279	24	*Argus*, Sept. 14, 1883.
279	28	*Free Press*, Ottawa, April 19, 1881.
280	39	O'Leary, pp. 66-67.
281	2	Berry, p. 252.
282	14	*Times*, Sept. 19, 1879.
282	21	*Armstrong Manuscript*, p. 73, Aug. 14, 1931.
283	28	*Ibid.*, pp. 77, 79.
285	5	*CPR Royal Commission*, Vol. 1, p. 161.
285	16	*Sentinel*, Nov. 5, 1880.
285	24	*CPR Royal Commission*, Vol. 1, p. 543, Kirkpatrick's testimony.
286	9	Keefer, *Address*.
286	24	*Armstrong Manuscript*, p. 109.
287	5	*Ibid.*
287	9	*Sentinel*, Nov. 12, 1880.
287	12	*Times*, July 20, 1880.
287	20	*Ibid.*, Sept. 4, 1880.
287	35	Rutledge, April 15, 1920, p. 21.
288	3	*Ibid.*
289	8	*Ibid.*
289	16	*Ibid.*
289	33	Walker, p. 384.
290	39	Fleming, *England and Canada*, p. 173.
291	13	Fitzgibbon, pp. 163-164.
291	26	*Times*, Aug. 2, 1881.
291	30	Rutledge, April 15, 1920, p. 66
292	2	*Sentinel*, Aug. 8, 1877.
292	24	*Globe*, Sept. 24, 1883.
293	21	*Armstrong Manuscript*, p. 101.
294	17	Rutledge, April 15, 1920, pp. 22 and 66.
294	34	*Armstrong Manuscript*, p. 85.
295	5	*Times*, Dec. 29, 1880.
295	22	*Sentinel*, Dec. 31, 1880.
295	34	*Times*, Aug. 14, 1880.
295	36	*Globe*, Sept. 24, 1883.
296	8	*Ibid.*
296	15	*Times*, Nov. 8, 1880.
296	31	*Ibid.*, Aug. 14, 1880.
298	26	*Ibid.*
298	32	*Ibid.*

339 21 Willson, *Lord Strathcona*, pp. 204-205.

339 40 *Hansard*, 1880, pp. 1467-1468, April 16.

340 4 *Ibid.*, p. 1626, April 20.

340 9 Fleming, *CPR Report*, 1880, App. 23, p. 353, Tupper to Fleming, April 15, 1880.

340 13 *Ibid.*, p. 354.

340 27 Harkin, p. 101.

340 30 *Ibid.*

340 40 Waite, pp. 148-149.

341 14 *Tupper Papers*, Vol. 5, Memorandum dated June 15, 1880.

341 21 *Campbell Papers*, Campbell to D. O. Mills, Aug. 2, 1880.

341 29 *Macdonald Papers*, Vol. 195, Campbell to Macdonald, July 15, 1880.

341 39 *Ibid.*, Vol. 519, Lorne to Macdonald, June 24, 1880.

342 12 *Ibid.*, June 26, 1880.

342 37 *Ibid.*, Vol. 127, McIntyre to Macdonald, July 5, 1880.

343 2 Collins, p. 177.

343 19 *Macdonald Papers*, Vol. 267, Stephen to Macdonald, July 9, 1880.

344 34 *Campbell Papers*, Onderdonk to Campbell, Aug. 3, 1880.

345 6 Saunders, p. 286.

346 2 *Macdonald Papers*, Vol. 267, Stephen to Macdonald, Sept. 27, 1880.

346 9 *Ibid.*

346 17 *Mail*, Sept. 17, 1880.

346 19 *Free Press*, Manitoba, Sept. 7, 1880.

346 22 *Daily Witness*, Sept. 23 ,1880.

346 25 *Mail*, Sept. 20, 1880.

346 28 *Bystander*, p. 403, August, 1880,

346 39 *Mail*, Sept. 20, 1880.

347 7 Quoted in *Daily Witness*, Sept. 18, 1880.

347 16 Quoted in *Free Press*, Ottawa, Oct. 2, 1880.

347 27 *Ibid.*

347 32 Quoted in *Daily Witness*, Sept. 14, 1880.

347 39 *Mail*, Sept. 28, 1880.

348 8 *Ibid.*

348 23 *Ibid.*

349 13 *Ibid.*, Sept. 27, 1880.

349 16 *Times*, Sept. 27, 1880.

349 34 Biggar, p. 218.

350 37 Preston, *Strathcona*, p. 132.

351 15 *Macdonald Papers*, Vol. 267, Stephen to Macdonald, Dec. 16, 1880.

351 19 *Ibid.*, Stephen to Rose, Dec. 16, 1880.

351 23 *Ibid.*

351 25 *Ibid.*, Stephen to Macdonald, Jan. 23, 1881.

351 30 *Ibid.*, Quoted in Rose to Stephen, Dec. 14, 1880.

351 35 *Ibid.*, Vol. 259, Morton, Rose & Co. to Sir John Rose, July 6, 1883.

351 35 *Ibid.*, P. deP. Grenfell to Macdonald, Nov. 7, 1882.

352 3 *Ibid.*, Vol. 267, Stephen to Macdonald, Nov. 7, 1880.

352 6 *Ibid.*, Dec. 16, 1880.

352 10 *Ibid.*, Rose to Stephen, Dec. 14, 1880.

352 24 *Ibid.*, Stephen to Macdonald, Sept. 27, 1880.

352 25 *Ibid.*, Oct. 9, 1880.

352 33 *Ibid.*, Oct. 18, 1880.

352 37 *Ibid.*

353 13 *Ibid.*, Nov. 13, 1880.

353 15 *Ibid.*

353 37 *Free Press*, Ottawa, Dec. 20, 1880.

354 3 *Daily Witness*, Dec. 13, 1880.

354 4 Quoted in *Times*, Dec. 14, 1880.

354 4 Quoted in *Times*, Dec. 24, 1880.

354 14 *Bystander*, Nov., 1880.

355 31 Quoted in Hutchison, p. 941.

355 35 *Free Press*, Ottawa, Dec. 20, 1880.

356 3 *Macdonald Papers*, Vol. 267, Stephen to Rt. Hon. W. E. Forster, Feb. 22, 1881.

356 17 *Daily Witness*, Dec. 15, 1880.

356 26 *Globe*, Jan. 5, 1881.

356 30 *Free Press*, Ottawa, Dec. 28, 1880.

356 33 *Globe*, St. Paul, Dec. 31, 1880, quoted in *Free Press*, Ottawa, Jan. 10, 1881.

357 10 *Free Press*, Manitoba, Nov. 23, 1880.

357 18 *Macdonald Papers*, Vol. 267, D. MacArthur to Macdonald, Dec. 24, 1880.

357 28 *Ibid.*, Stephen to Macdonald, Jan. 23, 1881.

page line

358　5　*Free Press*, Ottawa, Dec. 18, 1880.

358　10　*Citizen*, Jan. 12, 1881.

358　11　*Mail*, Dec. 14, 1880.

358　34　*Free Press*, Ottawa, Dec. 13, 1880.

358　38　*Ibid.*, Dec. 14, 1880.

359　2　*Ibid.*, Dec. 22, 1880.

359　35　Lyall, Vol. 1, p. 215.

360　12　*Free Press*, Ottawa, Dec. 6, 1880.

360　26　*Citizen*, Dec. 9, 1880.

361　17　*Hansard*, 1880-81, p. 2, Dec. 9.

362　12　Willison, p. 181.

362　20　Morton, p. 28.

363　31　*Macdonald Papers*, Vol. 267, Stephen to Macdonald, Dec. 16, 1880.

364　2　*Hansard*, 1880-81, p. 50.

364　18　*Bystander*, p. 578, Nov., 1880.

364　32　Ross, George, p. 116.

364　39　Harkin, p. 105.

365　8　*Hansard*, 1880-81, p. 19.

365　13　*Ibid.*, p. 39.

366　7　*Ibid.*, p. 74.

366　14　*Bystander*, p. 8, Jan., 1881.

366　20　*Hansard*, 1880-81, p. 75.

366　26　Ross, p. 142.

366　33　*Hansard*, 1880-81, p. 77.

367　2　*Ibid.*, p. 142.

367　12　*Ibid.*

367　27　*Ibid.*, p. 152.

367　35　*Ibid.*

367　40　*Daily Witness*, Dec. 18, 1880.

368　9　*Hansard*, 1880-81, p. 194.

369　4　*Macdonald Papers*, Vol. 127, Norquay to Macdonald, Dec. 2, 1880.

369　15　*CPR Archives*, Montreal, Memo from William Pearce, Nov., 1924.

369　26　*Free Press*, Ottawa, Dec. 21, 1880.

370　10　*Hansard*, 1880-81, p. 303.

370　19　*Mail*, Dec. 28, 1880.

370　38　*Hansard*, 1880-81, p. 423.

371　10　*Free Press*, Ottawa, Dec. 28, 1880.

371　22　*Hansard*, 1880-81, p. 302.

page line

371　35　*Mail*, Jan. 10, 1881.

372　2　Harkin, p. 107.

372　29　*Bystander*, p. 63, Feb., 1881.

373　2　*Hansard*, 1880-81, p. 246.

373　2　*Ibid.*, p. 269.

373　9　*Ibid.*, p. 281.

373　14　*Ibid.*, p. 295.

373　16　*Ibid.*, p. 312.

373　20　Ross, Margaret, p. 68.

373　24　*Hansard*, 1880-81, p. 320.

373　33　Ross, George, p. 119.

374　2　Pope, *Correspondence*, p. 277.

374　9　Saunders, p. 294.

374　15　*Free Press*, Ottawa, Jan. 21, 1881.

374　18　*Ibid.*, Jan. 8, 1881.

374　32　*Mail*, Jan. 15, 1881.

374　38　*Hansard*, 1880-81, p. 398.

375　28　Quoted in *Mail*, Jan. 12, 1881.

376　3　*Free Press*, Ottawa, Jan. 13, 1881.

376　21　*Ibid.*, Jan. 14, 1881.

376　33　*Hansard*, 1880-81, p. 471.

376　35　*Ibid.*, p. 469.

376　36　*Ibid.*, p. 472.

376　38　*Ibid.*, p. 473.

377　28　*Ibid.*, p. 488.

379　30　Macdonald's speech runs from p. 485 to p. 495 in *Hansard*, 1880-81.

379　35　*Canadian Illustrated News*, Jan. 29, 1881.

380　10　*Free Press*, Ottawa, Jan. 18, 1881.

380　24　*Hansard*, 1880-81, pp. 495 to 518, Blake's speech.

382　22　*Macdonald Papers*, Vol. 267, Stephen to Macdonald, Jan. 23, 1881.

382　30　*Free Press*, Ottawa, Jan. 31, 1881.

382　36　*Hansard*, 1880-81, p. 685.

383　4　*Ibid.*, p. 686.

383　34　*Ibid.*, p. 708.

386　6　Quoted *Free Press*, Ottawa, Jan. 29, 1881.

386　8　*Ibid.*, Jan. 21, 1881.

387　20　*Herald*, Cleveland, Dec. 17, 1880, quoted *Free Press*, Ottawa, Jan. 8, 1881.

388　8　*Free Press*, Ottawa, Feb. 1, 1881.

Bibliography

Unpublished Sources

Armstrong, Harry William Dudley	*Papers*, Public Archives of Canada.
Brown, George	*Papers*, PAC.
Bryce, Doctor George	*Papers*, Public Archives of Manitoba.
Campbell, Sir Alexander	*Papers*, Public Archives of Ontario.
Dufferin, First Marquess of, and Ava	*Papers* (microfilm), PAC.
Edgar, Sir James David	*Papers*, PAO.
Fawcett, Edgar	*Diary, Three Months on Survey, CPR-Bute Inlet, 1872*, Public Archives of British Columbia.
Fleming, Sir Sandford	*Papers*, PAC.
Guillet, Edwin C.	*Manuscript, The Pacific Scandal, 1948*, Toronto Public Library.
Hanington, Major C. F.	*Papers*, PABC.
Hargreaves, George	*Diary, Bute Inlet, 1872*, PABC.
Luxton, Norman H.	*Papers*, PAC.
Macdonald, Sir John A.	*Papers*, PAC.
Mackenzie, Alexander	*Papers*, PAC.
McLennan, Roderick	*Papers*, Toronto Public Library.
Mcquarrie, William	*Papers*, PAC.
Malhoit, Zéphirin	*Manuscript, Seventy Years of Growth with Canada*, PAC.
Moberly, Walter	*Diary*, Dec. 1871 to Feb. 1873, PABC.
Pearce, William	*Memo*, November 1924, CPR Archives, Montreal.
Rylatt, Robert M.	*Manuscript, Leaves From My Diary*, PABC.
Smith, Marcus	*Papers*, PAC and PABC.
Tupper, Sir Charles	*Papers*, PAC.

Public Documents

Canada	*Parliamentary Debates, 1870-72* and *Debates of the House of Commons of the Dominion of Canada, 1875-1881* (Hansard).
	Message to Parliament from the Governor-General (Lord Dufferin); Papers relative to the issue of a Commission to inquire into certain charges made against members of Her Majesty's Privy Council for Canada, respecting the grant of a charter and contract to the Canadian Pacific Railway Company, Ottawa, 1872.
	Report of the Royal Commissioners Appointed by

415

Commission, addressed to them under the Great Seal of Canada, bearing date the Fourteenth day of August, A.D., 1873, Ottawa, 1873.

Sessional Paper #19 1875, Message Relative to the Terms of Union with the Province of British Columbia, Ottawa, 1875.

Papers Connected with the Awarding of Section Fifteen of the Canada Pacific Railway, Ottawa, 1877.

Public Accounts Committee, House of Commons, 1877.

Reports and Minutes of Evidence Taken Before the Select Committee of the Senate Appointed to Inquire into and Report upon the Purchase of Lands at Fort William for a Terminus to the Canadian Pacific Railway, Ottawa, 1878.

First Report of the Select Standing Committee on Public Accounts in Reference to Expenditure on the Canadian Pacific Railway Between Fort William and Red River, Ottawa, 1879.

Report of the Canadian Pacific Railway Royal Commission Evidence, Ottawa, 1882, 3 Volumes.

Fleming, Sir Sandford   *Progress Report on the Canadian Pacific Railway Exploratory Survey*, Ottawa, 1872.

Canadian Pacific Railway, A Report of Progress on the Explorations and Surveys up to January, 1874, Ottawa, 1874.

Report on Surveys and Preliminary Operations of the Canadian Pacific Railway up to January, 1877, Ottawa, 1877.

Reports and Documents in Reference to the Location of the Line and a Western Terminal Harbour, Ottawa, 1878.

Report and Documents in Reference to the Canadian Pacific Railway, Ottawa, 1880.

Memorandum Addressed to the Honourable, The Minister of Railways and Canals by the Engineer-in-Chief of the Canadian Pacific Railway, Ottawa, 1880.

Letter to the Secretary of State, Canada, in Reference to the Report of the Canadian Pacific Royal Commission, Ottawa, 1882.

United States

Circuit Court of the United States for the District of Minnesota, Jesse P. Farley, complainant, and Norman W. Kittson, James J. Hill and the St. Paul, Minneapolis and Manitoba Railway Company, defendants, 15th day of July, A.D. 1882.

No. 6, Supreme Court of the United States, October Term, 1886, Jesse P. Farley, Appellant, vs. Norman W. Kittson, James J. Hill and The St. Paul, Minneapolis and Manitoba Railway Company (Appeal from the Circuit Court of the United States for the District of Minnesota).

Newspapers and Periodicals

Argus	Rat Portage 1883
British Colonist	Victoria 1871
Bystander	Toronto 1880-81
Canadian Illustrated News	Montreal 1873-81
Citizen	Ottawa 1873-81
Daily Witness	Montreal 1880-81
Free Press	Manitoba 1873-81 Ottawa 1880-81
Gazette	Montreal 1873-81 Picton 1873
Globe	Toronto 1871-81
Herald	Montreal 1873
Islander	Charlottetown 1870
Leader	Toronto 1870
Mail	Toronto 1873-81
Monetary Times	Toronto 1874-78
Nor'wester	Winnipeg 1874-75
Sentinel	Thunder Bay 1875-80
Times	Winnipeg 1879-81

Published Sources

Anon	*A Year in Manitoba*, London, 1881. Pamphlet. *Prince Arthur's Landing and the Terminus of the* CPR, Toronto, 1878, Pamphlet.
Allard, Jason O.	*Breaking Trail for Iron Horse*, as related to B. A. McKelvie, Maclean's, August 1, 1929.
Beaty, James	*The History of the Lake Superior Ring*, Toronto, 1874, Pamphlet.
Begg, Alexander	*History of the North-west*, 2 vols. Toronto, 1894.
Bernard, Kenneth	*Lord Strathcona*, The Wide World Magazine, March, 1907.
Berry, C. B.	*The Other Side, How It Struck Us*, London, 1880.
Biggar, E. B.	*Anecdotal Life of Sir John A. Macdonald*, Montreal, 1891.
Blake, Edward	*A National Sentiment*, Ottawa, 1874. Pamphlet Reprinted in Canadian Historical Review, September, 1921.
Boyd, John	*Sir George Etienne Cartier, Bart., His Life and Times*, Toronto, 1914.
Breton, Paul Emile, O.M.I.	*The Big Chief of the Prairies; The Life of Father Lacombe*, Edmonton, 1955.

417

Burpee, Lawrence J.   *Sandford Fleming, Empire Builder*, Toronto, 1915.

Butler, Sir William Francis   *The Great Lone Land*, London, 1872.

CPR   *Staff Bulletin*, Feb. 1, 1936.

Cambie, Henry J.   *Reminiscences of Pioneer Life in the West*, Journal of the Engineering Institute of Canada, Montreal, October, 1920.

Canniff, William   *Canadian Nationality: Its Growth and Development*, Toronto, 1875.

Careless, J. Maurice   *Brown of the Globe*, 2 vols., Toronto, 1959, reprinted 1963.

Carmichael Smyth, Major Robert   *The Employment of the People and the Capital of Great Britain in Her Own Colonies*, London, 1849. Pamphlet.

Clarke, Charles   *Sixty Years in Upper Canada*, Toronto, 1908.

Coffin, Charles C.   *The Seat of Empire*, Boston, 1871.

Collard, Edgar A.   *Canadian Yesterdays*, Toronto, 1955.

Collins, J. E.   *Canada Under the Administration of Lord Lorne*, Toronto, 1884.

Connery, David Pugsley   *National Gallery Honors Windsor Artist*, Border Cities Star, December 24, 1932.

Council of the Municipality of Shuniah, Thunder Bay   *The Question of the Terminus of the Branch of the Pacific Railway on the North Shore of Lake Superior Showing the Advantage of Thunder Bay over Nepigon Bay or any other point*, Ottawa, 1874, pamphlet.

Crawford, Robert   *Answer to pamphlet—The Question of the Terminus of the Branch of the Pacific Railway on the North Shore of Lake Superior Showing the Advantage of Thunder Bay over Nepigon Bay or any other point*, Ottawa, 1874, pamphlet.

Creighton, Donald   *John A. Macdonald, The Young Politician*, Vol. 1, Toronto, 1952.

    John A. Macdonald, The Old Chieftain, Vol. 2, Toronto, 1955.

D'Artigue, Jean   *Six Years in the Canadian North-West*, Toronto, 1882.

Dawson, S. J.   *Report on the Exploration of the Country Between Lake Superior and the Red River Settlement, and Between the Latter Place and the Assiniboine and Saskatchewan*, Toronto, 1859.

De Kiewiet, C. W. and Underhill, F. H. *Editors*   *Dufferin-Carnarvon Correspondence 1874-1878*, Toronto, 1955.

Dufferin, Marchioness of Dufferin and Ava   *My Canadian Journal 1872-8*, London, 1891.

Fitzgibbon, Mary   *A Trip to Manitoba, or Roughing It on the Line*, Toronto, 1880.

Fleming, Sandford   *England and Canada*, London, 1884.

	Practical Observations on the Construction of a Continuous Line of Railway from Canada to the Pacific Ocean on British Territory (Appendix to Henry Youle Hind's book *A Sketch of an Overland Route to British Columbia*, Toronto, 1864).
Fregeau, F.	*Reminiscences of Early Journalism in Fort William*, Thunder Bay Historical Society Annual Report and Papers 1911-12, Thunder Bay, 1913.
Gibbon, John Murray	*Steel of Empire*, Toronto, 1935.
Gilbert, Heather	*Awakening Continent, The Life of Lord Mount Stephen*, Vol. 1, Aberdeen, 1965.
Gladman, George	*Report on the Exploration of the Country Between Lake Superior and the Red River Settlement*, Toronto, 1958.
Glazebrook, C. P. de T.	*A History of Transportation in Canada*, 2 Vols. Toronto, 1938.
Gluek, Alvin C., Jr.	*Minnesota and the Manifest Destiny of the Canadian North West*, Toronto, 1965.
Gosnell, R. E.	*Sixty Years of Progress, British Columbia*, Vancouver and Victoria, 1913.
Grant, George Monro	*Ocean to Ocean*, Toronto, 1873.
	The Canada Pacific Railway, The Century Magazine, October, 1885.
Grant, William Lawson and Hamilton, Frederick	*George Monro Grant*, Toronto, 1905.
Ham, George H.	*Reminiscences of a Ranconteur*, Toronto, 1921.
Harkin, W. A., *Editor*	*Political Reminiscences of the Right Honourable Sir Charles Tupper, Bart.*, London, 1914.
Healy, W. J.	*Early Days in Winnipeg*, The Beaver, June, 1949.
Hill, Alex Staveley, D.C.L., Q.C., M.P.	*From Home to Home, Autumn Wanderings in the North-West in the Years 1881, 1882, 1883, 1884*, London, 1885.
Hind, Henry Youle	*The Climate of Western Canada*, Toronto, 1851.
	Report on the Assiniboine and Saskatchewan Exploring Expedition, Toronto, 1859.
	Narrative of the Canadian Red River Exploring Expedition of 1857 and of the Assiniboine and Saskatchewan Exploring Expedition of 1858, 2 Vols., London, 1860.
	A Sketch of an Overland Route to British Columbia, Toronto, 1862.
Hind, Henry Youle with Keefer, Thomas Robb, C. Hodgins, J. G. Perley, M. H. Murray, W.	*Eighty Years Progress of British North America*, London [Toronto Printing], 1863.
Horetzky, Charles	*Canada on the Pacific*, Montreal, 1874.

419

	Some Startling Facts Related to the Canadian Pacific Railway and the North West Lands, Ottawa, 1880, Pamphlet.
Hughes, Katherine	*Father Lacombe, The Black Robe Voyageur*, Toronto, 1920.
Hutchison, Paul P.	*Sir John J. C. Abbott*, Canadian Bar Review, Volume 26, 1948.
Irwin, Leonard B.	*Pacific Railway and Nationalism in the Canadian-American Northwest, 1845-1873*, Philadelphia, 1939.
Johnson, George	*Alphabet of First Things in Canada*, Ottawa, 1897.
Josephson, Matthew	*The Robber Barons*, New York, 1962 reprint.
Keefer, Thomas	*Address on the* CPR to the Annual Convention of American Society of Civil Engineers, Transactions, Vol. 19, August, 1888.
Lindley, Clara	*James J. and Mary T. Hill*, New York, 1948.
Longley, Honourable J. W.	*Sir Charles Tupper*, Toronto, 1916.
Longley, Ronald S.	*Sir Francis Hincks*, Toronto, 1943.
Lower, Arthur R. M.	*Canadians in the Making*, Toronto, 1958.
Lyall, Sir Alfred	*The Life of the Marquis of Dufferin and Ava*, 2 Vols., London, 1905.
MacDonell, Allan	*The North-West Transportation, Navigation and Railway Company: Its Objects*, Toronto, 1858, Prospectus.
Macgillivray, George	*A History of Fort William and Port Arthur Newspapers from 1875*, Toronto, 1968.
MacGregor, James G.	*Edmonton Trader*, Toronto, 1963.
MacKay, Douglas	*The Honourable Company*, New York, 1936.
MacPhail, Sir Andrew	*Sir Sandford Fleming*, Queen's Quarterly, Spring, 1929.
McDougall, J. Lorne	*Canadian Pacific, A Brief History*, Montreal, 1968.
McKellar, Peter	*How Nepigon Bay Lost the* CPR *Shipping Port on the Great Lakes*, Thunder Bay Historical Society Annual Report and Papers 1911-12, Thunder Bay, 1913.
McWilliams, Margaret	*Manitoba Milestones*, Toronto, 1928.
Macoun, John	*Autobiography of John Macoun*, M.A., *Canadian Explorer and Naturalist 1831-1920*, Ottawa, 1922.
Markwell, Mary	*An Adventure in Railway Building*, Saturday Night, March 1, 1930.
Meyers, L. W.	*Via the Fraser Canyon*, The Beaver, Winter, 1965.
Miller, Orlo	*A Century of Western Ontario: the Story of London "the Free Press" and Western Ontario 1849-1949*, Toronto, 1949.
Mitchell, Peter	*The West and North-west; notes of a holiday trip*, Montreal, 1880.
Moberly, Walter	*The Rocks and Rivers of British Columbia*, London, 1885.

	Picture of the Canadian Pacific Railway, Address December 8, 1908, to the Art, Historical and Scientific Association of Vancouver, Vancouver, 1909.
Moody, John	*The Railroad Builders*, The Chronicles of America Series, Volume 38, Toronto, 1919.
Morton, Henry James, *Editor*	*Canadian Men and Women of the Time*, Toronto, 1912.
Myers, Gustavus	*History of the Great American Fortunes*, New York, 1936 (reprint).
	History of Canadian Wealth, Chicago, 1914.
Notman, W. and Taylor, Fennings	*Portraits of British Americans*, 3 Vols. in 2, Montreal, 1865.
O'Leary, Peter	*Travels in Canada, the Red River Territory and the United States*, London, 1877.
Oberholtzer, Ellis P.	*Jay Cooke, Financier of the Civil War*, 2 Vols., New York, 1968, reprint from 1907, Philadelphia.
Ormsby, Margaret A.	*British Columbia: A History*, Toronto, 1958.
Palliser, John	*Journals, Detailed Reports and Observations Relative to the Exploration of British North America*, London, 1859.
	Further Papers Relative to the Exploration of British North America.
Perry, Mrs. F. C.	*First Newspaper Published in Thunder Bay*, Thunder Bay Historical Society Annual Report [and] Papers 1911-12, Thunder Bay, 1913.
Pope, Sir Joseph	*Correspondence of Sir John Macdonald; selections from the correspondence of the Right Honourable Sir J. A. Macdonald*, G.C.B., *First Prime Minister of the Dominion of Canada*, Toronto, 1921.
	Memoirs of the Right Honourable Sir John Alexander Macdonald, G.C.B., *First Prime Minister of the Dominion of Canada*, 2 vols., Ottawa, 1894, reprint Toronto, 1930.
Pope, Maurice, *Editor*	*Public Servant: The Memoirs of Sir Joseph Pope*, Toronto, 1960.
Porritt, Edward	*Sixty Years of Protection in Canada*, The Grain Growers Guide, Winnipeg, 1913.
Preston, W. T. R.	*Strathcona and the Making of Canada*, New York, 1915.
	My Generation of Politics and Politicians, Toronto, 1927.
Pyle, Joseph Gilpin	*The Life of James J. Hill*, 2 Vols., New York, 1916.
Rattray, W. J.	*The Scot in British North America*, 4 Vols., Toronto, 1880.
Robinson, Noel	*Blazing the Trail Through the Rockies*, Vancouver, 1915.

	Walter Moberly knew B.C. as 'Sea of Mountains', Daily Province, January 5, 1946.
Rose, George	*The Great Country, or Impressions of America*, London, 1868.
Rose, George Maclean	*A Cyclopaedia of Canadian Biography*, 2 Vols., Toronto, 1886.
Ross, George W.	*Getting Into Parliament and After*, Toronto, 1913.
Ross, Margaret	*Sir George W. Ross*, Toronto, 1923.
Rutledge, J. L.	*Binding the West with Bands of Steel, The Eventful Story of Michael John Haney*, Maclean's, April 1 and 15, 1920.
Saunders, E. M., D.D., Editor	*The Life and Letters of the Rt. Hon. Sir Charles Tupper, Bart.*, K.C.M.G., London, 1916.
Secretan, J. H. E., C.E.	*Canada's Great Highway: From the First Stake to the Last Spike*, Toronto, 1924.
Shaw, Charles Aeneas Hull, Raymond	*Tales of a Pioneer Surveyor*, Toronto, 1970.
Skelton, Oscar D.	*The Railway Builders, A Chronicle of Overland Highways*, Toronto, 1964, Chronicles of Canada series.
„ „ „ Shortt, Adam and Doughty, Arthur G. Editors	*Canada and Its Provinces, A History of the Canadian People and their institutions, by 100 Associates*, Vol. 9, Toronto, 1914.
Smith, Goldwin	*Reminiscences*, New York, 1910, Edited by Arnold Haultain.
	The Political Destiny of Canada, Toronto, 1878.
Smyth, Sir John	*Railroad Communication: A West Proposed Line of Steam Communication from London in England to China and the East Indies*, Toronto, 1845. Pamphlet.
Southesk, The Earl of	*Saskatchewan and the Rocky Mountains*, Toronto, 1875.
Spence, Thomas	*The Saskatchewan Country*, Montreal, 1877, Pamphlet.
Spry, Irene M.	*The Palliser Expedition*, Toronto, 1963.
Stanley, George F. G.	*The Birth of Western Canada, A History of the Riel Rebellion*, Toronto, 1936.
	Louis Riel, Toronto, 1963.
Stewart, George, Jr.	*Canada Under the Administration of the Earl of Dufferin*, London, 1878.
Sulma, Benjamin	*A British North American reply to a letter of 'Old Settler'*, London, 1877, Pamphlet.
Synge, Millington Henry	*Canada in 1848*, London, 1848, Pamphlet.
	Great Britain One Empire, On the Union of the Dominions of Great Britain, London, 1852, Pamphlet.
Thomson, Dale C.	*Alexander Mackenzie, Clear Grit*, Toronto, 1960.
Tolmie, William Fraser	*Canadian Pacific Railway Routes* (A selection of letters from the Colonist), Victoria, 1877, Pamphlet.

Trotter, Beecham and Hawkes, Arthur	*A Horseman in the West*, Toronto, 1925.
Trotter, Reginald George	*Canadian Federation, Its Origins and Achievements, A Study in National Building*, Toronto, 1924.
Trow, James	*A Trip to Manitoba*, Quebec, 1875.
Tuttle, Charles	*Tuttle's Popular History of the Dominion of Canada*, 2 Vols., Montreal, 1879.
Waite, P. B.	*Sir John A. Macdonald, The Man*, Dalhousie Review, Summer, 1967, Volume 47.
Walker, Frank Norman, Editor	*Daylight Through the Mountains, Letters and Labours of Civil Engineers Walter and Francis Shanly*, Montreal, 1957.
Wallace, W. Stewart, M.A.	*The Dictionary of Canadian Biography*, Toronto, 1926.
	The Growth of Canadian National Feeling, Toronto, 1927.
Watkin, Sir E. W.	*Canada and the States, Recollections, 1851 to 1866*, London, 1887.
Willison, Sir E. W.	*Reminiscences, Political and Personal*, Toronto, 1919.
Willson, Beckles	*Lord Strathcona, The Story of His Life*, London, 1902.
	The Life of Lord Strathcona and Mount Royal (1820-1914), Cassell, 1915.
Wilson, F. A. and Richards, Alfred B.	*Britain Redeemed and Canada Preserved*, London, 1850.
Wolesley, Garnet	*Narrative of the Red River Expedition by an Officer of the Expeditionary Force*, Blackwood's Edinburgh Magazine, January-June, 1871.
Young, Hon. James	*Public Men and Public Life in Canada*, 2 Vols., Toronto, 1912.

Acknowledgements

All of the work for this book was done in the public libraries and archives of Canada, and I owe a debt of thanks to the cheerful and helpful staff of people across the country who gave so much of their time to me and to Mr. Norman Kelly, who was my able research assistant for eighteen months. The Public Archives of Canada, where so many of the manuscript sources listed below were consulted, offers unparallelled facilities to the researcher. The staffs of the Metropolitan Toronto Central Public Library, especially that of its reference section, deserve my special gratitude. So does Willard Ireland, British Columbia's Chief Archivist, who placed so much material at my disposal at short notice and answered so many queries so efficiently. Mr. N. R. Crump, chairman of the board of the Canadian Pacific Railway, was good enough to facilitate Mr. Kelly's transcontinental trip along the route of the railway and also my own at a later date and to put at our disposal various personnel to explain the technical problems of railway construction and to give expert advice on the relevant sections of the research. I owe particular thanks to my former secretary, Ennis Halliday Armstrong, and to her successor, Anne Michie, for the enormous amount of work involved in transcribing notes, preparing the manuscript, checking sources and quotations and searching out hundreds of books, pamphlets, official documents and court records. Mrs. Michie also prepared the Bibliography. Mr. Kelly's notes were transcribed with great fortitude by Norma Carrier.

The manuscript, in an earlier draft, was given a professional reading by Professor Michael Bliss of the history department, University of Toronto, who made a great many valuable suggestions for changes, revisions and additions. I should also like to thank Dr. William Kilbourn, Dr. W. L. Morton, Norman Kelly, Major Courtney Bond and my wife, Janet, who all read the manuscript in one or more of its stages and who all made useful suggestions, many of which I was able to incorporate in the final draft. Longman's, Green, Toronto, was kind enough to allow me to read *Tales of a Pioneer Surveyor* in manuscript; my thanks go to Alistair Hunter of that firm and to the co-author, Raymond Hull. H. Travers Coleman of the CPR and that company's archivist, James C. Bonar, were both helpful to me. So was George Macgillivray, publisher of the Fort William *Times-Journal* and Mrs. Marian Childs of the Fort William Public Reference

Library. Barrett McMullen was kind enough to provide me with information about his grandfather, George W. McMullen; additional information came from David Taylor, Managing Director of the Picton Historical Society, and from Dick and Janet Lunn, authors of "The History of Picton County." Miss Penny Berton and Miss Pamela Berton both contributed special pieces of research to the book.

In a work of this complexity, errors are almost inevitable. For these and for the various judgements, I am alone responsible.

Index

Abbott, John J. C., 71, 78-80 *passim*, 95, 96, 116, 118, 132, 254, 371; and Pacific Scandal, 101-7; assists in forming Royal Commission (Pacific Scandal), 106-7; background and character, 122-3; drafts affidavit for Allan, 101-2; draws up CPR contract, 355; physical description, 123; testimony before Royal Commission (Pacific Scandal), 123-4

Alaska, 10, 210
Albert College, 44, 45
Alberta, 31, 36, 230
Albreda River, 51, 161
Alcohol; and railway camps, 291-2
Alert Bay, 205
Alexandria, 331
Alger, Horatio, 307
Allan, Andrew, 66
Allan, Sir Hugh, 70-109 *passim*, 116-25 *passim*, 129-32 *passim*, 148, 161, 172, 186, 248, 255, 281, 307, 319, 321, 346, 349, 355, 358, 367-8, 376, 382, 388; and Canada Pacific Railway Company, 66-72; and Cartier, 72-80; and McMullen, 82-6, 116; and Pacific Scandal, 139-45; annual income, 65-6; background, 66; downfall, 101; election pledges to Conservative Party, 76, 79, 80, 136; forms Canada Pacific Co., 71-2; physical description, 65; testimony to Royal Commission (Pacific Scandal), 120-2

Allan Line, 66-7, 122
Allard, Jason, 152
Anderson, Jack, 286
Andrews, Jones and Co., 279-80, 281
Anglin, Margaret, 362
Anglin, Timothy Warren, 362, 363, 368
Angus, Richard B., 320, 324, 328n, 335, 338, 344, 350-1, 356, 357
Archibald, Adams, 41
"Arid Belt," 35
Armstrong, Harry William Dudley, 152, 175, 282, 283, 286, 287, 290, 292-4 *passim*

Assiniboine River, 35, 224, 249
Astor, John Jacob, 310
Athabasca, 149, 157
Athabasca Pass, 160-3, 171-2, 271

Baird, Henry, 173-4
Baldwin engines, 220
Banff, 320
Bank of Montreal, 122, 140, 310, 321, 329, 334, 335
Barbados, 117
Baril Lake, 56
Barnes, John S., 313, 325
Barnum, Phineas T., 131
Barrie, 156
Beaty, James, 82; *The History of the Lake Superior Ring*, 232
Beaty, James Jr., 64
Beaubien, Louis, 118, 122
Beaudry, J. L., 104
Begbie, Matthew Baillie, 204
Bell, H. P., 151
Bengough, John Wilson, 98, 199
Bent, F. W., 297-8
Bethune, Dean John, 122
Big Bend, 171
Blackwoods Magazine, 39
Blaeberry River, 166
Blain, David, 135-6
Blake, Edward, 7, 23, 94-5, 98, 100, 107, 113, 127-32 *passim*, 134, 140, 197-208 *passim*, 339-40, 365-72 *passim*, 375-7, 379, 383, 388; and B.C., 197-8, 203; and session of 1880-81, 361-2; defeat in election of 1878, 263; public meetings of 1880, 371-2; resigns from Mackenzie's cabinet, 197-8; speech of Dec. 15, 1880, 366; speech of Nov. 3, 1873, 137-9; speech of Jan. 18, 1881, 380-2

Blakiston, Thomas, 33
Blumhart, William, 77
Bonheur, 285
Boston Bar, 205
Boultbee, Alfred, 363, 370
Bourgeau, Eugéne, 32, 33
Bowell, Mackenzie, 253-5 *passim*
Bracebridge, 279
Brainerd, 302
Brassey firm, 339, 341-2
Breckenridge, 222, 302
Brew, Chartres, 61

427

18, 25, 68, 70, 82-4 *passim*, 87, 96, 101, 104, 106, 116, 117-23 *passim*, 127, 131, 132, 142, 143, 161, 172; death, 97-8; physical description, 75; politically ruined by Allan, 72-80

Cartier, Jacques, 250

Cartwright, Sir Richard, 98, 200, 206, 209, 362, 363, 366-70 *passim*, 372, 375. 376; defeat in election of 1878, 263; physical description, 110; speech of Dec. 15, 1880, 366-7; speeches described, 127

Cascade Mountains, 180

Casey, George Elliott, 141

Casgrain, Philippe Baby, 363, 376

Cass, General George W., 10, 63, 70, 73, 75, 79, 85, 86 *n*, 101, 121, 131, 148

Central Ontario Railway, 144

Chapleau, Joseph Adolphe, 281, 374

Chapleau, Samuel St-Onge, 281, 298

Charles I (England), 114

Charlton (railway contractor), 245-6

Charlton, John, 370, 373

Chicago, 63, 75, 83

Chicago and Huron Shipping Canal, 63

Chicago Fire, 186

Chilanko River, 177

Chilcoten Indians, 180

Chilcoten Massacre (1864), 61

Chilcoten Plains, 175-6, 180, 195

Chilcoten River, 177

Chinese; in B.C., 189

Citizen (Ottawa), 206, 358

Clarke, Charles, 76, 77

Clear Grits, 16

Close, Patrick, 279, 280, 282

Club Cartier, 348

Coal, 305

Cockburn, James, 111-13 *passim*

Cody, Buffalo Bill, 19

Collingwood, 17, 26

Colonial Office, 47

Columbia River, 157, 159, 161, 166, 171

Commercial Bulletin (New York), 347

Confederation, 1, 7, 8, 20, 24, 27-9 *passim*, 43, 62, 73, 92, 108, 136, 140, 159, 189, 197, 198, 202, 207, 388

Confederation Life Association, 64

Conmee, James, 240

Conservative Party, 8, 15, 16, 21, 27, 64, 75, 77, 80, 81, 94, 98, 105, 120, 142, 262, 370

"Contract Forty-two," 278-82, 283, 296

Cook, James, 122

Cooke, Jay, 10, 63, 68-70 *passim*, 83, 86, 92, 186, 227, 232, 255, 341

Cooper, Alfred Thomas, 107

Cooper, Fairman and Co., 247-8

Cornish, Frank, 77

Countess of Dufferin (engine), 220, 286

Craigellachie, 18, 164

Cree Indians, 28

Crimean War, 165, 318

Cromwell, Oliver, 114

Crookston, 333

Cross Lake, 245, 247, 283, 285-7 *passim*, 297, 298

Crowley, Patrick, 291

Cunard, Samuel, 17

Cunningham, Robert, 133

Daily Mail (London), 12

Daily Standard (Victoria), 202

Daily Witness (Montreal), 107, 346, 348, 353, 367, 369

Dakota, 28, 57

Dalton, Thomas, 12

D'Artigue, John, 37

Davidson, Joseph, 233, 234, 236-8 *passim*

Davin, Nicholas Flood, 360

Dawson, Simon James, 35, 53, 57, 234, 276

Dawson Route, 52, 53-8, 190

Day, Charles Dewey, 106, 115, 116, 124

Day Book (Fort William), 235

Dean Inlet, 194, 206, 270

Deception, Lake, 285, 287

De Cosmos, Amor, 128, 190, 191, 194, 199, 348, 384

De Graff, 324-5

De Horsey, Admiral, 209, 210, 214, 216

Dewdney, Edgar, 151, 208, 209, 214, 216, 270, 363

Landry, Auguste, 363, 385
Langevin, Sir Hector Lewis, 79, 80, 95, 103, 104, 106, 118-9, 127, 259, 269, 270, 362, 367
Laurier, Sir Wilfrid, 230, 340, 362, 368, 371
Lavallée, Calixte, 19
Leader (Toronto), 24, 64, 82, 232
Leather Pass *see* Yellow Head Pass
L'Evénement (Quebec), 103
Liberal Party, 7, 16, 27, 71, 77, 82, 94, 96-8 *passim*, 103, 105, 107, 108, 110, 113, 114, 120, 128, 137, 138, 262, 364; railway policy, 189-90
Lillooet Indians, 180
Lisgar, 224
Lister, Joseph, 98
Litchfield, Edwin, 311, 314, 323, 329, 331, 333-4
Litchfield, 324
Littledon, E. G. D., 204
London, Ont., 77, 133
London and Southwestern Railway (England), 70
Long Lake, 153
Lorne, Marquis of, 341, 361, 388
Louis Philippe (France), 318
Lower Canada, 24

MacDonald, A. P., 241-2, 268, 270
Macdonald, Alec, 154
McDonald, Donald, 245-6
McDonald, Duncan, 268
Macdonald, Hugh, 99
Macdonald Hugh (son), 340
Macdonald, Sir John A., 6-11, 15, 16, 18, 22, 25, 27, 30, 60-5 *passim*, 68, 156-7, 172, 175, 184-91 *passim*, 198-200, 204, 237, 242, 250-60 *passim*, 272-3, 278-9, 317-23 *passim*, 360-85 *passim*, 388; alcoholism, 99-100; and Allan and associates, 81-8; and McMullen's blackmail attempt, 84-6; and Pacific Scandal, 91-145; and Stephen and associates, 338-59; attack on Donald Smith (1878), 255-6; character and personal life, 98-9; election of 1872, 73-80; election of 1878, 262-8; interview with Dufferin, Oct. 20, 1873, 124-5; nationalism of, 9; physical description, 98; session of

1873, 90-145; session of 1880-81, 360-8; speech of Nov. 3, 1873, 134-7; speech of Jan. 17, 1881, 377-9; telegrams of 1872, 104; testimony to Royal Commission (Pacific Scandal), 119-20; the "National Policy" of, 264-6, 339

McDonald, John J., 281, 298
Macdonald, Louisa, 98
Macdonald, Mary, 99
McDonald, Mitchell, 246
Macdonald, Sandfield, 92
Macdonald, Susan Agnes Bernard, Lady, 137, 156, 361, 380
Macdonell, Allan, 14-5, 16, 26, 375
McDougall, Mrs. David, 38
McDougall, George, 39
McDougall, John, 37
McGee, D'Arcy, 22, 29, 99
McGill University, 115
McIntyre, Duncan, 320, 342, 343, 345, 349, 350, 357
McKay, James, 231, 232
McKellar, Peter, 231-3 *passim*
Mackenzie Alexander, 6, 8, 16, 27, 82, 95, 100, 107, 133, 137, 143, 149, 175, 176, 185-91 *passim*, 195-209 *passim*, 212-20, 229, 232, 240, 242-60 *passim*, 269, 272, 275, 276, 278, 319, 330, 333, 338, 384, 388; and Carnarvon Terms, 195-8; and contract tenders, 240-1; and Great Depression (1878), 186-8; and Neebing Hotel case, 235-9; and Pacific Scandal, 111-5, 125-9; attitude to CPR, 186; attitude to patronage, 239-41; election of 1874, 184; election of 1878, 263-8; personal life, 185; physical description, 184; relations with Cambie, 214-6; relations with Dufferin, 196-7; session of 1880-81, 361-6, 373-6; speech of Jan. 12, 1881, 374-5

Mackenzie, Charles, 248
McLennan, Roderick, 154, 175, 227, 271
McLeod, Malcolm, 48, 49
McMullen, Daniel, 62
McMullen, George W., 62-3, 64, 67-75 *passim*, 78-88 *passim*, 96, 102-9 *passim*, 116-23 *passim*, 126, 130,

436

PIERRE BERTON, Canada's most widely read
historian, was born in the Yukon and educated at
UBC. Author of forty-seven books, he has received
three Governor General's awards for nonfiction,
two Nellies for broadcasting, two National Newspaper awards, the Stephen Leacock Medal for
Humour, and the National History Society's first
award for "distinguished achievement in
popularizing Canadian history." He holds eleven
honorary degrees, is a member of the Newsman's
Hall of Fame, and is a Companion of the Order of
Canada.